Christmas 2004.

To Darling Lydia,
Love BAMMA
xxx
xy

Christmas 2004.

To Darling Lydia,
Love BAMMA

GIANT BOOK
OF THE
HORSE

GIANT BOOK
OF THE
HORSE

Quantum Books

A QUANTUM BOOK

Published by
Quantum Publishing Ltd.
6 Blundell Street
London N7 9BH

Copyright © MCMXCIX
Quarto Publishing plc

This edition printed 2002

ISBN 1-86160-421-1

QUMGBH

Printed in Singapore by
Star Standard Industries Pte Ltd

CONTENTS

BREEDS OF THE WORLD   8

BRITAIN AND IRELAND   30

EUROPE   86

**RUSSIA, BALTIC STATES,
AND SCANDANAVIA**   158

THE AMERICAS 178

AUSTRALIA, ASIA AND AFRICA 218

LESSER-KNOWN BREEDS 232

BREEDS GLOSSARY 255

CARE AND MANAGEMENT 256

TACK AND EQUIPMENT 286

LEARNING TO RIDE 310

COMPETITIVE RIDING 344

INDEX 410

BREEDS OF
THE WORLD

EVOLUTION OF THE HORSE

All present-day strains and types of horses and ponies descend from the original wild ones which evolved, like other animals, by natural selection. Animals inherit their physical and mental features from their parents. Features, such as temperament, color, and size, are passed on by genes. Some genes are dominant and some recessive. The dominant genes override the recessive ones.

Eohippus

Genes can alter spontaneously in a random process called mutation. Without mutation, species stay genetically the same indefinitely. Mutation allows a species to evolve to suit a changing environment. Animals in which genes mutate to produce beneficial features, such as increased speed, may thrive.

The earliest ancestor
The horse developed from a fox-sized creature called Eohippus, which existed around 50 million years ago.

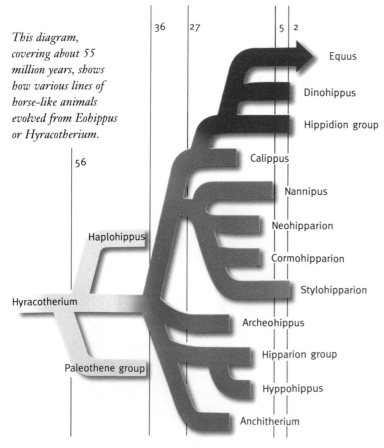

This diagram, covering about 55 million years, shows how various lines of horse-like animals evolved from Eohippus or Hyracotherium.

36 27 5 2

Equus

Dinohippus

Hippidion group

Calippus

Nannipus

Neohipparion

Cormohipparion

Stylohipparion

56

Haplohippus

Archeohippus

Hyracotherium

Hipparion group

Hyppohippus

Paleothene group

Anchitherium

Eohippus is the first creature which can be definitely likened to a horse and is regarded as the earliest direct horse ancestor. Fossils of Eohippus first appear clearly in the Eocene and have been found in both North America and Europe.

This small mammal walked on pads, like a dog, which were well suited to the soft wet ground of the swampy forests in which it lived. It had four toes on the forefeet and three on the hind, each ending in a little rounded nail or hoof, like the present-day tapir. Its teeth were smaller and sharper than those of today's horses, more suited to its diet of soft leaves. Eohippus would have hidden from its predators in the jungle-like undergrowth, rather than relying on speed to outrun them like the modern horse, so its coat was probably colored in a similar way to today's forest-dwelling animals – different shades of beige and brown with dappling and stripes for camouflage. Forest-living animals are often good jumpers, and it may be from this forest ancestry that some modern horses get their natural jumping ability.

As the Earth's climate changed, different species of animals and vegetation evolved. During the Miocene (from 26 million years ago to 7 million years ago), grassy plains developed across the American and Eurasian continents. Eohippus gave way to Parahippus, a larger grazing animal with a longer head and neck than Eohippus. Parahippus had bigger, stronger, prism-shaped teeth embedded in its jaw, which grew continuously to compensate for wear caused by eating the new, tough grasses: It also had longer legs and fewer toes on its feet to help it to run from predators on the grassy plains.

In the Pliocene (between 7 and 3 million years ago), the first one-toed ancestor, Pliohippus, appeared. The

The Somali Wild Ass is one of the rarest of equidae and is classified as endangered. It has been unofficially clocked by Land Rover as being able to gallop at 40mph. Note the primitive zebra markings on the legs and pale underbelly.

foot and leg had altered in structure so that the animal ran on the equivalent of the very end of our middle finger. The leg became supported by a spring system of tendons and ligaments. Pliohippus was the immediate forerunner of Equus – the modern horse.

Equus, which includes asses and zebras, appeared about one million years ago. The ultimate specialization for running speed had arrived and was well established on Earth half a million years before man's arrival.

MAPS

The country of origin of the horse is given for breeds throughout the book. This is shown on the small map at the top of the entry.

Left: The original situation of the earth's land mass meant there were ample migration routes for its creatures to spread.

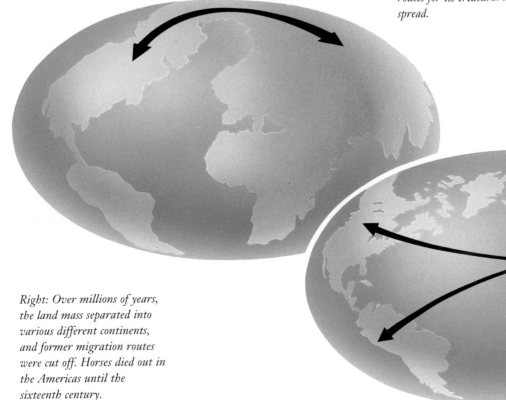

Right: Over millions of years, the land mass separated into various different continents, and former migration routes were cut off. Horses died out in the Americas until the sixteenth century.

Primitive horse types

There is considerable difference of opinion on the recent development of the horse. The most common view is that at the end of the last Ice Age, roughly 10,000 years ago, there were three main types of primitive horse and pony existing in Eurasia, all denominated *Equus caballus*, the scientific name given to the modern horse.

The **Forest Horse** (*Equus caballus sylvaticus*), also known as the Diluvian Horse, is probably the ancestor of all modern heavy horses. It was slow-moving and heavily built, with broad feet which were well adapted to its marshy European homeland. Its coat was thick and coarse, as was its mane, forelock, and tail. The Forest Horse probably had the phlegmatic temperament which most of our modern heavies possess and was resistant to wet and cold.

The **Asiatic Horse** (*Equus caballus przewalskii przewalskii* Poliakov) still exists today in zoos and safari parks and in carefully selected natural locations in eastern Asia. This type is also known as Przewalski's Horse as it was discovered in Mongolia in 1879 by the Polish explorer of that name. Although the Asiatic Horse is generally regarded as an ancestor of many modern breeds, it possesses 33 pairs of chromosomes compared to the modern horse's 32. The Asiatic Horse is resistant to cold, harsh weather. It stands around 13hh high and is sand-dun with a black mane and tail.

The third type was the **Tarpan** (*Equus caballus gmelini* Antonius). Its home was eastern Europe and on the southern Russian steppes. Its light build and speed were well suited to the open, grassy plains of this region. It is believed that many of our pony breeds, and light horse breeds descend in part from the Tarpan. It was very hardy, extremely strong, and aggressive.

Four basic types

By the time the horse was first truly domesticated 5,000 or 6,000 years ago, the three primitive equine types had produced four variants of themselves. Two northern pony types and two southern horse types commonly existed in Eurasia. They are generally given the names Pony Type 1, Pony Type 2, Horse Type 3, and Horse Type 4.

Pony Type 1 mainly lived in northwestern Europe and was small (around 12.1hh), chunky, tough, hardy and resistant to cold, wet, and windy weather. It was the archetypal Northern Pony also known as the Celtic and Plateau Pony. It is thought to have had a black mane, tail, and legs. Its body was brown to mouse, with mealy colored hair around the eyes, muzzle, belly, and between the thighs. Today, the Exmoor Pony and the

TIBETAN HORSE

In an age when the world seems to be fully mapped and explored, discoveries are still being made! As recently as 1995, two groups of horses were discovered in Tibet by the French explorer Michel Peissel. Scientific work is still being carried out on DNA taken from them to try to discover their genetic ancestry. Called the Riwoche (and featured in the rare breeds section), and the Nang-Chen, they may not, according to Peissel, be the only groups of horses or, indeed other undiscovered species, to exist in the most isolated parts of our planet.

The Icelandic Horse demonstrates Pony Type 1.

The Norwegian Fjord Pony, shown here, is believed to represent Pony Type 2.

HOT, WARM, AND COLDBLOOD

COLDBLOOD *Whether a horse breed is hot, warm, or cold blooded is decided by its temperament and physical characteristics. Horses and ponies suited to cold climates are built to retain body heat. Their bodies are rounder, and they have thicker coats of body hair.*

WARMBLOOD *Technically, warmblooded horses such as the Hanoverian and the Selle Français are crosses between hot-blooded and coldblooded horses.*

HOT-BLOOD *Horses and ponies from hot climates have more oval bodies with finer hair, and smaller heads with larger ears and open, flaring nostrils. Their legs are longer, and they carry their tails high, away from the body to facilitate heat loss.*

Icelandic Horse and similar types stem from it.

Pony Type 2 stood at around 14.1hh and, living in northern Europe and Asia, was very resistant to sub-zero temperatures, scant keep, bitter winds, and frost. It would have had a strong likeness in physique, temperament, and coloring to the Przewalski's Horse, with many of its genes. Its closest modern day relatives are larger and heavier ponies such as the Norwegian Fjord and the heavier types of Highland.

Horse Type 3, the desert/steppe horse, was very lean and spare to aid heat loss and had a great resistance to drought and heat. It had an oval, rather than rounded, body, a long slim neck, and a longish head. It had a fine coat, thin skin, and long legs, and stood at about 14.3hh. Horse Type 3 inhabited central Asia and central and western Europe. It probably contained a great deal of Tarpan blood and, in view of its Asian location, some Przewalski Horse genes. It must have been the closest ancestor of the old Turkmene horse and so, today, of the Akhal-Teké. The Barb and Iberian horses must also have generous amounts of its blood, as do the trotting breeds and even the more active type of heavy draft horse.

Horse Type 4, also known as the Proto-Arab, was also a desert horse, but a small one standing at about 12hh. Some claim that the modern Caspian is a direct

A modern type of Akhal-Teké descends from Horse Type 3.

A Managhi-type Arab represents the type which is believed to descend from Horse Type 4.

descendant from Horse Type 4. This type would have been greatly influenced by the Tarpan and developed to suit the desert environment in western Asia. It had fine skin, coat, and hair, and long, hard, tough legs. The head was small and the profile straight or slightly concave with a domed forehead. The body was short and compact, and the tail set and held high.

DOMESTICATION OF THE HORSE

It is generally accepted that the horse was the last animal to be successfully and widely domesticated, probably because it is highly strung, nervous and aggressive until tamed. There is no way of knowing exactly where and when horses were first domesticated, but it is believed to have been in the Far or Middle East.

Although the time of its general domestication is usually considered to have been between 5,000 and 6,000 years ago, there are cave paintings and rock carvings in Eurasia from before this time which seem to portray horses wearing simple harnesses.

Before the horse was used as a beast of burden, it was a prey animal for man. Horses would be used for hide, milk, blood, hair and bone. Early man would follow or herd his horses and other grazing animals, and eventually they became semidomesticated with the increase of sedentary agriculture. It was probably at this time that the potential usefulness of the horse's attributes of speed and strength became appreciated as potentially useful. They were used in much the same way as oxen and reindeer for carrying loads such as sleds and wheeled vehicles. Probably the first horse riders were the sick, injured, and elderly, who were hoisted up onto the beasts of burden.

A rock carving showing a horse wearing a simple harness.

The undomesticated zebra.

Horses at war

Early horses were usually much smaller than today's. It is only during the last couple of hundred years that riding horses over 15hh have become widespread. These smaller horses were better suited to pulling chariots than to riding. The speed and strength of horses when combined with wheeled vehicles for military purposes proved crucial to the dominance of some empires and civilizations. The horse is unique among domesticated animals in the influence it had on warfare.

Uncooperative cousins

Man has tried his hand at domesticating most potentially useful species during his brief history on Earth. Not all have proved as amenable as expected. The onager (Equus hemionus onager) or half-ass was domesticated by the Sumerians, Egyptians, and Romans among others, but never successfully. This animal is uncooperative and habitually bites and kicks,

Horses played an important part in early Olympic Games in ancient Greece.

As a vehicle for warfare, the horse was unsurpassed for thousands of years.

unlike the African domestic ass or donkey (Equus asinus), which is domesticated almost the world over. Similarly unsuccessful attempts have been made to domesticate zebras.

Horse power in the fields and on the roads

In agriculture the heavy jobs of working the land were originally done by the less valuable and more numerous oxen and donkeys. During the 19th century in Europe, however, faster and more efficient plows were drawn by the heavy horse, which possessed more power than donkeys and more speed than oxen. With the development of improved road surfaces, too, faster horse-drawn vehicles became possible.

The heyday of the coach for transportation, was the eighteenth and nineteenth centuries.

THE MODERN HORSE

Early horse breeding would have concentrated on building up numbers. As humans came to know the horses better, they would realize that some types of horse were better suited to certain jobs than others. Eventually, humans would notice that when some stallions mated with certain mares, they produced offspring which looked and behaved like their parents, enabling the breeder to forecast the nature of the foal. So they tried to promote the characteristics that they wanted, such as strength, by selectively breeding individuals. The property of being able to pass on characteristics reliably to offspring is called prepotency by breeders.

Creating horse breeds

Man creates a breed by choosing animals whose characteristics are desirable and mating them together. With this type of selective breeding, the members of the group will have identical, recognizable charac-teristics usually within about five generations. Once the inheritance of characteristics can be fairly reliably predicted in a reasonable number of matings, the group is said to be breeding true. Indeed, until a group of animals does breed true, it cannot be correctly described as a breed. Many of the newer types of horses have been designated as breeds, but are not yet true breeds in this sense, for example, the Palomino.

A modern breed is an artificial mating group selected by man and usually related by descent from a common ancestor. The members of a breed are enough alike genetically and in appearance and behavior to distinguish them from all other members of the species, and produce offspring strongly resembling themselves when mated.

The General Stud Book is the registry for the Thoroughbred breed.

A TROTTER

Norfolk Roadster and Hackneys with trotting ability.	*"Naturalized" North American types with good trotting gaits.*	*The Thoroughbred contributed size, quality, courage, and speed.*	*Morgan contributed trotting ability, and strength.*

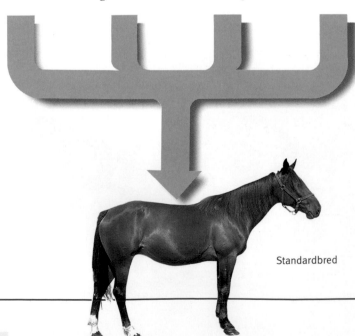

Standardbred

HOW TO ACHIEVE A CERTAIN BREED

When people want to create a breed of horse for a certain purpose, either for an activity or to have a particular appearance, they basically mate together mares and stallions which possess at least some of the characteristics they want.

Sometimes, an animal is strongly dominant in breeding, i.e. it passes on to its offspring most of its own characteristics, good and bad. Such animals are good for breeding as they reliably produce offspring like themselves. Dominant (called "prepotent") animals can be mares or stallions, but dominant stallions have more influence on a breed.

To produce good trotting horses, such as the Standardbred, a breeder mates together animals which are good at trotting; to create a breed for pulling heavy loads, animals which are heavy and very strong are mated together.

The modern competition warmblood was created initially by continental European nations to have "elastic," scopy gaits and a powerful jump – their aim was to produce world-class dressage and show (stadium) jumping horses.

MEASURING A HORSE IN HANDS

A "hand" is 4in (10cm), the approximate width of a man's hand. Horses and ponies are measured from the highest point of the withers down to the ground in a perpendicular line. Measuring sticks are calibrated in hands and inches. The animal is stood on level ground with both forelegs together and the stick placed next to its shoulder with the arm touching the top of its wither. The measurement is read in hands and inches, for example, 15.2hh (hands high) means 15 hands and 2 inches.

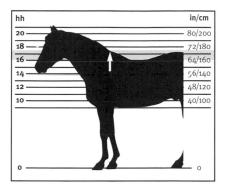

Horses are measured from the highest point of the withers.

HEIGHT BOXES
Throughout this book, height boxes are used to display the height range for a particular breed.

hh	in/cm
20	80/200
18	72/180
16	64/160
14	56/140
12	48/120
10	40/100
0	0

Modern breeds are usually managed by a breed society which maintains a stud book. This is a record book of animals belonging to the breed, with their pedigrees. The breed society decides which animals shall be admitted to the stud book and sets the standards for inclusion – such as height, color, markings, health, conformation, and performance. Animals may not be admitted to the stud book if they do not meet the requirements, even if their parents are fully registered in the stud book. Some breed societies insist on having horses blood-typed for authentication and identification purposes. Different breed societies have different criteria.

A type of horse or pony is a group of animals which look alike. They may not be genetically related and may or may not be part of any particular breed. They are usually defined by purpose or by color; for example, Hack, Hunter, Riding Horse, and Polo Pony.

POINTS OF THE HORSE

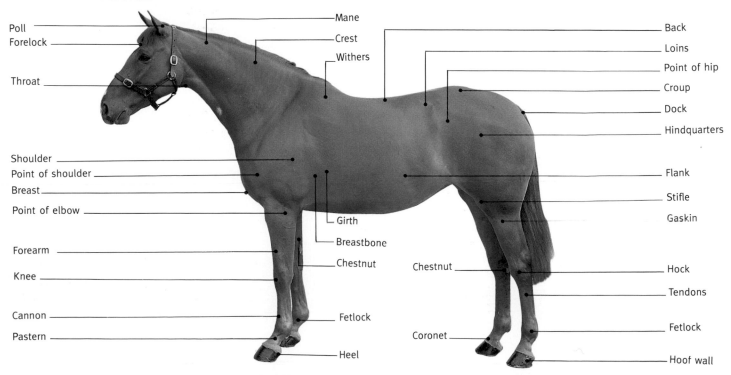

Poll
Forelock
Throat
Shoulder
Point of shoulder
Breast
Point of elbow
Forearm
Knee
Cannon
Pastern

Mane
Crest
Withers
Girth
Breastbone
Chestnut
Fetlock
Heel

Back
Loins
Point of hip
Croup
Dock
Hindquarters
Flank
Stifle
Gaskin
Chestnut
Coronet
Hock
Tendons
Fetlock
Hoof wall

GOOD CONFORMATION

Right: A basic method of gauging a horse's conformation is to compare sections of the body. Distances 1, 2, 4, and 5 should be about the same, with 3 about half of any of them. The distance from the point of the shoulder to the knee should be more than from the knee to the ground. The points of the hocks should be no higher than the front chestnuts.

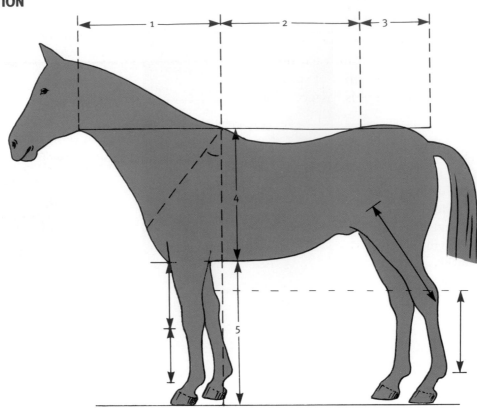

In riding breeds, the angle of the shoulder should be about 45° to the vertical, with the front hoof wall/pastern angle the same. The hind hoof wall/pastern angle can be slightly more upright. Harness breeds may have slightly more upright shoulders and pasterns.

THE HORSE'S GAITS

WALK This is the slowest gait. Horses always start a stride, in any gait, with a hind leg. The sequence for walk may be near (left) hind, near fore, off (right) hind, off fore, in a regular, four-beat rhythm, although some horses delay very slightly in the middle of the sequence. There is no moment of suspension in walk.

TROT An active, two-beat gait, the legs moving in diagonal pairs, the horse springing from one pair to another, with a moment of suspension when the horse has all four feet off the ground.

CANTER This is a three-beat gait, with a moment of suspension at the end of each stride, a stride being regarded as one full sequence. The horse may appear to "lead" or "point the way" with either foreleg. The sequence for off fore leading is near hind, off hind and near fore together, off fore, suspension.

GALLOP A very fast four-beat gait which is a natural extension of the canter. The sequence for off fore leading is near hind, off hind, near fore, and off fore, suspension.

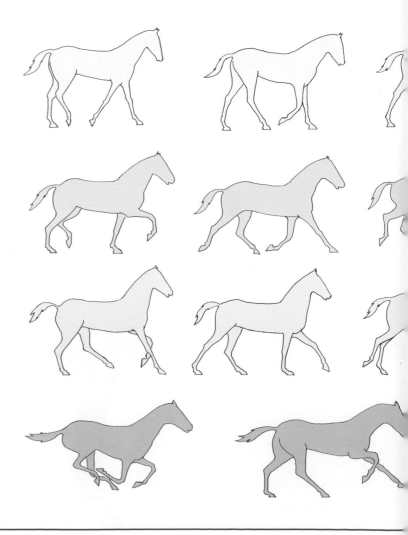

Conformation

Conformation is a horse's make and shape, which depends on its skeleton. There is a great variety of conformation in the horse world, but within each breed and type there is a common basic blueprint of shape.

The most important factor overall is balance. The lines of the body should flow and have a pleasing symmetry. All the horse's parts should seem to fit well together.

Horses with good conformation can be quite different shapes, even though they may be the same height. The Thoroughbred, at one extreme, has a light, sleek frame, long legs in relation to its trunk, a sloped shoulder for speed and a comfortable ride, and a long neck. The heavy draft horse, at the other end of the spectrum, has a much deeper trunk and shorter legs in proportion to its height; an "upright" shoulder to allow it to lift its knees and lean into a collar for pulling; a shorter, thicker neck; and a bigger head. Its limbs are generally much thicker than those of the Thoroughbred, and its hindquarters often slope down to the tail. There are many horses in between these two

No matter what type or breed a horse is, he must have good individual conformation and balance if he is to function well. This Cleveland Bay stallion shows that he can gallop well and freely despite being a moderately heavy breed, due to good make-up and shape.

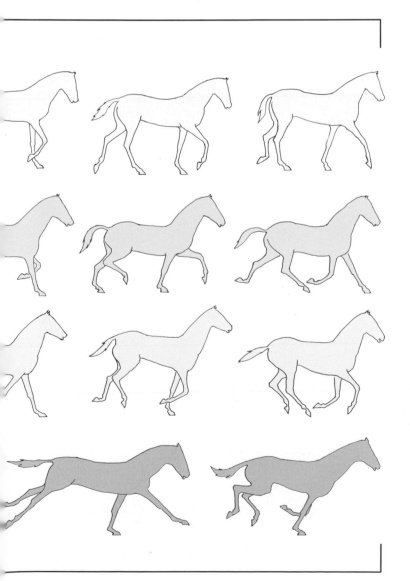

types. Competition warmbloods, for example, have a base of "heavy" blood plus Thoroughbred blood.

Action

A horse's action is the way in which it moves. Whatever the type of horse, a straight, true action is essential, with the hindlegs following exactly the same plane as the forelegs. When a horse with a good action is approaching you head on, its hindlegs should be barely visible to your eye. The exception to this is some breeds, such as the Andalusian or Paso Fino, in which an action called dishing is encouraged, in which the front hooves are thrown outward in an arc.

A horse with good action will move from its shoulders, not just the elbows, placing the fore hooves down well under the head. In riding breeds, at the natural walk, the hind hooves should land at least six inches (15 cm) ahead of the prints of the fore hooves – overtracking. At the trot they should land in the same prints – tracking up. However, heavy breeds will not always achieve these criteria because of their build.

Deviation from "straight" legs and true action places the horse at risk of self-inflicted injury (particularly strains, concussions, and sprains) as well as stumbling. A poor action is also a less efficient use of the horse's energy.

GOOD HORSE MANAGEMENT

The modern horse is a highly specialized grazing and running animal, perfectly fitted for a life on grassy plains. Early in its evolution, the horse's ancestors lived in swampy forests and browsed leaves from trees. Horses will still browse, but most prefer grazing.

Eating like a horse

To a horse, the most enjoyable thing in life is eating. As a large animal the horse requires a lot of food, but grass is generally not highly nutritious. It consists of roughage and water as well as nutrients, and this proportion varies with the season. A horse must consume a lot of grass to get enough nourishment to stay healthy and so must eat most of the time. Wild horses will eat for between about 15 and 18 hours each day, depending on the type of grazing available.

If a domesticated horse is stabled, it should be provided with a constant supply of food, usually hay or haylage. This prevents the horse from feeling hungry, uncomfortable, and bored. A horse with an erratic or spasmodic food supply will become stressed, which can cause colic – a potentially life-threatening digestive disturbance. Keeping a horse supplied with regular small amounts of food is known as trickle feeding.

Because we sometimes work horses harder than they would work themselves in nature, we sometimes need to provide them with more concentrated nourishment than hay or grass. Oats, corn, barley, and branded concentrated foods are popular supplementary foods. However, these are not natural foodstuffs and can cause digestive trouble if they are fed in large amounts.

Keep on moving

Exercise is extremely important for a horse's wellbeing. Horses are designed for a life on the move. The natural lifestyle of a horse is almost constant walking, eating as it goes, and domestic horses should be allowed to mimic this as far as possible, even if they are stabled. Two hours exercise a day, mostly walking with some trotting and perhaps cantering, is the minimum required to keep most stabled horses healthy and happy.

These Karabakh horses in their home environment have freedom, space, and company, and thrive on the sparse keep of their homeland.

Movement is essential to the horse for health and for mental contentment and satisfaction. Most love being exercised.

Strong as a horse

Horses are strong, athletic animals and can work much harder and get much fitter than most animals, including humans. A working horse, however, must be fit if it is to avoid injury. Fitness can be increased by gradually building up the severity and duration of the exercise. The body reacts to the increasing stresses placed upon it by strengthening itself enough to cope with the same amount of work next time.

If a horse is completely unfit (soft), it will take six weeks of walking, progressing to trotting and short canters, to get fit enough for lessons and schooling, half a day's hunting, or pleasure riding. A further six weeks of increasing work will get the horse fit for most jobs, and a full 16-week program, including specialized training for the horse's particular discipline, will have him fit for high level competition, three-day eventing, endurance rides, or races.

Feeding for fitness

A combination of gradually increasing exercise and careful feeding will produce a fit horse. In the past it was usual to cut down a horse's fibrous feed, such as hay, in favor of energy-giving concentrated grains when bringing him to fitness. This is now known to be wrong, because horses need nutritious fiber. Nutritionists now recommend that even the hardest-working horses should not have their hay ration cut to less than fifty percent of their daily feed allowance.

A veterinary surgeon can help devise a preventative medicine program for your horse to help you keep him in good health.

A little extra help

A preventive medicine program can be devised by a vet. It should cover essentials such as deworming, vaccinations, dental treatment, blood profiles to check on health and fitness, and an annual veterinary medical, particularly before starting a fitness regime. Even if your horse is simply a pleasure horse, he still needs proper care and veterinary attention to remain healthy.

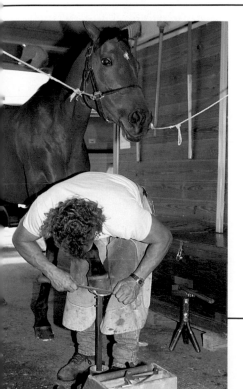

Strong horn and well-shaped feet are important features in any breed. Most working horses, however, still need the protection of properly made and fitted shoes.

SHOEING

Most working horses need shoes to prevent excessive wear of the feet which will make the horse footsore. Most shoes today are of mild steel, not iron as is popularly believed, although aluminum shoes (called plates) are normally used for racing because they are very light. Synthetic shoes are available but not widely used.

Shoeing is hard, dirty, and dangerous work. The blacksmith will remove the old shoes, trim off the excess horn which will have grown since last time the horse was shod, correctly shape and balance the feet, and adjust new shoes to fit, then nail them on.

The shoes can be adjusted hot (the metal is softened by heating in the forge which makes it easier to shape). They can also be adjusted cold, but this is more difficult.

COATS, COLORS, AND MARKINGS

The horse's coat insulates the body against extremes of temperature and the effects of the elements. It is water resistant and varies in texture according to the horse's genes and where he lives. Breeds which developed from stock which evolved in cold areas, for example, often have virtually waterproof coats, with a soft underlayer for extra insulation.

The domesticated horse has an extremely wide variety of coat colors and markings compared to his primitive ancestors. The variations in the domestic horse came about because of the interbreeding of the primitive types. The colors of the primitive ancestors comprised variations on dun ranging from yellow to uniform gray, and medium to dark brown. Shadings such as lighter underparts, muzzles, and eye area also occurred, along with a dorsal list or eel stripe down the back, and zebra markings on the legs.

This Sumba Pony shows a dark dorsal or eel stripe, or list, going all the way down his spine from poll (producing the dark mane) to tail.

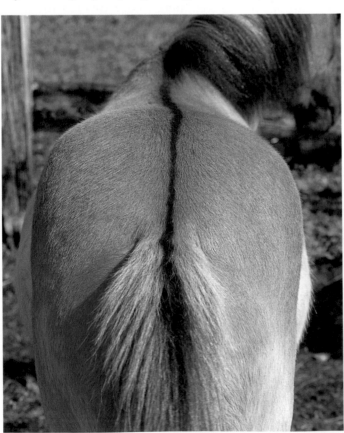

COAT COLORS

Within color categories there are different shades and varieties. Here, some of the most common ones are shown. If there is any doubt about the color of a horse, it is decided by the color of the points – the muzzle, tips of the ears, mane and tail, and lower part of the legs.

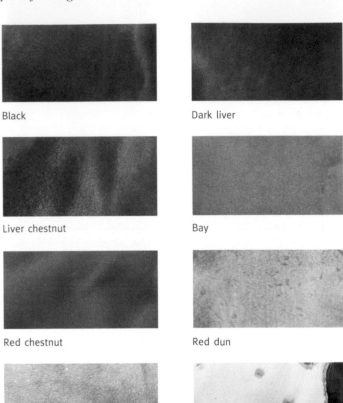

Black

Dark liver

Liver chestnut

Bay

Red chestnut

Red dun

Rose roan

Piebald

It is obvious from prehistoric paintings and carving that mottled, spotted, and sometimes striped horses were well known to prehistoric man, and ancient civilizations prized them highly. In fact, spotted and mottled horses were "all the rage" in Europe until about a couple of hundred years ago and crossed the Atlantic with the *conquistadores*. Such horses normally have vertically striped hooves.

Color is carried by a pigment called melanin in the skin; the color depends on the amount and type of melanin present. Breeding for color is not always easy. Although color is determined by genes, throwbacks and variations often occur.

Stories abound in the horse world about a horse's color or marking affecting its temperament, that chestnuts are highly strung, for example, but none of these myths have any basis in fact.

Skewbald

Leopard Appaloosa

Dappled beige dun

Dappled brown

Dappled chestnut

Cream

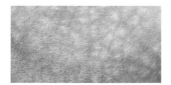

Palomino

Dappled gray

Fleabitten gray

Gray

ALBINO

White markings are areas with no pigment, and such markings do not appear to have existed in primitive and early strains. Albino horses with white coats, pink skin, and red eyes have no melanin at all. The skin under white hair is often susceptible to diseases such as mud fever, grease, or scratches, and to rain rash and sunburn. These conditions, however, are controllable with good management. White (creamy-yellow) hooves are no softer than dark ones.

FACIAL MARKINGS

Facial markings are an important means of identification. Some of the common ones are shown below. In the case of a star, the position, as well as size and shape, should be noted; a stripe should be classed as either narrow or broad.

White Face

Snip

Blaze

Star

Stripe

PSYCHOLOGY AND BEHAVIOR

Horses and ponies are by nature highly strung and reactive. It comes down to evolution. Horses evolved as prey animals and had to be constantly on the lookout for predators. Their natural habitat of steppes and grassy plains provides little or no cover, so the instinct to run at the first sign of danger developed as a defense. This instinct for flight has been changed little by 5,000 years of domestication. Even the most "bomb-proof" children's pony and the most obedient police horse will succumb to its instinct to run when frightened. This means that a rider must learn to be calm and quiet around horses.

The herd instinct

Horses live in herds as a form of defense. A lone animal is much more vulnerable to predators. Within the herd there is a strict but flexible hierarchy, although animals form strong individual friendships with each other which may complicate the picture. For example, a small animal low down the hierarchy may form a strong bond with a dominant animal. Different animals may be dominant in different facets of herd life. For example, one individual may be dominant over grazing, one over shelter. Fighting in established herds is rare. Not all horses crave close company, but they are usually friendly and tolerant toward each other and even those of other species – one reason for their successful domestication.

Learning experiences

Provided horses understand what their trainer wants, they learn very quickly. It is up to the trainer to make his or her requests clear. Horses can learn in "one take" and rarely forget an experience, though the same property which allows the horse to learn so well can have a negative result. Although some horses can get over a bad experience, such as a traffic accident or a bad fall, many may never completely recover. Trainers must be sure not to hurt or frighten a horse that is doing its best to cooperate; otherwise, the animal will always associate training with frustration, and will be unable to learn.

The horse's first line of defense against danger, usually a predator, is flight. They will run in a scattered bunch like this when frightened. They will normally only turn and fight when they have no escape route or must stand their ground such as when a mare defends her foal or a stallion his harem. When traveling from one grazing ground to another, they often go more or less in single file at a walk or canter. Feral horses don't seem to use the trot gait very often.

Horses are initially trained, in most westernized countries, on long-reins, like this, or a single (lunge or longe) rein.

Breaking in using a lunge rein

Using a lunge rein is a common way to "break in" or initially train horses in English-type equitation. The trainer stands with the horse on a long (lunge) rein, and works the horse mainly in circles around him or her.

At first the youngster is led with the trainer, and maybe an assistant, close to it, teaching it basic commands such as "walk," "trot," "canter," and "whoa" for stop.

Gradually, the trainer moves farther and farther away from the horse as it becomes used to the various commands. Lungeing, as it is called, teaches the horse to obey the voice and is a useful method of early training and fittening. It should not be overdone, however, as working in circles can be very hard work, particularly for young animals.

EQUINE COMMUNICATION

Horses communicate with each other, and with other animals and people, mainly by body language and facial expressions. They do, though, also use their voices.

Anger, dislike, or threat toward a particular individual is shown by the head outstretched, ears flat back, eyes angry, nostrils drawn back and wrinkled, and perhaps the teeth being bared ready to bite or warn.

Interest is shown by ears pricked (pointed) toward the interesting object or person, the eyes alert, the head held high if the object is distant or more flexed inward if it is near, and the nostrils open (flared) and perhaps quivering if the horse is near enough to smell the object or person.

Fear is shown by the ears being directed toward whatever the horse is afraid of. The eyes will look wide and alarmed, the nostrils will be wide open, and the skin will appear tightly drawn across the face. A sign of submission in youngsters, is the head outstretched and held fairly low, with the front teeth being gently snapped repeatedly together. This is called "mouthing."

The attitude of "flehmen" is when a horse is closely examining an odor. It breathes in the smell, then raises its head and turns its upper lip up to hold the smell in its air passages where the sensory Jacobsen's organ analyzes the odor.

Stallions herd their mares and offspring with a peculiar "snaking" motion. The head and neck are outstretched and held low as he goes along, usually at a trot, snaking his head and neck from side to side.

REACTING TO A THREAT
1 Startle response
2 Aggressive head thrust
3 Moving to attack
4 "Bottoms up" action –
warning
5 Fighting

LIFE CYCLE OF THE HORSE

The horse is a mammal. It gives birth to live young which suckle the dam (mother). Foals depend on their dams for a few months, although strong emotional bonds often exist long after practical independence is reached. Given reasonable care and good living conditions, both domestic and feral horses should be able to live well into their late teens and twenties.

Life span

To calculate the age of a horse in human terms, one year is usually thought of as four horse years. However, horses have a short adolescence, a long, active adulthood, and a short decline into old age. Domestic horses which are well cared for can live a long time. However, it is common for domesticated horses to be

A mare and foal should be left alone as much as possible for their first 24 hours.

MALE AND FEMALE DIFFERENCES

Although horses come in two sexes like other mammals, there are actually three "sexes" in the species because people are in the habit of castrating or gelding male horses.

A stallion is a male horse who has not been castrated/gelded. He has the full genital organs of penis and two testicles and, unless he has some disease or defect which prevents it, can mate and sire offspring. A gelding has a penis, but his testicles have been removed so he cannot reproduce.

A mare is a female horse with uterus and ovaries and can, again unless there is some disease or defect preventing it, mate and bear foals. Mares' udders are situated high up in between their hindlegs. They have two teats.

"Rig" is another term for describing a horse's sexual situation. A rig is a male horse who has "dropped" only one testicle during puberty; the other remains inside. Only the obvious testicle has been removed when the horse has been castrated, and the horse may then appear to be a gelding, but the remaining testicle still produces male hormones and the horse can mate and behave like a stallion. Rigs can, because of this, be quite dangerous.

A STALLION

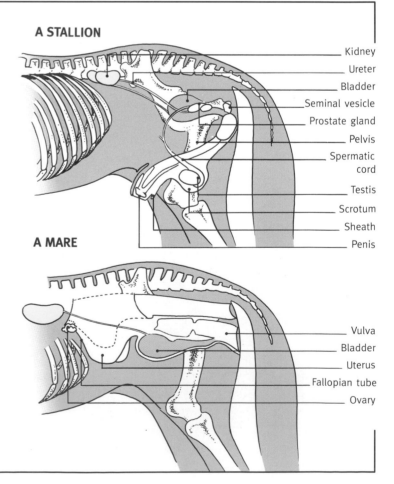

Kidney
Ureter
Bladder
Seminal vesicle
Prostate gland
Pelvis
Spermatic cord
Testis
Scrotum
Sheath
Penis

A MARE

Vulva
Bladder
Uterus
Fallopian tube
Ovary

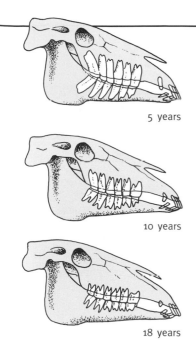

5 years

10 years

18 years

TEETH

A horse's age can be assessed fairly accurately up to about seven or eight years old by changes which occur over time to the pattern on the flat surfaces or tables of their incisor teeth. Horses have front incisor teeth to crop grass and leaves, and back molar teeth to grind them up. As the horse ages, the teeth become more triangular in shape and begin to slope outward more and more.

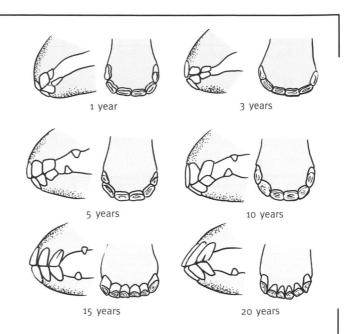

1 year

3 years

5 years

10 years

15 years

20 years

put down when they are no longer able to work or when they fall victim to diseases, usually between the age of 20 and 25.

Pregnancy and early life

A mare is in foal for a little over 11 months. In nature, foaling is geared to coincide with the growth of nutritious spring grasses. Most breeds have an official spring birth date. Some breeds, such as the Thoroughbred, have a mid-winter birth date (January 1 in the northern hemisphere and August 1 in the southern hemisphere). Thoroughbreds have their reproductive year brought forward artificially in order to have foals born as soon after that date as possible.

As a prey animal, a foal has to be able to keep up with the herd within a day. Most births take place at night to give the foal time to get to its feet, find its balance, and be able to run by day break.

In the wild foals suckle their dams for about a year, although they do start nibbling grass from the first day or so. Grass gradually replaces milk as the main foodstuff in the first year. Domestic foals are usually weaned at about six months.

Growing up and going to work

A horse matures between five and seven years of age, depending on the breed and the individual. A foal matures roughly from the ground up. The feet bones and legs are mature at about two to three years, and the spine is fully developed by five to seven years.

A reasonable age for a horse to begin real training for work is three years, when the work should be kept very light, gradually increasing as the horse matures,

With good care and fair work, horses can live useful, contented lives well into their twenties and even beyond.

and can be put into full work at six. A horse is considered to be in his prime between the age of eight and 12 years old. After about 17 years of age, his capacity for work will gradually wane.

Growing old

Old horses are prone, like old humans, to diseases of old age such as arthritis and rheumatism. An old horse may also become more sensitive to the weather and pests, and may slip down the herd hierarchy. Complete retirement may not always be the best option: the horse may feel unwanted and bored, particularly if he has been stabled for much of his life. In some cases it may actually be kinder to put down a horse, rather than to send him to a miserable retirement.

THE ROLE OF THE HORSE TODAY

In the Western world the working horse has largely been superseded by the combustion engine. Breweries still use heavy horses for some short-haul deliveries and for publicity purposes. Some farms still use heavy breeds for jobs on the land, and some towns use them for jobs in city parks. Horses are still an essential asset to the police in many countries.

Throughout eastern Europe, South America, Asia, and Africa, however, working horses (including donkeys and burros) are still in widespread use for transportation and agriculture.

Horses have played a crucial role in military campaigns throughout history. Now mainly confined to ceremonial roles, surprisingly some horses are still used in warfare in harness and to carry packs to transport arms and other supplies.

The main role of the horse in the West today is in pleasure and sport. Thoroughbred flat racing is big business in many places, including the U.S., Great

Many police forces rely on the versatility of the horse.

This horse is performing an old job – herding cattle.

Britain, Ireland, France, and Australasia. Steeple-chasing and its amateur version – point-to-point – are also popular. Other breeds that are used for ridden races in other countries include the Quarter Horse in the U.S. and the Arab in Asia. Harness racing, using the American Standardbred, is even more popular in the U.S. and Canada than mounted racing.

Since World War II, show jumping, eventing, dressage, carriage-driving, and endurance riding have boomed. The development of breeds suited to these sports has become important, particularly in Europe, Scandinavia, Australasia, and the Americas.

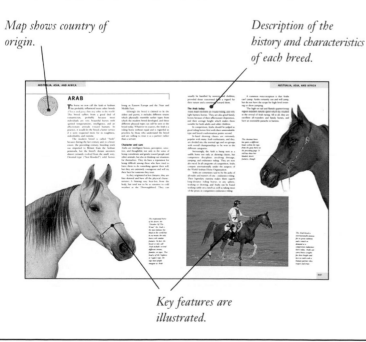

Above: Work in harness is still work for the horse, if sport for us.

Left: The working farm horse came into his own in the eighteenth and, particularly, the nineteenth centuries.

HOW TO USE THIS BOOK

This book is arranged according to the country of origin of each horse. Over 100 individual entries are illustrated, and arranged by geographical grouping. For each entry detailed information is provided on the origins, ancestry, breeding, history, and characteristics of that breed. This annotated example explains how the book is organized.

Map shows country of origin.

Description of the history and characteristics of each breed.

Ancestry box: explains the main known influences on the breed.

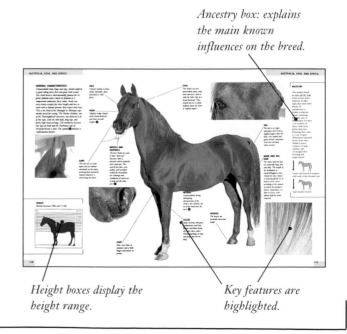

Key features are illustrated.

Height boxes display the height range.

Key features are highlighted.

BRITAIN AND IRELAND

CLYDESDALE

The Clydesdale is something of a paradox. It undoubtedly belongs to the category of heavy draft horse, and is extremely well suited to this job because of its strength and size, yet in appearance it looks the most elegant and refined of heavy breeds. Whereas some heavy draft breeds are small and chunky, resembling an English Bulldog in shape, the Clydesdale is a proud, finer animal without in any way appearing light or middleweight.

Compared with some other "heavies," the Clydesdale is a relatively young breed, its stud book having been started in 1878 by The Clydesdale Horse Society in Scotland, itself formed only the year before. The breed originated in the Clyde Valley when, in the late 17th and early 18th centuries, Flemish stallions (ancestors of the modern Brabant or Belgian Draft Horse) were imported from Flanders into Scotland to mate with the existing native draft mares. Those responsible for the importations are said to be a Lanarkshire farmer and successive Dukes of Hamilton. Other importations of these horses followed, and local farmers used their skills in gradually creating one of the world's most sought-after draft and heavy riding horses.

The need for more and better horses for transportation came about because of the expansion of the coal industry in Scotland. The fuel, a very heavy commodity, had to be transported to where there were no railroads, so roads had to be improved for more efficient transportation of home-produced and imported goods. Improved roads meant that horse-drawn vehicles could be used for long-distance journeys, so faster horses were needed. The farmers concerned were eager to meet this demand.

The long-legged build of the modern Clydesdale is clearly seen here, together with the large amount of white often seen on the legs and the light-colored belly – features which distinguish the breed. It is one of the taller heavy breeds.

The first farmer who brought over Flemish stallions chose wisely, because the Flemish horses belonged to what was already a well-established breed. The English horse we now call the Shire was still evolving into a fixed breed in the 17th century and was classed only as an ordinary carthorse, so it did not provide the reliability in breeding of the Brabant.

The Clydesdale was first exhibited under that name at the Glasgow Exhibition of 1826. In addition to performing heavy farm work, it was used for hauling coal on the docks and was also used by the railroads to shunt rolling stock and move transported goods.

William Aiton, an agricultural author writing in the late 18th century, described the Clydesdale as "the most valuable breed of draught horse in Britain, not only for farming business, but for every description of work where strength, agility and docility of temper are required." Other authorities from the period describe the breed as "worthy for the plough, the cart or the waggon," "strong, hardy, pulling true and rarely restive" and as having "the fastest natural paces of all the draught horses in Britain."

The excellence of the breed created a market for the horse worldwide, particularly in the developing countries of the United States, Canada, and Australia. Multiple teams of Clydesdales worked the vast prairies of North America and were the only significant heavy breed in Australia in the late 18th and 19th centuries.

Character and care

Clydesdales are strong, hardy horses with friendly, calm, and sociable temperaments. They are in no way sluggish, having a gaiety in their air and bearing. They have active, energetic gaits, and the horse dishes very slightly. Some have criticized the breed for a tendency toward weak joints; however, considerable emphasis is placed on the exceptionally good wearing qualities of the feet and limbs, so perhaps some critics have criticized perfectly good horses.

Heavy horses are not normally difficult to care for. They are obviously less susceptible to bad weather than their hotter-blooded relatives, but despite this, horses exported to hotter countries have adapted well, and the breed thrives all over the world.

The Clydesdale today

Although the Clydesdale's principal use as a

haulage and farm horse has greatly decreased in the 20th century, it is, in fact, enjoying a comeback as a publicity attraction. Traditional brewers and distillers used heavy horses for pulling their carts, and the Clydesdale finds a ready market in this field. Likewise, it is used in the parks and forests of its native land, where local and regional councils use it in the maintenance of these public areas.

For show, the horse is turned out in traditional heavy-horse style, with colored ribbons and other decorations. It is shown in-hand and in classes such as dray turnouts, as well as in competitive situations such as plowing and hauling contests.

Clydesdales enjoy popularity as working horses not only with breweries, as most "heavies," but also with local governments in its Scottish homeland. These two wait, patient and alert, in a park while their handler attends to his work.

CLYDESDALE

The Clydesdale, despite its undoubted heavy build, is one of the fastest and most active heavy horses in the world. It is one of the most popular working horses, given its sociable and calm temperament, and active gaits. The symbol **C** *indicates a conformation feature.*

BACK
Short and slightly hollow with broad, short loins.

SHOULDERS
Well sloped and muscular. **C**

QUARTERS
Well muscled, wide, long, and strong. **C**

COAT
The Clydesdale is very commonly roan, with bay (as here), brown, black, and chestnut also seen.

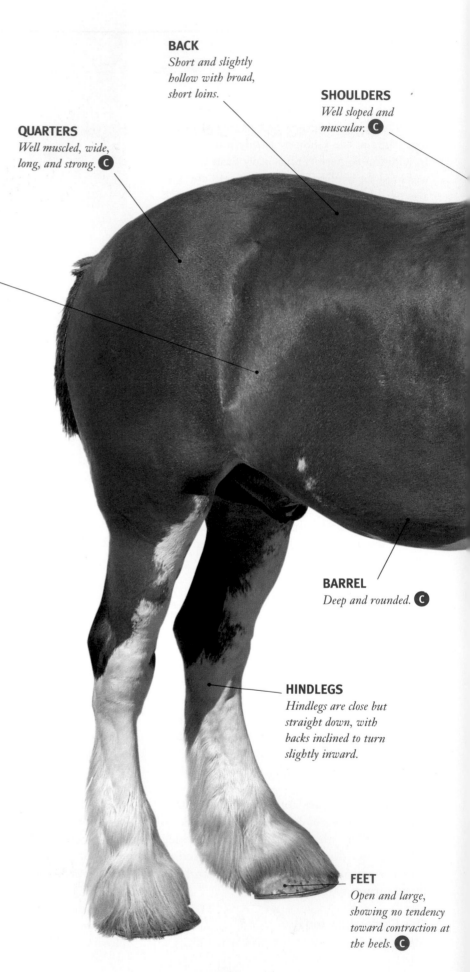

BARREL
Deep and rounded. **C**

HINDLEGS
Hindlegs are close but straight down, with backs inclined to turn slightly inward.

HEIGHT
Average 16.2hh, in males often 17hh, sometimes more.

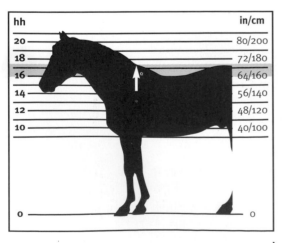

hh		in/cm
20		80/200
18		72/180
16		64/160
14		56/140
12		48/120
10		40/100
0		0

FEET
Open and large, showing no tendency toward contraction at the heels. **C**

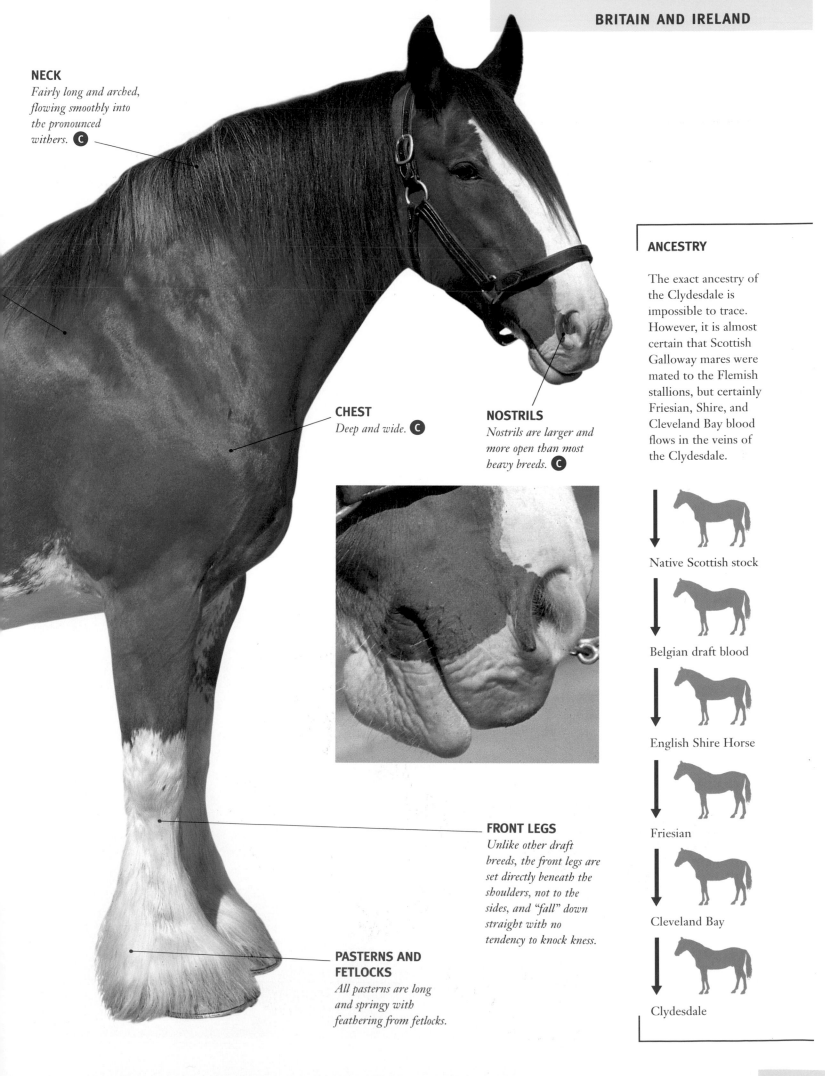

NECK
Fairly long and arched, flowing smoothly into the pronounced withers. **C**

CHEST
Deep and wide. **C**

NOSTRILS
Nostrils are larger and more open than most heavy breeds. **C**

FRONT LEGS
Unlike other draft breeds, the front legs are set directly beneath the shoulders, not to the sides, and "fall" down straight with no tendency to knock kness.

PASTERNS AND FETLOCKS
All pasterns are long and springy with feathering from fetlocks.

ANCESTRY

The exact ancestry of the Clydesdale is impossible to trace. However, it is almost certain that Scottish Galloway mares were mated to the Flemish stallions, but certainly Friesian, Shire, and Cleveland Bay blood flows in the veins of the Clydesdale.

Native Scottish stock

Belgian draft blood

English Shire Horse

Friesian

Cleveland Bay

Clydesdale

DALES PONY

ANCESTRY

The indigenous Celtic Pony was crossed with Friesian and probably French Ariègeois-cross horses brought over to England by the Romans. In the early 19th century, Welsh Cob blood was introduced, as was Clydesdale blood for added size. Although the size has remained in the Dales Pony, the heavy qualities of the Clydesdale have now disappeared.

Celtic Pony
Galloway ▼
Friesian/Ariègeois ▼
Welsh Cob ▼
Clydesdale ▼
Dales Pony

A strong but not coarse animal, the Dales Pony has played an important role in the history of England's economy: their trotting ability made them particularly sought-after as pack ponies able to carry heavy weights over very rough ground. Today, their stamina and calm temperament make them ideal for trekking, and as driving ponies.

The Dales Pony is the one native British breed which has never been truly wild. Although descended from the primitive Celtic Pony, it has received infusions of other blood.

The Dales Pony hails from the Yorkshire hills and dales on the eastern side of the Pennine hills which run down the northern half of England.

At one time there was little distinction between the Fell Pony (from the west of the Pennines) and the Dales Pony (from the east), and both types were informally known as Pennine ponies. The requirements of the regional human population, however, eventually formed the stock into different types.

In the past, Dales Ponies were known as superb trotting ponies and also for their ability to carry and pull stupendous amounts of weight. They have been used by the military for transporting ammunition, by farmers as all-round mounts, and for surface work in the coal-mining and lead-mining industries.

The ponies could cover a mile (1.6km) in three minutes, and could carry weights up to 220lb or 100kg, carried in a pannier on each side of the body. As pannier ponies, they went loose, supervised by a single rider known as a jagger.

Character and care

Dales are tough and hardy, with particularly hard legs and feet, and are able to withstand harsh outdoor conditions. They are quiet, but show intelligence and personality.

The Dales Pony today

Today, the Dales is coming into its own as a trekking and competition driving pony.

GENERAL CHARACTERISTICS

CONFORMATION Strongly built, this pony exudes strength with energy. The **legs** are sturdy with big, strong joints and a little silky feather around the fetlocks. The **feet** are hard and blue-ish. The **mane** and **tail** are thick and wavy.

HEAD The head is workmanlike, showing character and alertness. The pony has short **ears**, bright, lively **eyes**, and mobile **nostrils**.

COLOR Usually black with some browns, bays, and grays. Little white on feet and face.

HEIGHT Up to 14.2hh.

DARTMOOR PONY

The Dartmoor is an example of an indigenous breed which, although subject to infusions of other blood, has largely retained its original characteristics. It now makes an excellent children's and small harness pony.

ANCESTRY

Rather mixed for a native pony, the Dartmoor has, over the centuries, received infusions of Roadster, Welsh Cob, Arab, and, most recently, Thoroughbred blood.

Celtic Pony
British native types ▼
Roadsters/trotters ▼
Welsh Pony and ▼
Cob
Arab ▼
Thoroughbred ▼
Dartmoor

Both geographically and genetically, the Dartmoor Pony is a close neighbor of the Exmoor Pony, but there are obvious differences in both appearance and history which have produced two obviously different types of pony.

Exmoor is on the "arch" of the southwestern "foot" of England while Dartmoor is in the "heel." Both bleak and unforgiving, Dartmoor has higher tors or hills. The Dartmoor Pony has been subjected to many "improvements" over the centuries, made possible by the easier accessibility of Dartmoor than Exmoor, and today's pony can hardly be called either natural or indigenous since it has had so many infusions of various blood. It is, however, a superb example of a riding pony, and comes recommended as a child's first pony.

The Dartmoor Pony's habitat is wild and harsh, for the thin, acid soil which covers the elevated block of granite which forms Dartmoor supports only poor vegetation and scrub. The native pony is therefore tough and hardy, but even so, requires hay if it is to do well in the wild over winter. During World War II, Dartmoor was closed off except to troops, and the pony population was decimated by the severe climate over those years, only two stallions and 12 mares being found at the end of the War for inspection and registration. Since then, selective breeding and careful nurturing of the ponies have brought the Dartmoor back from danger and its future now seems assured.

GENERAL CHARACTERISTICS

CONFORMATION Full of real pony character, the Dartmoor is sturdy and well balanced, with slender but sturdy **legs** and tough, well-formed **feet**.

HEAD Small, with tiny, alert **ears**; large, kind **eyes**; and a very inquisitive **expression**.

COLOR Brown and bay are most common. Excessive white markings on legs and head discouraged.

HEIGHT Up to 12.2hh.

OTHER FEATURES The Dartmoor's distinguishing feature is its bloodhorse-like action. When moving, it hardly shows any knee flexion, having a free, long, and low stride.

Although herds of purebreds live on the moor, mares are usually put in foal to purebred stallions on farms and private studs, where most ponies are brought in for the winter.

Character and care
The Dartmoor is tough, strong and hardy with a quiet, sensible and kind nature.

The Dartmoor Pony today
The Dartmoor is used today as an ideal children's riding pony and in competitive driving.

SHETLAND PONY

The Shetland Pony from the islands of the same name in the far north of Scotland is a prime example of how a cold climate and appalling keep created a small, tough pony with all the features of coldblooded animals adept at reducing heat loss from their bodies. The Shetland Pony (formerly called the Zetland) has been exported all over the world and, even when kept in an environment very like its homeland, always seems to lose type very quickly when bred elsewhere. Of particular note in this respect is the American Shetland Pony, which has so developed that it hardly looks like its forebear at all.

The Shetland Islands are truly bleak and treeless, with a thin, acid soil which supports poor grasses and heather. Shetland Ponies are animals which have evolved to live off them. An 18th century horse book describes the Shetland Pony, "Summer or winter they . . . run upon the mountains, in some places like flocks; and if at any time in winter they are straitened for food, they will come from the hills, when the ebb is in the sea, and eat the seaweed. Winter storms and scarcity of food brings them so low

that they do not recover their strength till about the middle of June, when they are at their best." Despite these deprivations, Shetlands have always been long-lived ponies, often being good for riding at 24 years of age.

The Shetland's strength in relation to its diminutive body size (averaging 9 or 10 hands high, 36–40in (90–106cm) as the Shetland is usually measured in inches, not hands) is truly phenomenal. It has been said that a pony which a man could lift up in his arms could, in turn, carry him on a journey of 10 miles (16km) and back. One pony of 36in (91cm) in height is reported to have carried a man of 168lb (76kg) a distance of 40 miles (64km) in one day.

The origins of the Shetland Pony are obscure and subject to differences of opinion. Some believe that they came over from Scandinavia before the ice sheets retreated, others that they crossed the English Channel area before the British Isles became isolated from the rest of Europe. It is certain, however, that they have been present on their native islands for many thousands of years. There is archeological evidence of their existence there as far back as 500 B.C.

The Shetlands' uses traditionally have been as pack, harness, and riding ponies. They have been used in their islands' agriculture, principally for carting seaweed in huge panniers

The Shetland Pony is a true cold-climate equine, showing the rounded body, short legs, thick mane, forelock and tail hair, wide neck, and relatively large head which are all features that help retain heat in the body. The winter coat is very thick and water-resistant.

to spread on the poor land as fertilizer, carrying peat for kitchen fires in the same way, carrying people around the islands, and pulling carts and other vehicles. As the coal industry burgeoned in the 19th century, word of these immensely strong and tiny ponies spread, and most of the best stock was taken to work down in the mines, many never seeing daylight again.

Character and care

Their character is not always trustworthy. They can be domineering, independent, and headstrong. Not always docile, their occasional inclination to bite makes not all of them entirely suitable for children. However, when one of good temperament is found (and there are plenty), they make good children's mounts and family pets.

Because of their tremendous hardiness, Shetlands need little in the way of food and shelter, but they do need the regular attentions of a good farrier. Unfortunately, it is often very difficult to keep a Shetland Pony's weight down to healthy levels when it is removed from areas of sparse keep due to being unsuitably fed. Eating grass and other feed which is too rich for their constitutions, combined with too little exercise, can lead to laminitis, a crippling and potentially fatal foot disease. It is only in recent years that commercial feeds have been produced which are low enough in energy and protein to feed the ponies adequately, preventing both hunger and obesity while maintaining good health.

The Shetland Pony today

Although still used to some extent in its traditional roles on the Shetland Islands, the Shetland's role today is mainly as a children's pony, mainly because of its small size; however, some experts feel that the Shetland's chunky body makes it difficult for small children to get their legs around the pony.

Shetlands also make good harness ponies and are always favorites at driving events and in scurry racing. Some people keep them just as pets, and they are ever popular in circuses or as companions to lone horses. A few racing stables keep a "stable Shetland" as a companion for their horses, as most Shetlands, being of strong character, are quite able to keep big, fit Thoroughbreds in their place without resorting to physical violence. They usually have a quietening influence on excitable horses.

SHETLAND PONY

Shetlands are sturdy and heavy for their size. They have independent natures and are extremely resistant to very harsh weather. They are able to survive on very low nutrient keep or sparse grass. The symbol **C** *indicates a conformation feature.*

EARS
Typically the ears are very small to help prevent heat loss. **C**

HEAD
The head should not be too big, with a straight or concave face. **C**

NECK
The neck is short, deep, and strong. **C**

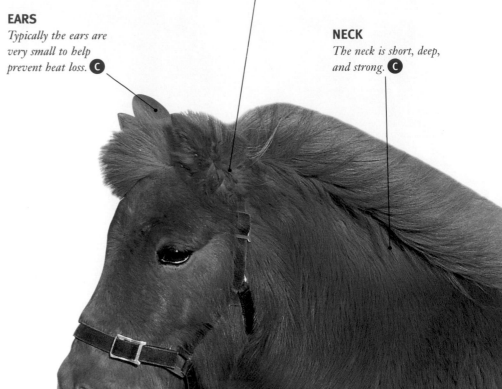

COLOR
Chestnut, bay, black, piebald, and skewbald are the most common.

FETLOCKS
There is some feathering around the fetlocks. **C**

HEIGHT
Measured in inches (or centimeters) rather than hands. The average height is 40 inches (101cm), but considerably smaller animals are quite usual.

hh	in/cm
20	**80**/200
18	**72**/180
16	**64**/160
14	**56**/140
12	**48**/120
10	**40**/100
0	0

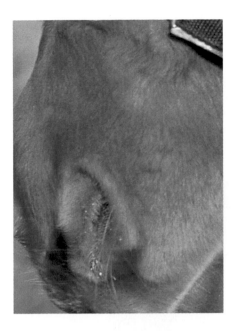

NOSTRILS

The nostrils are normally very small to prevent heat loss from exhaled air. **C**

COAT

The body coat is fairly fine and tough in summer and extremely thick, long, and dense in winter with an apparent soft underlayer for extra insulation.

BODY AND BACK

A rounded body with a short, often slightly hollow back. **C**

QUARTERS AND THIGHS

Strong, wide loins, broad, rounded quarters, and muscular thighs. **C**

ANCESTRY

In the absence of proof of any other theory, it is generally considered that the Shetland Pony is one of the purest descendants of the primitive Celtic Pony, of which the Exmoor Pony is another example.

Celtic Pony

Shetland

LEGS

The legs are short and strong. **C**

MANE AND TAIL HAIR

The Shetland Pony has thick, long forelock, mane, and tail hair.

EXMOOR PONY

The Exmoor is surely one of the purest pony breeds in the world today, resembling closely its prehistoric ancestors. The ponies still run free on Exmoor and retain their wild characteristics, yet make excellent family ponies if caught young.

ANCESTRY

A primitive type with hardly any other blood.

Ancient Celtic
Pony type ▼
Exmoor Pony

The Exmoor Pony is one of the most individual, ancient, and pure pony breeds. Its origins have been traced from a prehistoric, pre-Ice Age type of pony whose bones and fossils have been found in Alaska. The climate, coupled with danger from many predators, forged a tough, wild pony. As the Ice Age ended, this pony migrated across the Bering land bridge to Siberia, through the Urals, and westward through Europe. The pony crossed the land mass which has now become the English Channel into southern England.

Exmoor is a neighbor of Dartmoor in southwestern England and is just as wild. From the 11th century, it has been marked as a Royal Forest, used for hunting by royalty and the aristocracy. At one time the ponies belonged solely to the Crown, but now belong to the wardens, local farmers, and others.

Exmoor Ponies have been subjected to little outside blood. Some Welsh blood was introduced, which began a deterioration in some stock, but the effects were not long lasting.

World War II decimated Exmoor Pony numbers as many were slaughtered to feed the soldiers camped on the moor. After the War, restoration of the breed and numbers began. Some wild herds do still roam Exmoor, but most ponies are now bred on farms and private studs.

Character and care

Exmoors are tough and hardy, with a willing and hard-working nature – provided they are caught and broken in when young.

The Exmoor Pony today

The Exmoor is extensively used as a children's riding pony and for trekking. They are ideal for endurance riding due to their great stamina, and are also used in competitive driving trials.

GENERAL CHARACTERISTICS

CONFORMATION Exmoors are sturdy and thickset ponies, with full and wiry **manes** and **tails**. The **legs** are slender but strong with well-formed joints. The **feet** are small but very hard and rounded.

HEAD Sometimes fairly large. Thick, short **ears**, wide **forehead**. **Eyes**, known as "toad eyes," have protruding lids to protect the eyes from rain.

COLOR Bay, brown, or dun with "mealy" (oatmeal-colored) coloring around the eyes, muzzle, inside the flanks, and sometimes under the belly. No white anywhere. Black mane, forelock, and tail.

HEIGHT Up to 12.3hh for stallions, up to 12.2hh for mares.

FELL PONY

The Fell Pony is closely related to the Dales Pony, but is smaller and of purer blood. It comes from the western side of the Pennine hills, which run down the northern half of England. The Fell Pony is a true mountain and moorland pony, still bred and running free on the hills, although some are bred on farms and private studs. It is almost certainly descended from the Celtic Pony, and also contains Dutch Friesian blood introduced initially by the Romans. A now extinct breed to influence the Fell was the Scottish Galloway, a tough breed whose qualities have been inherited in full by today's Fell Pony.

The Fell Pony was used as an informal trotting-race pony, for sheep-herding and as a pack pony in the lead-mining industry. The Fell Pony transported lead in panniers weighing up to 110lb (50kg) each. The ponies walked in single file, herded by a single rider, covering up to 30 miles (48km) a day.

Character and care

The Fell Pony has an iron constitution, with great pony character and a wild air. It has a friendly, willing, yet determined, nature.

The Fell Pony today

The Fell Pony is widely used in England's Lake District as a trekking pony for tourists. It makes an excellent children's pony and is also good in harness. A few farmers still use Fell Ponies for herding sheep.

GENERAL CHARACTERISTICS

CONFORMATION Elegant but not fine, with a proud outlook, the Fell is a super type of pony. The action is showy with a long, smooth stride.

HEAD Well chiseled, with moderately wide-apart **ears**, broad **forehead**, and prominent, gentle, intelligent **eyes**. The head tapers slightly to the muzzle, the **profile** being straight to slightly convex.

COLOR Black is the most common, favorite color, but brown, bay, and gray occur. White markings are not favored, but a small star on the forehead and a little white on the feet is permitted.

HEIGHT Not exceeding 14hh.

The Fell Pony unmistakably resembles the Dutch Friesian, which influenced it considerably, but Celtic Pony toughness and sense remain, enhancing the good nature of the Friesian. Formerly an all-purpose farm pony, the Fell is now an excellent harness animal and children's mount.

SHIRE

When people think of the Shire Horse, they often imagine large, wise, plodding horses pulling a plow, or a scene set by a medieval castle, with huge horses standing patiently as knights in shining armor are hoisted on their backs. Nothing could be further from the truth.

The Shire Horse only evolved in England during the 19th century. During the preceding centuries, oxen were the animals mainly used for plowing and much of the country's general transportation requirements.

The Shire Horse only came to be called that in 1884, upon the formation of the Shire Horse Society. It is not, therefore, an old breed, but traces its origins back to the Old English Black Carthorse, ubiquitous in the 18th century. At the time most individuals of that breed were said to be common, ugly, sluggish, and bad-tempered. At one time, it was regarded a plus point if it could be said about a draft or harness horse for sale that it contained "no Black blood."

It was in the Midland counties of England – Lincolnshire, Leicestershire, Northamptonshire, Staffordshire, and Derbyshire – that the breeding of really big, heavy horses for agriculture and heavy haulage was concentrated, and these counties gave the modern breed its name in the 19th century. The heavy fenland soils and Midland clays were very tiring for horses to work, and it was felt that a big, strong horse was needed to cope with those conditions.

The breeders excelled themselves and ultimately produced the biggest and strongest breed of horse in the world. The average Shire stood over 18 hands high and weighed just over a ton. They were used by the breweries to transport drays of barrels to the ale houses and inns. The horses worked individually or in pairs, and many breweries still use Shires today. Short-haul deliveries (up to five miles/8km) are made much more economical if horse-drawn transportation is used, and this includes all the costs of the horses' accommodation, their feeding, harness, staff, maintenance of buildings, and veterinary fees. They also look much more attractive going down a main road than an 18-wheeler.

Shires are the tallest horses in the world. Known as "gentle giants," they were developed in England in the 19th century to meet the demand for a bigger, stronger animal to pull the heavier farm machinery and transportation vehicles coming into use.

Character and care

The Shire normally has a docile, patient temperament, often gentle and good-natured. They are coldblooded animals, not particularly sensitive to the weather, but like all horses and ponies, they do appreciate shelter from extremes of climate. Like other heavy horses in agriculture, they are often fed differently from light breeds, eating vast quantities of feeding straws, some grain concentrates, and hay and root vegetables of various kinds. Brewery horses often eat used hops and yeast and enjoy a daily allowance of about a bucket of beer, each horse making his preference known!

The Shire today

Although much decreased, the Shire's main use as a farm horse has not entirely ceased, and some true working Shires can still be found in various countries. It has been said that a Shire can plow deeper than a tractor and also, what the horse drops on the land fertilizes it.

   Without question, the Shire's main role today is as a dray horse, partly as a true working horse but also as a magnificent publicity symbol. Others are entered into competition: plowing matches are very popular, and the size and strength of the Shire makes it ideal for pulling contests. After a serious decline in its numbers in the 1950s, this noble breed is once again increasingly popular.

Today, the Shire is a very effective equine "public relations officer" for breweries and other commercial concerns. Shires work singly, or in pairs or teams, and are used for showing or for making short-haul deliveries.

Kindness and patience, qualities normally associated with the Shire, are well in evidence in the lovely expression on this horse's face.

HEAD

A slightly Roman (convex) profile, with a wise, proud look. Long ears, deep, soulful, and kind eyes. Wide forehead, pronounced jaw.

COLOR

Bay (often with pronounced dapples), brown, gray, or black, usually with considerable white on face and lower legs, but no white on the body.

SHIRE

The ultimate in massive musculature, strength, and sheer size and weight. The Shire combines height and strength without coarseness. Today's Shires have longer legs than earlier Shires, encouraged by breeders for increased height. Kindness and patience, qualities normally associated with the Shire, are well in evidence in the lovely expression on this horse's face. The symbol C *indicates a conformation feature.*

NOSTRILS AND LIPS

Nostrils wide and often large; thin lips, occasionally with whiskering.

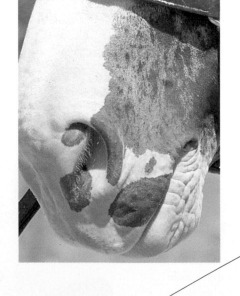

HEIGHT

Although the average height is often stated to be in the 17hh range, horses often reach 18hh and over. The Shire is the tallest horse in the world.

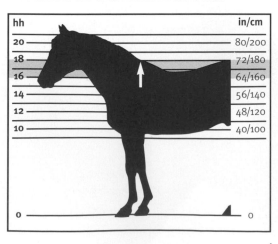

hh		in/cm
20		80/200
18		72/180
16		64/160
14		56/140
12		48/120
10		40/100
0		0

BARREL

The barrel is deep and well rounded. C

NECK AND SHOULDERS

The neck is long, arched, and strong, set smoothly into long, sloping, muscular shoulders. **C**

CHEST AND BACK

The chest is broad and deep, the back short. **C**

LOINS AND HINDQUARTERS

The loins and hindquarters are long, muscular, and rounded with a sloping croup. **C**

ANCESTRY

Not as old a breed as is generally believed, the Shire Horse was "manufactured" for a purpose, but can trace its antecedents back several centuries.

Old English Black Carthorse

Flemish

Friesian

Native heavy stock

Shire

LOWER LEGS AND FEET

The long, silky, straight hair on the lower legs is called "feather". The large feet are rounded, open, and strong. **C**

LEGS

The legs of present-day Shires are comparatively longer than those of the early Shires, due to being bred for increased height. **C**

CANNONS AND PASTERNS

Legs are strong with broad joints, fairly long cannons, and shortish pasterns. **C**

HACKNEY

ANCESTRY

The Hackney Horse
mainly includes
trotting blood of
various strains with
Oriental and
Thoroughbred
additions for quality
and spirit.

Early English trotting
strains
Danish ▼
Friesian ▼
Arab ▼
Yorkshire and ▼
Norfolk Trotters
Thoroughbred ▼
Hackney Horse

English trotting
strains
Fell Pony ▼
Welsh Mountain ▼
Pony
Hackney Pony

Hackney-type horses and ponies were used in
Britain in the Middle Ages, when they were
equally at home under saddle or between the
shafts. Their name is probably derived from the
French *haquenée*, in turn derived from *haque*
(meaning a riding horse, usually a gelding), from
which comes the English term "hack,"
describing a riding horse. The Hackney's main
gait was the trot, the gait both speedy for the
rider and energy-efficient for the horse.

The modern Hackney Horse traces back
to the Yorkshire and Norfolk Trotters of the
18th century. The Norfolk Trotter (or
Roadster) may descend from the Danish horses
brought to England by King Canute in the
11th century. The related Hackney Pony is also
based on trotting blood plus Fell and Welsh
Mountain blood. The Hackney Horse Society,
which also registers Hackney Ponies, has
administered the British stud book since 1883.

Character and care

The Hackney Horse and Hackney Pony are
spirited and energetic animals, not suited to
novice handlers. They have great stamina at a
fast trot and require expertise in their handling.

The Hackney today

These days, Hackneys are almost exclusively
used in the show ring, where their speed and
stamina is seldom displayed or tested. Some
Hackneys have been used in competitive
carriage-driving and show jumping.

GENERAL CHARACTERISTICS

CONFORMATION Today's Hackney presents an overall picture of fire and speed. Its conformation
suggests it is ideally suited to carriage work.

HEAD Small and carried high, it shows great
alertness and a certain arrogance. The **profile** is
slightly convex, the **ears** sharp and mobile, and the
eyes fiery and perceptive.

COLOR Mostly bay, brown, and black, with some
chestnuts and a few rare roans. White markings are
evident on head and legs.

HEIGHT Hackney Horses and Ponies range from
12hh to 15.2hh, the dividing line between the two
being drawn at 14hh.

OTHER FEATURES The Hackney's distinguishing
feature is the brilliantly extravagant, ground-covering
trot. The forelegs are brought up very high and
flexed at the knee, then flung out in full extension
right from the shoulder. At the point of complete
extension, the hoof appears to stop and hover in the
air for a second.

*The Hackney Horse,
and the Hackney
Pony, are show horses
par excellence. A
very specialized breed,
they are a "horseman's
Horse" and need
skilled handling to
control their
extravagant trotting
action and spirited
temperament.*

HIGHLAND PONY

ANCESTRY

Based on a Celtic
Pony type, the
Highland has
received many
infusions of blood
from other breeds.
The excellent but
now extinct Galloway
was bred extensively
with many Highlands,
and there have been
Percheron,
Clydesdale, Spanish,
Barb, and most
recently in the 19th
century, Arab
infusions. Through
all this, the Highland
has retained its good
qualities and is today
a recognizable type in
its own right.

Celtic Pony
Galloway ▼
Mixed European ▼
breeds
Clydesdale ▼
Barb ▼
Arab ▼
Highland

*One of Britain's large
native ponies, the
sturdy Highland is
particularly noted for
its kind temperament
and its "people skills,"
having traditionally
lived for centuries close
to its owners. It is still
used as an all-rounder,
from croft working to
trekking.*

Of all Britain's native mountain and moorland
ponies, the Scottish Highland Pony has
the most amiable temperament, possibly
because for many hundreds of years it has lived
in closer contact with people than most of the
other native breeds. Apart from in the Highlands themselves, types of Highland Pony are
also present on the islands of Skye, Jura, Uist,
Barra, Harris, Tiree, Lewis, Arran, Rhum,
Islay, and Mull – and in each of these different
locations, a slightly different type of Highland
Pony can be found. Traditionally, the ponies
have been made into what the local people
wanted and needed at the time.

Traditionally, there have been two main
types of Highland Pony, a small island type and
a larger, heavier mainland type known as a
Garron. Today, the Highland Pony Society
recognizes only one pony, and interbreeding
has largely done away with the two main types,
although both small and larger Highlands can
now be found. Highland Ponies have long been
used as general farm and estate ponies, and
they have also been extensively used in Scottish
military service.

Character and care

Highland Ponies are known for their extremely
kind and cooperative temperament, yet have
spirit and personality. Highlands are sturdy,
and do best outdoors on poorish keep.

The Highland Pony today

Highland Ponies are still used on crofts, farms,
and estates as well as in forestry, and as deer
ponies or in harness. They are also ideal as
trekking ponies and make excellent family pets.

GENERAL CHARACTERISTICS

CONFORMATION A stocky pony, well-balanced and
comfortable to ride. The **legs** are strongly muscled
and end in tough, well-shaped **feet**.

HEAD Short but broad. **Ears** short, **eyes** bright and
friendly, **profile** straight, **nostrils** open and mobile in
a neat **muzzle**.

COLOR A wide range of shades mostly within the
dun color, with names such as cream, fox, mouse,
gold, yellow, and gray. Conventional grays, blacks,
browns, bays, and chestnuts are also found.

HEIGHT From small, almost Shetland sizes (now
rare) to ponies not exceeding 14.2hh.

OTHER FEATURES Apart from an extremely kind
temperament and great strength, Highlands are
noted for their primitive markings, many of them
showing a marked eel stripe down the spine and
zebra marks on the insides of the legs.

THOROUGHBRED

The Thoroughbred was developed purely for racing, for the enjoyment of British royalty, aristocracy, and gentry. The sport spread and is now one of the most popular in the world.

The Thoroughbred can rightly be said to be the most important modern breed of horse. Its development over the last 250 years has been phenomenal. It was initially bred entirely for racing for the amusement of the British royalty, aristocracy, and gentry, but the popularity of the sport among the general public and the lure of gambling led to the spread of Thoroughbred racing and breeding to every continent of the world.

The most rapid development of the breed to its present levels of performance and recognizable characteristics took place mainly during the 19th century and the early part of the 20th century. Recently, a distinctive American type of Thoroughbred has emerged which is a horse with a high croup (with quarters higher than withers) and a longer hindleg which often swings slightly outward in action to create a longer stride.

The origins of the horse are in the Middle East, but it is generally accepted that the Thoroughbred breed stems from three Arab stallions imported into England – namely the Darley Arabian, the Godolphin Arab (or Barb), and the Byerley Turk. Of these three initial ancestors, probably only the Darley Arabian was a true Arab. The Godolphin was almost surely a Barb, and the Byerley Turk was almost certainly a Turkmene type.

Further importations of Oriental horses, largely Arabs, firmly established the Eastern-blood basis for the breed which, when mated with native British horses and ponies of colder blood and obviously different type, produced a horse of larger size, longer stride, more scope, and more speed.

Character and care

In temperament the Thoroughbred is not as consistent or amenable as its ancestor, the Arab, and needs very sensitive, skilled handling. In type it is variable, too; some individuals show cold blooded features such as rather large, plain heads and coarse hair while others show unmistakable Arab or Turk features.

Many expert horsemen and women prefer Thoroughbreds above all other breeds. Noted for courage, "heart," and for being highly strung, its temperament is often unstable, but it will give its all when handled and ridden by people whom it trusts and who can coax the best from it.

The Thoroughbred is now found throughout the world and, as a breed, is capable of adapting to most climates, although it does require protection from cold and wet, and from heat and flies in summer. It often needs a good deal of food to keep it in good condition and is not a suitable breed for an unknowledgeable owner or one with little time.

The Thoroughbred today

Like its ancestor the Arab, the Thoroughbred has been used to improve many breeds, not only riding breeds, but also high-quality carriage horses.

Its use today goes much farther than racing for which, however, it is still principally bred. It races on the flat and over hurdles and steeplechase obstacles, but also participates in show jumping, three-day eventing, dressage, and the hunting field. Many polo ponies are Thoroughbred, and the smaller representatives of the breed are also used to breed children's show ponies, as is its relative, the Arab.

The Thoroughbred was never bred for conformation as most other breeds are, but for performance, its job – racing – has produced its physique. In racing circles, animals for sale (usually as foals or yearlings) are usually assessed first from a sale catalog where pedigree is considered, then those with the purchaser's favored bloodlines will be chosen on conformation and action.

Although the wastage in the Thoroughbred racing industry is tremendous, some animals do survive to enter other spheres of work when they are older.

The head of the Thoroughbred oozes quality, elegance, and "breeding," with fine skin, "chiseled" features, and a somewhat superior air. Some Thoroughbreds are of difficult temperament, as no attention is paid to this in selection for breeding.

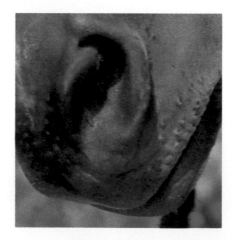

EYES
The eyes are large, usually with a "questing" look to them.

COAT
The Thoroughbred's ancestors evolved in hot climates, so the coat is fine and silky, as shown in the summer coat (above). The winter coat will be a little longer and thicker.

HEAD
The head is straight, lean, and elegant.

THOROUGHBRED
Elegant and refined, the Thoroughbred is often taken as the model for good riding conformation in other breeds. The Thoroughbred gives an overall picture of elegance, toughness, speed, and quality. The Thoroughbred has a "long and low" shape. This streamlined conformation, with its long, slender but strong legs, allows it to use its head and neck for effective balance at high speeds. The symbol **C** indicates a conformation feature.

WITHERS AND SHOULDER
The withers tend to be high, and the shoulder big and muscular. **C**

NOSTRILS
The nostrils are capable of opening wide ("flaring") to permit maximum air flow. This is essential for a horse bred for maximum physical effort at speed.

HEIGHT
Mostly between 15.2hh and 16.2hh.

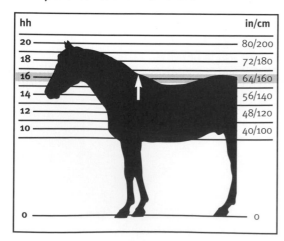

hh		in/cm
20		80/200
18		72/180
16		64/160
14		56/140
12		48/120
10		40/100
0		0

HOOVES
The hooves should be well conformed and tough, but many individuals have poor horn, low heels, and flat soles. **C**

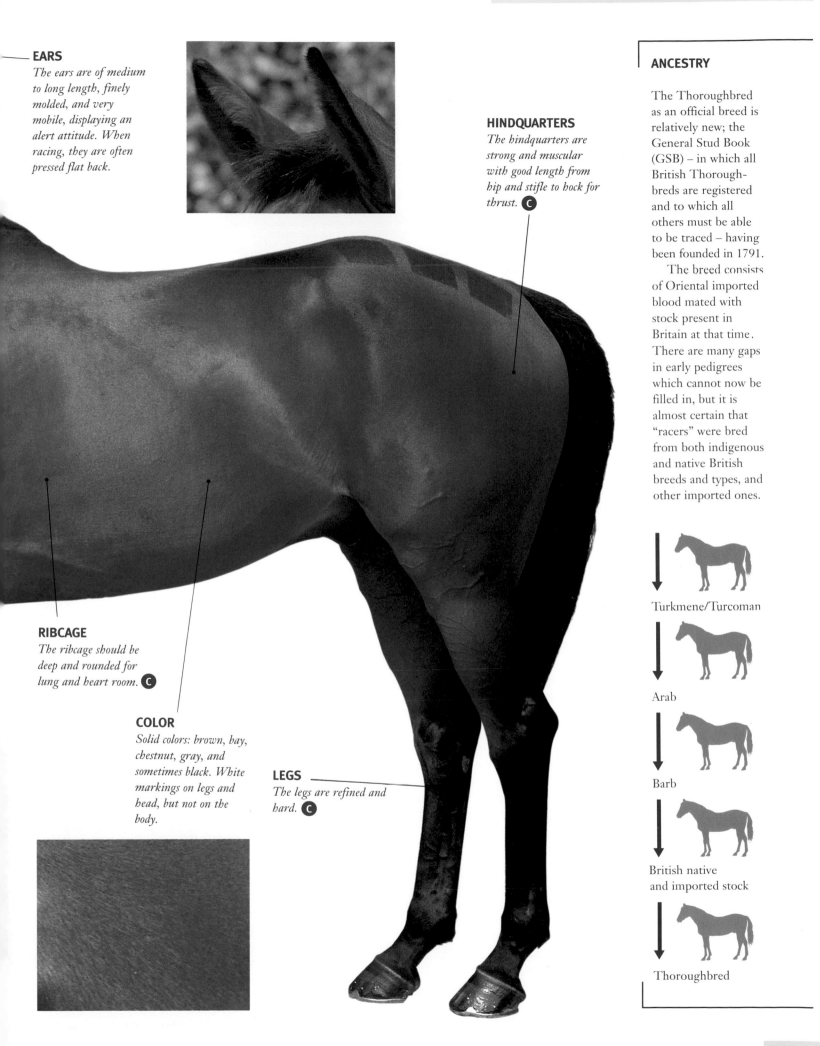

EARS
The ears are of medium to long length, finely molded, and very mobile, displaying an alert attitude. When racing, they are often pressed flat back.

HINDQUARTERS
The hindquarters are strong and muscular with good length from hip and stifle to hock for thrust. **C**

RIBCAGE
The ribcage should be deep and rounded for lung and heart room. **C**

COLOR
Solid colors: brown, bay, chestnut, gray, and sometimes black. White markings on legs and head, but not on the body.

LEGS
The legs are refined and hard. **C**

ANCESTRY

The Thoroughbred as an official breed is relatively new; the General Stud Book (GSB) – in which all British Thoroughbreds are registered and to which all others must be able to be traced – having been founded in 1791.

The breed consists of Oriental imported blood mated with stock present in Britain at that time. There are many gaps in early pedigrees which cannot now be filled in, but it is almost certain that "racers" were bred from both indigenous and native British breeds and types, and other imported ones.

Turkmene/Turcoman

Arab

Barb

British native and imported stock

Thoroughbred

NEW FOREST

One of Britain's larger native ponies, the New Forest enjoys popularity as an ideal mount for teenagers and smaller adults, and is an excellent ride-and-drive animal. There are still feral ponies running on the scrubland of the New Forest.

ANCESTRY

Basic Celtic Pony with Oriental and British native pony infusions from the 18th century onwards, particularly in the 19th century.

Celtic Pony
British native ▼
breeds
Arab ▼
Barb ▼
Thoroughbred ▼
New Forest

The New Forest pony is one of the largest, though probably the least hardy of Britain's native ponies, inhabiting as it does the mildest area where feral mountain and moorland ponies are to be found in the country. The New Forest in Hampshire, south England, consists mainly of open scrubland or very poor pasture or moorland interspersed with bogs. The ponies settling there probably come from the same Celtic Pony stock as all Britain's other indigenous ponies.

The earliest mention of ponies in the New Forest area dates to King Canute (or Knut) in the early 11th century. The area was afforested by William the Conqueror as a royal hunting reserve in 1072, local inhabitants retaining certain rights of grazing for ponies and other animals. The ponies were used historically for general purposes in farming and transport. By the 18th century, the New Forest pony was in decline. In the mid-18th century, an Oriental stallion called Marske was covering mares in the Forest for half a guinea; in the 19th century Arab and Barb stallions belonging to Queen Victoria were used on native mares to upgrade the stock. In addition, Dartmoor, Exmoor, Welsh, Fell, Dales and Highland blood has been used. It is a good cross with Thoroughbred or Arab stallions for breeding performance horses.

Character and care

Today's New Forest pony is a recognizable type of pony, and broken-in ponies exhibit a friendly, calm temperament. The breed is noted for strength, nimble-footedness, speed, and intelligence.

The New Forest today

The New Forest is mainly used for riding, although it goes well in harness. It is used for trekking and forest rides, and is an excellent Pony Club all-rounder and family pony for hacking, hunting, or competing.

GENERAL CHARACTERISTICS

CONFORMATION Has a long, low, smooth action. The **mane**, **forelock**, and **tail** are full. The **legs** are sturdy, straight, well muscled and quite slender, with well-formed, tough **feet**.

HEAD Of definite pony type, well set onto the neck. **Ears** medium length, **forehead**, quite broad, **eyes** generous and inquisitive, and fairly open **nostrils**.

COLOR Any color but particolors. Blue-eyed cream is also not allowed. White on head/legs permitted.

HEIGHT Up to 14.2hh.

SUFFOLK PUNCH

The Suffolk Punch is surprisingly small for a heavy horse, standing at an average of 16hh. It is very heavily muscled and compact, and low to the ground for its body type. It takes its name from the county of Suffolk, East Anglia, in the east of England, and from the old word Punch, meaning short and fat (muscle!).

The earliest written reference appears to be in 1506; it was possibly created in the 13th century by crossing heavy mares native to the east of England with imported French Norman horses. Norfolk Roadsters/Trotters (cob types) and the imported Flanders horses were also probably used. Some Thoroughbred blood was added in the 18th and 19th centuries.

The need for a smaller but agile heavy horse, with "clean" legs for working in the clay, and for better handiness around towns and cities brought the Suffolk Punch into being. The breed is renowned for working long hours with little refreshment or rest.

All present-day Suffolks descend from one nameless horse, believed to be a trotter foaled in 1768, and owned by Mr Thomas Crisp of Ufford (Orford), near Woodbridge, Suffolk. Some authorities also cite a horse called Blake's Farmer, foaled in 1760, as being an ancestor of all today's Suffolks. Both these horses were chestnut and seem to be responsible for passing on this colour to all Suffolk Punches.

Character and care
Suffolk Punches are tough, well-balanced, and extremely powerful, smaller-sized heavy horses. They are able to thrive on moderate rations, begin work at two years of age and work well into their twenties. They have, on the whole, kind natures and are willing workers.

The Suffolk Punch today
Suffolk Punches are today used mainly by breweries and for showing. A few are still used on the land in Britain, more so abroad.

GENERAL CHARACTERISTICS

CONFORMATION Very heavily muscled, short-legged horse. The **neck** is wide, arched and deep. The whole body from **shoulders** to **hindquarters** is very wide, yet short and compact, weight being the overall impression. The **legs** are straight and pillar-like. There is very little hair or feather around the heels. The **feet** are very strong, rounded and of medium size.

HEAD Medium to large, handsome, with a straight or slightly convex **profile**, wide-set **ears** aside a broad **forehead**, and generous, expressive **eyes**.

COLOR All Suffolk Punches are now varying shades of chestnut, usually lightening towards the feet, but with no white markings anywhere.

HEIGHT Averaging 15.3hh to 16.1hh, although some taller animals are found.

ANCESTRY

Almost certainly descended from the heavy cob-type horses of Suffolk of the 10th and 11th centuries, the Suffolk Punch has received infusions of trotting blood, almost certainly crosses of the imported Flanders heavy horses and, later, some Thoroughbred to add quality.

Native Suffolk heavy and cob stock
Flanders horses ▼
Norfolk Roadster ▼
Thoroughbred ▼
Suffolk Punch

One of the most distinctive breeds of heavy horse, the chunky, clean-legged Suffolk Punch combines strength of character with generosity of spirit. Although small for a heavy horse, the Punch is extremely strong and hardworking, and thrives on smaller food rations than other heavy breeds.

THE WELSH BREEDS

Wales must surely be one of the oldest horse-breeding countries in the Western world, and in such a tiny country are found four of the best and most popular breeds, the Welsh ponies and cobs.

The Welsh Pony and Cob Society stud book, first produced in 1902, is split into four sections: A, B, C, and D. The original wild Welsh pony, now called the Welsh Mountain Pony, is registered in Section A; the Welsh Pony in Section B; the Welsh Pony of Cob Type in Section C; and the Welsh Cob in Section D. All breeds in each category owe their origins to the Welsh Mountain Pony.

It is said of all of Britain's native ponies and cobs that they were present in the area at

The Welsh Mountain Pony is a favorite children's pony in many countries of the world. It has been successfully crossed with Arabs and Thoroughbreds to create larger show ponies. The trot, shown here, can be spectacular in all the "Welshmen."

the time the English Channel came into being, about 10,000 years ago when various land movements, together with the rising of the sea level as vast amounts of ice melted at the end of the last Ice Age, cut Great Britain and Ireland off from the rest of Europe.

The evolutionary route of the Welsh breeds probably stems from a primitive type – now called the Celtic Pony – which inhabited the north-western part of Europe from which the present regional types or breeds developed.

The oldest recorded reference to the existence and breeding of native stock in Wales comes from around 50 B.C., where it is noted that Julius Caesar founded a stud at Lake Bala

in Merionethshire and proceeded to introduce into the Welsh and other native British breeds Oriental and other equine stock brought over with his armies, with a view to producing larger animals for pack and general transportation. In turn, many native British horses and ponies were exported by the Romans to various parts of their empire.

In the 10th century, Welsh King Hywel Dda recognized the importance of horses to the life and economy of the Welsh people and introduced a strict and precise set of laws governing their value, breeding, sale, warranty regarding both physical and behavioral qualities, and use.

Running wild, the Welsh ponies provided an ever-present reservoir of stock for taming and general domestication, but they were also hunted for sport by Welsh farmers and others.

Although bred for all sorts of purposes, by the second half of the 19th century, the native Welsh Mountain Pony and the other "Welshmen" which had been bred from it had deteriorated in quality to such an extent that a ruling body was created to govern and preserve the breeds before they died out. The Welsh Pony and Cob Society was formed in 1901, its main objective being "the encouragement and improvement of Welsh Mountain Ponies, Welsh Ponies and Cobs."

WELSH MOUNTAIN PONY

The Welsh Mountain Pony is the foundation stock upon which the other three Welsh types are based. The Welsh Mountain Pony is the indigenous pony of Wales, and despite much abuse from both the weather and the human race, it has survived with all its best qualities of endurance, hardiness, quick-wittedness, and agility intact. Winters on the Welsh hills are severe and the keep minimal, so only those ponies which can convert practically nothing into useful energy and possess the sense to learn how to use their habitat to their best advantage have survived.

Although the ponies' former grazing grounds have been drastically reduced from what they were in previous centuries, the

Welsh Mountain Pony is still bred on the Welsh hills and increasingly in private studs.

Originally, the farmers themselves used the ponies, for they were able to carry a man all day on the hills, but also cross-bred them indiscriminately to produce anything big enough to be useful or salable. Unsuitable stallions and colts were turned out on the hills and helped to contribute off-type, "soft" and generally unsalable stock.

Small Arab and Thoroughbred stallions were also set loose in the hills, and although this resulted in a great improvement in general quality of the breeds, it also considerably reduced the hardiness of the ponies.

Two forerunners of the Welsh Pony and Cob Society, the Gower Union Pony Association and the Church Stretton Hill Pony Improvement Society, started an improvement program by banning from the hills all stallions and colts which did not pass inspection, selecting only the best of the native stallions. The Polo and Riding Pony Society (later The National Pony Society) began, at the end of the 19th century, to register Britain's native breeds, and local committees were asked to produce descriptions of their desired or existing type, which became the official standard by which future ponies were to be judged. The Welsh Pony and Cob Society subsequently introduced a premium award scheme. These measures undoubtedly saved the Welsh Mountain Pony from irretrievable deterioration. It says much for the dominance of the pony genes that, despite both indiscriminate and purposeful introductions of other blood, the Welsh native pony characteristics have come through to the pony of today.

Apart from being used by hill farmers, the Welsh Mountain Pony has been used extensively as a mine pony, and many have been exported over the world for use as riding or harness ponies.

Character and care

The Welsh Mountain Ponies are intelligent, surefooted, agile, and willing to work and please; they have innate pony sense. Their action is eye-catching, smooth, and flowing, with a good length of stride.

The Welsh Mountain Pony today

Welsh Mountain Ponies are possibly the most popular child's pony in Britain. They make excellent family ponies and pets, and are superb in harness.

WELSH PONY

The Welsh Pony has been almost exclusively bred in recent generations as a children's quality riding pony, the stud book describing it as having "quality riding action, adequate bone and substance, hardiness and constitution and pony character." It says much for the pony that, despite looking like a miniature Thoroughbred, that essential pony character nearly always comes through.

Welsh Ponies were originally produced by crossing the Welsh Mountain Pony with cob-type animals and by introducing Thoroughbred and Arab blood for extra quality. Like the Welsh Mountain Pony, limited numbers still roam and breed on the Welsh hills, but most are bred on studs and have been exported all over the world as riding ponies.

They have been used in the breeding of polo ponies, hunters and hacks, and their larger blood-brothers, the Welsh cobs. Traditionally, the Welsh Pony is normally too large to make a good mine pony, although it was used on the surface in coal mines for light hauling. It was also used for carrying and hauling Welsh slate from the quarries for the building trade.

A writer at the turn of this century noted that the Welsh Pony resembled a small middleweight hunter lacking the quality which the infusion of Arab and Thoroughbred blood had brought to the smaller Welsh Mountain Pony. Like the Mountain Pony, the Welsh Pony is a hardy animal which is noted for seldom going lame.

The Welsh Pony is a superb, active, tough, and patient children's pony. Based on the Welsh Mountain Pony, Thoroughbred and Arab blood was added, as was cob blood, to make a larger working pony for older children.

Character and care

The Welsh Pony is kind and spirited, with that peculiar Welsh character and common sense, while still being a "fun" pony for children and the family. Specifically a riding pony, it goes equally well and enthusiastically in harness and is noted for trying hard to please.

The Welsh Pony today

The Welsh Pony's role today is undoubtedly that of a child's riding pony and show pony; some are used to advantage in harness. They are good and willing jumpers, having superb riding conformation and action, resembling a Thoroughbred in a small package. They have stamina and can hunt all day and take part in endurance riding competitions at appropriate levels.

They, and the smaller Welsh Mountain Pony, provide specialist show ponies when crossed with Thoroughbreds or Arabs, the Welsh/Arab cross being well known and much sought after.

The Welsh Pony of Cob Type is a pony-sized animal with the build, strength, and character of the larger Welsh Cob. The least numerous of the Welsh breeds, it was developed mainly as a strong, fairly small harness animal.

WELSH PONY OF COB TYPE

The Welsh Pony of Cob Type is the least numerous of the Welsh breeds. It is a grand type of small cob with pony character. The same height as the Welsh Pony, it is stockier and stronger, and developed more as a harness than a riding pony, although it goes equally well under saddle.

Its origins are a mix of all the Welsh types. The Welsh Pony of Cob Type is really a miniature cob up to 13.2hh and differs from the Welsh Cob by height alone. Its numbers were reduced to an incredible seven after World War II – two stallions and five mares – but it has picked up greatly since then.

After World War II, riding as a pastime became more popular, and the demand for ponies of cob type could hardly be met. This fact saved the Welsh Pony of Cob Type from extinction. This pony/cob type was produced by crossing the Welsh Mountain Pony and Welsh Cob, both animals being of the same origin, but these days the Welsh Ponies of Cob Type are bred with each other, now that numbers are more plentiful.

Traditionally, the Welsh Pony of Cob Type was ideal for light farm work, being very strong for its height, and it was also used to cart slate from the mines and quarries. It was also used in small carts or traps for trips to market, or to chapel on a Sunday. Its strength and compact build made it ideal for pulling small vehicles along difficult, unpaved roads in its native hilly country. It would carry shorter family members out hunting and also took part in informal trotting races.

Its lively, energetic movement probably stems from its Hackney blood. This type of movement, together with its strength and agility, makes it ideal for carrying heavier riders over rough, hilly, and generally difficult terrain.

Character and care

The Welsh Pony of Cob Type has definite pony character, is lively, willing, enthusiastic, and amenable. It needs only basic care and a fairly frugal diet, doing best on sparse grassland.

The Welsh Pony of Cob Type today

The Welsh Pony of Cob Type makes an excellent family mount for young riders or smaller adults. As an all-round, ride-and-drive animal, it cannot be beaten. It is much in demand in today's tourist industry as a trekking pony, and it takes part in competitive driving. It is shown in performance classes, breed, and general pony showing classes.

WELSH COB

The Welsh Cob must be one of the most spectacular members of the equine race in the world, and although many have been exported all over the world, it is probably still not as fully appreciated as it should be. Anyone who has not witnessed the brilliant Trotting of the Cobs (specifically the stallions) at the major Welsh shows has missed a real treat. The power, fire, and pride of a Welsh Cob stallion trotting out for show in front of his rivals is an experience never to be forgotten.

The Welsh Cob probably came into existence in its present-day form in the 11th century. It was known then as the Powys Cob and also the mainly dun-colored Powys Rouncy. A Rouncy was a warhorse used by a knight's squire. In Norman times, superb Rouncies were bred in Norfolk; only the Powys Rouncy was held in higher esteem.

Prior to that development, Welsh Mountain Ponies had been crossed with stock imported by the Romans to create a larger, stronger animal – and Roman imports were brought from all over the empire. From the 11th to 13th centuries, however, Spanish/Andalusian and Barb horses were imported, while the Crusaders also brought home Arab horses, the spoils of war, which were almost certainly used on the existing native stock. The Welsh princes and tribal chieftains are believed to have ridden Powys horses into battle against the English, and their mounts were described by contemporary writers as being fleet of foot, good swimmers and jumpers, and able to carry considerable weight. In the 15th century, the poet Guto'r Glyn described at great length the animals which undoubtedly resembled today's Welsh Cobs.

In the 18th and 19th centuries, Hackney, Norfolk Roadster (a then-famous trotting breed), and Yorkshire Coach Horse blood was also introduced to the Welsh Cob. As often happens when native breeds are "improved," the use of too much non-cob blood was in danger of destroying the Welsh Cob's unique type. Several old and valued strains became almost extinct, and in the 1930s many breeders failed to register their stock. The decline was only halted when breeders began using only individuals showing the established cob type, eliminating untypical qualities and restoring the Welsh Cob to its former glory. The traditional homeland of the breed in recent centuries has been Cardiganshire (now part of Dyfed): there, the horse is known as the Cardi Cob and its breeders as Cardi Men.

Traditionally, Welsh Cobs were used as all-purpose light farm horses, herding sheep under saddle and taking the family to chapel in a cart, or farm goods to market, as well as doing light hauling around the farm. They were much in demand by tradesmen, local businessmen, doctors, and anyone else who wanted a stylish, fast animal to get them from place to

place. The Welsh Cob was also used extensively in surface work around coal mine heads and as a general pack animal, and it was greatly favored by the Army for both mounted infantry and for hauling weapons over rough, mountainous regions.

The Welsh Cob has always been renowned for stamina and its tremendous trotting ability. It is this ability which has peppered the stud book with many variations of names like Flyer, Comet, Meteor, and Express.

Character and care
Pride with gentleness, fire with amenability, and courage are the hallmarks of the Welsh Cob. Ever versatile, it is an excellent all-round family animal, athletic and sure-footed. Being tough and hardy, it is economical to keep.

The Welsh Cob today
Today, the Welsh Cob is increasingly seen in competitive driving trials. It makes an excellent jumper in the hunting field or in local-level cross-country or show jumping competitions.

Possibly the most impressive of the Welsh breeds, the Welsh Cob is full of quality, strength, and intelligence. The stallions have a fire and personality unique to their breed.

WELSH COB

The conformation of the Welsh Cob should be compact, well balanced, and strong. A true ride-and-drive animal, it has the strength for light farm work, the speed and stamina for harness transportation, and the activity and willingness for riding. A long, springy stride, with the forelegs reaching far out from the shoulder, with significant but not excessive knee action, and the hindlegs showing great flexion in the trot, the hindfeet reaching well under the body and powerfully thrusting the animal forward. The symbol **C** *indicates a conformation feature.*

EARS

The ears should be wide apart, shortish, sharp, and alert.

EYES

The eyes are large and "deep" with an interested expression.

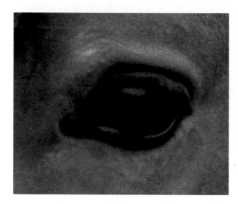

HEAD

The head is full of quality, the profile straight, and the nostrils capable of flaring widely. The jaw is open and strong. **C**

BODY AND CHEST

The body is deep through the girth. The chest is broad and generous. **C**

WITHERS

The withers are fairly pronounced. **C**

HEIGHT

There is no upper height limit, but the best animals seem to be around 15hh.

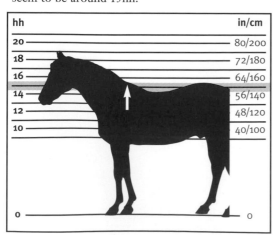

hh	in/cm
20	80/200
18	72/180
16	64/160
14	56/140
12	48/120
10	40/100
0	0

FEET AND FETLOCKS

There is some silky feather permitted around the fetlocks, and the feet are well rounded and hard. **C**

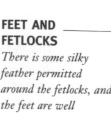

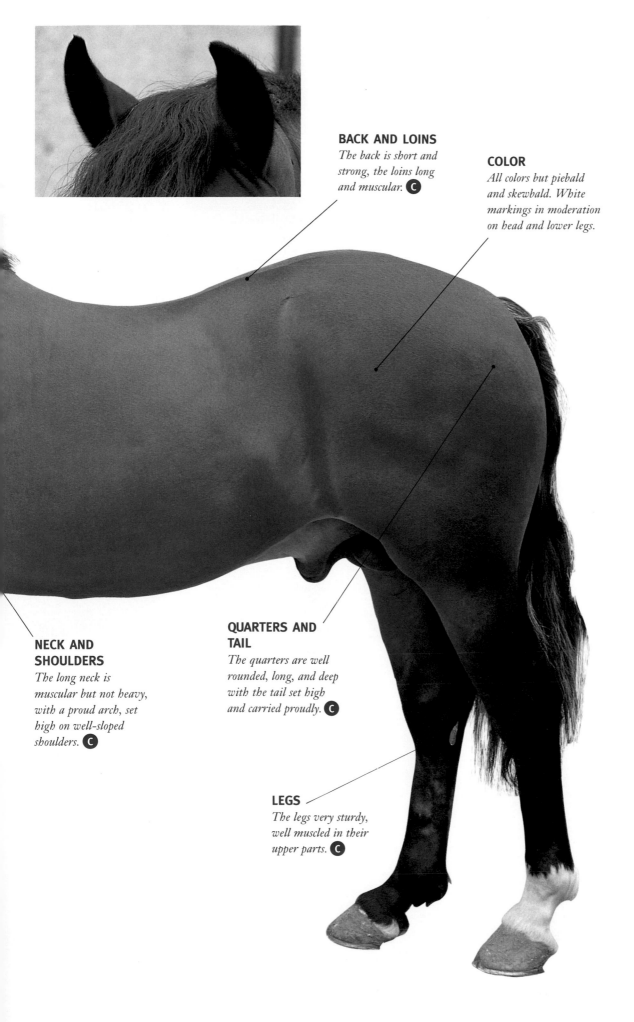

BACK AND LOINS

The back is short and strong, the loins long and muscular. **C**

COLOR

All colors but piebald and skewbald. White markings in moderation on head and lower legs.

NECK AND SHOULDERS

The long neck is muscular but not heavy, with a proud arch, set high on well-sloped shoulders. **C**

QUARTERS AND TAIL

The quarters are well rounded, long, and deep with the tail set high and carried proudly. **C**

LEGS

The legs very sturdy, well muscled in their upper parts. **C**

ANCESTRY

Based on the Welsh Mountain Pony. Over the centuries other blood has been introduced, but the Welsh Cob still retains the traditional type described by Roman and later historians.

Celtic Pony/Welsh Mountain Pony

Spanish/Andalusian

Hackney

Norfolk Roadster

Yorkshire Coach Horse

Oriental breeds

Welsh Cob

WELSH PONY OF COB TYPE

In build and type it is a scaled-down cob. The Section C is probably the most difficult of the Welsh ponies to breed as it cannot be produced with any certainty. It is very strong for its height and was developed as a small harness and light draft pony, although it is a good riding pony for teenagers and shorter adults. The symbol **C** *indicates a conformation feature.*

MANE AND TAIL
The mane and tail are full and generous and may be slightly wavy.

WITHERS
Moderately high and should not be too thick. **C**

LOINS
The loins may have a slight depression before rising to the croup. **C**

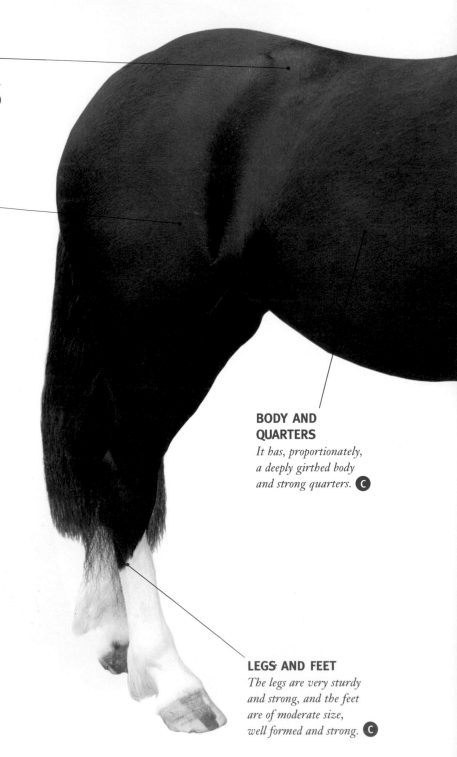

COLOR
All colors but piebald and skewbald are acceptable. It is preferred that they have only a little white on head and lower legs.

BODY AND QUARTERS
It has, proportionately, a deeply girthed body and strong quarters. **C**

HEIGHT
Not over 13.2hh.

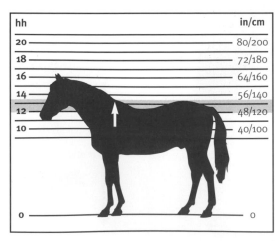

hh	in/cm
20	80/200
18	72/180
16	64/160
14	56/140
12	48/120
10	40/100
0	0

LEGS AND FEET
The legs are very sturdy and strong, and the feet are of moderate size, well formed and strong. **C**

NECK AND SHOULDERS

The neck is strong and muscular, often crested, set high on well-laid-back shoulders. **C**

HEAD

Should show quality and spirit, the profile being straight. There must be no coarseness about the head. **C**

EARS AND EYES

The ears are short, well pricked, and set wide apart. The eyes are widely spaced and prominent, with an interested expression.

ANCESTRY

As an amalgam of all the Welsh breeds, the Welsh Pony of Cob Type possesses primitive Celtic Pony blood, Arab and Thoroughbred blood, and also some Hackney blood, together with European and Oriental imports and the blood of other native types.

Celtic Pony

Welsh Mountain Pony

Welsh Cob

Spanish and European

Oriental

Native Welsh stock

Welsh Pony of Cob Type

63

WELSH PONY

The Welsh Pony has good riding conformation, a comfortable "ride," and the action to show or jump well. It has retained its Welsh quality and pony character, despite infusions of other blood. The symbol **C** *indicates a conformation feature.*

EARS
The ears of the Welsh Pony are short and pointed.

HEAD
Clean-cut Thoroughbred-type head, but often with slight dish.

NOSTRILS
Fine and open.

WITHERS AND CHEST
The withers are moderately pronounced and fine. The chest is deep and not too wide. **C**

FORELEGS
Set forward under the shoulder, straight and strong with long forearms. **C**

CANNONS AND KNEES
Short cannons, and broad, flat knees. **C**

HEIGHT
Not exceeding 13.2hh.

hh	in/cm
20	80/200
18	72/180
16	64/160
14	56/140
12	48/120
10	40/100
0	0

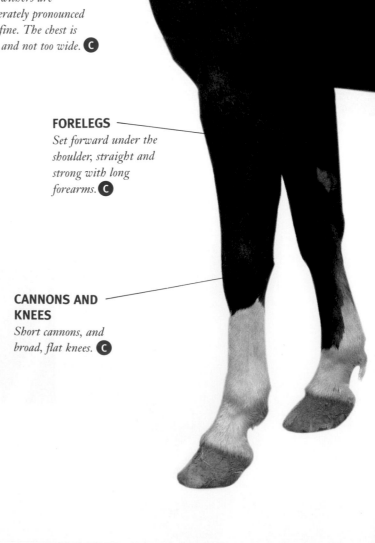

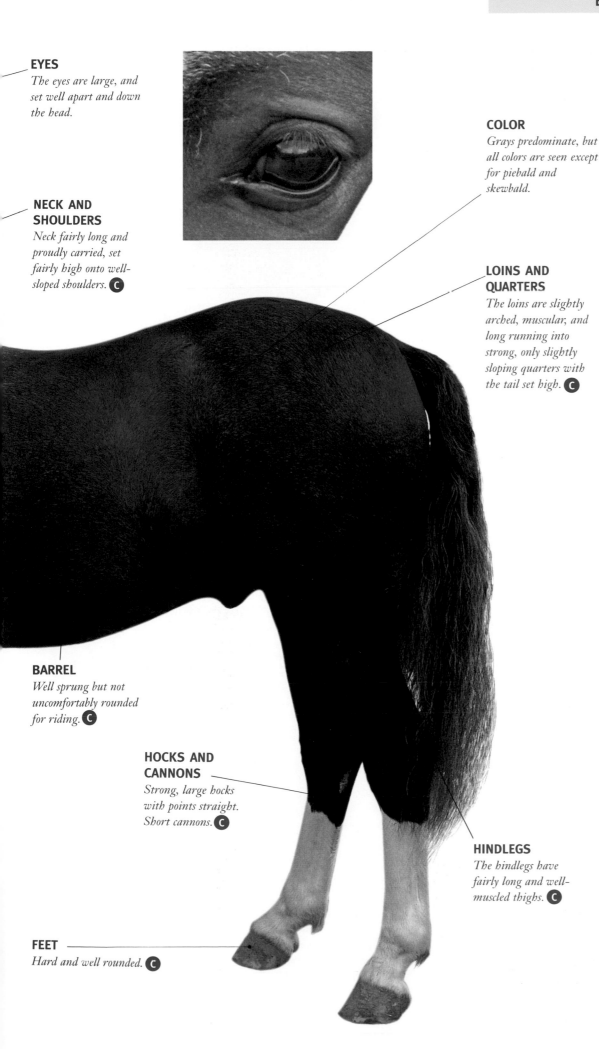

EYES

The eyes are large, and set well apart and down the head.

NECK AND SHOULDERS

Neck fairly long and proudly carried, set fairly high onto well-sloped shoulders. **C**

COLOR

Grays predominate, but all colors are seen except for piebald and skewbald.

LOINS AND QUARTERS

The loins are slightly arched, muscular, and long running into strong, only slightly sloping quarters with the tail set high. **C**

BARREL

Well sprung but not uncomfortably rounded for riding. **C**

HOCKS AND CANNONS

Strong, large hocks with points straight. Short cannons. **C**

HINDLEGS

The hindlegs have fairly long and well-muscled thighs. **C**

FEET

Hard and well rounded. **C**

ANCESTRY

Originating from the Welsh Mountain Pony, the Welsh Pony contains the blood of other Welsh types, plus Thoroughbred, Arab, and some Hackney. Throughout all the infusions of non-Welsh blood, it has retained its unique Welsh character.

Welsh Mountain Pony

Native non-Welsh stock

Hackney Pony

Arab

Thoroughbred

Welsh Pony

WELSH MOUNTAIN PONY

A very appealing pony and excellent as a riding pony for young children, Welsh Mountain Ponies also go well in harness. Many Section As look like small, sturdy Arabs due to the Arab blood in their ancestry, yet still have Celtic Pony characteristics. The symbol **C** *indicates a conformation feature.*

HEAD
Many ponies show their Arab ancestry. The face is often dished and the nostrils capable of flaring widely.

MUZZLE
The muzzle should be small, tapering, and soft.

EYES
Great personality is shown in the eyes, which are set well apart and down the head.

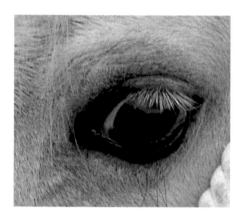

EARS
The ears are very short, well pricked, and alert.

HEIGHT
Not over 12hh.

hh		in/cm
20		80/200
18		72/180
16		64/160
14		56/140
12		48/120
10		40/100
0		0

LEGS AND FEET
The legs are sturdy, straight, and well muscled in forearm and gaskins, with broad, strong joints and small, rounded, hard feet. **C**

NECK AND SHOULDERS

The neck is of moderate length, quite arched, and set quite high on well-sloped shoulders. **C**

WITHERS

The withers are moderate but normally adequate to stabilize a saddle. **C**

COLOR

Grays predominate, mainly due to the pervading influence on the breed of one of its patriarchs, Dyoll Starlight, but all colors other than piebald and skewbald are accepted.

TAIL AND QUARTERS

The tail is set quite high on well-rounded, slightly sloping quarters. **C**

COAT

The winter coat is particularly thick and the mane and tail flowing, luxuriant, and slightly wavy.

BARREL

The barrel is particularly good, having well-sprung ribs, a short strong back, great depth through the girth, and strong loins. **C**

ANCESTRY

Some infusions of Thoroughbred and Arab blood during previous centuries have given the Welsh Mountain Pony the look of a stocky miniature Arab, and in addition to the stock of primitive Celtic Pony, other native pony blood is present.

Celtic Pony

Native pony

Thoroughbred

Arab

Barb

Welsh Mountain Pony

ANGLO-ARAB

The Anglo-Arab is a combination of two of the most aristocratic breeds in the world, the Arab and the Thoroughbred – the term "Anglo" comes from the fact that the Thoroughbred is an English breed.

In Britain, an Anglo-Arab must be the product of only Arab and Thoroughbred parents, yet other countries have introduced native blood into their Anglo-Arabs, notably the French with their superb French Anglo-Arab. However, there are usually stipulations as to the amount of Arab blood present in the breed, the figure normally being at least 25 percent. As the Anglo-Arab is a combination of two separate but established and prominent breeds, it is not usually regarded as an actual breed itself, one exception being the previously mentioned French Anglo-Arab. Other variations of the Anglo-Arab include the Gidran (Hungarian Anglo-Arab), the Shagya Arab of Hungary, the Russian Strelets Arab, and the Hispano-Arab of Spain (see also French Anglo-Arab).

Due to the phenomenal success of the English Thoroughbred, where speed, quality, scope of stride, and height are unsurpassed, some countries have been inclined to introduce too much Thoroughbred blood, which has undoubtedly reduced the toughness and endurance of the resulting stock, qualities which come from the Arab.

The Anglo-Arab is a top-quality riding horse with all the hallmarks of a hot-blood. A combination of the Arab and the Thoroughbred, the Anglo-Arab can take after either breed. This lovely horse is quite Thoroughbred in appearance.

True Anglo-Arabs are horses of outstanding quality, a good specimen having the qualities of both breeds. It is usual to mate an Arab stallion with a Thoroughbred mare, but the reverse may also be the case and two Anglo-Arabs may be mated together.

Character and care

A spirited, intelligent, courageous, and affectionate nature is characteristic of the best Anglo-Arabs. They have plenty of personality and tend to be "thinkers," unlike some Thoroughbreds. They should be cared for like any blood horse, requiring sensitivity and skill in handling plus plenty of exercise.

The Anglo-Arab today

Anglo-Arabs belong to the aristocrat group of riding horses. They make superb riding horses for most purposes, competitive or general, because their best representatives combine the athletic attributes of the Thoroughbred with the gentle intelligence of the Arab and have the courage of both breeds.

Anglo-Arabs have distinguished themselves in all sorts of competition. They make exquisite show hacks and riding horses, and although not of strict show hunter type, make excellent hunters in the field. They have distinguished themselves in eventing, show jumping, and in dressage, in endurance riding, and in racing. Anything its parent breeds can do, the Anglo-Arab can do as well.

Whereas Arabs are normally shown with full manes and tails, the Anglo-Arab can have its mane and tail trimmed and plaited or braided as a Thoroughbred or other show horse.

In the show ring, Anglo-Arabs excel in pleasure and riding horse classes and often have their own classes for in-hand showing. In performance-type competition, such as cross-country, jumping, and endurance, the Anglo-Arab often excels because it is fast and has tremendous stamina.

Due to the fact that the Anglo-Arab may take after either parent breed, it is a particularly interesting and exciting animal to breed and to own. The breed produces a great variety of individuals, all of which can truly be called aristocratic horses.

Anglo-Arabs excel in most spheres of competition. In action they should have a free-ranging stride like the Thoroughbred with the spring and comfort of the Arab.

ANGLO-ARAB

Ideally, the body should resemble the Thoroughbred, but the head and tail carriage should resemble the Arab's. This horse is a slightly different type of Anglo-Arab from the horse on the previous page. He is a little lighter in type, and although he is not markedly Arab, he shows more of an Arab look about the eyes and face. The symbol **C** *indicates a conformation feature.*

HEAD

Should show unmistakable Arab ancestry, but often not so marked as in the pure Arab. **C**

EARS

The ears are of moderate length, fine and pointed.

PROFILE

The profile may be straight, or dished (concave) as in the Arab. **C**

EYES

The eyes are soft and generous, showing pride, fire, and gentleness.

FACE AND NOSTRILS

The Anglo-Arab often has a more equable temperament than the sometimes-difficult Thoroughbred, often shown in the outgoing yet calm expression of the face, as here. The nostrils are mobile and capable of flaring widely.

HEIGHT

Wide range, from about 14.2hh to 16.1hh with some animals outside this range.

hh	in/cm
20	80/200
18	72/180
16	64/160
14	56/140
12	48/120
10	40/100
0	0

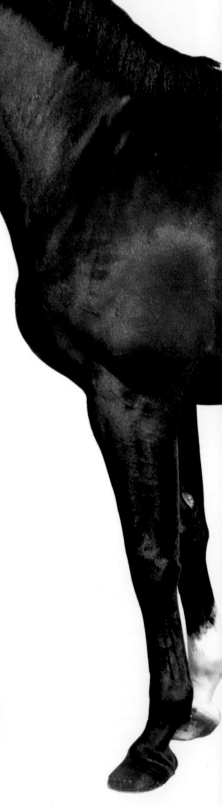

TAIL

Anglo-Arabs may inherit the high tail carriage of the Arab or, as here, the more restrained one of the Thoroughbred. Whereas Arabs appear in showing classes with "natural" manes and tails, Anglo-Arabs may be trimmed. The mane and tail hair is fine and silky.

COAT

As it is a hot-blooded horse, the coat is invariably short and fine in summer, slightly longer and denser in winter.

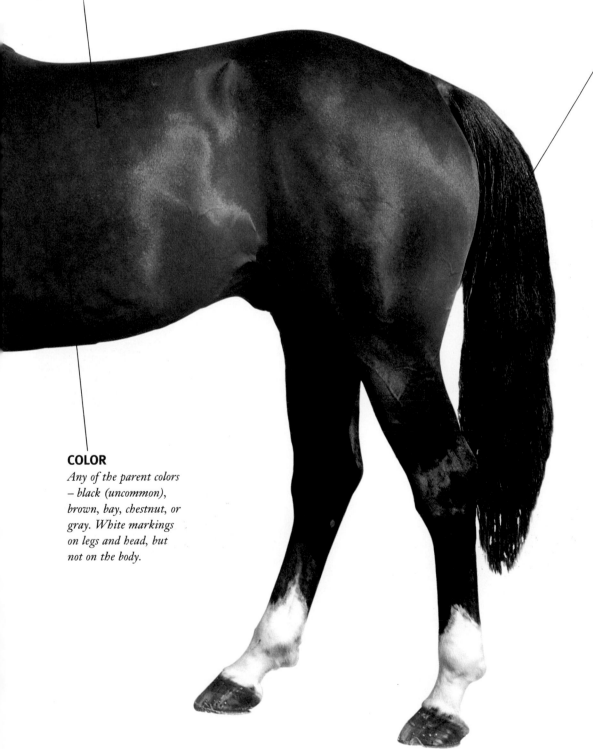

COLOR

Any of the parent colors – black (uncommon), brown, bay, chestnut, or gray. White markings on legs and head, but not on the body.

ANCESTRY

The true Anglo-Arab will have ancestors of only Thoroughbred or Arab blood, yet some countries have introduced a little other blood, usually their native horse or pony breeds. These are not pure Anglo-Arabs.

Thoroughbred

Arab

Anglo-Arab

IRISH DRAUGHT

The Irish Draught was developed by farmers as a general-purpose heavy to light draught animal for farm work, general harness work, riding, and hunting. It had to do everything from plowing and hauling, pulling a vehicle to market, and taking the family to church in the trap on Sundays, to galloping and jumping after hounds over Ireland's fearsome bogs, black-thorn hedges, and formidable banks. It is the perfect result of a cross between a performance horse with dash, and a breed with substance and common sense. Furthermore, when an Irish Draught is again crossed with a suitable Thoroughbred, the resulting progeny are often superb horses which can cross any country and jump the most fearsome obstacles when out hunting or in competition, both show jumping and cross-country disciplines. Many steeple-chasers also have a dash of Irish Draught blood in their veins.

The roots of the present-day Irish

Draught Horse go back to the 18th century, yet long before that, when the Celts populated Ireland, they brought various horses and ponies with them from Europe and in time these mated with the indigenous Irish stock of Celtic Pony. In the Middle Ages, the Norman English invaded Ireland, bringing with them heavy utility horses of European origin whose genes also went into the melting pot.

It is believed that Oriental and old Spanish blood came to Ireland with the Celts, who had access to such warmblooded horses on main-land Europe. Certainly, Ireland traded with the continent, particularly with Spain and France, and acquired their horses that way.

The 18th century saw further importations of Thoroughbred blood (which at that time included individuals of the Arab, Barb, and Turkmene breeds), and this trend continued into the 19th century. However, the Potato Famine of 1845–1846 decimated Ireland's

The Irish Draught is a quality, medium-heavy breed developed as an all-round working horse in Ireland. It is a good ride-and-drive animal and was also used extensively by the military as a pack horse.

economy, and horse breeding was affected, the numbers of the Irish Draught falling sharply. Later in that century, Clydesdales and Shires were introduced which considerably coarsened the Irish Draught stock, but early in the 20th century, the Irish government encouraged a return to quality by introducing inspections and registration schemes. In 1917 the Irish Draught stud book was started, mainly due to the horse's value to the British Army.

After the War, mechanism dealt the Irish Draught a further blow, both on farms and in military service, and it gradually declined once again, being restricted to minimal agricultural and trade use, as a hunter in its own right, and as a cross for the Thoroughbred to produce what has been called "the best cross-country horse in the world" – the Irish hunter. Then, in the 1970s, salvation came once again, this time in the guise of the new Irish Horse Board

which greatly encouraged and facilitated its breeding and use as a competition horse cross. Today's thriving competition and leisure horse markets, and the efforts of private breeders in Ireland and the UK, are maintaining the pure and cross-bred Irish Draught to cater for current requirements for a substantial but quality horse.

Character and care

Unexpectedly agile and enthusiastic for its type and weight, the Irish Draught is spirited and amenable, active, and courageous. It is athletic and has natural jumping ability and stamina.

The Irish Draught today

Its use today is mainly as a medium- to heavy-weight riding horse and hunter, and as breeding stock for hunters and competition horses.

IRISH DRAUGHT

Substantially built horse of medium draft type and weight, but showing obvious finer quality. The action of the Irish Draught belies its weight, being active, long, and scopy with moderate knee action, excellent reach, and agility. It has natural jumping ability. To meet the needs of today's competition horse market, the Irish Draught has received many infusions of Thoroughbred blood. These have created a slightly lighter horse without any loss of character, sensible nature, or hardiness. The symbol **C** *indicates a conformation feature.*

LOINS AND QUARTERS
Muscular loins and rather sloped but strong, deep quarters with a fairly low-set tail. **C**

BARREL AND BACK
The barrel is deep and slightly oval with a medium-length, straight back. **C**

WITHERS AND SHOULDERS
The withers are moderately prominent, and the shoulders slope above a broad, deep chest. **C**

COLOR
All solid colors, but black is rather rare. No particolors and little white on face or legs. Clean-legged with only a very slight silky feather allowed on the fetlocks. The coat is surprisingly fine for the horse's type.

FETLOCKS AND FEET
Although the breed was developed as a medium-type draft and working horse, it is clean-legged, having no significant amounts of long hair around the fetlocks and heels. **C**

HEIGHT
Normally between 15hh and 17hh.

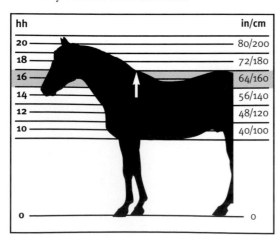

hh	in/cm
20	80/200
18	72/180
16	64/160
14	56/140
12	48/120
10	40/100
0	0

LEGS AND HOOVES
The legs are substantial and well muscled above the knee and hock, with large, flat joints, shortish but moderately sloped pasterns, and end in quite large and well-rounded hooves. **C**

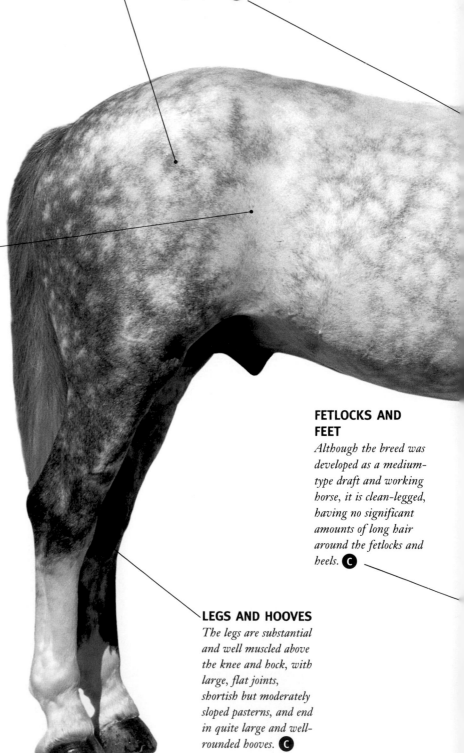

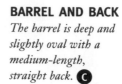

EARS AND EYES
Ears sharp and of moderate length, eyes wise and generous. **C**

PROFILE
Straight with broad forehead. **C**

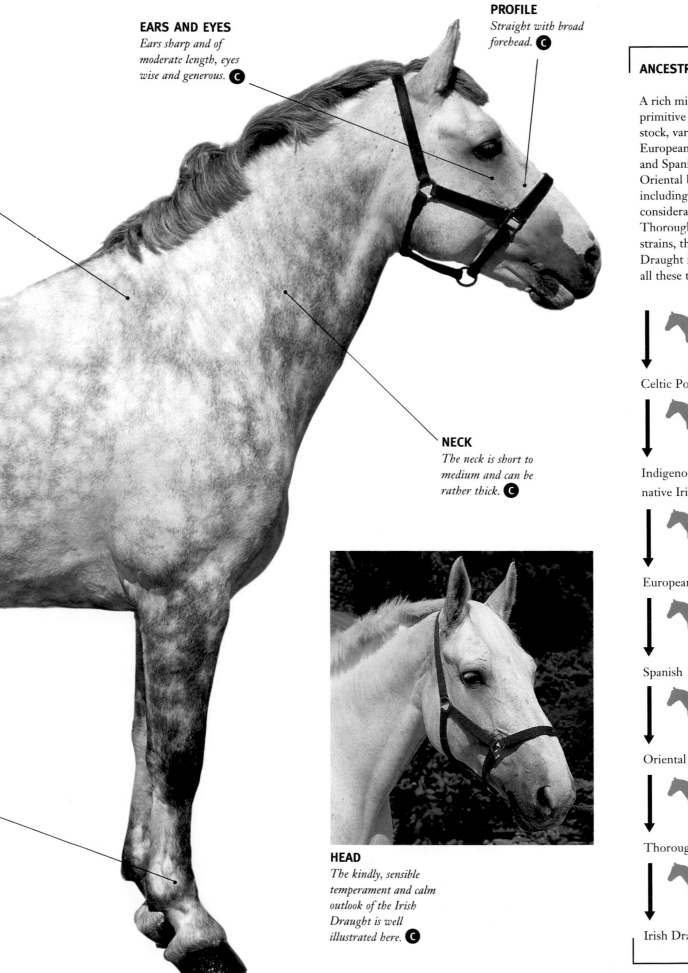

NECK
The neck is short to medium and can be rather thick. **C**

HEAD
The kindly, sensible temperament and calm outlook of the Irish Draught is well illustrated here. **C**

ANCESTRY

A rich mixture of primitive Celtic Pony stock, various European infusions, and Spanish and Oriental blood, including considerable Thoroughbred strains, the Irish Draught is a blend of all these types.

Celtic Pony

Indigenous and native Irish stock

European heavy blood

Spanish

Oriental

Thoroughbred

Irish Draught

75

CONNEMARA

The proud possession and creation of the Irish, the Connemara has had many infusions of other blood since its primitive and early domesticated origins. It has distinct pony character, and even "that Irish look," and makes an excellent larger riding pony.

Ireland is renowned for its history of horse-breeding, while the Irish have always been seen as fine judges of horseflesh. It is a little strange, then, that no true indigenous breed seems to have descended to the present day in its original form, as, for example, with the English Exmoor Pony or the Scottish Shetland. The Connemara pony, although superb in its own way, is a native breed rather than an indigenous breed.

The Connemara's ancestor, the famous Irish Hobbye of medieval times, was descended from an indigenous Irish type which in turn descended from the original Celtic Pony of northern Europe, mixed judiciously with other European imports. The Irish Hobbye was a coveted ambling/pacing mount of great speed, comfort, stamina, agility, and reliability – qualities required of any riding horse today.

The breed name of Connemara, indicating the district from which the pony came, is fairly recent in origin, having been in use for only a couple of hundred years, initially describing the region covering Connemara, Connaught, and Galway.

Connemara ponies have a natural proclivity for jumping – they possess good shoulders, hard legs, good action, and great stamina. All this is due in part to the random introductions of many other breeds over the centuries, most notably Arab, Barb, Norfolk Roadster, Hackney, Welsh Cob, Thoroughbred,

ANCESTRY

The Connemara stems from the ancient Celtic Pony, but in recent times has received blood from various other breeds. Nevertheless, it has achieved a recognizable character and retained its hardiness.

Celtic Pony
Irish Hobbye ▼
Iberian ▼
Oriental ▼
Roadster/Hackney ▼
Welsh Cob ▼
Irish Draught ▼
Clydesdale ▼
Thoroughbred ▼
Connemara

The head of this pony clearly shows Oriental influence. The quality and natural action of the Connemara make it a good cross with Thoroughbreds to produce performance horses, especially for riding and jumping.

Irish Draft, and the Clydesdale, which gave more substance and height to what many felt was a degenerating native pony. The knowledgeable Irish breeders were, however, capable of distilling all these ingredients into the excellent pony we know today.

Character and care

The Connemara is a tough, hardy pony which is not particularly susceptible to adverse weather conditions. It is sure-footed, and a willing worker, able to undertake almost any task. It is an ideal family pony as it is docile, patient, and easy to handle, with a good deal of fabled Irish charm.

The Connemara today

From its traditional role as a farm pony used for light work on the land, its main use today is as an excellent riding pony, hunter, hack, and trekking mount. When crossed with the Thoroughbred, the Connemara makes a superb competition horse.

GENERAL CHARACTERISTICS

CONFORMATION A quality riding pony. The **legs** are fairly short and strong, yet elegant, and the **feet** are tough and well formed. The Connemara seems to have a naturally well-balanced action.

HEAD Pony character with straight **profile**, small, fine **ears**, intelligent **eyes**, and mobile **nostrils.**

COLOR Mainly gray; all solid colors including dun.

HEIGHT From 13hh to 14.2hh.

COB

The cob, or riding cob as it used to be called, is essentially an English and Irish institution, particularly in the way in which it is regarded, presented, and shown.

The cob is basically a shortish, stocky animal with a substantial barrel, very deep through the girth, and with short, strong legs, "one at each corner," and it has a particular outlook on life which seems unique to the type. Definitely a type, cobs cannot be bred with any certainty – they just seem to pop up every now and again, and are the more valued for that. They come with some frequency from the Welsh Cob breed and often result from Irish Draught matings. Smallish heavy horses, too, have been known to produce cobs, but mate an undoubted cob-type mare with, say, a Welsh Cob, an Irish Draught, or a middle-weight Thoroughbred, and you are by no means sure to get a cob as a result.

Perhaps above all, the cob's particular intelligence and character single it out from other equines. Many have a great sense of humor and are basically pro-human to the point of really teaching or looking after novice, elderly, or incapacitated riders. The best are totally trustworthy and have been described as the Gentleman's Gentleman or, traditionally, as a Confidential Cob. The show-ring height limit is 15.1hh, which is just big enough for almost anyone to ride, yet small enough for those no longer young or not too athletic to mount without much difficulty. They are true family animals.

The head is workmanlike and very intelligent; the neck is short, shapely, and strong (the mane and forelock are always hogged or roached in the show ring); and the withers are of only moderate height but with long, powerful sloping shoulders. The back is short, the loins close coupled and powerful, with strong, rounded, muscular hindquarters and thighs. The legs are sturdy with very short cannons; the pasterns are of moderate length and well sloped to match the shoulders.

To ride a good cob gives one a feeling of supreme safety. They are active animals and try their best at whatever is asked of them and can be used for general riding and hacking, harness work, and make super hunters as well.

The term "Confidential Cob" aptly describes this animal. The best cobs have a stocky but not heavy body with shortish, strong legs, and a completely trustworthy nature: an ideal confidence-giver. The cob is of medium height, suitable for almost anyone to ride and goes well in harness.

BRITISH WARMBLOOD

The warmblooded competition horse *par excellence* which has been the mainstay of British teams in show jumping and eventing for generations, has been the Thoroughbred/Irish Draught cross. This is the type of horse which has won many Olympic, World, and European medals for Britain since competitive equestrianism became of serious significance around the middle of the 20th century. Other Thoroughbred crosses, such as Welsh Cob and native pony and cob, have also distinguished themselves competitively at home and abroad.

The British Warmblood is relatively new, but currently enjoys popularity as, particularly, a dressage horse and as a show jumper. Made up of continental European breeds, there is no consistent type at present, but strict testing guarantees that only high-quality animals are accepted into the registry.

The one discipline which has never been a British forté is dressage, and in an effort to improve this, continental European warmbloods began to gain favor in the British Isles about 30 years ago. Then, as the "continentals" – Germans, Belgians, Swedes, Dutch, Danish, and Swiss – began to steal the traditional British thunder in show jumping, it was felt that something had to be done about it. That something was a sudden swelling in the ranks of continental warmbloods imported to Britain and the formation of the British Warmblood Society in 1977.

Generally, the term "warmblood" is an "umbrella" one which covers various continental European breeds developed by different countries from performance bloodlines. Different breed societies have slightly different criteria as to what individual horses they will accept. So long as a horse meets the breed society's criteria of its home country, it can be accepted as a warmblood in Britain. Everyone understands a "warmblood" to be a horse of continental European origin, and not of the type of British and Irish cross mentioned in the first paragraph above (although those are technically warmblooded), so there is, in practice, no identity crisis.

The British Warmblood horse is currently extremely popular for dressage and show jumping. As it derives from so many different continental breeds, it is not possible to give it any clear breed standard. In conclusion, as a strict breed, it will be quite some time before a recognizable type emerges.

SHOW PONY

The creation of the British Show Pony (or Riding Pony) must rank as one of the great animal-breeding achievements of all time. The objective was to produce a miniature show hack for young riders, and this aim has been achieved perfectly, yet, as was always the intention, the pony character of the type has been retained.

The pony is a product of the 20th century, the super-refined type appearing in its latter half. It is based on native British pony blood, mainly Welsh, with Arab and Thoroughbred infusions. At first, many of these ponies, being a good three-quarters Thoroughbred, were unsuitable for any but very competent young riders. The temperament problems of the 1960s and 1970s had to be addressed, and now, although still sometimes a little highly strung, the ponies are temperamentally more suited to children, and a little less refined (or "spindly") than a decade or two ago.

The pony has been exported to many other countries to help in the foundation of their own native children's pony. The British version is divided into three height categories – up to 12.2hh, 12.2hh to 13.2hh, and 13.2hh to 14.2hh. All solid colors are acceptable including roans and palominos, but not particolors. White on legs and head is quite common.

In addition to the above height categories, there are categories for animals up to 15hh, which many contend are not ponies, despite having pony character, to help young riders make the sometimes difficult transition to horses and horse showing classes.

A high-class Show Pony has near perfect riding conformation, showing great refinement with pony character and providing young riders with the exhilarating ride of a Thoroughbred or Arab with the good manners and sensible outlook of its native pony ancestors.

Although many of these ponies live cosseted lives and are often never used for tough work such as hunting and jumping, those which retire from the show ring or take part in other activities show good stamina and soundness.

The Show Pony must be a small version of the adult's show horse, the hack, yet be a pony, and suitable for a child to ride. Despite having much Thoroughbred and Arab blood, it must retain pony character.

RIDING OR PLEASURE HORSE

Riding horses should be a pleasure to ride. Often of no particular breed, they should, to succeed in the show ring, show quality, co-operation, a good level of schooling or training, and an equable temperament. Shown in English-type or Western tack, the movements required to be shown (including jumping) vary nationally.

Show classes for Riding or Pleasure Horses are an extremely popular outlet for horses which do not seem to fit into any specific category or breed, and have opened a way of showing for riders with good riding animals which are of no specific type.

Having said that, in Great Britain official Riding Horse classes (run under the auspices of the British Show Hack, Cob and Riding Horse Association) are full of an increasingly recognizable type, part-way between show-hack type and show-hunter type. Horses which are too big for Large Hack classes often enter Riding Horse classes. The show Riding Horse has to walk, trot, canter, and gallop, but jumping is not required except in Working Riding Horse classes.

As all these classes and types of horse are so numerous and varied, it is not possible to give strict rules about the animals concerned. However, it is obvious that any Riding or Pleasure Horse (formal or informal) should be of good riding type with long, sloping shoulders and moderate to prominent withers which will produce the sort of action which is comfortable under saddle.

A horse ridden for pleasure should be very well trained, responsive, obedient, willing, and comfortable, with a degree of stamina depending on the work required.

BRITISH SPORTS HORSE

The British Sports Horse Registry is run in conjunction with the British Warmblood Society. It is an ideal outlet for animals whose pedigrees cannot be fully documented but who, in performance and/or appearance, appear to possess high quality performance ability. Approved animals must reach very high standards in relation to conformation, action, temperament, and character (just as high as those graded as British Warmbloods), and may be subsequently performance-tested. Entry in this register gives the seal of approval to animals which may otherwise not be able to be registered anywhere due to lack of formal documentation.

The British Sports Horse Registry means good performance animals which do not have fully documented pedigrees can be registered. Many top-class performers are British Sports Horses.

WORKING HUNTER

The Working Hunter class at shows is a useful class for animals which do not quite have the quality to win a pure showing class, yet make up for that with good jumping ability. In the Working Hunter classes in Britain and Ireland, the horses do have to jump a shortish course of natural fences rather than painted show jumps. Judging is based on conformation, action, and presentation, but also on jumping ability and way of going, which must be a free, hunting style and not the more formal show-jumping style.

The Working Hunter show type needs similar qualities to the show hunter proper. The horse must show a workmanlike, fluid, jump over natural-looking obstacles.

HUNTER

By definition, a hunter is any horse capable of carrying a rider to hounds. This can vary from a young child to an elderly person, and the animal can range from a little pony to a Shire or Thoroughbred.

Hunter classes in competitions are found in those countries which enjoy the sport of hunting, principally Ireland, Great Britain, the United States, Canada, the south-eastern states of Australia, Tasmania, and New Zealand.

Hunter classes are divided usually by the weight the horse is expected to carry, and also height classes and classes according to the horse's experience. Ladies' Hunters, as a category, are ridden side-saddle.

The show hunter is normally a good solid color, perhaps carrying a little white on lower legs and head, but as it is definitely a wide-ranging type, it has no specific breed characteristics, and it is unlikely that anyone is going to try to create a Hunter breed.

The show hunter, even the heavyweight, should carry a fair proportion of Thoroughbred blood, must have substance, stamina, excellent riding-horse conformation, strong, thrusting, and straight action with a strong back and powerful hindquarters. It must be well balanced and a comfortable ride, courageous, obedient, agile, must not "hot up" and must be robust enough to hunt up to two days a week for a six-month season.

In the show ring, hunters must exhibit excellent training, and much emphasis is placed on the ground-covering, controlled gallop. Specific performance requirements vary from country to country: for example, in Britain and Ireland, show hunters never jump and the judges always ride them at big shows, but in the U.S. they always jump and the judges never ride them.

Although, in practice, almost any animal can be used for hunting, the show hunter usually needs a large dose of Thoroughbred blood, even the heavyweight type. It must have quality, substance, and a strong, straight action, be obedient, comfortable to ride, and, very important, be controllable in often very exciting situations.

WORKING HUNTER PONY

The ideal Working Hunter Pony is a show pony of hunter type with the added performance factor of jumping. A mistake is often made when people enter fine-boned show ponies with plain or downright unattractive heads which would never win in their own category, but the Working Hunter Pony classes are not second bests for failed ponies of other categories. Much is left to the judge, however, and some will place a plain pony who performs really well above a better-looking, more "typey" pony who does not.

The Working Hunter Pony, at its best, should be of good show hunter pony type and must also have a bold, controllable, and well-mannered style of jumping and going between the jumps. It must give its rider a feeling of great confidence, the pair should look happy together and capable of going well across country following hounds.

These classes are extremely popular with children who do not wish to actually show jump and like showing but with that little bit extra as a performance element. The classes are usually well filled and attract large numbers of spectators.

Working Hunter Ponies are the junior version of the adult's Working Hunter. Its bold, calm outlook is ideal for a hunter, and its willingness and co-operation make it controllable by its young rider.

PONY OF HUNTER TYPE

The Riding Pony or, as it is usually called, the Show Pony, was created as a pony version of the show hack: but it was soon obvious that there was a slot available for more substantial ponies of hunter type to create a pony version of the adult show hunter.

These ponies, again, reproduce in miniature all the qualities of the show hunter. Initially a rather mixed bag, there has now evolved a correct hunter-type of pony which, while not showing the beauty and refinement of the show pony, appeals to those interested in

a more substantial pony which can probably go on to become a working hunter pony or an event pony. The animals competing are, however, of real quality and of excellent type for a child to hunt on.

Like its horse counterpart, the pony of hunter type is not required to jump in the show ring, but many do take part in other performance-type competitions.

HACK

The Hack is a peculiarly British type. The word derives from the old French *haquenai*, meaning a hired horse of poor quality, but over the years the hack came to mean a horse used for general riding but not hunting. This is still the meaning today: a hack must be comfortable, well mannered, and well-trained.

During the heyday of the hack, in the 19th and early 20th centuries, there were two main types of hack – covert hacks and park hacks. The covert hack was a horse with a good deal of Thoroughbred blood in it, good-looking, with quality and presence, on which the owner would ride to a meet of foxhounds, his groom having ridden his employer's hunter there earlier. The two would then change over, and the covert hack would be ridden home by the groom. The park hack was the prestigious, highly refined, and trained animal on which to be seen out and about. Park hacks had to be impeccably mannered and able to be ridden with one hand so that a gentleman could raise his hat to a lady or a lady could wave to her friends. A park hack was usually Thoroughbred or sometimes Anglo-Arab.

Today the hack is best exemplified by the various British and Irish categories of show hack, which are of old park hack type. The show hack should be of near perfect, light Thoroughbred conformation, with straight, low action of "elegant airiness" and of such a high standard of training that the rider can ride with one hand and have the horse under perfect control at all times. The horse should be capable of easy, collected gaits in walk, trot, and canter (hacks do not gallop or jump), and be able to stand and wait without moving a leg while the rider mounts and dismounts.

Hacks are ridden by the judge to test the ride and level of training – at major shows, there is often a conformation judge and a riding judge – and are stripped (the saddle removed) so that the conformation and in-hand action can be judged. They may also give an individual display.

There are three categories of show hack. The Small Hack, 14.2hh–15hh; the Large Hack, 15hh–15.3hh; and the Ladies Hack, 14.2hh–15.3hh, shown side-saddle. Any solid color, with moderate white markings on head and lower legs, is seen. Outside the show ring, color is unimportant.

In countries other than Britain, hacks may differ in type. In Europe, small Thoroughbreds with a little Arab blood are popular, while in the U.S., the Saddlebred type is regarded as the epitome of the quality riding horse.

Different countries have different types of hack class; but hacks anywhere are judged in the show ring on conformation, presence and type, action, manners, training, and quality of ride.

The show Hack is the quality, refined riding horse par excellence. Almost always of wholly Thoroughbred or Anglo-Arab blood, the horse must be superbly trained, very obedient, a good-looking animal of excellent conformation and with a beautiful, or at least, attractive head.

EUROPE

SELLE FRANCAIS

A high-quality riding horse, the Selle Français exhibits considerable variety of type within its breed. This horse resembles a middleweight Thoroughbred of good conformation. The Selle Français is an excellent performance horse.

Most breeds are created by mixing together horses or ponies of various types until a blend satisfactory to the breeder and the market is achieved, and the Selle Français is probably one of the more mixed breeds in the world. It was only in the 1950s that the French riding horse was given formal status as the Selle Français or French Saddle Horse, and it has proved to be an excellent riding and competition horse.

The foundation breed for the Selle Français is the Norman, bred in Normandy and certainly present in the Middle Ages, when heavy local mares were crossed with Arabs and other Oriental types brought to France after the Crusades. A useful warhorse was created from these mixes. In later centuries, the Norman deteriorated due to unsuitable and indiscriminate crossing with Danish and German carthorses, but from the 17th century to the early 19th century, in a successful effort to improve the breed, there were copious introductions of English Thoroughbred along with Arab and Norfolk Roadster blood to the Norman.

The resulting Anglo-Norman horse was the forerunner of the French Trotter, but significant amounts of its blood exist in today's Selle Français. In fact, two main types of Anglo-Norman were developed; one (containing also Percheron and Boulonnais blood) was for draft and cavalry use, and the other produced two sub-types, one for trotting and one for riding. The trotting strain appears to have gone from strength to strength, but the riding type was more difficult to establish as a quality riding horse, often inheriting the worst points of the Norman and the Thoroughbred.

Careful attention to suitably paired matings and study of the individual animals' dominant traits, however, eventually produced an excellent horse for general riding.

The original heavy draft type no longer exists, but its blood survives in a smaller version known as the Norman Cob. The riding type has been absorbed into the new breed now called the Selle Francais.

The Norman was only the foundation breed. Other infusions included native French breeds such as the Limousin, the Vendéen, and the Charentais. The Limousin, a heavyweight hunter type, was probably the best and most influential of the three. The breed appears to have begun life in the 8th century at the time of the Moorish invasions of southern France, which inevitably introduced considerable numbers of Arab horses to the local mares of the district. It appears to have undergone several changes of type, including the introduction of Anglo-Norman blood, to regain substance. In more recent times, it became a big, substantial horse, late-maturing and able to gallop and jump under considerable weight. It was later lightened and given more quality by introducing Arab blood again. The Vendéen and Charentais mares were heavy types upgraded by the use of Dutch, Norman, Anglo-Norman, Norfolk Roadster, Thorough-bred, Anglo-Arab, and Arab blood – a familiar but successful story.

The two breeds which are most influential in the breeding of the Selle Français are the English Thoroughbred and the Anglo-Norman, giving the Selle Français its athleticism, toughness, and common sense. At present, the stud book admits carefully selected mares and stallions of (in order of preference) Selle Français, Thoroughbred, Anglo-Arab, and Arab blood, with a small number of French Trotter stallions also being admitted. Future generations of Selle Français will probably show more uniformity of type, although some of the breed's enthusiasts feel that the different types now existing are a plus point since they can cater for varying tastes and requirements.

Character and care

Variable character is the dominant feature of the breed. In the main, the horses are docile but energetic, willing workers that are not hard to handle. Five types currently exist: the three mediumweight types are small (not exceeding 15.1hh), medium (15.1hh–16hh), and large (over 16hh), and the two heavyweight types are

small (up to 16hh) and large (over 16hh). They are divided according to their ability to carry weight.

The type of care they require should be determined by individual qualities, but basically they require the normal feeding, shelter, and other reasonable requirements of a halfbred riding horse, not being over-sensitive to weather or requiring great amounts of food.

The Selle Français today

The breed is basically bred as a competition horse and good general riding/leisure horse. Primarily intended as a show jumper, at which discipline it excels, it also produces excellent cross-country and event horses, and is a very good hunter. Numbers are exported through-out Europe for these purposes. It is also raced in non-Thoroughbred races both on the flat and over obstacles.

Miss Fan, ridden by Eddie Macken, here representing Ireland at Aachen in 1995, is a good example of a horse used for its original purpose – the Selle Français was principally developed as a show jumper.

SELLE FRANCAIS

This horse demonstrates excellent riding conformation, with his bold outlook, and should be highly placed in in-hand showing classes as well as in the performance field. The symbol **C** *indicates a conformation feature.*

HEAD

Generally tends to resemble the French Trotter, the profile being straight or slightly convex, a remnant characteristic of the Norman horse. **C**

WITHERS AND SHOULDERS

Prominent withers, well-laid-back shoulders with medium width chest. **C**

EARS AND EYES

The head is well set. The ears are long, the eyes are not prominent and sometimes rather small.

BARREL

The barrel is deep, oval, and substantial. **C**

HEIGHT

Overall, taking into account the different types, the height is from 15.1hh to over 16hh.

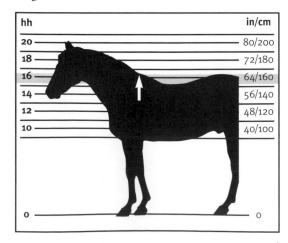

hh		in/cm
20		80/200
18		72/180
16		64/160
14		56/140
12		48/120
10		40/100
0		0

FEET

Tough, sometimes rather big feet. **C**

COLOR

This detail shows attractive dappling in a brown coat. Most of the breed are, however, chestnut, with bay, gray, and sometimes strawberry (red) roan occurring.

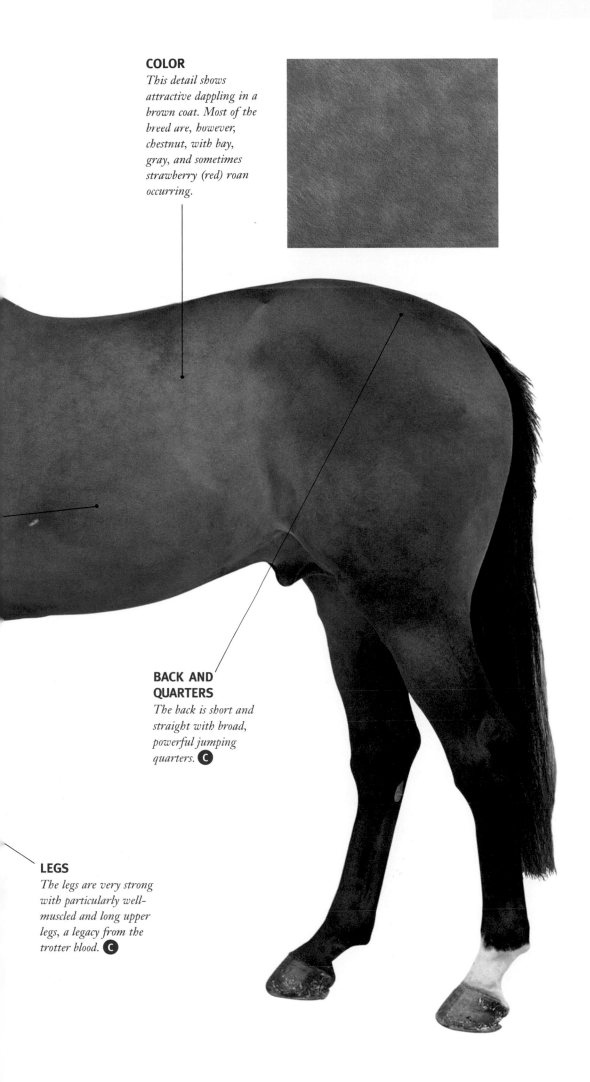

BACK AND QUARTERS

The back is short and straight with broad, powerful jumping quarters. **C**

LEGS

The legs are very strong with particularly well-muscled and long upper legs, a legacy from the trotter blood. **C**

ANCESTRY

Probably the pervading influences today are Norman and Thoroughbred, plus other Oriental strains and native French regional breeds. However, a strong Norfolk Roadster and Trotter influence remain.

Norman

Arab

Norfolk Roadster

Dutch and German cart breeds

French regional heavy breeds

Thoroughbred

Anglo-Arab

Selle Français

FRENCH TROTTER

Trotting races are an extremely popular sport in France, both in harness and under saddle. The sport became popular in the early 19th century, with the first trotting course opening at Cherbourg in 1836.

In those early days, the favored type of trotter was the Norman or Anglo-Norman, and it is said that the first trotting races were held to select suitable stud stallions, but the spectacle proved so popular that it took off as an entertainment in its own right.

The admirable Norman horse was initially crossed with the English Norfolk Roadster, but later in the 19th century, English Hackney and Russian Orlov Trotter blood was also introduced to create a blend of the best from around the world. Toward the end of the century, American Standardbred blood was introduced, which has had a noticeable and lasting influence on the breed.

In 1906, a stud book was opened for French trotting horses, although the French Trotter as a breed was not officially recognized as such until 1922. To be registered in the stud book, a horse had to be able to trot a kilometer in 1 minute 42 seconds. In 1941 the stud book was closed to horses other than those with registered parents. In recent years, however, some selected American Standardbred blood has been used again to help maintain quality and further increase speed, although the French Trotter is accepted as being as good as any other trotting breed in the world, including the Standardbred.

Character and care
The French Trotter is a horse of considerable quality with the appearance of a big and strong Thoroughbred. The harness trotters are slightly smaller than the ridden trotters. The temperament of the French Trotter is similar to that of the Thoroughbred with regard to both spirit and energy.

The French Trotter today
The French Trotter today is used almost exclusively as a trotting racer in harness and

ANCESTRY

Based on the Norman and Thoroughbred, the French Trotter also contains Norfolk Roadster, English halfbred stock, Hackney, Orlov Trotter, and later infusions of Thoroughbred with, significantly, American Standardbred blood.

Anglo-Norman
Norfolk Roadster ▼
English half- ▼
bred/hunter
Hackney ▼
Orlov ▼
Thoroughbred ▼
Standardbred ▼
French Trotter

Trotting races are particularly popular in France, both in harness and under saddle. This French Trotter clearly shows his Standardbred genes with the accompanying Thoroughbred influence.

In contrast to the horse on the previous page, this animal shows more of his French Norman ancestry with the longer back and more plebeian type.

The Anglo-Norman type of head with the very slightly convex profile, not uncommon in the French Trotter, is evident here, plus an honest and generous temperament.

under saddle. Horses which do not make the grade in racing do, however, make very good riding horses and seem to have an inborn jumping ability. The saddle-bred trotters are used at stud to sire competition and general riding horses; French Trotter blood is found in the Selle Français.

GENERAL CHARACTERISTICS

CONFORMATION The overall impression is that of a substantial Thoroughbred horse.

HEAD Quality, Thoroughbred-type head: straight **profile**, broad **forehead**, long, wide-apart **ears**, alert **eyes**, and flaring **nostrils**.

COLOR Chestnut, bay, and brown are the most common, with some roans, blacks, and the rare gray.

HEIGHT Averaging around 16.2hh.

CAMARGUE

ANCESTRY

Descended from the primitive French horse, the Camargue has undoubtedly received infusions of Barb and Arab blood centuries ago and, more recently, Thoroughbred, more Arab, and French Postier-Breton – but to little effect.

Primitive French horse
Barb ▼
Arab ▼
Thoroughbred ▼
Postier-Breton ▼
Camargue

No one seems to know just how long Camargue horses have inhabited the salt marshes of their homeland in south-eastern France. They are believed to descend from the primitive Diluvial Horse, but from their type, particularly their heads, they seem to have a good deal of Barb blood.

The horses of the Camargue in south-eastern France spend much of their time up to their knees in salt water, grazing on reeds and sparse coastal grasses, yet they have lived and thrived there for many thousands of years, though now numbering less than 500. The Camargue region on the Rhône delta, is open, exposed, and hot in summer and cold in winter.

The Camargue horses are probably descendants of the primitive Diluvial Horse. From their heads, it would appear that they also have Barb and other Oriental blood in them.

In the 19th century, other blood was introduced by local residents – Arab, Anglo-Arab, Thoroughbred, and the French Postier-Breton – but these seem to have had no lasting effect on the Camargue horse. Annual round-ups of the herds take place in the fall for the selection of riding animals, while culling of sub-standard colts and stallions has improved the breed.

Character and care

Once broken in, the Camargue makes a docile and willing riding horse, while remaining independent and spirited. It is late to mature, but is long-lived.

The Camargue today

The Camargue is used mainly for herding the wild black bulls of its homeland, which are often exported to Spain for bullfighting there. With an increase in tourist traffic in the region, the horse is often pressed into service as a trekking mount.

GENERAL CHARACTERISTICS

CONFORMATION The Camargue has a primitive, wild quality. The **tail** is set low and, like the **mane** and **forelock**, is long and thick. The **legs** are sturdy and strong, and the **feet** extremely hard and well formed.

HEAD Rather plain and big with short, broad **ears**, pronounced, heavy **jaws**, and expressive, soulful **eyes** set well to the side of the broad **forehead**.

COLOR Almost always white-gray. Like with the Lipizzaner, the foals are born dark but lighten with age. Bay and brown sometimes occur.

HEIGHT Around 13.1hh to 14.2hh.

FRENCH ANGLO-ARAB

The Anglo-Arab horse is one of the best all-round high-class riding horses in the world. It is a composite breed containing Arab blood and that of the Thoroughbred – an English breed, hence the term "Anglo."

The French Anglo-Arab dates from about the 1830s when a French veterinary surgeon, E. Gayot, decided to create a formal Anglo-Arab breed, first at the stud of Le Pin and then at the stud at Pompadour. He selected the Arab stallion Massoud, the Turkish stallion Aslan, and three English Thoroughbred mares.

This does not mean that M. Gayot introduced Arab blood into the country. Oriental strains were already present in France's native stock. Napoleon was a great fan of the Arab and founded studs for purebred and part-bred breeding at Pau and Tarbes in southwestern France; indeed, his famous white charger, Marengo, was probably a pure-bred Arab.

Today, the French Anglo-Arab is bred using Arab, Anglo-Arab, and Thoroughbred blood, and to be eligible for registration in the stud book a horse must have at least 25 percent Arab blood and the absence of any other than Thoroughbred and Arab blood for at least six generations.

Character and care

The best examples of the French Anglo-Arab combine the Arab's intelligence, good nature, and stamina, and the scope, size, and speed of the Thoroughbred. They require sensitive, knowledgeable handling.

The French Anglo-Arab today

The French Anglo-Arab is a high-quality riding horse which excels at show jumping, dressage, eventing, racing on the flat and over jumps, endurance riding, showing, and hunting.

GENERAL CHARACTERISTICS

CONFORMATION Strongly built, but with an overall impression of aristocracy and pride without the arrogance of some Thoroughbreds.

HEAD The head has a straight or slightly convex **profile**; finely chiseled **ears**; knowing **eyes**; and a slightly tapering **muzzle** with fine, mobile **nostrils**.

COLOR All solid colors, although chestnut is very common. White markings on legs and head.

HEIGHT A wide range, from about 15.2hh to 16.3hh.

The French Anglo-Arab is one of the highest quality performance horses in the world. Bred with thoroughness and care, the breed was intended as a top-class officer's charger. Today, it is a superb competition horse in all disciplines, although it is not used extensively in harness.

ANCESTRY

Indigenous French stock containing infusions of Oriental blood formed the basic foundation, with Arab, Turk, and Thoroughbred blood used in the 19th century to found the specific breed.

Tarbes, Limousin, and other native breeds
Iberian ▼
Oriental ▼
Arab ▼
Turk ▼
Thoroughbred ▼
French Anglo-Arab

PERCHERON

Undoubtedly a heavy horse of good draft type, this Percheron has well-balanced conformation and shows the breed's calm temperament and strength. He is clean-legged, without significant feathering around the fetlocks.

Along with the Scottish Clydesdale, the French Percheron is the most popular draft breed of horse working in the world today. It is exported and bred throughout Europe and the United States. It is heavier and "chunkier" than the Clydesdale, but just as active and elegant, mainly due to considerable infusions of Arab blood.

The breed comes from the La Perche district of Normandy, one of the oldest horse-breeding regions of the world. The Percheron, now noted for heavy draft work, was, centuries ago, lighter than its modern representatives, and was almost certainly used for riding and light draft work. It is believed that in the 8th century Arab and other Oriental horses, taken as booty from the Saracens following their defeat at the Battle of Poitiers, were mated with native heavy and cob stock, producing the first of the Percheron horses.

In the Middle Ages, the Crusaders' Oriental prizes of war, again mainly Barbs and Arabs, filtered into the region to provide another infusion of Eastern genes. Also around this time, Spanish blood was introduced by the Comte de Perche who brought Spanish horses home with him from his forays into Spain. Later, the Comte de Rotrou imported Andalusian stallions which were used on

Percheron mares. In the 18th century, Arabs and the new English Thoroughbreds were also imported and used. In 1820, two gray Arab stallions were imported into the La Perche area and used extensively on existing stock, and it is from these two that the present-day gray color of the Percheron stems.

By the middle of the 19th century, the old strains of Percheron blood had almost disappeared and the stock was augmented by bringing in heavy mares from neighboring Brittany to mix with the remnants of the old Percheron. It was the advent of railroads which greatly decreased the demand for the old, lighter Percheron horse. Breeders from the tiny La Perche region looked to agriculture for new markets and began concentrating on producing vanners and heavier horses for heavy agricultural work. At the close of the 19th century, heavy horses from Brittany, Caux, and Picardy were brought to the Percheron's home area and were introduced into the breed, eventually producing the type of Percheron that is familiar today.

Throughout the centuries, the Percheron has changed type (there are still heavy and lighter-heavy types today), size, and jobs with great adaptability and always seems to have been the amenable, active, kind, energetic, and elegant horse which has made it so immensely popular. It has always been used for light and heavy draft work, as a vanner, for pulling urban buses, and by armies for heavy artillery and transport work. In the 19th century some enthusiasts retained the lighter strains for trotting competitions. The breed is, in fact, noted for being able to maintain a fast trot while pulling a heavy load and is said to be able to average 35 miles (56km) a day in this way with no problem.

Character and care

The Percheron is noted for its equable temperament, its intelligence, ease of handling, and willingness to work. It is an elegant type of heavy horse due to the constant infusions of Oriental-type blood over the centuries. It is energetic and active, with a long, low, free stride showing little knee action.

Although undoubtedly now a heavy breed, it definitely shows its lighter and particularly its Oriental ancestry in its carriage, the set of the head and facial expression, and the lack of feather on the lower legs.

Like any heavy breed, it is resistant to most weather conditions and, for its size, does not need excessive amounts of food to keep it in good condition. However, it does have relatively fine skin, and its coat is quite fine and satiny, even in winter, which is unusual in a heavy horse and may denote a certain lack of hardiness in extremes of weather, yet Percheron horses have been exported all over the world and have always appeared to adapt well to their new climate.

The Percheron today

Today, Percherons are used widely by the brewing companies in most Western countries. Their elegance, docility, and arresting appearance make them ideal for this purpose. Some are certainly still used in agriculture, particularly in less well-developed countries. They are also useful for any short-haul heavy road transportation job, for example, for logging in many countries' forestry businesses. The lighter versions of Percheron are even used under saddle as heavyweight riding horses, and the breed makes an excellent foundation for breeding up quality, substantial competition horses, hunters, and driving animals.

Percherons are still used as working horses in agriculture and haulage in France and other countries, and in shows and competitions. Their good temperament and energy make them popular workhorses.

PERCHERON

Some Percherons are even used as heavy riding horses. This horse shows a lighter type than the gray on the previous page and would not look out of place under saddle. The Percheron's ground-eating stride and riding-horse action should be mentioned as being unique among "heavies." The symbol **C** *indicates a conformation feature.*

COAT AND COLOR

Although most Percherons are gray or black, chestnut is occasionally acceptable if the horse is particularly good. This horse is a dark liver shade of chestnut.

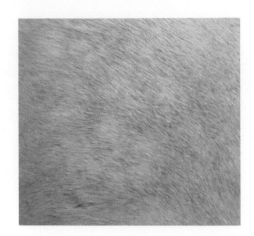

LOINS AND QUARTERS

Well-muscled, broad loins, a noticeable croup, and strong, deep, somewhat sloping quarters. **C**

TAIL

In many countries, it is traditional to dock the tail or nick the muscles. However, this is not a breed requirement and it is illegal in other countries. **C**

HEIGHT

There is a smaller recognized variety which stands between 14.3hh and 16.1hh and a larger one, which stands between 16.1hh and 17.3hh, although taller horses are certainly found.

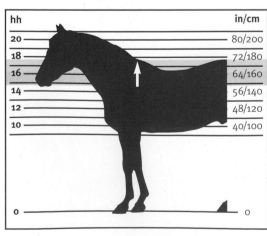

hh		in/cm
20		80/200
18		72/180
16		64/160
14		56/140
12		48/120
10		40/100
0		0

LEGS AND HOOVES

The legs are short and robust with exceptionally hard, well-formed hooves of tough horn. **C**

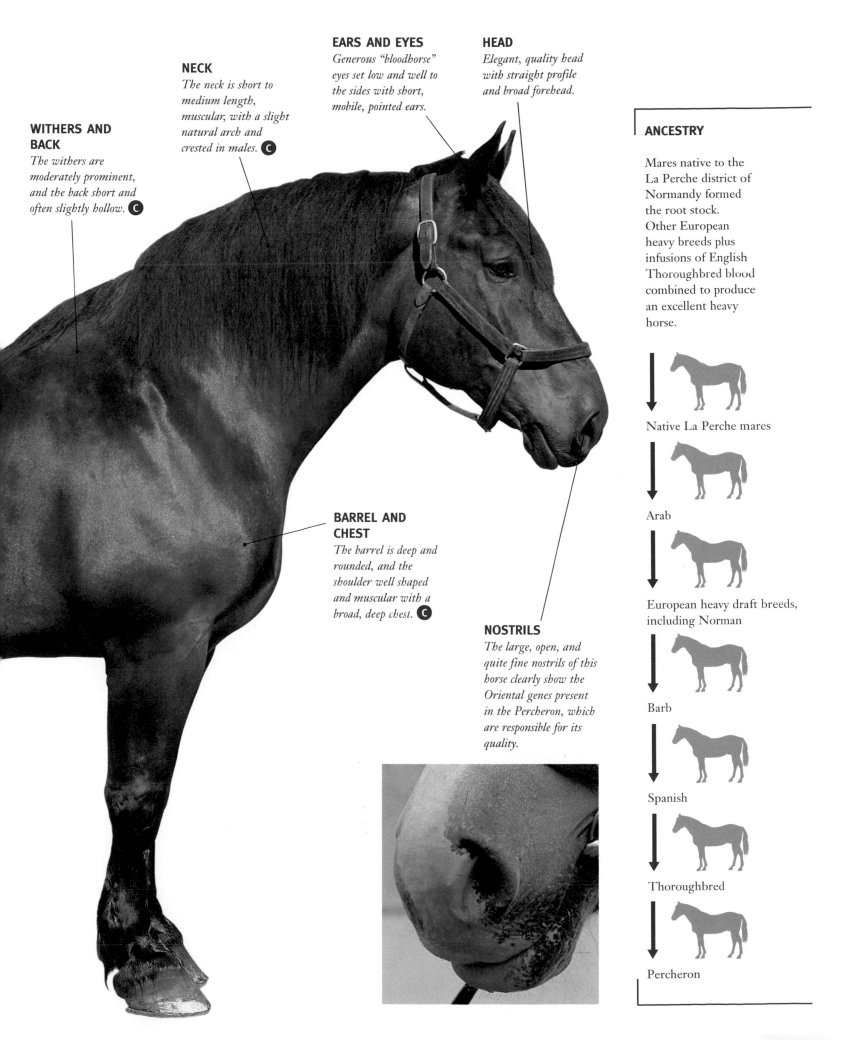

NECK

The neck is short to medium length, muscular, with a slight natural arch and crested in males. **C**

EARS AND EYES

Generous "bloodhorse" eyes set low and well to the sides with short, mobile, pointed ears.

HEAD

Elegant, quality head with straight profile and broad forehead.

WITHERS AND BACK

The withers are moderately prominent, and the back short and often slightly hollow. **C**

BARREL AND CHEST

The barrel is deep and rounded, and the shoulder well shaped and muscular with a broad, deep chest. **C**

NOSTRILS

The large, open, and quite fine nostrils of this horse clearly show the Oriental genes present in the Percheron, which are responsible for its quality.

ANCESTRY

Mares native to the La Perche district of Normandy formed the root stock. Other European heavy breeds plus infusions of English Thoroughbred blood combined to produce an excellent heavy horse.

Native La Perche mares

Arab

European heavy draft breeds, including Norman

Barb

Spanish

Thoroughbred

Percheron

BRETON

The Breton draft horse is a recently formed breed from Brittany in the northwest of France. There is a heavy and a smaller, more active strain within the same stud book.

The history of its foundation stock goes back 4,000 years, when Asian stock was brought to Europe by the Aryans. In the Middle Ages, the horses found in the Brittany area were much sought by armies due to their ground-covering and comfortable gait. The horses had an attractive, easy-to-handle nature and great stamina.

The Crusaders' Oriental horses, brought back to France from the East, were introduced into the Brittany horse, and from the cross there developed two types of horse, the Sommier, used mainly as a strong but slow pack horse, and the Roussin, used mainly as a long-distance riding horse and as a warhorse. These two types were popular for centuries in general agricultural work and for collecting seaweed for fertilizer from the Breton shores.

In the 18th century the Sommier and the Roussin were crossed with other breeds (specifically the Ardennais, Percheron, and Boulonnais) to create a heavier, stronger type of animal, the Draught or Grand Breton. Then, in the 19th century, Norfolk Roadster and Hackney blood were crossed into the lighter animals, producing a smart, substantial animal used for light draft, military, and coaching purposes, the Postier-Breton.

ANCESTRY

Originally founded from small Asian heavy horses and local indigenous types. Oriental blood was initially introduced, with later additions of Ardennais, Boulonnais, Percheron, Norfolk Roadster, and Hackney.

Asian and indigenous stock
Oriental ▼
Ardennais ▼
Boulonnais ▼
Percheron ▼
Norfolk Roaster ▼
Hackney ▼
Grand Breton/
Postier-Breton

Character and care

Both types of Breton have amenable temperaments and endurance abilities. The Postier-Breton is clean-legged; the Grand Breton is an early maturing, powerfully muscled animal.

The Breton today

The Grand Breton is used for heavy draft work; the Postier-Breton is for light draft work on farms and vineyards.

GENERAL CHARACTERISTICS

CONFORMATION Although both the Grand Breton and Postier-Breton are similar in type, the differences lie in the smaller, lighter build of the Postier and its more active gaits.

HEAD Squarish and large with heavy **jaws**, but with a friendly **expression**, short, mobile **ears**, and small, bright **eyes**. The **nostrils** are large and open.

COLOR Usually chestnut or red roan, but other roans, bay, and gray occur.

HEIGHT 15hh to 16hh, the Postier-Breton being the smaller of the two types.

The exact origins of the Grand Breton and the lighter Postier-Breton are subject to speculation. Having gone through many changes and developments, both sorts are still used for work, and the larger Grand Breton is used for meat production.

NORMAN COB

The Norman Cob is aptly named, showing the true cob type and clean legs but in a bigger body. It is still actively used as a working horse in France, mainly in agriculture and transportation.

ANCESTRY

Old Norman stock forms the basis of this unusual horse, with additions of Oriental and Norfolk Trotter blood.

Anglo-Norman
Norfolk Trotter/ ▼
Roadster
Native stock ▼
Norman Cob

The Norman Cob is a true cob in appearance, but is considerably larger than the true cob type. In fact, the Norman Cob resembles the old-fashioned type of cob due to the fact that its tail is usually docked, a practice which is illegal in Britain but not in France.

Normandy has always been a noted horse-breeding area, which has produced superb horses for thousands of years. The Norman horse was the basis for the Anglo-Norman, which has itself formed the progenitor base for riding and light harness horses. The Norman Cob was created in the 17th century specifically for riding, carriage work, and light draft work. Today, it is a good, all-round animal, big and stocky enough to be useful in draft work, yet it is also a pleasurable ride.

In France, state studs make Norman Cob stallions available to private breeders as well as using them on their own establishments, and the breed is still actively bred and highly regarded.

Character and care

The Norman Cob is a tough, hardy animal with strength, stamina, and is "nice to know." Even the heavier individuals show quality and are not ponderous or sluggish.

The Norman Cob today

Today, the Norman Cob is used as a light to medium draft horse, although the stockier ones are strong enough to perform heavy agricultural work. The breed is mainly used in its homeland, where it can be found working on farms.

GENERAL CHARACTERISTICS

CONFORMATION Stocky but not coarse, the Norman Cob is a quality draft horse of real cob, rather than heavy-horse, build. It is also an attractive energetic mover.

HEAD The head is held high and proudly, the **ears** are medium to short, and the **forehead** broad between bright, mischievous **eyes**. The **muzzle** is small, and the **nostrils** tend to be likewise.

COLOR Chestnut, brown, and bay are the usual colors with occasional roans and grays.

HEIGHT From 15.3hh to as tall as 16.3hh, which is unusual in a cob type.

ARDENNAIS

This example of the heavy draft Ardennais is not the usual strawberry roan, but more bay with just a hint of roan. Despite various other infusions, the Ardennais still retains an air of antiquity about it.

ANCESTRY

Based on primitive indigenous stock, the Ardennais also contains Oriental and Thoroughbred blood with Brabant, Boulonnais, and Percheron infusions.

Prehistoric Diluvial/ Solutré Horse
Oriental ▼
Thoroughbred ▼
Brabant ▼
Boulonnais ▼
Percheron ▼
Ardennais

The Ardennais comes from the Ardennes region on the borders of France and Belgium, but it is generally regarded as a French breed. It is one of the oldest breeds of heavy draft horses in the world, being directly descended from the prehistoric Diluvial Horse of Solutré. It was particularly praised and valued by the Romans. The Ardennais has never been a very tall horse and probably formed one of the base progenitor types for the so-called Great Horse of the knights of the Middle Ages.

In previous centuries, the Ardennais has been shorter and less massive than it is now, its present-day shape and size having come about by introductions of Belgian Brabant blood for increased height and musculature at the expense of stamina, vigor, energy, and action.

The Ardennais has often been used as a cavalry horse, and Napoleon used them in his Russian campaign in 1812, where the breed survived the horrific Russian winter better than the other breeds. In World War I, Ardennais were used extensively as artillery wheelers.

In the early 19th century, Thoroughbred and Arab blood were, somewhat surprisingly, introduced into the breed, together with French Boulonnais and Percheron blood, resulting in variations in type. The three types of Ardennais now in existence are the old, original type of around 15hh which live in small numbers in the mountains; the Trait du Nord type, which is bigger, heavier, and more

widespread; and the Auxois, a very heavy type probably containing less original Ardennais blood than the other two types.

Character and care

Unmistakably a heavy draft animal, the Ardennais of any type has a primitive air to it, yet it is tractable and easy to work with.

The Ardennais today

The Ardennais is used in heavy draft work, including short-haul transportation and farming.

GENERAL CHARACTERISTICS

CONFORMATION One of the heaviest, if not the tallest, types of draft horse, the overall impression given by the Ardennais is one of great strength combined with docility. The breed has a quick, energetic action.

HEAD Can be quite light and finer than expected, with an alert, friendly **expression**, wide-apart **ears**, flat **forehead**, prominent **eyes**, and a straight **profile**.

COLOR A distinctive feature of the Ardennais is its very common strawberry roan color with black points. All other colors except black are accepted.

HEIGHT From 15hh to 16hh.

FRIESIAN

The Friesian is now being recognized as one of the old, original Haute Ecole breeds. In Holland, it is also a much-loved and showy carriage horse with remarkable trotting ability.

ANCESTRY

Descended from the local primitive horse, the Friesian received Oriental and Andalusian crosses during the time of the Crusades. Oldenburg blood was brought in to revive the breed in the early 19th century.

Primitive local horse
Oriental ▼
Andalusian ▼
Oldenburg ▼
Friesian

The Friesian horse, or Harddraver, is at last being acknowledged as one of the original royal horses of Europe, albeit not so well known as its colleagues, the Andalusian, Lusitano, and Lipizzaner. Royal horses are breeds or types favored by royalty for their type and bearing.

The Friesian hails from the coastal Friesland province of Holland, and its old name, Harddraver, means "good trotter" in Dutch. Coldblooded horse remains from 3,000 years ago found in the area prove the existence of similar ancestral horses in Friesland from which the modern Friesian is descended.

The Romans respected the then rather ugly Friesian as an excellent working horse, and it went to Britain with the Frieslanders who were pressed into service as cavalrymen with the Roman armies. It was used in the formation of Britain's Fell and Dales ponies, as well as influencing most of the world's trotting breeds.

Used as an excellent hack, the Friesian was also popular on farms and was used in the formation of the German Oldenburg breed. Just before World War I, the only Friesians in existence were three stallions and a few quality mares. Judicious crossing and selective breeding with the Oldenburg restored the Friesian.

Character and care

A light to mediumweight horse, having a proud yet gentle bearing. Most are fairly tractable, if energetic and enthusiastic. It is hardy and a good all-rounder.

The Friesian today

The Friesian has spread throughout the world; its presence and active, showy trot in harness makes it very popular in show rings and in the festivals of its homeland. The Friesian is also being revived as a *Haute Ecole* horse.

GENERAL CHARACTERISTICS

CONFORMATION An elegant quality horse. The very profuse wavy **mane** and **tail** are worn long as trimming is not officially allowed.

HEAD Rather long and narrow with flaring **nostrils**. The facial **expression** is appealing.

COLOR Exclusively black with only a tiny white star permitted on the forehead.

HEIGHT 15hh or a little over.

DUTCH WARMBLOOD

If any breed can be said to have experienced a meteoric rise to fame, it must be the Dutch Warmblood competition horse. It is a new breed, its stud book in The Netherlands only having been started in 1958, but it is now established as one of the most successful, popular, and sought-after competition and riding horses in the world.

It is very much a product of the 20th century, as are most warmblood competition horses, but whereas many existed in a slightly different form before this century, the Dutch Warmblood did not. Although it was created by the Dutch, it is really a European product, containing not only Dutch but also British, Spanish, French, and German breeds.

Its foundation breed is the Gelderlander plus its heavier companion, the Groningen. Both are old breeds known to have existed in The Netherlands and surrounding regions since before the Middle Ages. The Gelderlander has Andalusian, Neapolitan (Italian), Norman, Norfolk Roadster, Oldenburg, Holstein, Anglo-

Norman, Hackney, and Thoroughbred blood in it, whereas the Groningen was created by crossing Friesian and Oldenburg stock.

Although the Dutch began breeding their Warmblood later than in most other European countries, they set out with enthusiasm to breed a show jumper – which has subsequently turned out to be a superb dressage horse.

The Gelderlander and the Groningen both had desirable traits in common: they had stylish action, good basic conformation, substance with quality and presence, the ability to thrive on moderate keep, and a docile, co-operative temperament. Initially the two breeds were mated together, but Thoroughbred blood was soon introduced to add quality and spirit and to correct the sometimes long backs, short necks, and poor fronts which cropped up. The rather high harness action was also leveled out by Thoroughbred blood, and subsequent difficulties of temperament were eliminated by not only bringing in more Dutch native blood, but by using Selle Français and Hanoverian

The Dutch Warmblood was developed mainly as a show jumper and dressage horse. Midnight Madness, shown here in competition ridden by Britain's Michael Whitaker, exhibits all the scope and power needed by a world-class show jumper today.

This attractive Dutch Warmblood, like the best warmblood performance horses, shows the type and quality of a middleweight Thoroughbred.

blood to refine the resulting stock without producing the sometimes difficult Thorough-bred temperament.

Considering its youth, the Dutch Warm-blood is now an established type popular on both sides of the Atlantic and often up among the winners in international competition.

Character and care

Most Dutch Warmbloods have an excellent temperament, being normally quiet, willing, intelligent, and with enough spirit and energy to command attention and perform the work required of them. They are noted especially for their flowing gaits which make them a pleasure to ride and attractive to watch.

They require the normal care given to hard-working, athletic horses, and despite being top-level competition animals, they are still quite easy for the moderately experienced handler to ride and look after.

The Dutch Warmblood today

The Dutch Warmblood's main use is as a show jumper, dressage, and general riding horse. Because of its amenable temperament, sound conformation, and superb action, it can also be used as a carriage-driving horse, in competition or otherwise.

The workmanlike yet elegant head of this Dutch Warmblood shows the interested nature and calm temperament demanded by breeders and riders alike.

DUTCH WARMBLOOD

The Dutch Warmblood has less heavy blood in its veins than some other warmbloods. The Thoroughbred and related influence of lighter types of warmblood are evident in this attractive horse. The Dutch Warmblood's action is particularly notable, being long, free, and possessing the elasticity demanded of today's performance horses, particularly in dressage. The symbol **C** *indicates a conformation feature.*

COAT AND COLOR
The Dutch Warmblood is mainly bay and brown: this coat is an attractive red chestnut. Gray and black may also occur.

LOINS AND QUARTERS
Long, muscular loins and powerful, deep quarters with slightly sloping croup. **C**

SHOULDERS AND WITHERS
Well-sloped and strong shoulders, with prominent withers. **C**

BACK
Short, strong, and level back. **C**

TAIL
Often set quite high and proudly carried. **C**

LEGS AND FEET
Legs are long and muscular. The feet are strong and well formed. **C**

HEIGHT
Around or above 16hh.

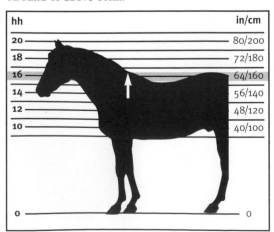

hh	in/cm
20	80/200
18	72/180
16	64/160
14	56/140
12	48/120
10	40/100
0	0

HEAD
The workmanlike yet elegant head of this Dutch Warmblood shows the interested nature and calm temperament demanded by breeders and riders alike. **C**

EYES
Alert but calm, interested expression on the face and in the large, friendly eyes.

ANCESTRY

The Dutch Warmblood is mainly made up of the two Dutch native breeds, the Groningen and the Gelderlander, the latter itself having a complex ancestry. Thoroughbred and other warmblood types have been used to refine the breed to adjust temperament and conformation.

Groningen

Gelderlander

Thoroughbred

Hanoverian

Selle Français

Dutch Warmblood

NECK
Medium to long neck of riding horse type, well developed and gently arched at the throat. **C**

EARS
Medium-length ears which are well-pointed, wide-set, and mobile.

SWISS WARMBLOOD

Switzerland's version of the warmblooded competition horse is based on her own excellent old breed, the Einsiedler, from the Swiss canton of Eisiedeln. The Einsiedler was a strong horse used for both riding and driving. Benedictine monks were breeding horses in the region in 1064, keeping well-documented records on their improvement of local horses.

In more recent centuries, Norman and Hackney blood was introduced into the Einsiedler and, later, Anglo-Norman blood as well. In the 20th century, the Selle Français and French Anglo-Arab were used. In the 1960s, when it was decided to produce a world-class competition horse, Swedish, Hanoverian, Holstein, Trakehner, and Thoroughbred blood were brought in with the intention of creating the Swiss Warmblood, a stylish dual-purpose horse, mainly a riding and competition horse for dressage and show jumping, but also a competitive carriage-driving horse. At first, stallions were imported for breeding, but as the breed developed, Swiss Warmblood stallions started to be used, and this practice continues at the National Stud at Avenches.

ANCESTRY

Based on old Einsiedler blood, several European breeds were introduced in the 19th and 20th centuries to create a strong, athletic performance and general riding horse which could also be used in light harness.

Einsiedler
Norman ▼
Hackney ▼
Anglo-Norman ▼
Thoroughbred ▼
Several European ▼
warmblood breeds
Swiss Warmblood

Character and care

The Swiss Warmblood is a quality horse with free, supple gaits and a proven talent for dressage and show jumping. It has a docile, kind temperament and is a willing, co-operative worker.

The Swiss Warmblood today

The Swiss Warmblood is used as a general all-round riding horse, with the best and most talented individuals competing on equal terms with the best competition horses in the world. In light harness, the breed is elegant and stylish.

GENERAL CHARACTERISTICS

CONFORMATION An elegant quality horse, resembling a middleweight Thoroughbred.

HEAD Well-proportioned and attractive with a straight or slightly convex **profile**. The **ears** are of medium length, the **eyes** are wide apart, and the **muzzle** is sensitive with flaring **nostrils**.

COLOR All solid colors permitted, with white on the head and legs.

HEIGHT Averages at around 16hh.

One of the younger European warmblood breeds, the Swiss Warmblood, formed from several breeds, is an elegant, stylish, and successful competition horse, particularly in dressage. Attempts are now being made to make the breed self-sufficient with little outside blood likely to be used in future.

ITALIAN HEAVY DRAFT

Local native stock was mated initially with Arab, Hackney, and English Thoroughbred, with later introductions of Brabant, Boulonnais, Ardennais, and Percheron. Ultimately, the Postier-Breton was used extensively to achieve the current type.

Local native stock
Arab ▼
Hackney ▼
Thoroughbred ▼
Brabant and French ▼
heavy breeds
Postier-Breton ▼
Italian Heavy Draft

The Italians have never had much inclination to breed massive, phlegmatic horses, so even when they produced their own heavy draft type, they went for a smallish animal with a lively action and bright temperament.

The Italian Heavy Draft is a newish breed, having only been developed in 1860 when the state stud at Ferrara began crossing stallions from the Po Delta region with native mares, and also introducing Arab, English Thorough-bred, and Hackney blood into the breed.

At the beginning of the 20th century, greater size and strength were required, and so more massive breeds were introduced into the Italian Heavy Draft – the Belgian Brabant was tried, as were the French Boulonnais, Ardennais, and Percheron. Results did not please, however, and it was not until the lighter, more active Postier-Breton was tried that a type evolved which everyone was happy with.

Character and care

The Italian Heavy Draft is a distinctive breed with a friendly, calm nature and lively but docile temperament, although some individuals are notably highly strung. It is a smallish, energetic, and quite fast draft horse, fairly hardy and easy to care for.

The Italian Heavy Draft today

Although some are still used in agriculture, the breed's main use today is as a meat animal.

GENERAL CHARACTERISTICS

CONFORMATION The **neck** is short, strong, and broad at the base, bearing a full **mane**. The **legs** are short and sturdy but not massively heavy, with strong joints and some feathering on the lower legs.

HEAD Quite fine and small for a heavy draft breed. It has small, pricked **ears**, a broad **forehead**, kind, lively **eyes**, and flaring **nostrils**.

COLOR Many chestnuts, with flaxen, full mane, forelock, and tail. Red roan and bay also occur. There are distinctive coat shadings and patterns in many of the solid-colored horses.

HEIGHT From 14.2hh to 16hh.

Though undoubtedly a heavy horse, the Italian Heavy Draft has a lively nature and plenty of personality. The breed is active, energetic, and full of compact strength.

SALERNO

ANCESTRY

Neapolitan blood
forms the basis of the
Salerno, with much
Andalusian, Arab, and
modern
Thoroughbred
infusions.

Neapolitan
Andalusian ▼
Arabian ▼
Thoroughbred ▼
Salerno

Italy has long been a horse-breeding country. Before the Romans dominated the Western world, the Etruscans bred horses there, while in the 20th century Italy had become the producer of some of the best racing Thoroughbreds of all time, largely through Federico Tesio, who bred such world-beaters as Ribot and Nearco. Another Federico, this time Caprilli, the famous innovator of the forward seat for the Italian cavalry which has become the basis of modern jumping and cross-country riding, must have been very familiar with the Salerno breed, which was used extensively as a cavalry horse in the 20th century.

The now extinct Neapolitan was one of the famous *Haute Ecole* breeds of the Renaissance period. It was a highly fashionable horse among the royalty and aristocracy of the time. Based on Andalusian, Barb, and Arab blood, it is said that the breed was almost indistinguishable from the Iberian horses of the day.

The Neapolitan horse formed the base stock for the Salerno, which was itself developed in the Campania district by heavily infusing the Neapolitan with Andalusian blood and other Oriental strains. The breed was favored by King Charles III of Naples and later of Spain, but internal unrest in the country meant that in 1874 the Salerno's special breeding program was ended.

At the beginning of the 20th century, the breeding program was resumed. Arab and Thoroughbred blood was introduced into the remaining stock, and the horse was carefully developed, initially as an excellent carriage horse and then, with the introduction of more and more English Thoroughbred blood, as a quality saddle horse with excellent jumping abilities and stamina. The Italian cavalry enthusiastically adopted the new Salerno as a cavalry mount, as it had both the speed and stamina to go across country and over jumps.

Character and care

The Salerno is spirited and lively, but has a level, tractable nature. It requires careful handling, but is not normally difficult or unduly sensitive.

The Salerno today

The Salerno is almost exclusively used as a leisure and competition horse because of its excellent jumping ability. It is also being used as the foundation for Italy's new modern sports horse breed, the Italian Saddle Horse.

The Salerno was established in its modern form by the middle of the 20th century. It was a favored mount of the Italian cavalry for the sports of cross-country riding and show jumping.

GENERAL CHARACTERISTICS

CONFORMATION The Salerno resembles a middle-weight Thoroughbred horse. The **legs** are hard, but with stronger **feet** than found in many Thoroughbreds.

HEAD Again, a Thoroughbred appearance: elegant, with a straight **profile**, longish **ears**, a broad, squarish **forehead**, alert **eyes**, and flaring **nostrils**.

COLOR Any solid color. White permitted on legs and head.

HEIGHT Averages around 16.1hh, although some individuals are taller.

The head and facial expression reveal the elegance expected of an Italian breed, plus spirit. Some Salernos need tactful handling, but most are cooperative and even-tempered.

Originally of old Neapolitan stock (said to be very similar to the Andalusian), today's Salerno looks nothing like its Iberian forebears due to copious infusions of Arab and, particularly, Thoroughbred blood, used to create a modern, quality riding horse.

LIPIZZANER

The Lipizzaner is probably most famous today for its performances at the Spanish Riding School in Vienna where the "dancing white stallions" perform Haute Ecole *classical airs or movements. The air shown here is* pesade, *the ultimate in the collection.*

After the Arab and the Thoroughbred, the Lipizzaner is probably the most famous breed of horse in the world, and that is due almost entirely to its prominence as an *Haute Ecole* riding horse at the Spanish Riding School of Vienna in Austria. The Spanish Riding School was so titled not because it originated in Spain (it did not) nor because it promoted Spanish-style riding principles, but because of the ancestry of the breed and type of horse used there in the past.

Like most European breeds, the Lipizzaner is heavily indebted to the old Spanish (Iberian) horse, the Andalusian, and Lusitano, for many of its desirable qualities. Without all this Spanish blood, the Lipizzaner as a recognizable and highly regarded breed would simply not have evolved.

The name of the Lipizzaner breed itself comes from the stud at Lipizza or Lipica, formerly in Italy but now in the Karst region of northwestern Slovenia. It is true to say that most breeds are named after the geographical area from which they originate, yet the origins of the Lipizzaner go back even farther to the Moorish occupation of Spain from A.D. 711, when the invaders brought with them to the Iberian peninsula Arab and Barb (Berber) horses, crossing them with native heavy horses and the old Spanish type. The result of the Moors' horse-breeding activities was the Andalusian, which is the main progenitor of the Lipizzaner.

When the Hapsburg Archduke Charles II of Austria, son of the Holy Roman Emperor Ferdinand I, inherited the Austro-Hungarian-Spanish empire in 1564, his new possessions included Lipizza. Classical *manège* riding was very much in fashion in the 16th century, and Archduke Charles wanted to have the best horses in the world capable of carrying out the demanding airs or movements. He waited until 1580 before founding his stud, and in July of that year began importing the best Andalusian stallions and mares Spain had to offer. He wanted to stock his own stables with his own Spanish horses so as to be able to breed them and not be dependent on imports.

Very soon the stud in Lipizza was stocked with horses of fine Spanish blood. This is significant because, no matter what the subsequent name of the breed, it is the Spanish genes it contained which influenced subsequent produce, and the Lipizzaner breed contained all the qualities found in the Spanish horses – nobility, pride, sensitivity, affectionate temperament, agility, and courage. Furthermore, the lofty, naturally cadenced action of the Spanish types had not been bred out by the significant infusions of Oriental blood, and this action was one of the main requirements of the classical *manège*, the other being the very strong haunches that are demanded in the *Haute Ecole* movements.

The Lipizzaner was, however, expected to produce not only riding horses but also to produce quality carriage horses which, because of the different strains in its foundation stock and the differing types evident in the breed, it was well able to do.

The Spanish Riding School was set up in

The rounded lines of old Iberian-type conformation are still obvious in this modern Lipizzaner; plus the strength and musculature to enable the horse to perform taxing classical airs and also to work in draft.

1572 for the purpose of instructing noblemen in the art of classical riding. Initially the lessons took place in a wooden structure, but the beautiful building which is still standing today was commissioned in 1735 by Emperor Charles VI. Charles VI was extremely interested not only in the riding skills taught at the school but also in the scientific and practical aspects of breeding, and greatly fostered these pursuits with his considerable resources of land, money, and horses.

German, Italian (including Neapolitan), Danish, and Kladruber breeds were crossed with the Lipizza stock down the centuries. By the 19th century, some Arab blood was also being used.

With the fall of the Austro-Hungarian empire, the stud at Lipizza was moved to Piber in Austria, but during World War II, the breed was evacuated farther west, mainly to Germany, to avoid capture by the Russian army. Today, Lipizzaners are again bred at Piber and also at Lipizza and Babolna (where the Hungarians breed their favored bigger, freer-moving strain), as well as in Italy, Romania, the Czech Republic, and Slovakia. The breed is very popular in the U.S., but has a limited number of representatives in Britain.

Character and care

A gentle but proud temperament is the hallmark of the Lipizzaner. The horse is willing, intelligent, and possesses stamina as well as strength, agility, and natural balance.

The Lipizzaner today

The Lipizzaner is almost exclusively used as a *Haute Ecole* horse both at the Spanish Riding School in Vienna where its training sessions and displays are always sold out. The Lipizzaner has also always been popular, along with its relatives, the Andalusians and Lusitanos, in circuses around the world.

The breed makes an excellent carriage horse and is used as such in Hungary. It is also sometimes used in general draft work.

The Lipizzaner is a late-maturing breed and serious work requiring strength and mature physique cannot be asked of the horse until it is usually seven or eight years of age. It takes seven years to train a Lipizzaner fully in *Haute Ecole* equitation, but they are a long-lived breed, and stallions can give top-level performances even when well into their twenties.

LIPIZZANER

The Lipizzaner is a very well-balanced horse showing its Iberian ancestry in its overall curvaceous, pleasing outline. This horse is somewhat lighter in type than the horse in the photograph on the preceding page. Basically, though, the old traditional conformation, perhaps with a little more "quality," is maintained. Excellent individual balance is essential for Haute Ecole *work. The symbol*  *indicates a conformation feature.*

COLOR

A peculiarity of the breed is that they are nearly all gray. Foals are born black, but whiten with age. Traditionally, a bay Lipizzaner is always kept at the Spanish Riding School to indicate the breed's links with the past, when bay, brown, black, and roan horses were also common.

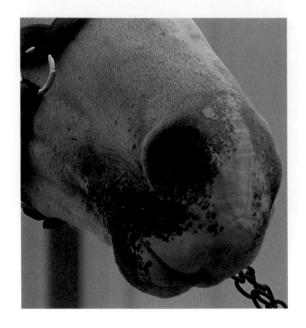

NOSTRILS

The nostrils are open and mobile.

WITHERS AND BACK

The withers are usually low and broad, the back rather long but shapely and strong, though occasionally a little hollow.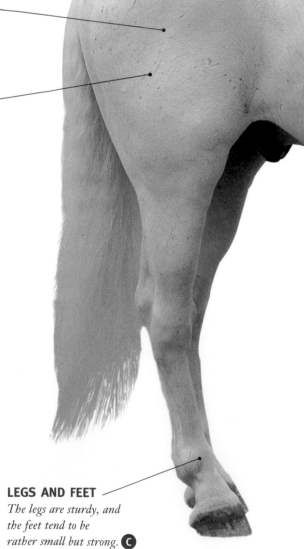

LOINS

The loins are strong and broad.

QUARTERS AND TAIL

The quarters are strong, rounded, and very muscular with a well-carried tail.

HEIGHT

About 15hh to 16.1hh, although taller animals can be found.

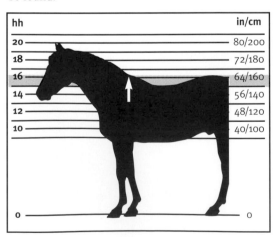

hh	in/cm
20	80/200
18	72/180
16	64/160
14	56/140
12	48/120
10	40/100
0	0

LEGS AND FEET

The legs are sturdy, and the feet tend to be rather small but strong.

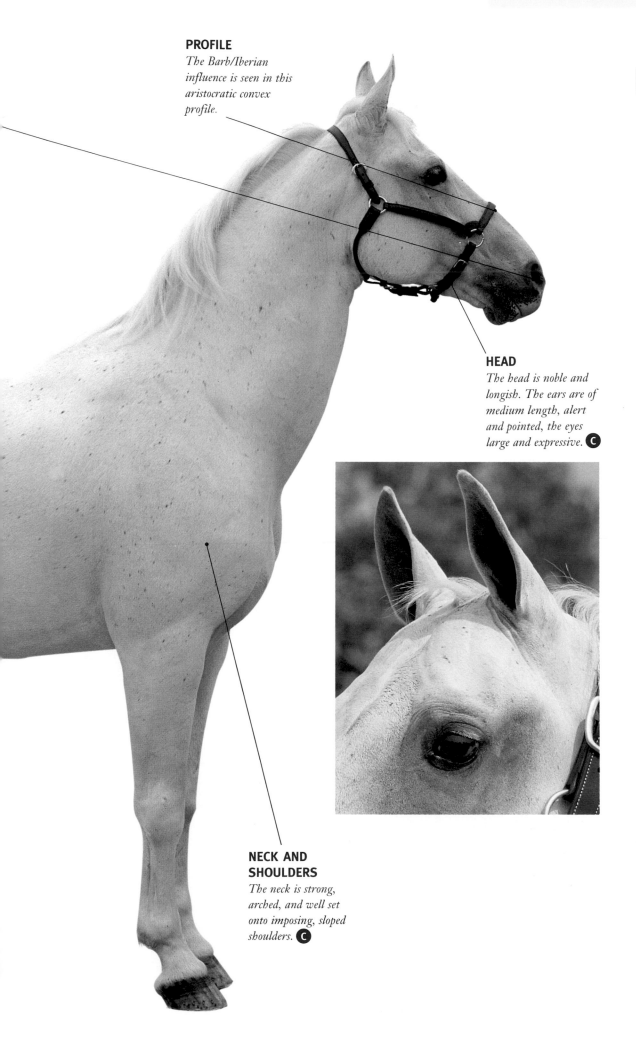

PROFILE
The Barb/Iberian influence is seen in this aristocratic convex profile.

HEAD
The head is noble and longish. The ears are of medium length, alert and pointed, the eyes large and expressive. **C**

NECK AND SHOULDERS
The neck is strong, arched, and well set onto imposing, sloped shoulders. **C**

ANCESTRY

A blend of breeds containing large amounts of old Spanish blood make up the Lipizzaner, which has been bred true to type for centuries. Today, both the riding and the larger, freer-moving carriage horses are bred from different types within the breed.

Spanish (Iberian)

Native heavy stock

Barb (Berber)

Arab

Andalusian

mixed European including Neapolitan and Kladruber blood

Lipizzaner

117

HAFLINGER

The origins of the Haflinger pony are rather obscure. One theory states that in 1342 King Louis IV of Germany sent a stallion from Burgundy as a wedding present to his son, Louis of Brandenburg. The stallion was mated with the local mares, which were of Oriental origin, inhabiting the southern Alps at that time. The resulting stock evolved into the Haflinger breed.

The second theory is that the Haflinger descended from the Oriental horses left behind in the Tyrol after the Ostrogoths were driven north across the Alps by the Byzantine forces in A.D. 555. This would explain the obvious Arab content of the Haflinger.

What is known about the Haflinger is that the modern breed, does descend from an Arab stallion, El Bedavi XXII, brought into the region in 1868 to upgrade the rather coarse stock present there at that time. All modern Haflingers can be traced back to him.

Over the centuries the border between Italy and Austria has changed many times, but today, the Haflinger is regarded as an Austrian breed, with the closely related, slightly bigger Avelignese, as its Italian counterpart. The two breeds are regarded as more or less identical.

Today, the Haflinger is found in Austria, Switzerland, Germany, and Italy, and is popular in other European countries. It is a solid mountain pony used in forestry and farming. In Austria, breeding is closely monitored by the state, and Haflingers are bred by both state studs and private owners.

ANCESTRY

Believed to have originated from local heavy-type ponies with subsequent Oriental input.

Heavy indigenous pony stock
Oriental ▼
Alpine Heavy ▼
Horse
Related pony ▼
breeds
Arab ▼
Modern Haflinger

Character and care
Haflingers are docile yet bright, friendly, and trusting toward humans. They are late-maturing but extremely hardy, and have great stamina and strength.

The Haflinger today
The Haflinger is still used in forestry and farming in the Alps, and is equally at home in harness pulling sleighs, carts, or carriages, and under saddle. It is also a popular family pony.

GENERAL CHARACTERISTICS

CONFORMATION Of heavy type with an Arab look to the head, the Haflinger is chunky and compact, possessing great strength and endurance.

HEAD The head is very elegant and aristocratic for what is essentially a heavy breed. It is wedge shaped with short, pointed **ears**; expressive, deep **eyes**; a straight or concave **profile**; and a neat **muzzle** with fine, mobile **nostrils**.

COLOR All shades of chestnut with eye-catching flaxen mane, forelock, and tail. White markings are usual on the head, but extremely rare on the legs.

HEIGHT Up to 14hh.

Founded hundreds of years ago as a small, sturdy, working horse, the modern Haflinger has survived border changes in its home region between Austria and Italy. It remains an extremely popular large working pony and is especially useful as a family pony, since it is noted for liking people.

NORIKER

The Noriker is a medium-sized heavy-type horse whose forebears were introduced into its homeland by the Romans. It is ideal for farm, forestry, and transportation work in tricky mountain country, a role it still fulfills today.

ANCESTRY

An ancient breed founded on Roman imports bred with local stock. Some Andalusian and Neapolitan blood runs in its veins with, in the South German strain, added infusions of Norman, Cleveland Bay, Holstein, Hungarian, Clydesdale, and Oldenburg.

Native stock
Roman imports ▼
Neapolitan ▼
Andalusian ▼
Noriker

The Noriker (or Pinzgauer, Oberlander, or South German Coldblood) is an ancient breed founded from various heavy horses introduced into its homeland some 2,000 years ago by the Romans, who had named the province Noricum. The province was made up of roughly the area occupied by today's Styria and Carinthia in Austria. In time a strong, sure-footed, and hardy draft animal was developed, ideally suited to agricultural work in the harsh climate of the mountainous terrain.

In the 16th century, the breed was given more agility and presence by the introduction of Andalusian and Neapolitan blood. Later, in the 19th century, Norman, Cleveland Bay, Holstein, Hungarian, Clydesdale, and Oldenburg blood was introduced into the South German strain of Noriker, which considerably lightened the local stock.

There are five recognizable strains of Noriker today, but all can be described as being smallish carthorses, able to work the mountainous terrain of southern Europe where they play an important agricultural role.

Character and care

A carthorse with an active movement, and strong, calm, and quiet.

The Noriker today

The Noriker, in all its forms, is mainly used in agriculture and in forestry

GENERAL CHARACTERISTICS

CONFORMATION The **neck** is short and thick and the **shoulders** well muscled and strong. The **tail** is low set, and both **mane** and tail are thick and often wavy. The **legs** are sturdy with moderate feathering.

HEAD Slightly heavy with a convex **profile**. The **ears** are short, the **eye** kind, and the **nostrils** open.

COLOR Bay, chestnut (often with flaxen mane and tail), roan, brown, black, or spotted. Rarely gray or dappled gray.

HEIGHT From 15.1hh to 16.2hh.

BRABANT

A major influence on most of the world's heavy breeds, the Brabant became even more popular than the old Flanders Horse in the development of heavy breeds in the 19th century. A powerful horse, with a willing temperament, its blood is still used in warmblood breeding.

The Brabant (also known as the Belgian Heavy Draft Horse or Brabançon) from Belgium can truly be described as the Arab of the heavy horse world, in that it has influenced just about every other heavy breed in the world. Its excellent physique and temperament plus its prepotent genes have meant it has been in demand for centuries, both in its own right as an improver of other heavy breeds and as basic foundation stock for lighter draft, carriage, or riding breeds, principally continental European warmblood competition and performance horses.

The Brabant is not, unfortunately, appreciated enough in its homeland (or in Ireland and Britain, despite its having significantly influenced the Shire, Clydesdale, and Irish Draft), but is very popular in other European countries, Australia, and America.

The Brabant is of ancient lineage, the only older breed being the French Ardennes from which the Brabant is derived, hence the charac-teristic strawberry (red) roan coat color. The French Ardennes is believed to be descended from the primitive Forest Horse of the Quaternary period, whose fossilized remains have been found along the eastern bank of the River Meuse.

Serious breeding of the Brabant's ancestors was already well established in Brabant and Flanders in the 10th century. The fertile, heavy soils of the area needed horses of great and compact strength with economical, energy-saving action but nevertheless ample knee and hock action to lift the massive legs out of the clay-like mud when it was wet. The indigenous horses undoubtedly evolved naturally with such action, and the early breeders had the wisdom and knowledge to breed it into their home-bred stock. Subsequent breeders down the centuries have jealously guarded the type and heritage of the Flanders horse, not using foreign stock to dilute its qualities.

So popular was the Brabant in the Middle

Ages that the breed was exported all over Europe, a considerable feat in those days. It contributed greatly to the now more-or-less extinct Rhenish horse of the Rhine Valley in Germany, but its genes still run in that country's superb warmbloods. Russia imported, her share of Flanders horses for work, crossing them with their native stock.

In the 17th century there was a short-lived attempt to alter the characteristics of the breed to make it appeal to an even wider market, but the results were not successful and the experiment soon ceased. Since then, only pure Brabant/Flanders lines have been bred together which has resulted in a breed which always "breeds true" within itself and stamps its qualities on other breeds with which it is crossed elsewhere.

The name Brabant became more popular than that of Flanders in the late 19th century, by which time breeders had formally determined the characteristics of the breed. Three different bloodlines were amalgamated to create the modern Brabant: the Gros de la Dendre strain (muscular and very strong with massive legs), the Gris de Nivelles (with presence and good conformation), and the

Colosses de la Mehaigne (a big type with an enthusiastic nature).

Character and care

The dominant characteristics of the Brabant are its docile temperament, its strength, and its weight. It has been described as phlegmatic, even sluggish, but almost always good-natured. As for pulling power, it is almost impossible to beat, its nearest rival in strength being the English Shire. It is an early-maturing and long-lived horse, obedient, unflappable, extremely strong and reliable, and willing to work hard.

It has a strong constitution and is very hardy, requiring only moderate amounts of food considering its size and body mass.

The Brabant today

In common with all heavy breeds, the Brabant is used mainly for heavy agricultural and haulage work – short-haul road transportation, logging, estate work, and as a dray horse. It is enthusiastically received in the show ring, either in showing classes or in publicity displays. The Brabant is still used as a foundation stock in warmblood breeding.

A Belgian Brabant fulfilling his original role as a working horse, here in Colorado. The breed is still used in agriculture and forestry, as a cart horse, and in other jobs, and is well received in shows and displays.

BRABANT

The Brabant has a massively muscled body with an unmistakable impression of strength, weight, and power. This modern Brabant, with his lighter type and longer legs, takes after the Gris de Nivelles strain, showing good conformation and presence. He also shows a primitive coloring tendency to lighter underparts. The Brabant is noted for pre-potency in breeding and for breeding true to type. Its great strength, willingness, and good nature are highly prized. The symbol **C** *indicates a conformation feature.*

QUARTERS AND TAIL
The quarters are strongly muscled and the tail well set. **C**

BARREL AND BACK
The barrel is rounded and deep, the back very short and strong. **C**

COAT AND COLOR
This sorrel/light chestnut coat color is usually accompanied by a flaxen (lighter or "blond") mane, tail, and lower legs – and often the belly is paler, too.

LEGS
The legs are very strong, with long, muscular upper legs for leverage and big, flat joints. **C**

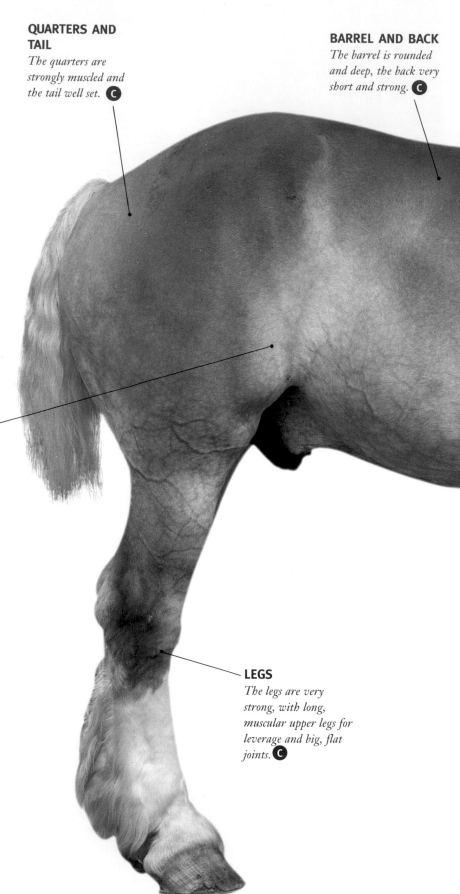

HEIGHT
Ranges from 15.3hh to 17hh.

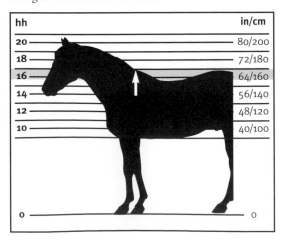

hh	in/cm
20	80/200
18	72/180
16	64/160
14	56/140
12	48/120
10	40/100
0	0

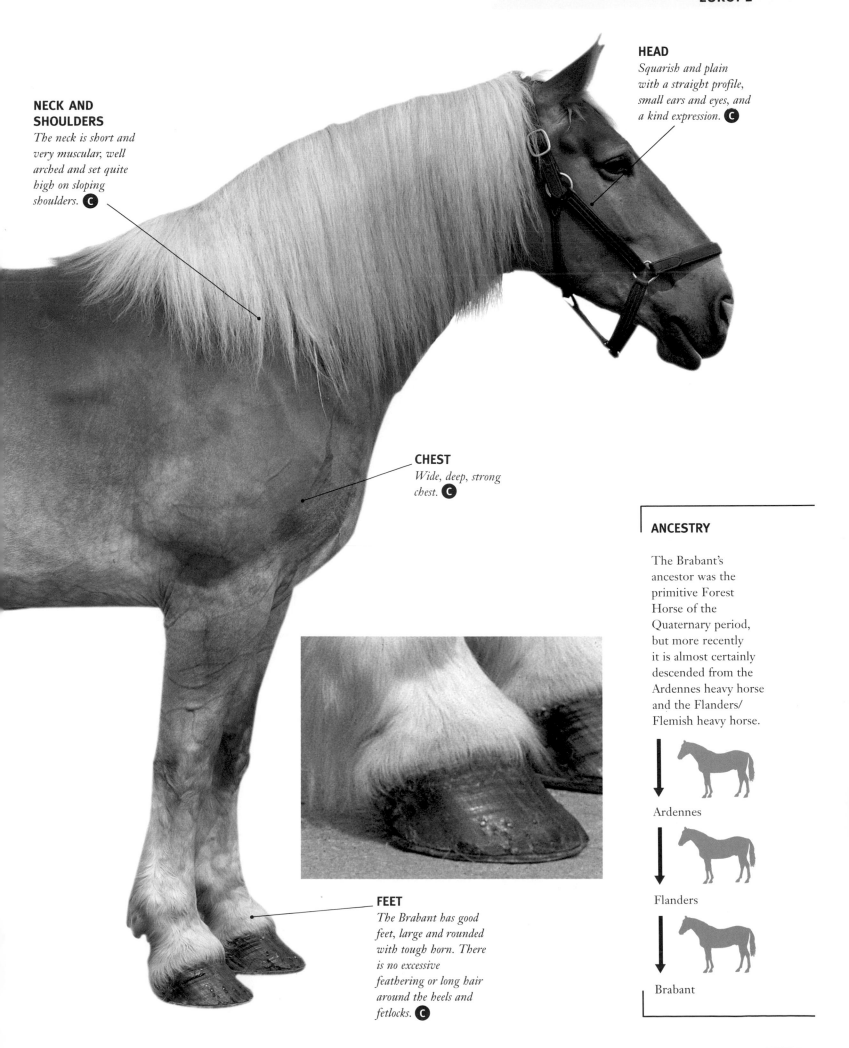

NECK AND SHOULDERS
The neck is short and very muscular, well arched and set quite high on sloping shoulders. **C**

HEAD
Squarish and plain with a straight profile, small ears and eyes, and a kind expression. **C**

CHEST
Wide, deep, strong chest. **C**

FEET
The Brabant has good feet, large and rounded with tough horn. There is no excessive feathering or long hair around the heels and fetlocks. **C**

ANCESTRY

The Brabant's ancestor was the primitive Forest Horse of the Quaternary period, but more recently it is almost certainly descended from the Ardennes heavy horse and the Flanders/ Flemish heavy horse.

Ardennes

Flanders

Brabant

KONIK

Poland's Konik pony is a virtually direct, though probably a little heavier, descendant from the wild Tarpan. It has been used to "reconstitute" the now extinct Tarpan, the results of this breeding project running free in the ancient Bialowieza forest in Poland.

ANCESTRY

The Konik is believed to contain a large amount of original Tarpan blood, with some Arab and other local infusions.

Tarpan
Arab ▼
Native pony stock ▼
Konik

The Polish Konik pony is much closer to its ancestors than other ponies. The word "konik" means "little horse" in Polish; it does not denote a specific breed, and there are various strains (about five) of Konik. The type normally referred to as the formal Konik breed is believed to have descended from the original wild Tarpan of Eastern Europe, which was an Oriental type of small horse with a fine head and the primitive markings of a dorsal stripe and zebra markings on the legs.

The wild Tarpan was hunted to extinction late in the 19th century, but efforts were later made to gather together the Konik ponies descended from it, in order to collect as many Tarpan genes as possible. The ancient wood of Bialowieza was made into a national reserve, and the Konik ponies were turned free there. Today, the descendants of the Konik ponies (referred to as reconstituted Tarpans) still roam in Bialowieza, and possess the Tarpan coloring and many of its characteristics. Koniks are used on Polish farms mainly to the east of the River San.

Character and care

Late-maturing but very long-lived, the Konik survives on little keep and can live out all year round. Although most are easy to handle, some retain the wild streak of the Tarpan and may be independent and difficult.

The Konik today

Mostly used for farm work, though the more amenable ones are used as children's ponies. The Konik has been used in the formation of many Eastern European and Russian breeds.

GENERAL CHARACTERISTICS

CONFORMATION The **neck** is quite long for the size of animal, but well-shaped and muscular, held quite high, with a long, generous **mane**. The **legs** are of pony type, sturdy and strong, with small, tough **feet** with a little feathering.

HEAD Can sometimes be heavy but not ugly, with a lively **expression**, short, pricked pony **ears**, searching **eyes**, and a small **muzzle** with flaring **nostrils**.

COLOR Mostly mouse-gray or dun, both often with a blueish tinge, and bay. There is a dark dorsal stripe and sometimes zebra markings on the legs.

HEIGHT From 12.3hh to 13.3hh.

WIELKOPOLSKI

Poland is one of the great horse-breeding countries of the world. The Polish-bred Arab is famous for its hardiness and quality, but Poland's newest creation, the Wielkopolski, is an excellent light draft, riding, and competition horse.

As a breed, it has only a short history, being formed after World War II. It is closely related to the Trakehner, but is mainly based on indigenous Polish and Eastern European stock crossed with Arab, Thoroughbred, and West European strains. Its native content includes two Polish warmblood horses, the Masuren and the Poznan.

The Masuren is an old breed containing much Trakehner blood, and for many generations it has been used as a riding horse and hunter. The Poznan is a slightly heavier horse, mainly used for agricultural purposes. It contains Trakehner, indigenous (Konik) pony, Thoroughbred, Arab, and Hanoverian blood.

Both the old Masuren and Poznan breeds are no longer formally recognized by the Polish, although limited numbers remain living alongside their descendant, the Wielkopolski. The Wielkopolski is a middle-weight quality riding and light draft horse. The stallions must pass stringent performance and conformation tests before being allowed to breed.

Character and care

The Wielkopolski is of sturdy middle-weight build with a gentle temperament. It is intelligent, quiet, and hard-working, with good stamina.

The Wielkopolski today

The Wielkopolski is being developed specifically as a quality modern competition horse, yet it also makes a good carriage horse, and is still used for light draft work.

ANCESTRY

The Wielkopolski is a true representative of its part of the world, containing both Eastern and Western European strains with a strong reliance on its native regional breeds and types.

Konik
Masuren ▼
Poznan ▼
Trakehner ▼
Hanoverian ▼
Thoroughbred ▼
Arab ▼
Wielkopolski

GENERAL CHARACTERISTICS

CONFORMATION The impression is that of a middle-weight riding/carriage horse.

HEAD The head is workmanlike rather than elegant, with moderately long **ears**, expressive, lively **eyes** aside a medium-width **forehead**, and open **nostrils**. The **profile** is usually straight.

COLOR All solid colors.

HEIGHT From 16hh to 16.2hh.

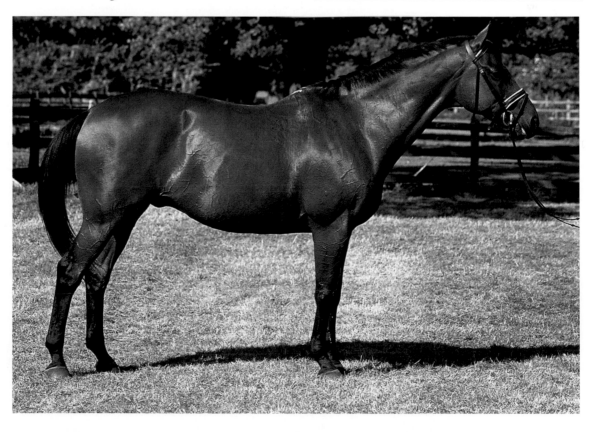

The Wielkopolski is one of the youngest breeds in the world, being developed since World War II, in Poland, as a quality, modern competition horse. Its gene pool includes two Polish warmblood breeds, the Masuren and the Poznan.

MALOPOLSKI

The Malopolski, or Polish Anglo-Arab, is another horse created by the skillful and horse-loving Poles to meet modern demands for a quality riding and competition horse.

The Malopolski comes from the same progenitor base as its now fairly distant relative, the Wielkopolski, containing Masuren and Poznan blood. The Masuren and the Poznan were two of many regional types of horse which are not really recognized as separate breeds now, having been incorporated into the Wielkopolski and the Malopolski stud books, but are, nevertheless, still recognized by their local breeders and enthusiasts.

The Malopolski has received much more Arab blood than the Wielkopolski, and this shows in the horse's bearing, temperament, and general appearance. Local stock has been infused with a good deal of Thoroughbred, Hungarian Furioso, and Hungarian Gidran blood, producing a popular, successful, and well-balanced horse.

There are two types of Malopolski: the Darbowski-Tarnowski is strongly based on the Gidran and the Sadecki on the Furioso. Within the breed, therefore, there is no strict uniformity, but overall it is a very popular horse which finds a ready market.

Character and care

The Malopolski is courageous, spirited, and energetic, yet it has a calm and even temperament. It is noted for great stamina and is a good jumper. Being a quality horse, it requires fairly skillful management.

The Malopolski today

The Malopolski is used today as a superior riding and competition horse. It also goes well as a carriage horse.

ANCESTRY

The Malopolski is based on native stock with considerable infusions of Thoroughbred, Arab, and Anglo-Arab blood

Native Polish stock
Thoroughbred ▼
Arab ▼
Anglo-Arab ▼
Malopolski

GENERAL CHARACTERISTICS

CONFORMATION Arabic in general appearance, with many Arab features, such as high-set **tail** and long **legs**.

HEAD Well-proportioned with, in the Darbowski-Tarnowski, a slight "dish" – an Arab feature. The **ears** are of medium-length and active, the **forehead** broad with the **eyes** set well down and to the side. The **muzzle** tapers to flaring **nostrils**.

COLOR All solid colors including roan.

HEIGHT From 15.3hh to 16.2hh.

The horse shown here resembles a substantial Thoroughbred more than his Arab forebears, the Malopolski also being known as the Polish Anglo-Arab. It is an excellent performance horse, going well in light harness as well as under saddle.

HUCUL

The Huçul is descended from the wild Tarpan, but contains more native pony blood than its close relation, the Konik, and a good deal of Arab blood. It has an exceptionally willing temperament, is very quiet, and prefers to live out in all weather.

ANCESTRY

Descended from the Tarpan, the Huçul contains some native pony blood and a great deal of Arab blood.

Tarpan
Native Polish pony ▼
stock
Arab ▼
Huçul

The Polish Huçul (or Huzul) pony is closely related to the Konik and, both being descended from the original wild Tarpan of Eastern Europe, often throws up Tarpan features, particularly in the shape of the head and in the coloring.

The Huçul is said to be more willing to work and associate with humans than some Koniks, and it has been formally bred since the 19th century. Because of its ancient lineage, it has attracted the interest of equestrians and zoologists in other countries, and there are Huçul breeding centers outside Poland.

The homeland of the Huçul is the Carpathian mountain range in the south of the country, and the pony is often called the Carpathian Pony. Unlike the Konik, it has been infused with generous amounts of Arab blood, so now it does not closely resemble the original wild type. It is bred nowadays at the Siary Stud near Gorlice.

Character and care

This pony has more pony characteristics and personality than its relative, the Konik, which is more like a small horse. The Huçul is said to be fearless, and is most willing to work, its small size and well-balanced, compact body making it ideal for work in its native mountainous region. It also has a very docile temperament.

It has been described as making "an art of starvation"; in other words, it appears to be able to live well on very poor keep and is undemanding to care for, living out (and preferring to do so) in all weathers, despite the very harsh climate in the Carpathians.

The Huçul today

The Huçul is bred as a small harness pony for general farm work. It is also used as a children's pony, being quiet and willing to please.

GENERAL CHARACTERISTICS

CONFORMATION Very similar to the Konik, with a full **mane** and **tail**. Its action is smoother and higher than that of the Konik's.

HEAD A short, wedge-shaped head with a snub **muzzle** and straight **profile**. The **ears** are small and pointed and the **eyes** rather small.

COLOR Usually bay or light chestnut with flaxen mane and tail, but duns and mouse-grays also occur.

HEAD 12hh to 13hh.

TRAKEHNER

Like all warmbloods, the Trakehner was developed as a high-class competition horse. It is noted for its sheer class, being in general the lightest and most Thoroughbred in type of all today's warmbloods. This is Perow (ridden by M. Gibson) competing for the U.S. in the 1996 Olympic dressage competition.

The Trakehner (or East Prussian) has one of the most dramatic histories of any breed of horse. Generally regarded as the highest quality and most valuable of the warmblood breeds, the Trakehner took its name from the stud founded by King Frederick Wilhelm I in 1732 at Trakehnen in the province of East Prussia, now in Poland. The stud was set in 14,000 acres (5,670 hectares) of some of the loveliest country in the world and was once known as the Newmarket of East Prussia. Throughout its history, it was evacuated on four occasions to avoid invading armies, and after the fourth evacuation (fleeing the advancing Russian army during World War II), there was no going back. The stud was tragically destroyed.

Of the approximately 58,000 horses present in the stud at the time of the Russian invasion, many thousands were taken on foot, usually unshod, on a 900-mile (1,448km) trek to west Germany during the harsh winter of 1944–45. They had hardly anything to eat,

virtually no shelter, and broodmares were harnessed to their owners' wooden carts overnight in freezing conditions. As a result of these harsh conditions, most of the foals were born dead, and many of the other animals and their owners died from malnutrition, sickness, and injury. In total, less than a thousand animals finally made it to safety.

In its heyday, there were 400 broodmares at Trakehnen, and the stud was an important source of revenue for the farmers in the area. Between the two World Wars, the province of East Prussia annually exported no less than 32,000 horses. Up to World War II, the breeding association consisted of 10,000 members with 20,000 registered mares. Four state studs bred horses for the army from more than 33,000 broodmares and 500 stallions, demonstrating how perfect this vast and beautiful area of Eastern Europe was for breeding horses, which thrived on its natural juicy grass, its clement climate, and its wide, open space, that underestimated and sometimes scarce commodity so essential to horses.

The Trakehner was based on two old wild and semi-wild types indigenous to East Prussia – the Panje and Schweiken ponies, themselves descended from the truly wild Tarpan, an Oriental type of which large herds were known once to have roamed the vast forests of Eastern Europe and the steppes of northern and eastern Asia.

In the early 13th century, Prince Konrad of Masovia requested the Knights of the Teutonic Order to colonize and Christianize Prussia and its inhabitants, the Pruzzens. The knights carried out the royal edict, building many garrisons and forts and to a large extent civilizing the area.

The knights' horses, of Oriental and Spanish extraction, and the region's native ponies were systematically bred together to produce heavy farm animals and lighter riding types, and over the years the East Prussian type of horse was gradually developed and refined by the knights. Then came two major disasters, the demise of the power of the knights and their need for mounts, and the Black Death which decimated the local population. In the early 18th century, King Frederick Wilhelm I took the advice of Prince Leopold von Anhalt-Dessau, and decided to revitalize the region. He ordered that the swampy land be drained and established Trakehnen, encouraging the establishment of other studs.

By the 18th century, the heavy type of horse had almost disappeared, but a few remained; there were more of the riding type left, and of this uneven herd 1,101, including 513 mares, were assembled at Trakehnen and bred together to supply horses for the royal stables. At the beginning, breeding at the stud was un-skilled and haphazard, with mixed blood and breeds being bought in from almost every-where. The results were disastrous, and the best were often sold off for economic reasons – the equine version of selling the family silver.

After the death of King Frederick the Great (the son of King Frederick Wilhelm I), the stud passed out of royal ownership to the Prussian state, and very gradually, the old East Prussian horse, albeit somewhat smaller than before, began to re-emerge. Infusions of Thoroughbred and Arab were added to the stock, and by the 19th century, quality Trakehner horses fulfilling the requirements of the army for quality mounts and officers' chargers were being bred.

The breed was, like other breeds, affected by mechanization and subsequently came to be produced for leisure riding, light carriage and harness work, and competition/performance riding. The double elk-antler brand on the horse's thigh is now taken to identify a riding horse of the highest quality. The breed thrives again and is now administered in Germany by a well-organized society. Like all warmbloods, it undergoes very strict selection tests to maintain standards. It is also bred in many other countries and is a much sought-after horse.

Character and care

Trakehners are extremely courageous, spirited yet calm, affectionate toward people, tough, and full of quality. Resembling a light- to middle-weight Thoroughbred or, occasionally, Anglo-Arab, they epitomize all that is required in a quality riding horse without the sometimes difficult temperament of the Thoroughbred.

The Trakehner should be treated as a Thoroughbred. It is relatively easy to handle and is rewarding to own and ride.

The Trakehner today

The Trakehner has come through difficult times to shine as the performance and competition horse *par excellence*. It is exported and bred all over the world, and is often used in preference to the Thoroughbred or Arab to bring lightness and quality to other breeds due to its established type, athletic abilities, and equable temperament.

The quality and aristocratic outlook of the Trakehner are well illustrated here – with the straight profile of the Thoroughbred, a fine, tapered neck; long, very mobile ears; and spirited eyes set on either side of a broad forehead.

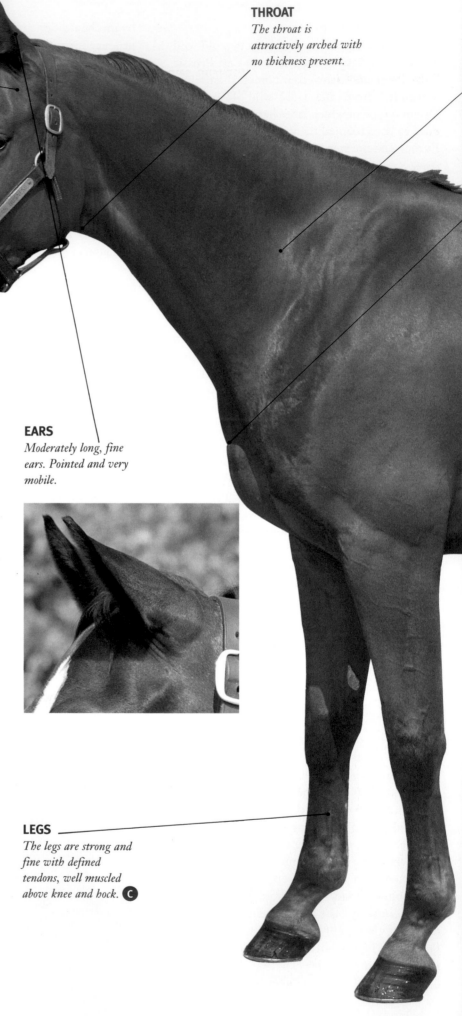

HEAD
The head of this Trakehner resembles a middleweight Thoroughbred horse, showing quality with interest and intelligence. **C**

EYES
Deep, kind, and spirited eyes, set well to the sides of the broad forehead.

PROFILE AND MUZZLE
Straight profile, with head tapering slightly to fine, sensitive muzzle with open, mobile nostrils.

THROAT
The throat is attractively arched with no thickness present.

EARS
Moderately long, fine ears. Pointed and very mobile.

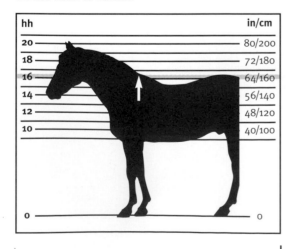

LEGS
The legs are strong and fine with defined tendons, well muscled above knee and hock. **C**

TRAKEHNER
Of all the warmblood breeds, the Trakehner is probably the best suited for eventing, being the fastest and most Thoroughbred of them all, yet with a dash of heavy or pony blood. Such a combination traditionally provides speed and jumping ability with agility and common sense. The symbol **C** *indicates a conformation feature.*

HEIGHT
About 16hh to 16.2hh.

hh	in/cm
20	80/200
18	72/180
16	64/160
14	56/140
12	48/120
10	40/100
0	0

NECK AND SHOULDERS
A well-developed neck set onto well laid-back "riding" shoulders. **C**

CHEST
Moderately broad, deep, and well muscled. **C**

WITHERS AND BACK
The withers are high to moderate, with a straight, short, and strong back. **C**

QUARTERS AND TAIL
Slightly sloping quarters with well-set tail, proudly carried. **C**

COLOR
The colors of the Trakehner are brown, bay, chestnut (as here), and black. Gray occurs rarely, and roans or particolors are never seen.

PASTERNS
Sloping pasterns above feet which are larger and stronger than in the past. **C**

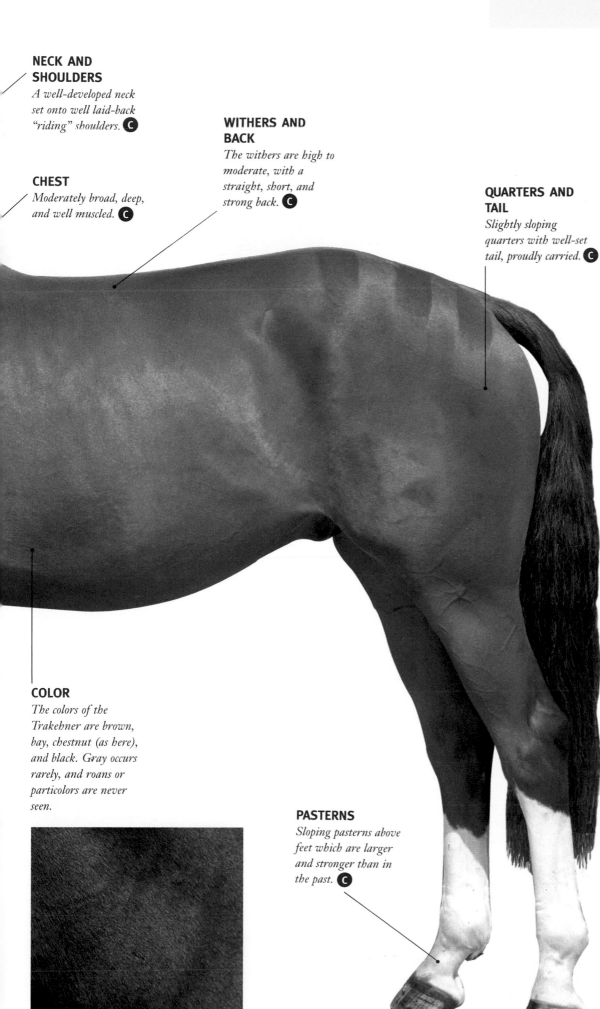

ANCESTRY

Based on indigenous feral blood, much mixed blood was introduced in the Middle Ages and again in the 18th century. Subsequently, the old East Prussian type was selected and infused with English Thoroughbred and Arab blood.

Tarpan

Panje and Schweiken

Mixed European (including Spanish) and Oriental

Old East Prussian

Thoroughbred

Arab

Trakehner

131

OLDENBURG

The Oldenburg has an older lineage than most warmbloods and is the heaviest of the modern warmblood breeds. Originally a substantial quality coach horse, it has been lightened and is now a superb carriage horse as well as being a good show jumper and dressage horse.

ANCESTRY

The Oldenburg is based on the old Friesian type with subsequent additions of many other breeds to give it height and strength.

Friesian
English halfbred ▼
Arab ▼
Barb ▼
Early ▼
Thoroughbred
Cleveland Bay ▼
Yorkshire Coach ▼
Horse
Norman/Anglo- ▼
Norman
Hanoverian ▼
Trakehner ▼
Modern ▼
Thoroughbred
Oldenburg

The biggest and heaviest of modern warmbloods, the Oldenburg from northwestern Germany has an older traceable history than many other warmblood breeds. It is named after its founder, Count Anton von Oldenburg (1603–67), who was a keen horsebreeder. He crossed Friesian mares with the half Oriental stallion, Kranich, adding Iberian and Neapolitan blood to create a substantial coach horse.

In later centuries, Arab, Barb, and Thoroughbred blood was added, and by the 19th century, the Cleveland Bay had an important influence on the breed, as did the Yorkshire Coach Horse. Norman, Anglo-Norman, and Hanoverian blood was also used at around that time in order to fulfill military requirements for a strong artillery horse.

After World War II, increased mechanization largely ousted the working horse, so Oldenburg breeders lightened their horse to cater for the increasing leisure pursuit of riding. Further Thoroughbred blood was brought in, together with Trakehner and Anglo-Norman blood, and the breed has developed to take its own place in the growing field of competitive riding. Over the past couple of decades, history has repeated itself in that the Oldenburg is once again being used as an excellent carriage horse.

Character and care

The Oldenburg is a big horse with a large frame. It resembles a heavyweight hunter type with obvious Thoroughbred content. It is not quite so hardy or enduring as most other warmbloods, but its strength, early maturity and longevity, height, and long, active stride mean that it remains always in demand.

The Oldenburg today

As a carriage-driving horse for competition or ceremony, the Oldenburg is hard to beat. It is also a good show jumper and is often used in dressage competitions.

GENERAL CHARACTERISTICS

CONFORMATION The horse gives the impression of a quality halfbred of heavy type.

HEAD A quality, workmanlike head with a thick but well-arched **throat**, longish, pointed **ears**, a slightly convex **profile**, and flaring **nostrils**.

COLOR Mainly black, brown, and bay.

HEIGHT From about 16.2hh to 17.2hh.

EAST FRIESIAN

Today's East Friesian bears little resemblance to its original "brother" breed, the Oldenburg. It contains lighter blood, introduced after World War II, to create the refinement preferred by its Eastern European breeders for general riding and for competition purposes.

ANCESTRY

A mix of European breeds; however, the East Friesian has more Arab and Hanoverian blood than its close relative, the Oldenburg.

Old Friesian
English halfbred ▼
Oriental ▼
Thoroughbred ▼
Cleveland Bay ▼
Yorkshire Coach ▼
Horse
Polish/Hungarian/ ▼
French breeds
Arab ▼
Hanoverian ▼
East Friesian

The East Friesian is a blood brother of the Oldenburg, and both were regarded as one breed for about 300 years until World War II split Germany in two. The East Friesian stems from stock left in eastern Germany, which was identical to that from which the Oldenburg was developed farther to the west.

Historically, Eastern European horse breeders have usually been excellent, tending to favor a lighter and more Oriental type of blood horse. Therefore, when the East Friesian stock was being further refined, its breeders turned to the Arab, to add quality, spirit, and a lighter frame to the existing breed.

Arabs from the Babolna Stud in Hungary, one of the best and oldest in Europe, were used, and the stallion Gazal had a particular influence on the breed. Horses from Poland were also used. The East Friesian is a good example of how a breed can change and be changed until it bears virtually no resemblance to its original stock. Since the end of World War II, the lighter type of Hanoverian has also been used to slant the East Friesian more toward the modern competition horse market.

Character and care

The East Friesian is a quality all-rounder, being spirited, courageous, good-natured, and energetic. It is strong and has excellent stamina, but like similar breeds, it needs reasonable shelter, feeding, and health maintenance.

The East Friesian today

The East Friesian is used as a riding horse for general riding and competition purposes, and it is also used as a light harness horse.

GENERAL CHARACTERISTICS

CONFORMATION A well-balanced, quality horse resembling a lightweight halfbred type of horse.

HEAD The considerable use of Arab blood has given the East Friesian a distinctively knowing, perceptive look about the head which, however, is not typically Arab, but more Anglo-Arab. The **ears** are of medium length and pointed, the **forehead** broad, and the large, generous **eyes** set well to its sides. The **profile** is straight, and the **nostrils** are open and flaring.

COLOR Bay, brown, black, chestnut, or gray. White is permitted on head and legs.

HEIGHT From 15.2hh to 16.1hh.

HANOVERIAN

The Hanoverian warmblood must surely be the most popular competition horse in the world today and is found in most international show jumping and dressage teams. Being a product of German thoroughness, it has been carefully bred for about 300 years for differing but specific purposes. It is descended from rather unprepossessing foundation stock which was improved through the addition of suitable Thoroughbred, Arab, and Trakehner blood.

The origins of the Hanoverian can be traced to the Battle of Poitiers in A.D. 732, where the Franks defeated the Saracens. The Frankish horses were of mixed blood, and types stemming from the southern and eastern European horses of the pre-Christian era interbred with native horses kept by a tribe called the Tencteri, who had settled in the Rhine Valley in about A.D. 100. Little is known of the Tencteri, except that they had the reputation of loving their horses and having a well-organized rudimentary cavalry.

From the 8th century, these horses developed into the so-called Great Horse of the knights of the Middle Ages, a stout cob type which was undoubtedly bred with the famous Flanders horses.

As methods of warfare changed, so the horses had to change with them to remain useful, and the Hanoverian's predecessors were bred to be taller and more active than the cob types. By the 17th century, three main types of horse were being bred for military use: the Danish, the Mecklenburg, and of course, the Hanoverian. All three horses were still rather heavy in type.

History then took an unexpected turn which was to be of particular benefit to the Hanoverian breed when the House of Hanover ascended to the British throne. Prince George Louis, Elector of Hanover, was crowned King George I in 1714 and William IV – the last of the Hanoverians – died in 1837, so for 123 years the Hanoverian horse received constant nurturing from its royal overseas benefactors. Early English Thoroughbred and Cleveland Bay stock was sent to Hanover for mating with

The Hanoverian is probably the most sought-after warmblood today. It is noted for its long, "scopy" action, substance, and generally excellent conformation, and excels as a dressage, show jumping, and riding horse.

the existing Hanoverian breed which, at the beginning of the 18th century, was still pretty heavy in type, to produce horses suitable for agricultural and coaching use.

George II was so keen on the advancement of the Hanoverian that in 1735 he founded the national stud for the breed at Celle. Fourteen black Holstein stallions were provided to inject new blood into the existing stock. The Holsteins were of a heavy type, containing some Oriental, Spanish, and Neapolitan blood.

The Neapolitan, an Italian creation containing Spanish, Oriental, and a great deal of heavy blood, dated back to the Middle Ages and by the 17th century was all the rage in Europe for *manège* riding, and display and parade purposes, being big and fiery, yet gentle and kind, with a proud head-carriage, lofty action, and strong hindquarters. They were nimble-footed and, through the Holstein stallions at Celle, brought these qualities to the heavy Hanoverians.

When lighter carriage horses were desired, Thoroughbred blood was successfully used, and some of the resulting horses were exported to Britain to pull the royal carriages. Back in Germany the Hanoverian became much sought-after as an army mount, but the input of Thoroughbred blood was restricted for fear of making the breed too light.

The breed survived World War I in its heavy form, but by the end of World War II the heavy Hanoverian was no longer needed for transportation and agriculture. In the post-War years, leisure and competition riding grew in popularity, so once again, the Hanoverian was adapted to match the new requirements. Thoroughbred and Arab blood was reintroduced into the breed, as was the lighter Trakehner stock, which resulted in the superb competition horse we have today.

Character and care

The main requirement of the Hanoverian is an equable temperament, and in the demanding selection tests the animals undergo before being allowed to breed, this point is given great consideration, and those of doubtful temperament are discarded from the breeding program. The typical Hanoverian horse should have a grand outlook, demonstrating self-confidence and natural pride without being hot or difficult.

Their action is ideal for dressage and show jumping, being free, supple, and with good flexion in knee and hock.

In general, they are managed like halfbred horses (which in effect they are), adapting, in either circumstance, to being stabled or put out to field.

The Hanoverian today

Today's Hanoverian is used almost entirely for competitive dressage, show jumping, and as a general riding horse, although some are used as carriage-driving horses.

Only those Hanoverians with a considerable amount of Thoroughbred blood have the necessary speed for cross-country competitions such as eventing.

The Hanoverian Grunox Tecrent (ridden by Monika Theodorescu) competing in Aachen in 1996. Many top dressage horses are Hanoverian, having the action plus the temperament for this sport.

HANOVERIAN

In looks, Hanoverians resemble medium- to heavyweight Thoroughbred/quality halfbred hunter types. Originally bred from rather unprepossessing early warhorses of small build, the modern Hanoverian has gradually been changed and improved, according to market demand, over a period of about 300 years. It is one of the most mixed-blood breeds in the world. The action of the Hanoverian is ideal for dressage and show jumping, being free, supple, and with good flexion in knee and hock. The symbol **C** *indicates a conformation feature.*

LEGS

The Hanoverian is bred to have particularly good legs, to give it the elastic, long-reaching stride for which it is known. Hanoverians frequently have a good deal of white on the legs. **C**

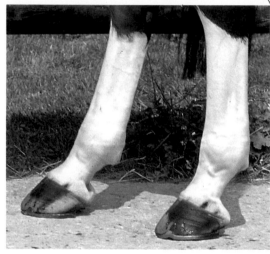

HEIGHT

Usually between 15.2hh and 17hh, average being around the 16hh mark.

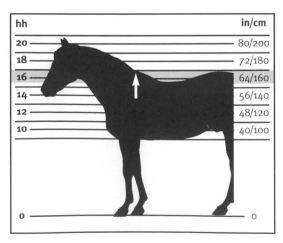

hh		in/cm
20		80/200
18		72/180
16		64/160
14		56/140
12		48/120
10		40/100
0		0

COLOR

The Hanoverian comes in all solid colors, this color being an attractive golden bay. They often have substantial white on lower legs, sometimes on the face.

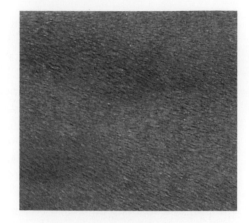

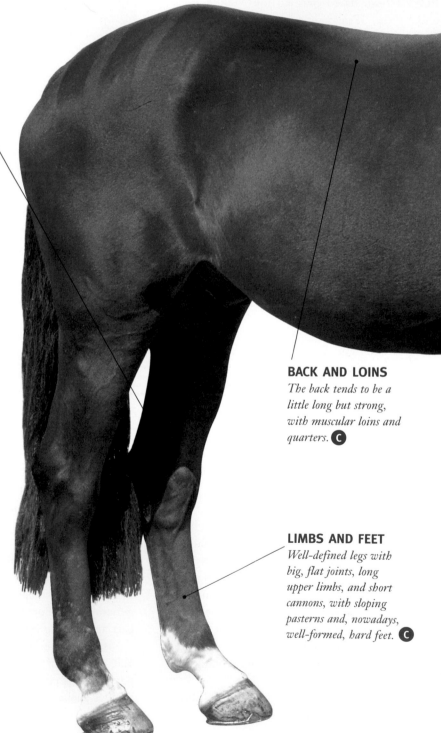

BACK AND LOINS

The back tends to be a little long but strong, with muscular loins and quarters. **C**

LIMBS AND FEET

Well-defined legs with big, flat joints, long upper limbs, and short cannons, with sloping pasterns and, nowadays, well-formed, hard feet. **C**

WITHERS AND SHOULDERS

The withers are quite pronounced above well-sloped, big shoulders. **C**

NECK

The neck is medium to long, well-developed, and graceful. **C**

CHEST

The chest is deep and well-muscled. **C**

HEAD

Medium-size head with straight or convex profile. This horse has a lighter and more Thoroughbred-type head than some, showing the quality and placid nature of most of the breed. **C**

EARS AND EYES

Ears are of medium length, fine and pointed, eyes generous in expression and size, well set to the side of the head.

ANCESTRY

A very mixed heritage makes up the Hanoverian: the breed is a careful blend of many types which has been changed as required down the ages.

European indigenous stock

Oriental/Spanish

Holstein/Thoroughbred

Cleveland Bay

Andalusian

Arab

Trakehner

Modern Hanoverian

137

SCHLESWIG HEAVY DRAFT

ANCESTRY

Native heavy stock was mated extensively with Danish Jutland stock to produce the early Schleswig. Suffolk Punch, Cleveland Bay, and Yorkshire Coach Horse blood was used in the 19th century, with Thoroughbred additions. Most recently, Breton, Boulonnais, and once again, Jutland crosses have been introduced to the breed.

Native heavy stock
Jutland ▼
Suffolk Punch ▼
Cleveland Bay ▼
Yorkshire Coach ▼
Horse
Thoroughbred ▼
Breton ▼
Boulonnais ▼
Modern Jutland ▼
Schleswig Heavy
Draft

A smallish heavy-type horse, the Schleswig Heavy Draft has been the subject of some controversy as to whether or not it should be called a true heavy horse, because of its lack of height and cob-like character. Although originally based on native heavy stock, the breed as it is now known, was only developed during the 19th century. The present breed was created to meet the demands for strong, fast draft power and, along with many other heavy draft breeds, it was carefully bred for military and general heavy draft work.

The Schleswig's immediate neighbor from Denmark, the Jutland, had a lasting influence on the breed, a situation greatly facilitated by the fact that the province of Schleswig-Holstein in northern Germany, where the Schleswig Heavy Draft comes from, was once owned by Denmark. Both the Jutland and the Schleswig were influenced by the stallion Oppenheim LXII, who was brought to Schleswig-Holstein in 1860 and was almost certainly a Suffolk Punch.

Toward the end of the 19th century, considerable Thoroughbred blood was intro-duced to lighten the breed. In this century, however, faults such as an over-long, rather weak back and soft feet were causing concern, so further crosses, this time of Breton and Boulonnais, were added to eliminate these defects. More recently, Jutland blood has again been introduced.

Character and care

The Schleswig looks like a cross between a heavy horse and a large cob. It has a lively temperament and energetic movement, and is a willing, hard worker.

The Schleswig today

The Schleswig is mainly used as a heavy draft horse on farms in Germany.

GENERAL CHARACTERISTICS

CONFORMATION A heavy cob-type horse.

HEAD Rather plain, yet with a lively, inquiring look. The **ears** are medium length, well pricked, and wide set, the **eyes** small but not mean.

COLOR Usually chestnut, particularly an attractive chocolate color, with a wavy flaxen mane and tail, but bay and gray sometimes occur.

HEIGHT From 15.1hh to 16.1hh.

Initially a rather ponderous heavy breed, the Schleswig Heavy Draft has been lightened and bred for more activity and now has a definite cob-like appearance. It has an interesting history and retains its popularity as a farm horse in Europe.

WESTPHALIAN

The modern Westphalian is yet another top-quality German horse which has been refined from an older version of the breed to produce what is required by today's market – a superb riding and competition horse.

The Westphalian was first named as a formal breed in 1826 with the formation of the breed association in Westphalia, in Germany. Early stock used in the formation of the breed was based on indigenous stock mixed with mainly Thoroughbred blood. Breeding the Westphalian became more concentrated at the end of World War II. The choice of Thoroughbred and Arab blood for speed, courage, stamina, and quality, plus the popular Hanoverian blood for common sense and willingness, proved excellent in combination with the breeders' existing stock.

The Westphalian first came to the attention of the competition horse world in the late 1970s. One of their number, Roman, won the World Show Jumping Championship in 1978, and then in the 1982 World Championships, Westphalians again won the jumping with Fire and the dressage with Ahlerich.

Bred for the modern performance horse market, the Westphalian contains fewer other breeds in its make-up than some warmbloods. It is a multi-talented horse, being used for carriage driving, general riding and harness work, and especially for show jumping and dressage.

Character and care

The Westphalian has a courageous, spirited temperament, yet is docile and willing.

The Westphalian today

Today the breed is used for general riding and harness work, including competitive carriage driving. It is most talented, however, in the fields of show jumping and dressage, and some even have the speed for eventing.

GENERAL CHARACTERISTICS

CONFORMATION A well-balanced, quality middle-weight horse of varying type due to the stud book's not being closed to further infusions of desirable outside blood.

HEAD An intelligent head. The **ears** are of medium length, the **eyes** show courage and friendliness, the **profile** is straight, and the entire head is more workmanlike than beautiful.

COLOR All solid colors. White allowed on head and legs.

HEIGHT From 15.2hh to 16.2hh.

ANCESTRY

Native Westphalian stock plus early Thoroughbred blood has been combined with Hanoverian, Arab, and modern Thoroughbred.

Native stock
Early ▼
Thoroughbred
Hanoverian ▼
Arab ▼
Modern ▼
Thoroughbred
Westphalian

HOLSTEIN

The Holstein is often referred to as the Hanoverian's big cousin, but although there is Holstein blood in the Hanoverian, the Holstein's origins are considerably different. It is known to have been bred from around the turn of the 13th century at a monastery in the marshy district northeast of the Elbe estuary in present-day Schleswig-Holstein, Germany. Descended from a primitive indigenous type known as the Marsh Horse, the Holstein's initial use was as a heavy-type agricultural and coach horse.

Throughout the Middle Ages, the Holstein was selectively bred to produce a popular warhorse and tourney horse. In later centuries it was used as a cavalry, heavy gun, and transport horse by the military, and was so in demand that it was exported to France and England for similar uses.

The Holstein was always a big and strong but not cumbersome horse used mainly for draft or heavy riders. It was admired as a tough coach horse, able to withstand hard work and long distances, aided by its natural stamina. On the farm it was noted as an excellent all-rounder able to do most jobs from plowing to cart and carriage pulling and riding.

Over the centuries other breeds and types have been introduced into the Holstein, such as the Andalusian, Neapolitan, and Oriental. Therefore, while retaining its strength, length of stride, and toughness, the Holstein acquired elegance together with willingness and energy and a certain quality and presence, making it an imposing, as well as a reliable, horse.

From the 16th to the 18th century, Holsteiners were much in demand and were exported all over Europe, particularly to France. They were expensive and owning one had cachet – not without reason. The demand

Originally a large agricultural and coach horse, the Holstein is often tall and rangy with considerable substance. The horse shown here is closer to the type popular in the 19th century than most modern Holsteins.

for them far outstripped the supply of good horses being exported, and being bred for quantity instead of quality, the breed deteriorated until, in the early 19th century, measures were taken to halt the decline.

The main route to improvement lay via the English breed so highly regarded at the time, the Yorkshire Coach Horse. This horse was a cross between the Cleveland Bay and the Thoroughbred. The breed had its own society and registry, and the object of its breeders was to produce a horse which stood very high at the shoulder (most were 17hh or more), combining quality with a sufficiency of substance.

Yorkshire Coach Horses were imported into Germany for introduction into the Holstein breed. It was an experiment which worked well. The Holstein improved in appearance and constitution while retaining its original appearance and character.

In common with many of the heavy breeds, the Holstein was dealt a severe blow in breeding in the years following the end of World War II. With the advent of mechanization, heavy horses were no longer so much in demand. The Holstein was, however, essentially so sound that the recent introduction of Thoroughbred and Trakehner blood has lightened the horse, which is now used in carriage work and riding.

Character and care

The Holstein has an excellent temperament and is of a different makeup to other warmbloods, retaining the big, rangy, substantial build, yet conforming to the requirements of those who want a large, elegant, and not unduly fine performance horse.

The breed is tough and hardy, having been traditionally kept outdoors in swampy marshland. The inclusion of more Thoroughbred blood today, though, demands that the Holstein should be properly sheltered in severe weather conditions.

The Holstein today

Today, the Holstein is used for carriage-driving, show jumping (for which it seems to have a natural talent), eventing (where its great stride eats up the cross-country miles and often makes light of huge fences), and also in dressage, where its height and quality give it a commanding presence. It is also used by the military for parade purposes.

The modern Holstein excels at show jumping, with its big, rangy build and long, well-balanced stride. Here, the Holstein show jumper, Classic Touch, ridden for Germany by Ludger Beerbaum in the 1992 Olympic Games, ably demonstrates the breed's expertise in these sequence shots of clearing a fence.

HOLSTEIN

The overall impression created by the Holstein is that of a tall and substantial quality horse. This Holstein horse is a good example of the type most wanted today – still with the height and obviously the scope, but lighter and with Thoroughbred blood well in evidence. Apart from the overall impression of quality and toughness in a big package, the main feature of the Holstein is its strong, well-balanced, long stride. The symbol **C** *indicates a conformation feature.*

COAT AND COLOR
This coat is a markedly dappled gray. Other colors seen are all the solid colors with little or no white.

HEIGHT
Between 16hh and 17hh.

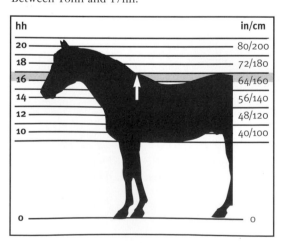

hh		in/cm
20		80/200
18		72/180
16		64/160
14		56/140
12		48/120
10		40/100
0		0

QUARTERS AND TAIL
The quarters are powerful, wide, deep, and slightly sloped with a well-set tail. **C**

WITHERS, BACK, AND LOINS
The withers can be quite high; the back is level and often quite long, but the horse is well ribbed-up and the loins long, slightly arched, and broad. **C**

CHEST AND GIRTH
The chest is deep and broad, and the girth area deep and substantial. **C**

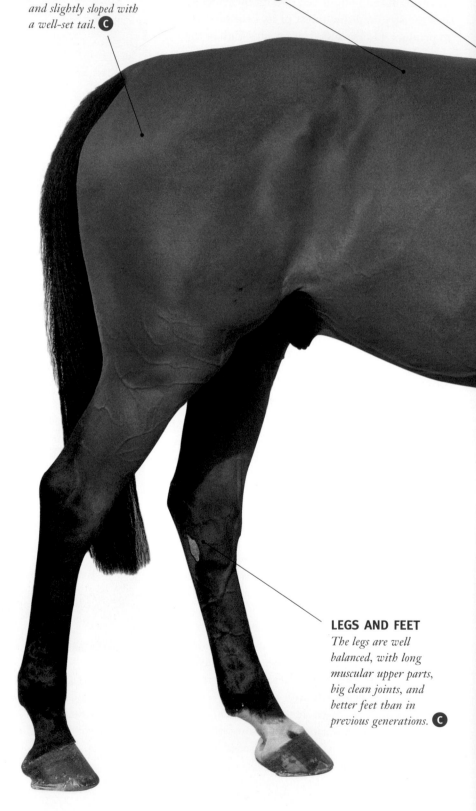

LEGS AND FEET
The legs are well balanced, with long muscular upper parts, big clean joints, and better feet than in previous generations. **C**

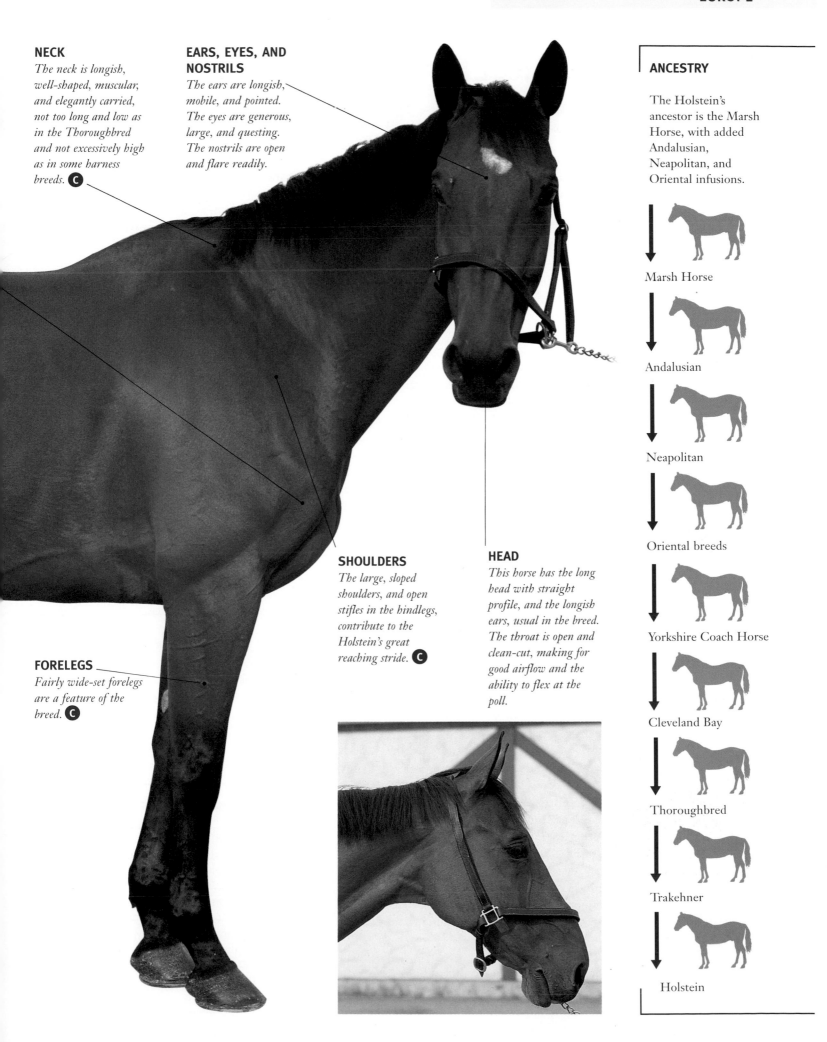

NECK

The neck is longish, well-shaped, muscular, and elegantly carried, not too long and low as in the Thoroughbred and not excessively high as in some harness breeds. **C**

EARS, EYES, AND NOSTRILS

The ears are longish, mobile, and pointed. The eyes are generous, large, and questing. The nostrils are open and flare readily.

SHOULDERS

The large, sloped shoulders, and open stifles in the hindlegs, contribute to the Holstein's great reaching stride. **C**

HEAD

This horse has the long head with straight profile, and the longish ears, usual in the breed. The throat is open and clean-cut, making for good airflow and the ability to flex at the poll.

FORELEGS

Fairly wide-set forelegs are a feature of the breed. **C**

ANCESTRY

The Holstein's ancestor is the Marsh Horse, with added Andalusian, Neapolitan, and Oriental infusions.

Marsh Horse

Andalusian

Neapolitan

Oriental breeds

Yorkshire Coach Horse

Cleveland Bay

Thoroughbred

Trakehner

Holstein

143

MECKLENBURG

The main purpose of horse breeding in Germany up until World War II was to produce horses primarily for military service, but which could also be put to domestic use. The state studs largely control the stallions, while private owners keep the mares.

In earlier centuries, heavy-type cobs had been used in warfare to carry armored knights, and the Mecklenburg's ancestors fall into this category. It was later "bred up" using warm-blood stallions to create a suitable cavalry horse.

In the 18th century the Mecklenburg was particularly prized as a substantial carriage horse of considerable strength, stamina, and soundness with an equable temperament. During the latter half of the 19th century, however, it deteriorated somewhat, due to the random introduction of substandard Thoroughbred blood.

By World War II the Mecklenburg had developed into a cavalry-type, medium-weight riding horse, with sturdy legs and an easy action. The breed's homeland was in what was to become East Germany, and it was there that a stud was founded at Schwerin, where the Mecklenburg's transformation into a modern leisure and sports horse was undertaken.

In the 1960s and early 1970s, two Anglo-Arab stallions were used on Mecklenburg mares to introduce fire into its slightly phlegmatic temperament, and it was subsequently crossed heavily with the Hanoverian.

Character and care
Today's Mecklenburg is specifically a riding and carriage horse, strong and bold but with a tractable and quiet temperament.

The Mecklenburg today
The Mecklenburg's main use today is as a leisure and competition riding horse.

ANCESTRY

The Mecklenburg's ancestors can be traced back to the 14th century. Low-grade Thoroughbred blood was introduced in the late 19th century, and in the 20th century, Anglo-Arab and Hanoverian blood has been used extensively.

Native heavy horse
Thoroughbred ▼
Anglo-Arab ▼
Hanoverian ▼
Mecklenburg

GENERAL CHARACTERISTICS

CONFORMATION The **neck** is quite long, the **chest** is broad and deep, and the **legs** are sturdy with rounded, tough **feet**.

HEAD Of average size, workmanlike, and with a straight **profile**. The **ears** are of medium length, and the **eyes** are calm and bold.

COLOR Usually bay, brown, black, or chestnut with white allowed on head and legs.

HEIGHT Averages between 15.3hh and 16.1hh.

KARACABEY

Turkey, the homeland of the Karacabey, is very well supplied with horses. It is believed that there are over a million of them in the country, and they are used mainly for transportation and in agriculture. Of the various types in Turkey now, the Karacabey is the only one breeding true to type, and it is generally regarded as being the native Turkish horse.

The origins of the Karacabey are still recent, going back to the beginning of this century, when native Turkish mares were crossed with Nonius stallions imported from Hungary. At the same time, a significant amount of Arab blood was also added to give quality, refinement, and stamina to the breed.

Character and care
The Karacabey is a warmblood, versatile with good conformation. It has a steady, even temperament, and is a willing worker.

The Karacabey today
The breed is very versatile. In Turkey it is used as a riding horse, a cavalry mount, a light draft horse, and as a pack horse.

ANCESTRY

The Karacabey is a very young breed. Native Turkish mares were mated with Nonius stallions, then Arab blood.

Native Turkish mares
Nonius ▼
Arab ▼
Karacabey

GENERAL CHARACTERISTICS

CONFORMATION The **neck** is strong and well proportioned with a slight arch, the **legs** are strong and quite long with pleasing conformation.

HEAD Straight **profile** with medium-length **ears**.

COLOR Bay, brown, black, gray, chestnut, or roan. Some white markings on lower legs and head.

HEIGHT 15.1hh to 16.1hh.

KLADRUBER

ANCESTRY

Alpine mares were bred with Barb and Turk stallions. Later, Andalusian, Lipizzaner, and Neapolitan blood was introduced. In this century, Anglo-Norman, Hanoverian, and Oldenburg blood was used to revive the breed's numbers.

Alpine heavy mares
Barb ▼
Turk ▼
Andalusian ▼
Neapolitan ▼
Lipizzaner ▼
Anglo-Norman ▼
Hanoverian ▼
Oldenburg ▼
Modern Kladruber

This historic coach breed is held in great affection. An impressive, distinctive type of horse, the Kladruber contains, on its native heavy base, much old Spanish blood, only receiving crosses of other breeds of necessity after World War II.

The Kladruber of Bohemia in the former Czechoslovakia was founded in 1597 by the Emperor Maximilian II of Austria. Its home, the Kladrub Stud, is still operational today.

Heavy mares from the Alps were initially mated with Barbs and Turks, and later, Andalusian stallions imported from Spain were also used, as were Lipizzaners and Neapolitans. In the Kladruber's formative years, the breed was the subject of very careful selective breeding, and animals were specifically bred as parade or coach horses for the Imperial Austrian court of Vienna. The horses were mainly gray, but some blacks were also bred.

World War II ravaged Kladruber stocks; to revive the breed, Anglo-Normans, Hanoverians, and Oldenburgs were mated with existing Kladrubers. The breed is once again thriving, with both gray and black strains being found.

Character and care

The Kladruber is a strong, active horse, long-lived, calm, and amenable.

GENERAL CHARACTERISTICS

CONFORMATION The **neck** is deep and muscular, the **legs** are strong with broad, flat joints and with very little hair on the fetlocks – the Kladruber's action is moderately high, and the **feet** are of medium size and well formed.

HEAD A classical look to the head indicates the horse's origins. The **ears** are of medium length, the **eyes** large and with an appealing expression, the **forehead** broad, and the **nostrils** open.

COLOR Almost always gray, but blacks are still bred.

HEIGHT In the past Kladrubers were 18hh, but today's representatives of the breed are about 16.2hh to 17hh.

The Kladruber today

The Kladruber was formerly the classic coach horse; today's smaller animal is an excellent riding and draft horse.

SHAGYA ARAB

A riding horse of the highest quality, the Hungarian Shagya deserves to be better known outside its home country. Technically a part-bred Arab, the Shagya is today virtually a large Arab, but with more substance – a very desirable mount.

O ne of the highest quality yet most under-rated horse breeds is the Hungarian Shagya Arab. Though strongly Arab in appearance and character, it is a part-bred, with a strong preponderance of Arab blood.

Mezőhegyes, the oldest stud in Hungary, was founded in 1785; the Babolna Stud was founded four years later, and this stud is the home of the superb Shagya Arab. In 1816 a military edict was passed to the effect that the broodmares at Babolna must be mated with Oriental stallions to provide light cavalry and harness horses. Stallions of mixed Oriental blood were used as well as Old Spanish crosses.

The results following the 1816 edict were so satisfactory that a generation later it was decided that Babolna should concentrate on producing horses of exclusively Arab blood, and these became the forerunners of today's Shagya, descending from an Arab stallion of that name who was imported to Babolna from Syria in 1836 as a six year old. At 15.2½hh, Shagya was big for an Arab. He was of the Seglawy or Siglavi strain, which embodied the most "traditional" Arab appearance, with a delicate, dished head; a crested, arched neck; and a high-set banner-like tail.

Character and care

In appearance and constitution, Shagyas are just like big, substantial Arabs. They are

ANCESTRY

Based on indigenous Hungarian mares but with Oriental infusions, the Shagya is a high-quality horse of marked Arab type.

Hungarian (inc. Tarpan and Mongolian and some heavy blood)
Mixed Oriental ▼
strains
Old Spanish ▼
Thoroughbred ▼
Arabian ▼
Shagya Arab

GENERAL CHARACTERISTICS

CONFORMATION In appearance, the Shagya is of typical Arab conformation, but with rather more substance. As with all Arabs, the **mane**, **forelock**, and **tail** are of long, straight, and silky hair. Altogether, the Shagya Arab is a horse of superb quality.

HEAD Typically beautiful with wide-set, pointed **ears**; large, gentle **eyes** aside a broad, slightly domed **forehead**; a small **muzzle** with fine, flaring **nostrils**; and a characteristic arch to the throat.

COLOR Most Shagyas inherit their founding father's satiny gray coat, but all Arab colors can be found, including the rare black, inherited from "The Black Pearl of Hungary," the perfect stallion O'Bajan XIII (foaled in 1949), at stud in Babolna.

HEIGHT From 14.2hh to 15.2hh.

intelligent, kind-natured, spirited yet gentle, and enthusiastic. They also have great toughness, speed, and stamina.

The Shagya Arab today

Traditionally bred for the cavalry, today Shagya Arabs are superb riding, light driving, and competition horses.

NONIUS

ANCESTRY

The founding sire was of Anglo-Norman and Norfolk Roadster blood, while the founding mares came from the Arab, Andalusian, Lipizzaner, Norman, and Kladruber breeds, with some English halfbreds. Later, Thoroughbred and Arab blood was introduced to the already established Nonius breed.

Anglo-Norman
Norfolk Roadster ▼
Arab ▼
Andalusian ▼
Lipizzaner ▼
Norman ▼
Kladruber ▼
English halfbred ▼
Thoroughbred ▼
Nonius

In one regard, and that is in the prepotency of its founding stallion, the Nonius breed of Hungary can be said to resemble the American Morgan. Nonius Senior, the founding stallion of the breed, stamped his stock unmistakably with his own type, and to this day, all Nonius horses look very much alike.

The breed came about as a result of a fairly unprepossessing-looking Anglo-Norman stallion (Nonius Senior) being captured by the Hungarian cavalry in 1813 from the French stud Rosières following Napoleon's defeat at Leipzig. Nonius Senior's sire, Orion, was apparently not full Thoroughbred, but a halfbred, the other half probably being Norfolk Roadster, and his dam was an old-type Norman mare who was said to be common but a good broodmare.

Nonius Senior himself was not attractive and had several significant faults such as poor hindquarters, a long, weak back, and a short neck with a plain head, big ears, and piggy eyes. What the Hungarians saw in him is hard to understand but perhaps they had a sixth sense, because he was to found one of their most useful breeds. Nonius Senior turned out to have a tractable temperament and willing nature, and was popular with his handlers.

Nonius Senior was put to all sorts of mares – Arabs, Lipizzaners, Andalusians, Kladrubers, Normans, and English halfbreds – and the results were invariably the image of their sire. When the staff at the famous Mezőhegyes Stud saw what a fertile and prepotent sire he was, they planned a daring program of close in-breeding to Nonius Senior to fix the type he threw. He was mated back to many of his own carefully selected daughters, and the Nonius stamp continued. Not only did his daughters pass on his characteristics, but his sons did, too, and he sired many superb stallions to carry on his excellent work. He was a young horse when captured and lived to be 22 years of age, dying in 1832 after a very long and prolific stud career.

In the late 19th century, a refining influence was felt necessary, so Thoroughbred and Arab blood was introduced into the breed.

There are now two types of Nonius: the large type, derived from the Anglo-Norman, is an excellent carriage horse, but is also used for riding and farm work. The small Nonius, containing more Arab and Thoroughbred blood, is mainly a riding horse, but is also used for light draft work.

Character and care

The Nonius of both types is a calm, easy-to-handle horse, which is willing to please. They are late maturing but generally long lived.

The Nonius today

The Nonius was formerly used extensively by the Hungarian army. Today both types of Nonius are versatile all-rounders.

GENERAL CHARACTERISTICS

CONFORMATION The Nonius is not a beautiful horse, but the conformation faults of the past have now been largely overcome.

HEAD The head is a little long and plain. The **ears** are of medium length, the **eyes** bigger and more generous than in earlier generations, and the **profile** straight or slightly convex. The **expression** is very honest and friendly.

COLOR Black, dark brown, or bay. A little white on head and lower legs may sometimes be seen.

HEIGHT The large Nonius stands between 15.3hh and 16.2hh, while the small Nonius stands between 14.2hh and 15.3hh.

A popular and generally useful breed. All Nonius horses to this day look extremely like their unprepossessing founding stallion, the Anglo-Norman Nonius Senior, abducted by the Hungarians from France.

FURIOSO

The Furioso is a quality, responsive, intelligent breed, being a substantial halfbred type and a very good all-round sports and carriage horse. It continues to receive infusions of carefully selected Thoroughbred blood in view of the type of competition horse currently in demand.

ANCESTRY

English stallions of Thoroughbred and Norfolk Roadster blood were used on mares of Nonius and Arab blood. Thoroughbred genes were reintroduced in the 19th century and are still being used today.

Nonius/native
Hungarian ▼
Arab ▼
Early ▼
Thoroughbred
Norfolk Roaster ▼
Thoroughbred ▼
Furioso

The Furioso, or Furioso North Star, may have a slightly strange name, but, like other Hungarian breeds, it takes its name from the stallion (or in this case, stallions) who founded it. Nowadays the breed is simply known as the Furioso.

The Furioso is only about 150 years old, but it is firmly established as a great favorite in Hungary and Eastern Europe.

The Furioso is a substantial middle-weight plus Thoroughbred type. The Hungarians like quality, responsive, and intelligent horses, and the Furioso shows all these qualities.

One of Hungary's most famous studs, the Mezöhegyes Stud, founded by the Hapsburg Emperor Joseph II in 1785, first developed the Nonius and later the Furioso and North Star breeds, following the importation of those stallions in 1840 and 1843 respectively. Furioso was an English Thoroughbred and North Star an English Norfolk Roadster. These two stallions were mated with Nonius and Arab mares to produce two distinct breeds, but by 1885 the offspring started to be interbred and are now blended into the one breed, with the Furioso being the dominant type.

Character and care

Thoroughbred by nature, the Furioso is a sub-stantial middle-weight horse, intelligent with a cooperative and pleasant temperament.

The Furioso today

The Furioso is a good all-round riding horse, used for most saddle pursuits from general riding to steeplechasing, having excellent jumping abilities. It also makes an excellent carriage horse with great stamina and retains the coach-horse type of action with knee lift inherited from its Nonius forebears.

GENERAL CHARACTERISTICS

CONFORMATION Resembling a middle-weight Thoroughbred or halfbred horse, the Furioso has a pleasing, proud appearance.

HEAD Very Thoroughbred in character. The **ears** are of medium length, the **eyes** courageous and inquiring, and the **profile** straight. The **muzzle** is rather squarish with large, open **nostrils**.

COLOR Almost always brown, bay, or black. Very rarely carries any white.

HEIGHT Averages at around 16.1hh.

ANCESTRY

A strong Arab base, but a great deal of Thoroughbred blood has subsequently been added.

Arab
Native Hungarian ▼
Spanish ▼
Thoroughbred ▼
Gidran

GIDRAN

The Gidran, or Hungarian Anglo-Arab, can be traced back to an Arab stallion of the Seglawy (or Siglavi) strain called Gidran Senior, who was imported from the Middle East into Hungary in 1816. He was mated with a Spanish mare called Arrogante and the resulting foal, named Gidran II, is generally regarded as the foundation sire of the breed, although another Arab stallion of the same name, bred at Hungary's Babolna Stud, was also used extensively in the formative years.

From the outset, the Gidran was intended as a cavalry horse, and as Arabs were too small for European cavalry use, other blood was used in its formation. Mares of native Hungarian mixed blood, together with Spanish mares, were used as foundation mares, and these were mated with English Thoroughbreds and half-breds to give extra height and scope to their offspring. The breed is now a quality saddle horse, excellent for today's sports horse market.

Character and care

The Gidran has a hot and difficult temperament, but it is an excellent jumper: fast, bold, and keen.

The Gidran today

Used as a riding and competition horse. It is exported within Eastern Europe for competition purposes and for improving other breeds.

GENERAL CHARACTERISTICS

CONFORMATION A quality Thoroughbred-type horse in appearance, the Gidran often shows its Arab ancestry and spirit.

HEAD Often beautiful and characteristic of a quality blood horse. Its **ears** are well pricked, with **eyes** set well to the sides of a broad **forehead**. The **profile** is straight or slightly concave, the **muzzle** is "tight," and the **nostrils** capable of flaring readily and widely.

COLOR Nearly always chestnut.

HEIGHT Usually between 16.1hh and 17hh.

ANCESTRY

Old Iberian blood was combined with Arab and Barb blood in the breeding of the Carthusian, which escaped the introduction of heavier blood introduced into other Andalusian strains.

Iberian
Barb ▼
Arab ▼
Carthusian

CARTHUSIAN

The Carthusian monks of Jerez de la Frontera had been using selective breeding to produce top-class Iberian horses since 1476, when Don Alvaro Obertus de Valeto be-queathed to them 10,000 acres (4,050 hectares) of prime land in Jerez.

So zealous were the monks in their quest to breed and preserve the pure old Spanish horse that they refused to obey a royal edict enforcing the introduction of Neapolitan blood.

When, in the Peninsular Wars of 1808–14, Napoleon stole most of the best Andalusian stock, the Carthusian monks gathered together what remained and continued to breed them selectively with their own existing stock. Today, Carthusians are still bred by a few rich families, and some state studs, and the breed's lines can be traced back to those so carefully preserved by the monks.

Character and care

Proud, gentle, and intelligent, the Carthusian has all the qualities of the Andalusian breed.

GENERAL CHARACTERISTICS

CONFORMATION The **neck** is proudly arched and set on high, sloping shoulders. The **legs** are strong and fine, and the **feet** well formed.

HEAD A little smaller than the Andalusian. The **forehead** is broad and the **profile** straight in the upper part. The **muzzle** is long and tapering with a little hollow just below the nostrils. The pricked **ears** are set wide apart, the **eyes** bold, large, and alert.

COLOR Most Carthusians are gray, but chestnut and black also occur.

HEIGHT 15.2hh or smaller.

The Carthusian today

Used for riding and light draft work, including work in the bullring and *Haute Ecole* displays.

ANDALUSIAN

Shown here is an Andalusian of the older type, with his rounded outline and powerful hindquarters. This type of horse finds it relatively easy to move in the highly collected way needed for Haute Ecole *airs, although today's Andalusians sometimes have more Thoroughbred blood to add height and refinement.*

The modern Andalusian is probably one of the purest and oldest breeds or strains in the world. Along with its blood-brothers, the Lusitano, the Carthusian, the Altér Real, the Castilian, the Extremeño, and the Zapatero, the Andalusian represents almost exactly the type of horse depicted in Iberian prehistoric cave art. All are based on a still-existing primitive type, the Sorraia, found at one time throughout the whole of Iberia.

Over the ages, various peoples and their horses invaded and traded with the civilizations currently present in Iberia. Outcrossings began thousands of years before the Moors invaded in A.D. 711, mainly with Oriental types. Boundaries have changed within the peninsula, too, accounting for the different names being given to various areas at different times in history, and thus the different names for what is

essentially the same breed of horse. At one time, before the Middle Ages and during the period of the Arab empire, almost the whole of the peninsula was called Andalusia and its horses Andalusians. Lusitania, for example, was the Roman name for roughly present-day Portugal.

Iberia was a noted horse-breeding area during its time as a Roman province, when Arab, Barb, and other Oriental strains were brought there, and many thousands of years before that it contained horses of typical Spanish or Iberian type – high-headed, convex profile, compact, strong build, and high action, proud and gentle.

Today's Andalusian is a major world breed which has influenced many others and is very highly prized in Spain, especially in Andalucia in the heart of old Spain – Jerez de la Frontera,

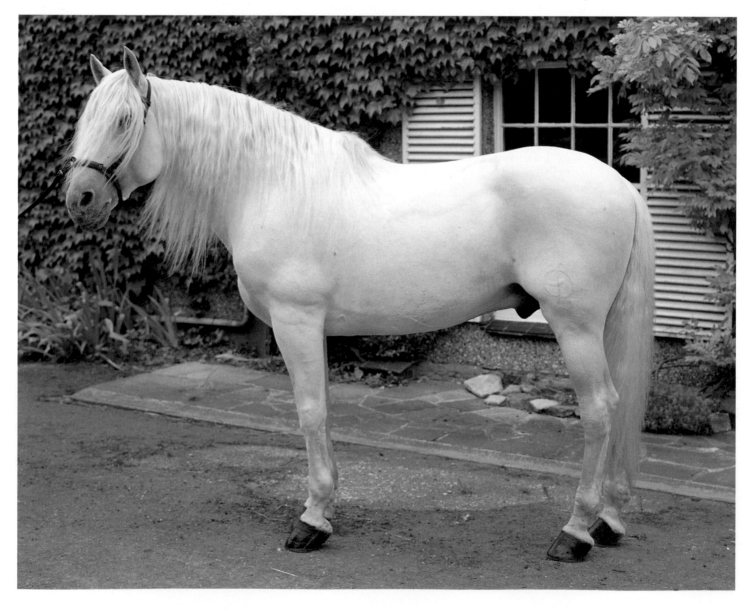

The Spanish Trot, shown here, is, with the Spanish Walk, not accepted in competition dressage as a required movement, since the horse is not collected or "on the bit." It is, however, a valuable training movement for making the shoulders more supple and freer.

Seville, and Cordoba. It was taken to the Americas, by the *conquistadores*, and has influenced American breeds, and many of Europe's.

As a warhorse, it had all the qualities of conformation needed to perform the battlefield maneuvers necessary of a knight's mount (Babieca, the mount of Spain's hero, El Cid, was an Andalusian) and also possessed endurance with a pleasant temperament. The height of its systematic breeding stretched from the 15th to the 18th centuries. In order to introduce height and more weight to the breed, heavier stallions were used, which almost decimated the breed's highly prized qualities of fire and pride with docility and tractability, and contaminated its compact conformation and proud action. During his Iberian campaigns, Napoleon and his officers took most of the best remaining strains, and the breed was in real danger of dying out. Mercifully, the Carthusian monks of Castello, Jerez, and Seville, who had bred the best and purest Andalusians from the 15th century, salvaged the best of what remained and selectively bred them to maintain the continuity of the breed. Most of today's best horses can be traced back to the Carthusian monks' lines.

Character and care

Pride, courage, and spirit combined with docility and affection toward people typify the Andalusian's character. Small children habitually ride them in Spain, yet they possess all the fire and presence demanded by an expert horseman of a display or parade horse.

The Andalusian today

The Andalusian is mainly used for display purposes and for bullfighting. The agility and power of the breed ideally suit it to the intricate movements needed of a bullfighting horse, from which some *Haute Ecole* airs derive.

It is difficult to import the best examples of a breed which is jealously guarded in its homeland, but the breed is gradually spreading, and there are a limited number of Andalusians in Britain, more in the United States. Andalusians have the conformation and power to make good jumpers. They are athletic, energetic horses with ideal gaits for advanced dressage, but apart from being superb general riding and carriage horses, they are used in showing classes, both in hand and under saddle.

ANDALUSIAN

An Andalusian of the more modern type, lighter and with longer legs, but still showing that old nobility which made the breed such a huge favorite in the bullrings and classical riding schools of the Europe of centuries ago. Ever popular in its homeland, today the breed enjoys renewed popularity elsewhere. The action is characteristic: purposeful, showy walk; high, lofty trot with a tendency to dish; natural "rocking horse" canter. The symbol **C** *indicates a conformation feature.*

COLOR
Gray (predominantly), bay, an auburn-brown shade, some chestnuts and roans.

LOINS AND QUARTERS
The loins and quarters are strong and muscular. **C**

BACK
Compact, well balanced, and sturdy with a straight, fairly short back. **C**

MANE AND TAIL
The luxuriant, often wavy mane and tail are a feature of the breed, and much prized. In former times, manes and tails sweeping the ground were not unknown.

LEGS
The legs are elegant yet strong with short cannons. **C**

HEIGHT
Average 15.1hh to 15.3hh.

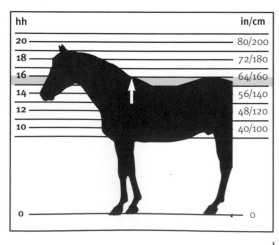

hh	in/cm
20	80/200
18	72/180
16	64/160
14	56/140
12	48/120
10	40/100
0	0

HEAD AND NECK

The powerful, crested neck and the aristocratic outlook of the Andalusian are both obvious here. The breed has fire and quality with a gentle, equable temperament. **C**

EARS AND EYES

The ears are medium length and expressive. Eyes are proud yet gentle, large, and appealing.

HEAD

Set onto the neck at such an angle as to make collection easy and natural. **C**

CHEST AND SHOULDERS

The chest is broad and deep with laid-back shoulders on which the neck is set high. **C**

PROFILE AND NOSTRILS

The profile is convex (characteristically) or straight. The nostrils are capable of flaring fully. **C**

COAT

Dense coat, short in summer and slightly longer in winter, particularly in colder countries.

ANCESTRY

Like many horses not officially designated as warmblooded, this is exactly what the Andalusian is. The native Spanish horse, the Ginete, and the native ponies, the Garrano and the more primitive Sorraia, mated with Barbs and Arabs and produced this lovely horse, which has been carefully and selectively bred as a breed in its own right for centuries.

Spanish horse

Garrano

Sorraia

Barb

Arab

Andalusian

ALTER REAL

The Altér Real is the second of Portugal's aristocratic *Haute Ecole* and bullfighting horses, but unfortunately it suffered in Napoleon's Peninsular Wars much more than its brothers, the Lusitano and Andalusian.

The Altér Real was founded on the blood of 300 Andalusian mares imported from Jerez by the Portuguese royal house of Braganza to found a stud at Vila de Portel in the Alentejo province in the south of the country, specifically to provide the royal court in Lisbon with good *Haute Ecole* and carriage horses.

After eight years, the stud was moved to the small town of Altér do Chao in the Alentejo, which subsequently gave the horse its name, *Real* meaning "royal" in Portuguese.

Breeding was successful, and the Altér Real thrived until the Peninsular Wars, when the stud was ransacked and the best horses stolen by Napoleon's troops. The abdication of King Miguel in 1832 further damaged the breed, since much of the stud's land was confiscated from the crown following his abdication. Later, efforts to reinstate and "improve" the Altér Real by the introduction of English Thoroughbred, Hanoverian, Norman, and Arab blood led to the weakening of both the type and the character of the breed.

The subsequent reintroduction of Carthusian-Andalusian blood from the stud of the Spanish Zapata family late in the 19th century began to reverse the decline, but when in the early 20th century, the Portuguese monarchy was abolished, the Altér Real's stud records were destroyed, the stock dispersed, and the stallions removed for gelding.

Today, the breed owes its existence to only one man, Dr. Ruy d'Andrade, who was able to acquire two stallions and a few mares. An expert breeder and lover of the true Iberian horse, he built up a small but top quality stud of Altér Real horses which he passed to the Portuguese Ministry of Agriculture in the middle of the 20th century.

The breed has since been owned and administered by the state and is now highly regarded and thriving again.

Character and care

The Altér Real is a true old Iberian type of horse to look at, but its sometimes excitable temperament (not typical of the Andalusian or,

ANCESTRY

Misfortune has introduced much undesirable blood into the breed which is now, however, recovering due to selective breeding for the old Iberian type.

Andalusian
English ▼
Thoroughbred
Norman ▼
Hanoverian ▼
Arab ▼
Carthusian- ▼
Andalusian
Altér Real

Not so well known as its Iberian brother breeds, the Andalusian and Lusitano, the Altér Real suffered in the early 19th century by the introduction of much undesirable blood. Dedicated breeding for the old type by Dr. Ruy d'Andrade saved the Altér Real, which is today bred by the Portuguese state.

Due to unsuitable infusions in the past, the temperament of some Altér Reals is somewhat excitable, requiring skilled handling. The breed is, however, intelligent, tough, and hardy.

especially, the Lusitano) bears witness to the indiscriminate breeding and introduction of poor-quality, outside blood in the early 19th century. It can require skilled handling by competent horsemen.

It is intelligent, quick to learn, and responsive, but fiery to some extent, very self-aware, and spirited. It is tough and hardy.

The Altér Real today

The Altér Real is used as a riding and light draft horse, mainly for *Haute Ecole* displays, and is used extensively for such purposes by the Portuguese army.

GENERAL CHARACTERISTICS

CONFORMATION The short **neck** is substantial and arched, tapering to a shapely **throat**. The upper **legs**, particularly the **thighs**, are powerfully muscled, and the legs in general are hard and tough. The high-stepping action comes from the long pasterns and very strong, thrusting hocks. The **feet** are slightly small but well-shaped and tough.

HEAD Full of old-type quality, with a slightly convex **profile** and a gentle taper to the **muzzle**. The **ears** are of medium length, the **eyes** expressive and somewhat arrogant.

COLOR Nearly always bay.

HEIGHT The average height is between 15hh and 16hh.

OTHER FEATURES An impressive horse, full of quality and fire, the Altér Real is immensely strong and powerful and, due to its high-stepping action and high, wide front, looks considerably bigger when ridden than it actually is.

LUSITANO

The Lusitano was one of the favored royal horses of Europe with its traditional rounded outline, sloping croup, and gently convex profile. Never bred in the same numbers as its blood-brother, the Spanish Andalusian, it is used as much or more for work rather than being mainly a parade or display mount.

ANCESTRY

Like the other Iberian breeds, the Lusitano is based on the primitive Sorraia pony which still exists in the peninsula. In the past, some Oriental blood was used, but today only horses showing true Iberian characteristics are used in breeding, and no significant outside blood has been mixed into the breed for many generations.

Sorraia
Oriental ▼
Garrano ▼
Old Spanish ▼
Lusitano

The Lusitano, like the Andalusian, is descended from the old Iberian saddle horse. Named after its country of origin, Lusitania being the Roman name for Portugal, this name only came into use as a description of Portugal's Iberian horses in the early 20th century, and was officially adopted in 1966.

The Lusitano is bred mainly in the agricultural heartland of Portugal, and the fertile south and west around the River Tagus, for participation in the *corrida* or bullfight. In Portugal the bull is not killed, the whole fight takes place on horseback, and it is a major disgrace if the horse is injured. The horses are highly prized, painstakingly schooled, and are the epitome of agility, courage, and grace. Their temperament is spirited, willing and cooperative.

In addition, the stallions are normally schooled to the highest standards of *Haute Ecole* before being sent out to stud. The Lusitano is a late-maturing but long-lived breed, and is generally not broken in until at least three and a half years of age. Fighting horses are retained entire, since it is generally considered that geldings lack the courage, sensitivity, interest, and spark needed to face up to the bull.

Character and care

The Lusitano is a proud, gentle, nimble, and extremely well-balanced horse. It is most courageous and willing and obedient by nature.

The Lusitano today

The Lusitano is mainly bred for bullfighting and the associated schooling in *Haute Ecole*, and is used for general farm work.

GENERAL CHARACTERISTICS

CONFORMATION The **neck** is carried high and is muscular and well-developed. The **legs** are well-developed and muscular in their upper parts with hard, round, and rather small **feet**.

HEAD The **profile** is slightly convex with a rounded, tapering **muzzle**. The **ears** are moderately long, finely sculpted, and mobile; the **eyes** are almond-shaped, alert, and with a bright, deep quality. The **nostrils** are open and mobile.

COLOR Gray, brown, bay, and chestnut are the most common colors.

HEIGHT 15hh to 16hh.

EAST BULGARIAN

When Bulgaria decided to create her own quality riding and light draft horse, the result was a horse of symmetry and visual appeal as well as of competence in performance.

The East Bulgarian was founded toward the end of the 19th century at the Kaiuk and Vassil Kolarov stud farms. Unusually, the foundation stock does not seem to have included native Bulgarian horses or ponies. Instead, English Thoroughbreds, English halfbreds, Arabs, and Anglo-Arabs were selected and bred together.

Once the required characteristics had been obtained, the breeders restricted themselves to English Thoroughbreds for further development and upgrading. The Thoroughbred still continues to be used, but more usually individuals of the now-established breed are mated together.

Character and care

The East Bulgarian is a quality, well-built horse of elegance and proud bearing, with a supple stride. It has a quiet but lively temperament, and is kind-natured, enthusiastic, and tough.

The East Bulgarian today

The East Bulgarian is a versatile horse. It is used under saddle for general leisure riding, and as a competition horse; and in harness as a carriage-driving horse.

GENERAL CHARACTERISTICS

CONFORMATION Of middleweight Thoroughbred type with elegance and strength. The **legs** are fine and hard, well muscled in their upper parts, and the **feet** are better than in those belonging to the pure Thoroughbred.

HEAD Of Thoroughbred type, the head is elegant and attention-drawing. The **expression** is proud and calm, the mobile **ears** of medium length, the **eyes** alert, and the **profile** straight, with open, flaring **nostrils**.

COLOR Usually chestnut and black, but bay and brown are also found. Gray is rare. Little white is sometimes found on legs or head.

HEIGHT 15hh to 16hh.

ANCESTRY

English Thoroughbreds and halfbreds were mated with Arabs and European Anglo-Arabs to create the breed, and now only Thoroughbred blood is used for further upgrading.

English Thoroughbred
English halfbred ▼
Arab ▼
Anglo-Arab ▼
East Bulgarian

DANUBIAN

The Danubian has no pretensions toward being a competition or performance horse, being created as a general riding and strong light draft horse. It was founded at the start of the 20th century by crossing original-type Nonius stallions with Gidran mares.

The resulting stock were compact, strongly built horses, which were upgraded with the addition of further Anglo-Arab and Thoroughbred blood, and the Danubian today is a popular riding and light harness horse in Bulgaria. Despite the Arab and Thoroughbred blood in its veins, it is a workmanlike and rather plain animal, having inherited the rather unglamorous characteristics of the Nonius.

Character and care

The Danubian is a rather cob-like horse in many respects, with a docile temperament.

The Danubian today

Used as a general riding and light draft horse,

GENERAL CHARACTERISTICS

CONFORMATION Compact and solidly built, with a "cobby" look to it.

HEAD Workmanlike and well proportioned, with a straight **profile**. The **ears** are of medium length, the **eyes** perhaps a little small but lively, and the expression alert and amenable. **Nostrils** are slightly small but open.

COLOR Nearly always black or dark chestnut.

HEIGHT Generally about 15.2hh.

the Danubian is not intended as a competition horse. However, when the mares are mated with Thoroughbred horses, they produce good performance horses.

ANCESTRY

Nonius and Gidran stock form the basis for the Danubian, with later additions of continental Anglo-Arab and Thoroughbred blood.

Nonius
Gidran ▼
Anglo-Arab ▼
Thoroughbred ▼
Danubian

RUSSIA, BALTIC STATES, AND SCANDINAVIA

ORLOV TROTTER

The Orlov, or Orloff, Trotter was founded in 1777, when Count Alexei Grigorievich Orlov played a role in the succession of Catherine the Great. As a reward, Catherine made him Commander of the Russian fleet. Count Orlov defeated the Turkish fleet at Chesme in 1770, and was presented by the Turkish admiral with an Arab stallion, Smetanka.

Smetanka had one season at the Orlov Stud and left only a handful of progeny from Danish, Dutch Harddraver, Mecklenburg, English Thoroughbred, and Arab mares, but the following year a Danish mare foaled a very moderate colt named Polkan. He was mated with a Danish mare, and the result was an outstanding trotting stallion named Bars I, regarded as the founding father of the Orlov Trotter.

Count Orlov worked on developing the Orlov breed of trotters at his new stud at Khrenov. Bars I was used on a variety of mares – Arabs, Dutch, Danish, English halfbreds, Polish, Russian, and Mecklenburg and their crosses – breeding selectively for quality, strength, stamina, and trotting ability. Within a few generations, the Orlov Trotter had become the fastest and most popular trotting breed in the world. Today, most Orlov Trotters cannot compete with the Standardbred or the French Trotter, but new infusions of Standardbred blood are being judiciously used with Orlovs to create the Russian or Métis Trotter.

Character and care
The Orlov Trotter is a strong, tough horse with a docile yet lively temperament.

The Orlov Trotter today
The Orlov Trotter is raced, and is also widely used as a farm horse.

GENERAL CHARACTERISTICS

CONFORMATION A well-balanced, lightly framed horse, with many individuals showing their Oriental ancestry.

HEAD The best examples of the breed have an elegant head with a straight or slightly concave **profile**. The **ears** and **eyes** are Arab in appearance, with flaring **nostrils** and a squarish **muzzle**.

COLOR Mostly gray, but black and bay also occur.

HEIGHT Quite varied in range, from 15.2hh to 17hh.

ANCESTRY

An Arab base on a variety of European breeds, with modern infusions of American Standardbred.

Arab
Dutch ▼
Danish ▼
Russian ▼
Polish ▼
Mecklenburg ▼
English ▼
(Thoroughbred/
Norfolk Roadster)
Standardbred ▼
Orlov Trotter

This brown gelding shows the short front, upright shoulder, and long, sturdy legs typical of harness racers. The Orlov Trotter was the fastest trotting racer in the world before the advent of the Standardbred, and Orlov races are still a major entertainment in Russia and surrounding countries.

DON

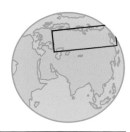

ANCESTRY

Indigenous Steppe horses were mated with various Asian and Oriental strains to create the earlier type of Don associated with the Cossacks. Later, Orlov, Thoroughbred, and Strelets Arab blood was added.

Indigenous Russian
Steppe horse
Turkmene ▼
Karabakh ▼
Karabair ▼
Persian Arab ▼
Orlov ▼
Strelets Arab ▼
Thoroughbred ▼
Modern Don

The Don comes from the area around the Rivers Don and Volga on the bleak Russian Steppes where the Cossacks came from. Indeed, the Don was the Cossacks' mount. It was a small, exceptionally tough and wiry horse, highly independent with incredible stamina and seemingly impervious to the vicious Russian winter. It descended from the indigenous Steppe horse which ran free in the Caucasus Mountains, appearing to thrive on whatever food it could forage.

As far back as the 18th century, the need for selective breeding for improvement was recognized among the Don's owners and breeders, so Persian Arab and other Oriental stallions were introduced into the herds which ran on the Steppes. In the 19th century, the Orlov Trotter, Thoroughbred, and Russian Strelets Arab stallions were run with the mare herds to heighten, refine, and correct the Don's physique.

Character and care

The modern Don is still tough and strong with an independent character. It is bred in large numbers in the Steppes, where it can run free and needs little care from humans.

The Don today

These days the Don is mainly used for endurance riding, for which it is admirably suited. It is also used to infuse stamina and hardiness into other breeds.

GENERAL CHARACTERISTICS

CONFORMATION The Don's conformation problems have still not been entirely overcome. The structure of its hip joint and angle of the pelvis often interfere with free movement, and its action can, therefore, be short and somewhat jarring.

HEAD The **ears** are smallish, shapely, and pricked; the **eyes** large and expressive; and the **profile** straight with open **nostrils**.

COLOR Usually brown or chestnut but bay, black, and gray sometimes occur. There is often a metallic sheen to the coat.

HEIGHT Between 15.2hh to 15.3hh.

The Don was the horse of the Cossack cavalry that made history in the war with Napoleon. He disastrously under-estimated both the merciless Russian winter and the sheer toughness of the Don horses. Independent, tough, and strong, the Don is still used for endurance riding.

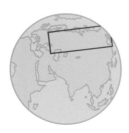

BUDYONNY

The Budyonny, Budenny, or Budyonovsky horse is one of the newer Russian breeds, created after the Russian Revolution. One of the people's heroes of the Revolution was Marshal Budyonny, whose aim was to create the perfect cavalry horse. It had to have stamina, toughness, an equable temperament, courage, and physical prowess involving both speed and jumping ability. The military stud farm at Rostov was chosen as the location for the development of the breed, which was to be named after its instigator, Marshal Budyonny.

Using Thoroughbred stallions on Don mares proved successful; other breeds, particularly the Kazakh and Kirgiz from Mongolia, were not so successful. Chernomor mares (similar to Dons, but smaller and lighter) were also tried with more success. The breed type was quickly fixed and by 1948 was already breeding true to type, when it was officially recognized.

Character and care

The Budyonny is a kind-natured, patient, intelligent horse, but it has, nevertheless, spirit, courage, and enthusiasm as well as speed, stamina, and jumping ability. Although fre-

quently bred on the state studs, large herds of the Budyonny still run free under the care of a groom and, as such, remain hardy and tough.

The Budyonny today

An excellent, all-round competition horse, the Budyonny also goes well in light harness. It excels at both endurance riding and racing.

ANCESTRY

Thoroughbred stallions on Don mares are the main foundation of this breed, with additions of Kazakh, Kirgiz, and Chernomor blood.

Don
Kazakh ▼
Kirgiz ▼
Chernomor ▼
Thoroughbred ▼
Budyonny

GENERAL CHARACTERISTICS

CONFORMATION The faults present in the Don's conformation can be seen to a lesser extent in the Budyonny.

HEAD A head showing definite Thoroughbred ancestry. The **ears** are fine and of medium length, the **eyes** bold and generous, the **profile** straight or slightly concave, and the **nostrils** open and flaring.

COLOR Most Budyonnys are chestnut, but other solid colors occur, although rarely.

HEIGHT Usually around 16hh.

The Thoroughbred quality of the modern Budyonny is clearly seen in this horse. A true product of the East, the breed also contains Don, Kazakh, Kirgiz, and Chernomor blood. Intended as the perfect cavalry mount, the Budyonny today is a high-quality competition horse.

METIS TROTTER

With its powerful, straight shoulders, high croup, and long legs, this horse is unmistakably a fast harness racer. Bred to rival the Standardbred, it contains many of its genes, plus those of the famous Orlov Trotter, and its speeds currently fall between those two breeds.

ANCESTRY

The Métis Trotter is a straight cross between the Orlov Trotter and the American Standardbred.

Orlov Trotter
Standardbred ▼
Métis Trotter

When one is accustomed to being the best in the world, it goes very hard to be usurped, and early in the 20th century the Russians realized that their world-famous, record-breaking, and hitherto invincible racing trotter, the Orlov, was being beaten hands down by the American Standardbred. Instead of getting mad, they decided to get even, and so they went straight to the source of their problem and started buying American Standardbreds. They mated them with their beloved Orlovs and came up not with an improved Orlov, but with a new breed of faster trotter, the Russian or Métis Trotter.

Sadly, despite nearly a hundred years of crossing and selective breeding using the very best trotting blood from both the Standardbred and the Orlov, the Métis Trotter is still not as fast as the Standardbred, but it is faster than the pure Orlov. In 1949 the Métis Trotter was recognized as a breed in its own right.

Character and care
The Métis Trotter is an even-natured horse, very energetic, courageous, and fast with good stamina. In Russia it receives the type of care expected of a valuable and valued racehorse – good stabling, feeding, and general care.

GENERAL CHARACTERISTICS

CONFORMATION The Métis Trotter resembles a tough, quality halfbred with powerful, sometimes croup-high **hindquarters**, a fairly straight **neck** but well-balanced physique. The Métis Trotter's trotting action exhibits the defect known as "dishing" in both the fore- and hindlegs, the forelegs being slightly knock-kneed and the hindlegs being "cow-hocked."

HEAD The head is not as fine as one might expect. The **ears** are moderately long and are well shaped, the **eyes** are sometimes a little small, and the **profile** is straight or slightly convex.

COLOR All solid colors are present in the breed.

HEIGHT Between 15.1hh and 15.3hh.

The Métis Trotter today
Specifically bred for racing at a fast trot, this is almost exclusively what the Métis Trotter is used for.

TERSKY

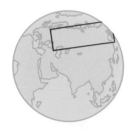

The strong Arab character of the modern Tersky is obvious in this beautiful horse. As well as this Arab type, there are two other types of Tersky. They are all excellent performance horses and the particularly beautiful ones find work in the circus.

ANCESTRY

Native Ukrainian mares and indigenous old-type Terskys were initially put to the Strelets Arab. Later, Kabardin, Don, Arab, and Thoroughbred blood was used to refine the breed.

Old-type Tersky native mares
Strelets Arab ▼
Kabardin ▼
Don ▼
Shagya Arab ▼
Thoroughbred ▼
Modern Tersky

The Tersky, Tersk, Terskij, or Terek is one of the beauties of the horse world, but it is also an excellent performance horse.

The modern breed was created early in the 20th century as an Arab-type horse for military use, which seems a little strange as Russia already had an excellent part-bred Arab type, the Strelets Arab, which has now been more or less completely absorbed into the Tersky. The Strelets Arab was based on native Ukrainian mares and Oriental, mainly Arab, stallions. It contained some high-caste Arab blood (now passed on to the Tersky) as stallions from England's Crabbet Park Stud, Poland's Janow Podlaski Stud, and Hungary's Babolna Stud were all brought to Russia to form the Strelets Arab.

The old-type Tersky horse was used by the Cossacks because it was tough and enduring, but in the 20th century Marshal Budyonny refined the breed by adding more Kabardin, Don, Arab, and Thoroughbred blood.

There are three types of horse within the breed: a light, fine, Arab-looking type; a more substantial intermediate type; and a thicker-set type with sturdier legs and a longer body.

Character and care

The Tersky has a gentle yet spirited temperament, intelligence, stamina, excellent jumping ability, and speed.

The Tersky today

The Tersky is a high-class sporting horse, excelling at jumping and endurance riding. It is in demand for dressage and, because of its beauty, for circus work.

GENERAL CHARACTERISTICS

CONFORMATION All three types of Tersky are very Arab-looking in appearance, showing all typically Arab characteristics.

HEAD A quality head, finely chiseled, with longish **ears**, a dished **profile**, liquid **eyes**, and readily flaring **nostrils**.

COLOR Gray with a metallic silver sheen.

HEIGHT Not a tall horse, between 14.3hh and 15.1hh, but can look and "ride" much bigger.

KABARDIN

The Kabardin is an extremely adaptable animal which can live on sea-level plains or high in the mountains. The Kabardin originally came from the North Caucasus mountains, where it was an old and established breed. It is a strange mixture of Oriental characteristics, being fine skinned with long, mobile ears and open nostrils, and those of horses found in colder climes, which the North Caucasus Mountains certainly are.

It is a descendant, as are many Eastern European horses, of the wild Tarpan. As with other Russian breeds, it remained unchanged until the Russian Revolution, after which it was mixed with Karabakh, Turkmene, Persian, and Arab strains to give it more scope and height for riding, pack, and agricultural work. Kabardins are bred at two main studs in their native country, and are also bred and used extensively in neighboring states. Extremely fertile, they are also used to produce milk.

The breed is very popular in its homeland, the Republic of Kabardin-Balkar. As a mountain horse, it is extremely sure-footed, nimble, sensible, and intelligent enough to pick its own way to find a safe route. It can work in snow and in deep, fast-flowing water and can trot all day, as it is well endowed with stamina.

Character and care
The Kabardin has an equable and willing temperament, very sensible and intelligent. It is long-lived, strong, and enduring. It lives outdoors and is given extra feed in winter.

The Kabardin today
Although an excellent light to medium draft horse, the Kabardin is regarded principally as a riding horse and is still used extensively for transportation in its mountain home. Elsewhere, it is a very good sports horse and has been used in the development of other breeds.

GENERAL CHARACTERISTICS

CONFORMATION Oriental in appearance, with a smooth and comfortable action.

HEAD Quite long with a slightly convex **profile**, thin **skin**, and with pronounced **jaws**. The **ears** are quite long with noticeably inward-turning points and are set quite close together. The **eyes** are fairly small and the **nostrils** open.

COLOR Bay, brown, and black, occasionally gray, but never white.

HEIGHT Between 142.hh and 15.1hh.

ANCESTRY

Descended from the wild Tarpan, in the early 20th century Karabakh, Turkmene, Persian, and Arab strains were infused into the local indigenous stock.

Tarpan
Karabakh ▼
Turkmene ▼
Persian ▼
Arab ▼
Kabardin

The Kabardin is said to be the safest and most reliable mountain horse in the world. An unusual mixture of Oriental and colder-blooded features combine to create great stamina and hardiness in this breed.

UKRAINIAN RIDING HORSE

A young breed, having been developed as a quality performance horse only since World War II, the Ukrainian Riding Horse is also used for light harness work and in agriculture depending on type. It regularly represents the Ukraine in competitive events.

ANCESTRY

Local native mares and Nonius, Furioso North Star, and Gidran mares were mated with Trakehner, Hanoverian, and Thoroughbred stallions to produce this breed.

Native mares
Nonius ▼
Furioso North Star ▼
Gidran ▼
Thoroughbred ▼
Trakehner ▼
Hanoverian ▼
Ukrainian Riding
Horse

The Ukrainian Riding Horse was founded after World War II by crossing large Nonius, Furioso North Star, Gidran, and local native mares with Trakehner, Hanoverian, and English Thoroughbred stallions. All excellent breeds in their own right, this mixture was almost bound to produce a good sporting horse if the right mating selections were made, and this is exactly what happened. Once a good base was formed, development continued with further infusion of Thoroughbred and Hanoverian blood.

The original purpose for this new breed was to create a high-class riding and competition horse, and this aim has now been achieved. The colts begin work very young, at just 18 months of age, and are tested for individual talent and aptitude in racing, dressage, show jumping, and cross-country. The best are normally kept for breeding, not necessarily after a competitive career.

Character and care
The Ukrainian Riding Horse is a mixture of excellent riding and competition breeds, most of which are bred for good temperament. The Ukrainian Riding Horse has picked up this

trait, being kind-natured, obliging, and a willing worker. It is a quality warmblood horse with strength, stamina, and scope.

The Ukrainian Riding Horse today
Principally a high-class competition horse, the Ukrainian Riding Horse is used for general pleasure riding, light harness work such as carriage-driving, and also in agriculture, depending on individual type and build.

GENERAL CHARACTERISTICS

CONFORMATION As this breed was developed from quality horses, the Ukrainian Riding Horse exudes elegance and refinement.

HEAD Occasionally rather large, with a straight **profile**, pricked **ears**, alert **eyes**, and open **nostrils**.

COLOR Usually chestnut, but bay and black are also found.

HEIGHT Up to 16.1hh.

LATVIAN

ANCESTRY

Descended from the
Northern Europe
Forest Horse and the
Tarpan/Arab-based
Zemaituka pony.
Three types now
exist, due to varying
infusions of Finnish
Heavy Draft,
Swedish Ardennes,
Hanoverian,
Oldenburg, Norfolk
Roadster,
Thoroughbred, and
Arab blood.

Primitive Forest
coldblood
Zemaituka ▼
(Tarpan/Arab)
Finnish Heavy ▼
Draft/Swedish
Ardennes
Hanoverian/ ▼
Oldenburg
Norfolk Roadster ▼
Thoroughbred/ ▼
Arab
Latvian

The Latvian probably descended from the prehistoric Forest Horse of Northern Europe, which was a heavy draft horse. Some experts, however, believe it is based on a tough and spirited pony indigenous to Lithuania, the Zemaituka (based on Tarpan and Arab blood).

The Latvian now occurs in three types, due to the different breeds introduced into it. The heavy type, the Latvian Draft; a standard or intermediate type, the Latvian Harness Horse; and a lighter type, the Latvian Riding Horse. The Draft is the original type from which the others have been developed.

The Finnish Draft Horse, Oldenburg, and Swedish Ardennes were introduced into the Draft type for more substance and strength. It can be used as a heavyweight riding horse.

The Latvian Harness Horse was developed in the 1920s by infusing Hanoverian blood into some strains; others received Anglo-Norman, Oldenburg, and Norfolk Roadster blood to create a slightly heavier type. Both types are used for riding and competition.

The Latvian Riding Horse, a more recent development, contains substantial crosses of Thoroughbred and Arab blood, and often resembles a warmblood trotting horse.

Character and care

Latvians have a quiet, relaxed temperament. They are very strong with a great deal of stamina.

The Latvian today

The Latvian, in its different types, is used for every job from heavy farm work to competition riding. The breed is popular with farmers and leisure riders alike.

GENERAL CHARACTERISTICS

CONFORMATION The physical differences in the Latvian apply only to type. Generally, the overall conformation is such that, whatever its type, a Latvian is easily recognizable as a Latvian.

HEAD Rather long and proud, with a straight **profile**; small, pointed **ears**; large, gentle **eyes**; and big **nostrils**. The mane and forelock are full.

COLOR Black, brown, bay, and chestnut occur, with the occasional gray being found.

HEIGHT Between 15.1hh and 16hh.

The Latvian is a stronger breed than its appearance would indicate. Developed for about 300 years mainly as a draft animal, there are now, due to the mingling of other breeds, draft, harness, and heavyweight riding types. All combine a quiet temperament with strength and stamina.

KARABAKH

The Karabakh horse, although of pony size, comes from the Karabakh Mountains of Azerbaijan. Karabakhs look like Arabs, which isn't surprising as both horses come from the same genetic type.

The Karabakh's existence was documented as far back as the 4th century A.D., and it has remained popular ever since as a riding mount. In the 18th century, it was suddenly very much in demand and was exported to many other Asian and European countries.

Today, it is said that no pure Karabakhs are left because in the past the breed was diluted by Persian, Turkmene, and Arab blood.

Character and care

The Karabakh is a spirited and refined hot-blood horse. It is beautiful, calm, and gentle, but also has energy and stamina. Like all true mountain breeds, it is sensible and very sure-footed with an innate sense of direction.

ANCESTRY

An ancient hot-blood type, the Karabakh has been mixed with Persian, Turkmene, and Arab blood.

Old Karabakh
Persian ▼
Turkmene ▼
Arab ▼
Modern Karabakh

The Karabakh today

Used largely for racing, it also makes an excellent small riding and pack horse. It is also popular for mounted ball games.

GENERAL CHARACTERISTICS

CONFORMATION The Karabakh looks like a hot-blood horse of Arab extraction, it is refined and small with long **legs**, often ending in blue-black **feet**.

HEAD Oriental in type, it is quite small with a straight **profile**, pointed **ears**, large **eyes**, and a soft, fine **muzzle**.

COLOR Like some other Russian breeds, the Karabakh has a beautiful metallic golden sheen to its coat. It is usually golden dun with black points, often with a dark eel stripe down its spine. Some white markings may occur. Other colors are chestnut, bay, and gray.

HEIGHT Around 14.1hh.

The long legs, spare frame, and high-set, sparse tail declare this horse's Oriental genes. A small mountain horse, its talents include racing, pack work, and mounted games.

SWEDISH WARMBLOOD

Sweden is a country very much in the North of Europe, so its indigenous stock will have been the northern coldblooded pony and horse types. When in the 17th century a superior type of cavalry horse was required, the Royal Stud at Flyinge began to cross the native stock with a very wide variety of other European breeds, including Iberian, Friesian, Arabs, and Barbs.

This process continued for many generations, and as time went on the breed was refined with later additions of Hanoverian, Trakehner, English Thoroughbred, and selected Arab blood. Today, the breed is quite self-sufficient and is still being bred at Flyinge.

The Swedish Warmblood is now one of the most successful competition horses in the world and has repeatedly won Olympic medals in the three disciplines of dressage, eventing, and show jumping. It is also a superb competitive carriage-driving horse.

The stud book was started in 1874, and before being registered, individual horses must pass extremely rigorous tests covering conformation, action, temperament, and general performance. Inspectors travel the country to inspect privately bred animals. Both private- and state-bred animals are graded according to quality and may be upgraded or downgraded, or even removed entirely from the breeding register, according to their performance in the field or at stud.

Character and care

Swedish Warmbloods are tractable and intelligent. They have excellent jumping ability, flowing, elastic gaits, and plenty of speed and stamina for horse trials.

The Swedish Warmblood today

Mainly bred for competition purposes, those not quite up to standard are used as general riding and leisure horses.

GENERAL CHARACTERISTICS

CONFORMATION The **neck** is long, crested, and well muscled, set on long, sloping shoulders. The **legs** are quite long and well muscled in their upper parts, and the **feet** are strong and well formed.

HEAD Intelligent expression, long **ears**, alert, bold **eyes**, and a straight **profile**.

COLOR All solid colors, but black is rare.

HEIGHT Usually 16.1hh to 17hh, but quite a few animals are smaller.

ANCESTRY

Indigenous Swedish pony and horse types were initially mated with Iberian, Friesian, Arab, and Barb stallions. In the 20th century, Thoroughbred, Hanoverian, and Trakehner blood was introduced for further refinement of the breed.

Indigenous Swedish stock
Iberian ▼
Friesian ▼
Arab ▼
Barb ▼
Hanoverian ▼
Trakehner ▼
Thoroughbred ▼
Swedish Warmblood

Formerly a superior cavalry horse, the Swedish Warmblood is today one of the most successful competition horses in the world. It is one of the few warmbloods fast enough for eventing and is also an excellent competitive carriage-driving horse.

GOTLAND

Almost a victim of its own popularity, the Götland or Skogruss pony was saved from seriously depleted numbers, due to export, by government action in the 1950s. It now thrives as a riding and performance pony, and also competes in trotting races.

ANCESTRY

An ancient breed descended from the Tarpan containing small amounts of Oriental blood.

Tarpan
Indigenous ▼
Swedish pony
Oriental ▼
Gotland

The Gotland, or Skogruss, pony is one of the most ancient breeds in the world. Along with the Bosnian, the Konik, and the Huçul, it is a direct descendant of the original wild Tarpan, sharing many of its characteristics.

The Gotland pony has run wild on the Swedish island of that same name since prehistoric times, and there is still a herd running wild there today, although many are now selectively bred on the mainland.

The ponies bred on the mainland are not exactly pure, since they have had moderate infusions of Oriental blood. In the past, the pony was used on farms and for transportation, but numbers fell in the 20th century due to mechanization. At that same time the ponies became a popular export, to the extent that their numbers in Sweden fell sharply. This resulted in the Swedish government forming the Swedish Pony Association in the 1950s to promote and encourage breeding.

The pony is sometimes called the Skogruss because that means, aptly, "little horse of the woods."

Character and care

The Gotland is an attractive pony, possessing much native craftiness, and some have a strong independent, stubborn streak. Most, however, are tractable and willing. They are surprisingly good jumpers.

The Gotland today

The Gotland is popular in trotting races and as a general riding pony for children. It also goes well harnessed to a light vehicle.

GENERAL CHARACTERISTICS

CONFORMATION The tail, mane, and forelock are long and full. The **legs** are sometimes rather fine for the pony's build, but well muscled with good joints and strong tendons. The **feet** are tough, small, and well shaped.

HEAD Small with broad, pricked **ears**; a wide **forehead**; large, generous **eyes**; and a straight **profile**.

COLOR The most common colors are black and bay. Many have the eel stripe down the spine.

HEIGHT 12hh to 13.1hh.

NORTHLANDS

The Northlands pony is little known outside Norway, its homeland. It belongs to the North European type of prehistoric Celtic Pony and closely resembles the Scottish Shetland Pony.

Until the 1920s, this pony was used and bred by Norwegian farmers. No particular selection policies were followed, but the pony remained true to its type.

By the 1940s, however, numbers had fallen to a mere 43, but a particularly fine stallion, Rimfakse, brought the breed back from almost certain extinction. Some credit must also go to the worldwide increase in riding as a leisure activity, because the Northlands had all the good qualities of a children's riding pony, and interest in the breed from other countries meant that it was bred for export.

Character and care

The Northlands is a quiet-natured pony, but energetic and not at all lazy. It is strong and tough, requiring only minimal care to keep it in good health and condition. Like all such ponies, it seems able to live well on frugal keep and to be fairly impervious to bad weather.

The Northlands today

The Northlands is mainly used as a children's riding pony, but in its homeland it is still used for farm work.

GENERAL CHARACTERISTICS

CONFORMATION A typical Celtic/North European type of pony. The **legs** are strong and not too fine, well muscled with well-formed joints, and small, tough **feet**.

HEAD Well-proportioned but sometimes a little big, with short, pricked **ears**, large expressive **eyes**, a straight **profile**, and rather small **nostrils**.

COLOR Chestnut, gray, bay, and brown. No significant white.

HEIGHT Around 13.2hh to 14.2hh.

ANCESTRY

The indigenous pony of Norway, the Northlands belongs to the Celtic Pony group with some Tarpan blood.

Celtic Pony
Tarpan ▼
Northlands

A typical North European pony, the Northlands is somewhat overshadowed by the famous Fjord. This kind-natured, willing, and active pony is popular as a children's mount and as a farm worker on ground too difficult for machinery.

DOLE-GUDBRANDSDAL

The Døle-Gudbrandsdal is very similar to the British Dales Pony, and it is likely that they stem from the same prehistoric ancestor. The Døle-Gudbrandsdal comes in varying but recognizable types within the breed, partly as a result of its being a dual breed (the Døle and Gudbrandsdal were originally separate breeds which have now become amalgamated), but also because other types of blood have been introduced into it, from heavy draft blood to trotting, Thoroughbred, and Arab blood, making it a versatile breed which can do many jobs.

Its offshoot, the Døle Trotter, is the result of extensive crossing with Thoroughbreds, and its races are very popular in Norway.

Døle-Gudbrandsdal numbers were depleted by the end of World War II, but in the 1960s state studs were established throughout Norway, and the Døle-Gudbrandsdal was one of the breeds they fostered, resulting in an increase in both its numbers and popularity.

Character and care
A patient, kind temperament is combined with energy, stamina, and strength. It requires minimal care, doing well on meager feed.

The Døle-Gudbrandsdal today
The Døle-Gudbrandsdal is still used in harness by Norwegian farmers for general farm work and in forestry, while its trotter strain is raced very regularly with great popularity.

GENERAL CHARACTERISTICS

CONFORMATION Very much like the British Dales Pony, sharing all of its characteristics.

HEAD Variable. Can be heavy and Roman-nosed, or lighter with a straight **profile**. The **ears** are short and mobile, the **eyes** gentle and inquiring, and the **nostrils** open.

COLOR Mainly black and brown with some bay. Palomino and gray occur rarely.

HEIGHT From 14.2hh to 15.1hh.

ANCESTRY

Belonging to the Celtic Pony group, there is almost certainly Friesian blood present, with other additions to create different types within the dual breed.

Celtic Pony
Friesian ▼
Heavy Draft ▼
Norfolk Trotter ▼
Døle ▼
Gudbrandsdal ▼
Arab ▼
Thoroughbred ▼
Døle-Gudbrandsdal

A combination of two breeds, the Døle and the Gudbrandsdal, this breed has also had infusions of other breeds which has created varying types within it. An offshoot of the breed, the result of extensive Thoroughbred crosses, is the Døle Trotter, shown here.

FJORD

If ever a breed of pony was instantly recognizable, it must be the Norwegian Fjord pony. Its color, markings, and the still-followed ancient method of trimming the mane are unique in the equine world.

The Fjord has been known in Norway for thousands of years. The Vikings made full use of it for battle, as shown by the many carvings on Viking runestones, and they used the blood-thirsty practice of horse-fighting to select the best stallions for use and breeding.

Other northern European breeds of pony have Fjord blood in them, notably Britain's Highland Pony and the Icelandic Pony. They have also been exported to many European countries, particularly those with no good native ponies of their own. The Fjord, or Vestland, as it is sometimes known, is very common throughout Scandinavia and appears in several similar varieties.

Character and care

The Fjord is an ancient type of pony resembling Przewalski's Horse, which may well have been its ancestor. Its coloring and markings are primitive, and it is a true representative of the Celtic Pony group.

It has a kind and willing nature, but some are said to be stubborn. It is very strong and tough, and has great stamina.

The Fjord today

The Fjord is a sure-footed and fearless mountain pony. It is still used for plowing on rough terrain, but is more popular as a trekking pony. It also takes part in Fjord trotting races, long-distance events, and competitive driving.

GENERAL CHARACTERISTICS

CONFORMATION A full-length **eel stripe** runs down the Fjord from the poll right down to the tip of the dock. There is a middle, black layer to the **mane**, starting as a central black lock in the forelock, from where it runs down the mane, down the back, and continues again as a black stripe down the center of the tail hair. The upright mane is cut in the ancient way so that the outer, silver layers are slightly shorter than the middle black layer, making the neck appear more crested than it actually is.

HEAD The head is wide, the **ears** short and pointed and wide apart above a broad **forehead**. Large, expressive and gentle **eyes**. The **nostrils** are open, but the **muzzle** sometimes has a stubby appearance.

COLOR Very distinctive. Nearly always yellow- or cream-dun with a mane in three layers (see above). Zebra marks often appear on the limbs. May have white on the head.

HEIGHT 13hh to 14.2hh.

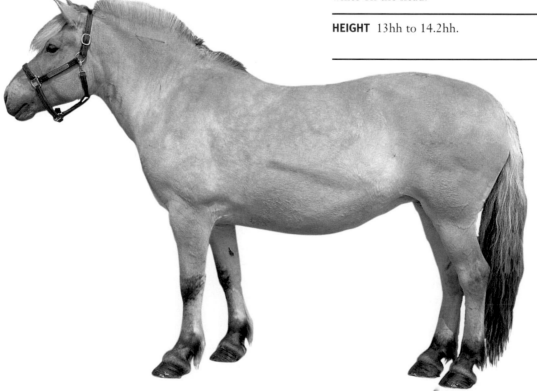

A highly distinctive breed, the Fjord from Norway is of ancient lineage and probably existed in its present form at least 2,000 years B.C. Its primitive markings, with an eel stripe from the poll to the tip of the tail and sometimes zebra marks on the legs, are remarkable.

DANISH WARMBLOOD

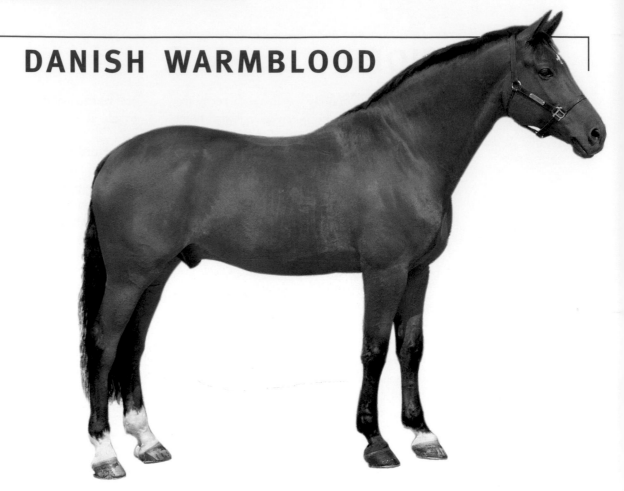

One of the few European warmblood breeds with no Hanoverian blood, the Danish Warmblood nevertheless contains many warmblood and Oriental genes. These have created a hugely successful competition and performance horse in the modern continental European mold.

ANCESTRY

Over the centuries German and Danish mares were mated with Iberian, Neapolitan, Dutch, and Turk horses. The Dutch Warmblood was created by breeding the resulting mares with Thoroughbred, Trakehner, Anglo-Norman, Wielkopolski, and Malapolski stallions.

German and Danish
native mares
Iberian ▼
Neapolitan ▼
Dutch ▼
Turk ▼
Thoroughbred ▼
Trakehner ▼
Anglo-Norman ▼
Wielkopolski ▼
Malapolski ▼
Danish Warmblood

The Danish Warmblood, along with the Swedish, the Hanoverian, and the Dutch, is one of the world's premier warmbloods. Holstein, now again in Germany, was Danish land until seized by Prussia in 1864, and this gave Denmark access to German breeds. Monasteries often seem to have taken particular interest in breeding horses, and the Cistercian monks in what is now Holstein bred horses from the early 14th century, putting mares of large German breeds (such as the old Holstein) to high-quality old Iberian stallions.

The great Royal Fredericksborg Stud was founded near Copenhagen in 1562, mainly on the Neapolitan and Andalusian breeds, but Denmark's native small coldblood horse and also her larger Jutland carthorse were also mated there with Iberian, Dutch, Turk, and later, Thoroughbred stallions. To create a suitable, indeed superlative, competition horse from their largely Fredericksborg-Thoroughbred mares in the mid-20th century, the Danes chose mainly Anglo-Norman, Thoroughbred, Trakehner, Wielkopolski, and Malapolski stallions for breeding. Unusually in warmblood breeding, the Hanoverian was not used.

Character and care

Danish Warmblood horses are hugely successful at the highest level of equestrian competition, in dressage and show jumping in particular. Their temperament is almost always equable and willing, yet they possess spirit, courage, and individuality. Their action is particularly supple, elastic, and flowing.

The Danish Warmblood today

Bred specifically for competition, those which do not make the grade make excellent general riding horses.

GENERAL CHARACTERISTICS

CONFORMATION Extremely hard to fault. The **legs** especially are virtually perfect, the correct length for the horse, well-muscled in their upper parts, substantial yet refined, with big, clean joints and excellent, well-made **feet**.

HEAD The head shows intelligence and courage. The **ears** are longish and fine, the **eyes** generous and expressive.

COLOR All solid colors, bay being most common. Some white is permitted on head and legs.

HEIGHT Consistently between 16.1hh and 16.2hh.

FREDERIKSBORG

The old type of Frederiksborg was a Haute Ecole *horse* par excellence. *The modern version, shown here, is primarily a superb carriage horse, but increasing infusions of Thoroughbred blood will probably, in time, make it into a competition warmblood.*

ANCESTRY

The Royal Frederiksborg Stud was begun with Neapolitan and Iberian stallions used on native Danish, Jutland, and Holstein mares. Old Iberian, Dutch, Turk, and early Thoroughbred stallions were also used, and this blood made up the original Frederiksborg. Today's Frederiksborg was revived with Oldenburg, Friesian, Thoroughbred, and Arab blood. Thoroughbred blood is continuing to be infused.

Andalusian
Neapolitan ▼
Danish/Jutland ▼
Holstein ▼
Iberian ▼
Dutch ▼
Turk ▼
Early ▼
Thoroughbred
Oldenburg ▼
Friesian ▼
Arab ▼
Modern ▼
Thoroughbred
Modern
Frederiksborg

Today, when we talk about *Haute Ecole* horses, we mention Lipizzaners, Lusitanos, and Andalusians. In fact, when *Haute Ecole* was at the height of its popularity in the 19th century, the Frederiksborg was one of the most popular horses used in its disciplines.

The Royal Frederiksborg Stud, near Copenhagen, had been founded in 1562 by King Frederik II. The purpose was to breed horses with the strength and spirit for *Haute Ecole*, the speed and stamina needed as an officer's charger, and to serve as carriage horses for state occasions.

The main breed bred there was the Frederiksborg which, for several hundred years, was regarded as the perfect example of a *Haute Ecole* horse. Sadly the Danes could not resist the demand from other countries, and unwisely sold too many of their prime breeding stock. The stock significantly depleted; the Fredericksborg Stud took to breeding Thoroughbreds, but in 1862 was closed.

A few of the old-type Frederiksborgs remained in Denmark, nurtured by private breeders, but it was not until about 75 years later that Frederiksborgs began to reappear and be registered once again in the stud book. The breed had to be bred up again, with Oldenburg, Friesian, Thoroughbred, and Arab blood.

Recently, more Thoroughbred blood has been used in the Frederiksborg to bring it into line with modern riding and competition needs.

Character and care

The Frederiksborg is rather plain, but is strong and agile with an equable temperament.

The Frederiksborg today

A good riding horse, the Frederiksborg is also a quality carriage horse. It is still used by Danish farmers for medium draft work.

GENERAL CHARACTERISTICS

CONFORMATION The **neck** is substantial and fairly short, set and carried high on a deep, broad **chest**. The **legs** are rather long but well set and strongly made, and the **action** is straight and fairly high, with a particularly good trot.

HEAD The head is honest and intelligent. The **ears** are readily pricked and the **eyes** friendly.

COLOR Almost always chestnut.

HEIGHT From 15.1hh to 16.1hh.

KNABSTRUP

Formerly a victim of breeding almost entirely for eye-catching color and markings, the Knabstrup is now bred more judiciously and makes a good middle-weight riding horse. Due to its coloring, it is still in demand for circus work.

ANCESTRY

The old breed was based on Frederiksborg and Iberian blood. Today, Thoroughbred blood is being used to upgrade the breed.

Frederiksborg
Iberian ▼
Thoroughbred ▼
Modern Knabstrup

The Knabstrup of Denmark is over 200 years old, but having gone from great popularity to near obscurity, it is now swinging back into favor. A particular characteristic of the Knabstrup is its spotted coat. The horse's early ancestors were forest-dwellers, and spotted horses appear in prehistoric cave paintings.

In the 16th and 17th centuries, spotted horses were fashionable in European courts. One spotted Iberian mare was sold by her Spanish owner to a Danish butcher called Flaebe. Of great stamina and speed, she was sold to Major Villars Lunn, a noted breeder of riding horses, and, at his Knabstrup estate, was mated with a palomino Frederiksborg stallion. In 1813 Flaebehoppen foaled a multicolored spotted colt with a metallic sheen to his coat. Named Flaebehingsten, he founded the Knabstrup breed.

As often happens when a horse is bred for color, the Knabstrup had by the 19th century deteriorated, becoming coarse, disproportionate, and with differing types developing within the one breed. The breed eventually developed into a strong, plain harness type. Recently, the addition of Thoroughbred blood has resulted in a much improved animal.

Character and care

A quality riding horse, the Knabstrup is intelligent, perceptive, tractable, and easy to handle.

The Knabstrup today

The Knabstrup is used for general riding and showing in breed classes. Because of its spotted coat, it is in demand for circus work.

GENERAL CHARACTERISTICS

CONFORMATION There is nothing Oriental or refined in the Knabstrup, but today's horse remains solid and dependable; a comfortable ride.

HEAD The head is set onto the neck with a noticeable arch to the clean **throat**. The **ears** are pricked, the **eyes** friendly and intelligent, the **profile** straight, and the squarish **muzzle** sensitive with open **nostrils**.

COLOR A wide variety of different spots and splashes on a white or roan background. Some, however, still show the all-over spotting of the old Knabstrup. The mane and tail are sparse.

HEIGHT Between 15.2hh and 15.3hh.

ICELANDIC

Iceland is one country which never seems to have acquired an indigenous pony. The well-known Icelandic Horse is the result of the interbreeding of many different strains and types descended from northern Europe's Celtic Pony, which was brought to the island in the 9th century with the Norse settlers from the Scandinavian countries. It also is possible that various Celts also migrated there. The ponies interbred quite freely, forming an extremely hardy native animal, eventually recognizable as a specific breed. The Icelandic Horse has been used for farm work and racing, and also transportation, essential when the roads are completely impassable to vehicles in winter.

The introduction of Oriental blood to improve the breed was a failure; hot Oriental blood was an unsuitable cross for animals living in a harsh climate. These days the ponies usually live in a half wild state and survive winter with no supplementary feeding, scraping away at the snow and frost and foraging on what they can. Cattle are unable to survive the Icelandic winters, so the ponies have always been kept for meat as well as for work.

In the early part of this century, Icelandic Horses provided a useful export trade when they were sold to the British as mine ponies and small pack ponies.

Character and care

The Icelandic Horse is unsurprisingly tough and hardy, requiring almost no special care.

It is very strong and sound, quiet to handle, inquisitive, friendly, yet independent.

The Icelandic today

Today, the ponies find a fairly ready market outside their homeland for they excel as children's ponies and are popular as trekking mounts. They are also outstanding as endurance rides. They are still used by farmers in Iceland for a variety of farming tasks.

GENERAL CHARACTERISTICS

CONFORMATION The Icelandic Horse is stocky and strongly built. The **neck** is short and thick, and the **legs** are short and sturdy, with short cannons and extremely tough **feet**.

HEAD Undeniably big and plain. **Ears** are short and pricked, **eyes** friendly and expressive. The pony has a shock of hair for the **forelock** and **mane**, and the **tail** is equally long and full, for cold-weather protection.

COLOR Almost any color can be found, and there are many variations and combinations.

HEIGHT From 12hh to 13.2hh.

OTHER FEATURES The Icelandic Horse is a five-gaited horse. Its most distinctive gait is the tølt, a running walk as fast as the canter.

In centuries past, the main method of selecting Icelandic stallions for breeding was to set them against each other in fights. Today, modern methods are used, with emphasis on selecting for quality of gaits, one of which is the tølt, a very fast, comfortable running walk. Tough and hardy, and possessing a remarkable homing instinct, the breed excels at trekking and endurance rides, and is still used for farming.

THE AMERICAS

QUARTER HORSE

The Quarter Horse is noted for a sharp, intelligent, yet calm outlook on life. Small-muzzled, the head is short and broad, and carried on a muscular, fairly straight neck.

The American Quarter Horse is said to be able to "fly for as long as he can hold his breath" and "turn on a dime and toss you back nine cents change." These two sayings sum up perfectly the outstanding qualities which have made the Quarter Horse, according to its proponents, one of the most popular horses in the world – lightning sprinting speed and incredible agility. Its fans claim it is the fastest horse in the world – over a quarter of a mile (400m). Enthusiasts of the breed also maintain that it can do more jobs better than any other horse in existence. Remarks like these give the animal a lot to live up to, but the Quarter Horse seems to manage that with no problem.

Traditionally, the Quarter Horse was developed in the 17th century, when British and European settlers brought over their horses and ponies, but found that the Iberian and Oriental horses brought in the 15th and 16th centuries by the *conquistadores* were already very much established in the colonies, both in wild and domesticated form.

North America is a land of varied climate and geography, ideal for the development of just about every breed of horse and pony imaginable. Settlers landing in the Carolinas and Virginia were faced with the task of clearing land from the virgin forests and wilderness for their homesteads, but there was more to life than just hard work. They also wished to be entertained and had brought over with them an enthusiasm for horse-racing.

Initially, the settlers raced their horses and ponies down village streets and cleared paths for racing which tended to be about quarter of a mile long. At first, due to the amount of work

which had to be carried out on the land, their horses had to be able to perform a variety of tasks, but over time a type was developed from mating imports with the already present stock, which specialized in lightning standing starts. Horses successful at this skill came to be known as "quarter pathers," and were bred specifically for village races.

In time, the quarter pathers came to be raced on specially created racecourses, yet they also came to be recognized for their "cow sense," seeming to know instinctively how to work cattle. These attributes of speed, fast standing starts, general agility, and an instinct for working with cattle are all traits of the Iberian horse, used as it was back in Europe for working cattle and for participating in bullfights, so it is not surprising that Iberian blood was handed out in generous degree to the new-forming American breed, the Quarter Horse. These important qualities of speed and general agility were selectively bred by the settlers and their descendants, and over time there developed a horse which has become a specialist in these skills.

A major step forward in the development of the Quarter Horse was the importation from England in the mid-18th century of a small Thoroughbred stallion called Janus, a grandson of the Godolphin Barb. His strength was racing at speed over distances of around four miles (6.5km), yet he sired many short-distance sprinters and Thoroughbreds as well as quarter pathers. Janus was at stud in North Carolina and Virginia for only four years, but he must have been extremely virile. He has had a lasting influence over the breed, with most of today's foundation sire lines tracing back to him. He also sired many famous Thoroughbred stallions and mares, including winners of the Kentucky Derby.

Character and care

Quarter Horses are noted for extremely fast standing starts, great speed over short distances, agility, and cow sense. In addition, they are known for their docile and willing temperament while being, at the same time, lively, energetic, and happy to try anything.

They are usually kept in very varying conditions, from being fully stabled at luxury racing establishments, to running out on the range in the western parts of the United States. In practice, being halfbred or warmblooded, they are not difficult to care for and are physically tough.

The Quarter Horse today

Quarter Horse racing is very big business in the U.S. and other countries, including Australia. The breed certainly excels at this sport. In the U.S., it is also used as a cow pony and a rodeo horse. As a trail horse for novice or expert alike, it is hard to beat a Quarter Horse, and it also makes an excellent all-round family horse, both under saddle, Western or English, or in harness, although not many appear to work between the shafts. Its attributes also suit it for polo, which it seems to really enjoy, and for show jumping. It is found mainly in the United States, as well as Canada, Australia, and some European countries.

Although primarily developed as a short-distance racehorse, the Quarter Horse is as well known for its skills in Western riding disciplines. It is particularly noted for its inherent "cow sense."

QUARTER HORSE

The most obvious trait of the Quarter Horse is its exceptionally muscular and big-boned build, which is particularly noticeable in the shoulders and the hindquarters and thighs. The modern type is not quite as chunky as the old type, which seems to be going out of fashion. The Quarter Horse is expected to gallop fast and perform sharp, rapid twists and turns in the course of its work. Its muscular, chunky build facilitates a free, straight stride and exceptionally nimble action. The symbol **C** *indicates a conformation feature.*

COLOR

The Quarter Horse comes in all solid colors. There are variations of dun and roan-based colors (as here), with distinctive names, in the breed.

HEIGHT

Larger than in the past, at between 15hh and 16hh.

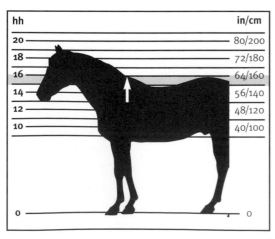

hh	in/cm
20	80/200
18	72/180
16	64/160
14	56/140
12	48/120
10	40/100
0	0

LEGS AND FEET

In the past, some show horses were bred with too-small feet, but this tendency is now being rectified, and the Quarter Horse has hard, tough legs and feet. Some white is permitted on the lower legs. **C**

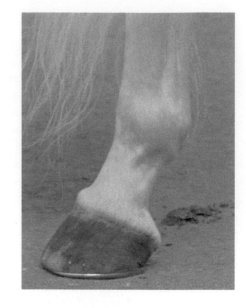

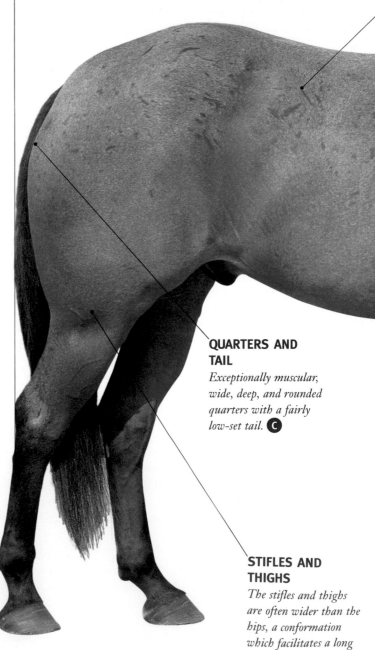

QUARTERS AND TAIL

Exceptionally muscular, wide, deep, and rounded quarters with a fairly low-set tail. **C**

STIFLES AND THIGHS

The stifles and thighs are often wider than the hips, a conformation which facilitates a long stride and great thrust from behind. **C**

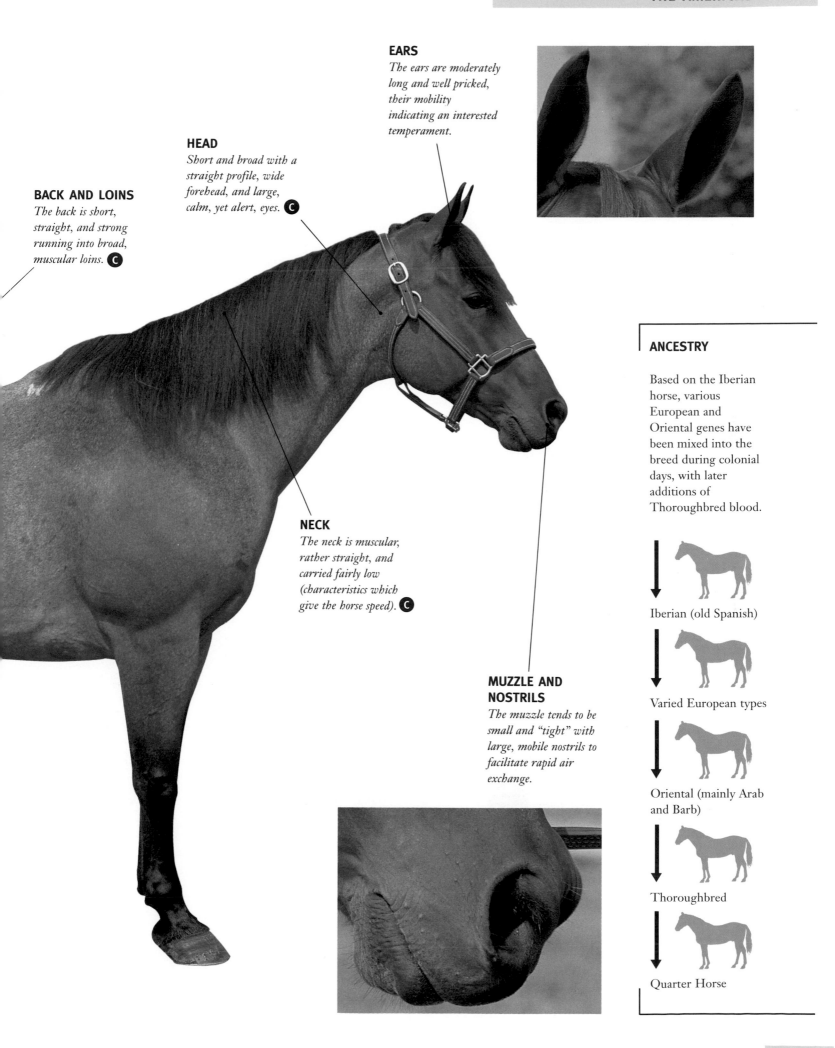

EARS
The ears are moderately long and well pricked, their mobility indicating an interested temperament.

HEAD
Short and broad with a straight profile, wide forehead, and large, calm, yet alert, eyes. **C**

BACK AND LOINS
The back is short, straight, and strong running into broad, muscular loins. **C**

NECK
The neck is muscular, rather straight, and carried fairly low (characteristics which give the horse speed). **C**

MUZZLE AND NOSTRILS
The muzzle tends to be small and "tight" with large, mobile nostrils to facilitate rapid air exchange.

ANCESTRY

Based on the Iberian horse, various European and Oriental genes have been mixed into the breed during colonial days, with later additions of Thoroughbred blood.

Iberian (old Spanish)

Varied European types

Oriental (mainly Arab and Barb)

Thoroughbred

Quarter Horse

SADDLEBRED

The Saddlebred is one of the most glamorous, lovable and, indeed, loving horses in the world. Apart from its supremely stylish appearance and spirited nature, it has one of the kindest temperaments of any horse.

It was developed as an obedient, enduring working horse in the southern states (initially and principally Kentucky, where its forerunner was called the Kentucky Saddler). Here, plantation owners often needed to be in the saddle from dawn to dusk, supervising their vast plantations.

The horse had to be extremely comfortable for the long hours under saddle and also fast, but the gallop was not a practical gait for its job, so two other gaits were developed in addition to walk, trot, and canter. This was not difficult due to the breed's pacing and ambling ancestors from Spain and England. The horses are said to be "three-gaited" and "five-gaited": the three-gaited horses show the walk, trot, and canter, and the five-gaited horses show the "slow gait" and the "rack."

Character and care

The Saddlebred is fiery, spirited, and proud, yet so gentle that it can be handled and ridden by children.

ANCESTRY

Distant ancestors include trotting and pacing breeds brought from England and Europe by settlers. The Narragansett Pacer (developed on Rhode Island in the 17th century), the Canadian Pacer, the Morgan, and the Thoroughbred were also used. Blended together, these breeds and types produced a truly distinctive, quality riding horse.

English/European trotters and pacers
Narragansett Pacer ▼
Canadian Pacer ▼
Morgan ▼
Thoroughbred ▼
Saddlebred

The Saddlebred appearance is very distinctive, with its long legs, high head, and its artificially nicked and set tail. The breed is produced mainly for the show ring, both in harness and under saddle. In the latter, it is shown in both three-gaited and five-gaited classes.

The Saddlebred today

The Saddlebred is almost exclusively bred and produced for specialized Saddlebred classes in the American show ring in both ridden and Fine Harness classes, although it would be able to compete with any other horse in any field. Some make excellent jumpers.

Its very high, exaggerated action is encouraged by maintaining the feet very long (sometimes they are artificially built up), by fitting heavy shoes, and by training. Also, the muscles under the dock are nicked (an illegal practice in most countries on humane grounds). This nicking produces the unnaturally stiff and high tail carriage still seen in most (but nowadays not all) Saddlebreds and maintained by the horse wearing a tail-brace when stabled; these practices prevent the horse from lowering his tail and deprive the horse of its natural use. The American Saddle Seat, in which the rider sits well back behind the horse's center of balance with the feet well forward, is used for this breed. Until these practices are at least modified, if not abolished, the breed will not gain true recognition for its superb qualities in the wider horse world.

GENERAL CHARACTERISTICS

CONFORMATION A truly beautiful (and capable) horse with a temperament to match and quite extraordinary presence and expression. Its long and elegant **neck** is set and carried very high, the high **withers** running smoothly into the back atop long, sloping **shoulders** which are narrow at the tops and wider at the base, creating open elbows and a fluid, free action. The **barrel** and **back** are quite long, the former well sprung and the latter strong and level, with wide, powerful loins and flat quarters with a naturally high-set **tail**. The **legs** are fine, tough, and strong, well muscled, with long, sloping pasterns and hard **feet**.

HEAD Small and narrow, alert and intelligent, and carried very high. **Ears** pointed, fine, and close-set. **Eyes** proud without arrogance, and yet gentle. **Profile** is straight and **nostrils** big and open. **Throat** is clean and arched.

COLOR All solid colors, including palomino, occasionally roan. Some white may be seen on head and lower legs. Very fine, silky coat and mane/tail hair.

HEIGHT 15hh to 16.1hh.

OTHER FEATURES The breed's gaits distinguish it from others. The "slow gait" (also known as the running walk, stepping pace, and slow rack) is a very old gait seen in many east Asian breeds and old European and English breeds: the feet on one side move one after the other, followed by the feet on the other side, in a smooth, running walk. The "rack" is a much faster version of the same gait and looks spectacular with the horse's high action.

The aristocratic, proud, sometimes even arrogant, head of the Saddlebred may belie its kind, often affectionate temperament. The breed is noted for intelligence and alertness without being prone to "hotting up."

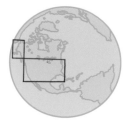

APPALOOSA

The Nez Percé tribe developed the forebears of the modern breed of Appaloosa, one of the most popular in America. An Appaloosa does not necessarily have to be spotted; but, if it is not, the skin must be mottled beneath the coat hair; the hooves must be striped, and there must be white sclera around the eyes.

The Appaloosa can truly be said to be the horse of the Americas because it was bred by the native American tribe, the Nez Percé from the northwest of the United States, from stock brought by the *conquistadores*.

The horse's ancestors were forest-dwelling animals that would have had mottling and possibly striping on their coats which camouflaged them in the dappled shade of trees, protecting them against predators. Their modern-day Appaloosa descendants have inherited the genes for patterned coats.

It is known that Cro-Magnon man was familiar with spotted horses and has left cave drawings of them. They were much prized in Asia and up until the late 19th century in Europe, when they seem to have gone out of fashion. Now, though, the Appaloosa is enjoying renewed favor, not only for parade or display work, for which its coat is ideally suited, but also as a working and competition horse.

A horse does not have to be spotted to be an Appaloosa. Those that are not must, however, have three other requirements: they must have the white sclera around the eyes, mottled skin beneath the coat hair, and striping on the hooves.

There are many variations of mottling and spotting in the breed, but for ease of classification there are six main coat patterns. The *leopard* pattern has chestnut, brown, or black spots all over the body on a white coat, the *snowflake* has white spots on a chestnut, brown, or black coat; the *blanket* pattern has a large white area over the horse's loins, croup, and thighs and is of two types – spotted with chestnut, brown, or black, or unmarked with no spots or mottles. The *frosted* pattern is a dark coat bearing a few white spots on the hips and loins, and the *marble* variation is a dark coat in the foal changing through speckling and splashing to almost white in the older horse, apart from the retention of dark markings on the head and legs.

The variations to the main patterns include roan coats (chestnut or gray mixed in with white hairs) and light (not white) spots.

Character and care

Appaloosas make ideal family ponies and horses because of their sweet temperaments

Appaloosas are of compact, well-muscled build, the Quarter Horse-type conformation being generally favored. Emphasis is laid on strong, correct legs and feet, because most of the breed work as stock or pleasure horses, or compete in various events, especially Western-style ones.

and physical hardiness. They are agile, fast, and have considerable stamina, yet at the same time are docile and enthusiastic, fun to work, and not difficult to care for.

The Appaloosa today

Appaloosas make good general riding horses, and harness horses although few seem to work in harness. In competition, the Appaloosa is judged firstly as a good riding horse.

Appaloosas are used in the United States in various Western riding classes and classes such as roping, cow pony, and barrel racing, as well as various style classes.

In Britain the breed is improving all the time, with more breeders breeding for quality and not merely color, so Appaloosas are being increasingly seen in Riding Horse, Colored Horse, and Family Horse classes as well as general ability classes such as cross-country events, show jumping, and dressage. In Australia, the breed is very popular, and there as in the U.S., the Appaloosa is used as a racehorse in addition to its other talents.

The breed has a generally calm, willing temperament. Appaloosas look good in either Western, native American, or English-style tack.

APPALOOSA

The Appaloosa was bred for color rather than temperament. However, as a breed, it is known for its generally calm, willing, good-natured temperament. Appaloosas look good in either Western, native American, or English-style tack. With most breeds, horses that show the whites of the eyes are traditionally noted for being bad-tempered. However, this is certainly not the case with the Appaloosa! The symbol **C** *indicates a conformation feature.*

COAT AND COLOR

Although there are six main coat patterns within the breed, the many variations of mottling, splashing, and spotting can sometimes make it hard to name a color or pattern exactly. This, though, is the blanket pattern with a large white area over the hindquarters.

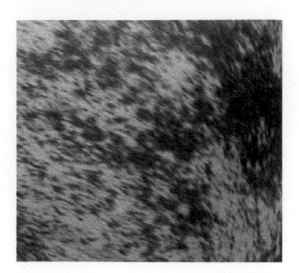

HINDQUARTERS AND LIMBS

Powerful hindquarters, and strong, well-set limbs. **C**

MANE AND TAIL HAIR

A feature of the breed is the rather sparse mane, forelock, and tail hair. This attractive individual has a fuller tail than many Appaloosas.

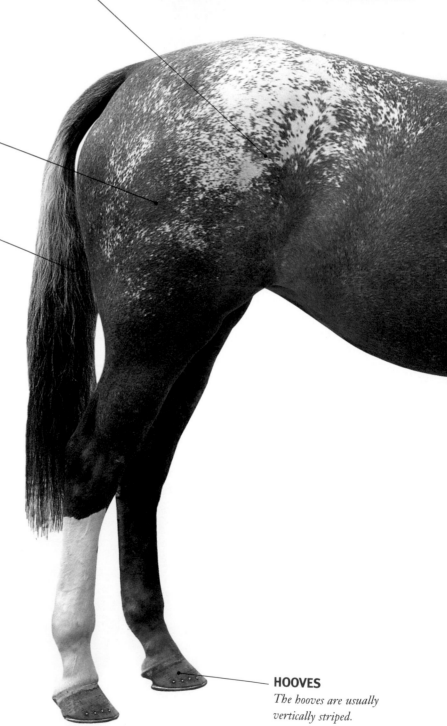

HEIGHT

Mainly 14.2hh and 15.2hh.

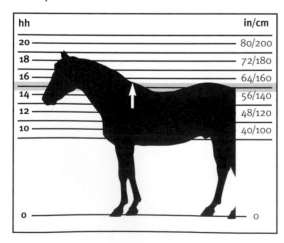

hh	in/cm
20	80/200
18	72/180
16	64/160
14	56/140
12	48/120
10	40/100
0	0

HOOVES

The hooves are usually vertically striped.

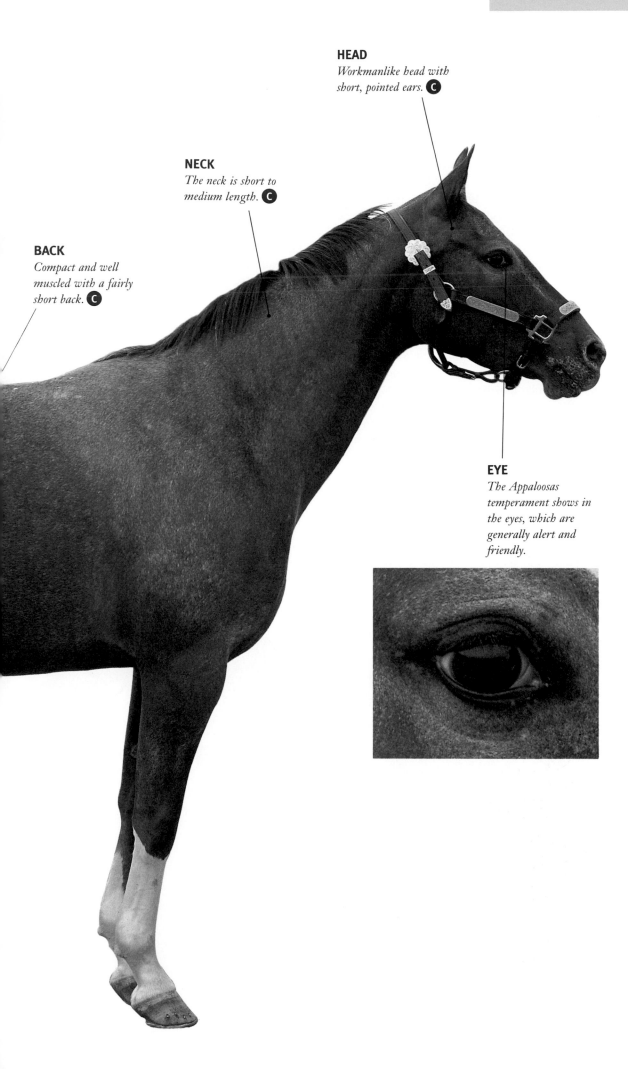

HEAD
Workmanlike head with short, pointed ears. **C**

NECK
The neck is short to medium length. **C**

BACK
Compact and well muscled with a fairly short back. **C**

EYE
The Appaloosas temperament shows in the eyes, which are generally alert and friendly.

ANCESTRY

Spotted and mottled horses were prized among ancient civilizations, and Appaloosas are not the only types with these colorings. Most types originated in Asia, spread to Europe, and were taken from there to the Americas by the *conquistadores*. Mainly of Oriental-type ancestry, they do however possess some colder-type blood, probably from European ancestors, as shown by their stockier build.

Arab

Barb

Turk

Old Spanish

Appaloosa

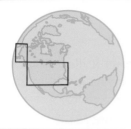

TENNESSEE WALKING HORSE

Like other Deep South breeds, the Tennessee, or Plantation, Walking Horse, was developed in the 17th century by plantation owners to carry them for long hours at a fast, easy gait around their extensive farms. The "Walker," as the breed is generally known today, is used as an all-round riding and harness horse, being more robust and less elegant than the American Saddlebred.

Like the Morgan, the Walker owes its existence to one prepotent stallion called Black Allan, who was by a Standardbred stallion. He was foaled in 1886 and, having been discarded as a harness horse because of his strange walk, he was taken to Tennessee while still a young horse, where he founded a distinctive and highly popular new breed based on his "defect."

Black Allan enjoyed a long and distinguished stud career. He was unfailingly prepotent, transmitting his type – and his walk – to his offspring.

Character and care

The Tennessee Walking Horse is often compared to the Saddlebred, but is a much less stylish horse. Its temperament is kind and tractable, and its distinctive gaits, particularly its running walk, are very much desired.

The Tennessee Walking Horse today

Although bred extensively for the show ring, the Tennessee Walking Horse is also used as a general riding and harness horse.

GENERAL CHARACTERISTICS

CONFORMATION The **neck** is long, arched, and muscular, carried high, and its broad base is set high on the **chest**, which is deep and broad. The horse's **gaits** are distinctive and naturally inherited, although brought out by training. The two walks (the flat-footed walk and the famous running walk) are described as "a basic, loose, four-cornered lick, a 1-2-3-4 beat with each of the horse's feet hitting the ground separately at regular intervals." Both gaits are supremely comfortable and are said to convert even the most sceptical rider.

HEAD Rather large and plain, with pricked **ears**, straight **profile**, gentle **eyes**, and big **nostrils**.

COLOR Many blacks, with chestnut, bay, brown, gray, and roan. Some white on head and lower legs is permitted.

HEIGHT Not less than 15.2hh.

ANCESTRY

A breed created by settlers and pioneers, the Tennessee Walking Horse is founded on Standardbred and Morgan blood with Narragansett Pacer, Saddlebred, Thoroughbred, and Canadian Pacer infusions.

Standardbred
Morgan ▼
Narragansett Pacer ▼
Saddlebred ▼
Canadian Pacer ▼
Thoroughbred ▼
Tennessee Walking Horse

Famous for its fast, running walk, this breed is extremely popular as a show and general pleasure and harness horse. Having an equable temperament and being easy to care for, the Tennessee Walking Horse is a rewarding yet not too demanding horse to own.

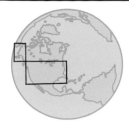

PONY OF THE AMERICAS

Just as the British produced their miniature Thoroughbred riding pony for young riders, so has America created her own breed of pony, the Pony of the Americas.

The Pony of the Americas is based on two quite diverse breeds, the Celtic Pony-type Scottish Shetland Pony from Britain and the Iberian-based American Appaloosa. In the 1950s, horse-breeder Leslie Boomhower of Iowa mated a Shetland stallion with an Appaloosa mare, and the result was Black Hand I, who was a replica of his dam. He proved to be so successful in the show ring and popular with youngsters that eventually he was used to found America's first pony breed.

The pony is required to have Appaloosa coloring and patterns with the conformation of a miniature Arab/Quarter Horse cross, and although foals may be provisionally registered provided one parent is already registered as a Pony of the Americas (POA), a pony must be three years old before it can be fully registered. The aim is to produce a miniature horse rather than an animal with pony character. Also, the trot is required to show a high action with a certain lift to the knee: the long and low gait of Thoroughbred- and Arab-type horses is not what is wanted.

Character and care

The Pony of the Americas is specifically bred to be a small horse rather than a true pony. It is quiet and docile and an excellent all-rounder. It is tough and hardy, undemanding to care for, and easy for children to handle.

The Pony of the Americas today

The Pony of the Americas is suitable as a general riding animal by children and can also be ridden by small adults. It is versatile enough to be used for a variety of jobs – trekking, jumping, endurance riding, show jumping, trotting races, and even for pony flat racing.

GENERAL CHARACTERISTICS

CONFORMATION In an effort to create a fixed and recognizable type, strict standards are now being applied to the Pony of the Americas. To create a miniature horse of Quarter Horse/Arab type is the breeders' ultimate aim.

HEAD An Arab-like head, wedge-shaped with small, pricked **ears**, broad **forehead**, large, generous **eyes**, and a small **muzzle** with flaring **nostrils**: some, however, can be a little heavier and coarser.

COLOR All Appaloosa variations.

HEIGHT 11.2hh to 13.2hh.

ANCESTRY

Founded on Shetland and Appaloosa blood, there is now a good deal of Quarter Horse and Arab in the breed, and these founding breeds will predominate, but any pony meeting the admittedly strict registration requirements should be eligible, regardless of background.

Shetland
Appaloosa ▼
Quarter Horse ▼
Arab ▼
Pony of the Americas

Developed to be a small horse rather than a true pony, the Pony of the Americas is increasingly popular as a riding animal for children, teenagers, and smaller adults. Its high action and Appaloosa color patterns make it quite distinctive.

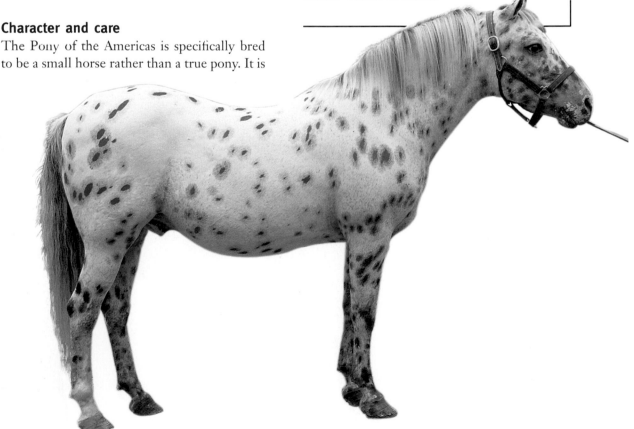

STANDARDBRED

The Standardbred is the fastest trotting and pacing harness racer in the world. It has been bred with the most painstaking care and precision for one purpose only, to trot or pace harnessed to an ultralight, two-wheeled racing sulky for one mile (1.6km) to a minimum standard time. This aim has produced a definite breed of horse with predictable abilities and qualities of physique and temperament.

The standard times set in 1879 required a horse to cover a mile in two minutes and 30 seconds. This speed was required for registration purposes, although today pedigree alone is usually the only necessary criterion. The standard times today require a two-year-old trotter or pacer to do the mile in two minutes and 20 seconds, or two minutes and 15 seconds for horses of three years or more. Horses go much faster these days, partly because of the continued selection for speed, but also because of the improved racetrack surfaces and harness and sulky design. Niatross, a Standardbred stallion, introduced a new era in the sport in 1980 when he completed a time trial in one minute and 49.5 seconds, and speeds are edging faster all the time.

The difference between trotting and pacing is that in trotting the horse moves in a diagonal gait, the hind foot on one side and the forefoot on the other landing simultaneously; when the horse is pacing the hind and forefeet on the same side hit the ground simultaneously. Pacers are slightly faster than trotters because the suspension phase of their gait (the period the horse is traveling through the air with no feet on the ground) is fractionally longer than in the trot gait, so they have that bit of extra time in the air without being stopped by the ground, that has a braking effect each time a foot hits it.

Most horses race in either the trot or the pace, but a few have been successful in both gaits. Although it is generally believed that whereas the trot is natural to a horse and the pace is not, many horses pace naturally from birth, and this is brought out and developed by training in a hobble harness, which is fastened around the upper legs to maintain the gait.

Trotting races originated in the 17th century when people used horses and light carriages to get them around on unpaved tracks which served as roads. Later, as roads improved and horses and vehicles were used more, people took a natural pride in their roadsters (road horses), and impromptu friendly races took place whenever one family tried to overtake another. Trotting races were, therefore, the logical development of people's natural competitiveness.

In the early 19th century, more attention was paid to breeding for speed, and on June 11,

The Standardbred is the world's best harness racer. The breed's development was phenomenal and precise – to produce animals that naturally pace or trot, pacers being marginally faster than trotters, with speeds today of less than 2 minutes for a mile (1.6km) being not uncommon.

1806, the *New York Commercial Advertiser* carried the following race account: "*Fast trotting* – Yesterday afternoon the Haerlem race course of *one mile's distance*, was trotted around in *two minutes and fifty-nine seconds* by a horse called *Yankey*, from New-Haven, a rate of speed, it is believed, never before-excelled in this country, and fully equal to any thing recorded in the English Sporting Calendars."

Yankey's record was the first time a horse had trotted a mile in less than three minutes, and harness racing continued to gain popularity, with contestants using a high-wheeled, heavy cart. To differentiate harness racing from mounted racing, the harness racing standards were set in 1879, and the name Standardbred was established, differentiating it from the more speedy Thoroughbred, which was favored for mounted racing. In 1892 pneumatic-tire bicycle sulkies made their debut, which resulted almost immediately in a near four-second reduction in trotting and pacing times.

The Standardbred can be traced back to the English Thoroughbred stallion, Messenger, who in 1788 was imported to Philadelphia. Interestingly enough, he traced back to two notable stallions: the first being Norfolk Roadster type, Blaze, who sired the famous Old Shales, founding father of the Norfolk Roadster and Hackney breeds, and the second being Sampson, an influential stallion in all trotting and pacing breeds who passed on his trotting and pacing abilities to all his progeny. Morgan blood has also been used in the development of the Standardbred.

Character and care

The Standardbred, although undoubtedly a "blood" horse, is tough with great stamina, and although it requires reasonable care, it does not require excess cosseting. It is docile and easy to handle, willing, enthusiastic, and energetic, with a natural competitive streak.

The Standardbred today

The Standardbred's main role today is participating in trotting and pacing races, which take part in its homeland, the United States, but also in Scandinavia, Canada, Australia, and New Zealand. Those horses not used for racing, or which are just not fast enough, make excellent riding horses and seem particularly suited to endurance riding and hunting because of their stamina. Although they make good event horses, they are not quite as fast as the Thoroughbred, which still dominate the top levels of the sport.

In the U.S., harness racing – both pacing and trotting – appears to be more popular than Thoroughbred racing. Such races are also popular in Canada, Scandinavia, Australia, and New Zealand. The Standardbred has been used to improve other trotting breeds throughout the world.

STANDARDBRED

The horse resembles a middleweight Thoroughbred type, being more robust and sturdy than the average Thoroughbred and with less fire. This lovely horse is very correct and clearly shows the Thoroughbred ancestry of the breed. A peculiarity of the breed is that it is almost always significantly croup-high, the croup being 1in (2.5cm) or sometimes 2in (5cm) higher than the withers; a conformation which, combined with powerful quarters, provides great thrust from behind. In riding horses this conformation is uncomfortable for riders, who feel as if they are going downhill. The trotting or pacing action must be free and perfectly straight, for economy of energy and to prevent self-inflicted knocks at speed around the tight turns of the racetracks. The symbol **C** *indicates a conformation feature.*

COAT AND COLOR

Most Standardbreds have a brown body color, as here, and also bay where the mane and tail are black. Blacks (as in the main photograph), chestnuts, and more rarely, grays and roans also occur.

LOINS AND QUARTERS

Strong, wide loins, long, deep, and very powerful quarters with a slight slope to the tail. **C**

JOINTS AND CANNONS

The joints are big and strong with well-defined tendons and short cannons. **C**

HEIGHT

About 14.1hh to 16.1hh, the average height being around 15.2hh.

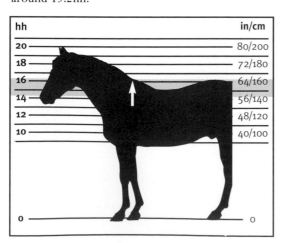

hh	in/cm
20	80/200
18	72/180
16	64/160
14	56/140
12	48/120
10	40/100
0	0

LEGS

The legs are shorter than the Thoroughbred's, and the upper parts, particularly the thighs, are very well developed. **C**

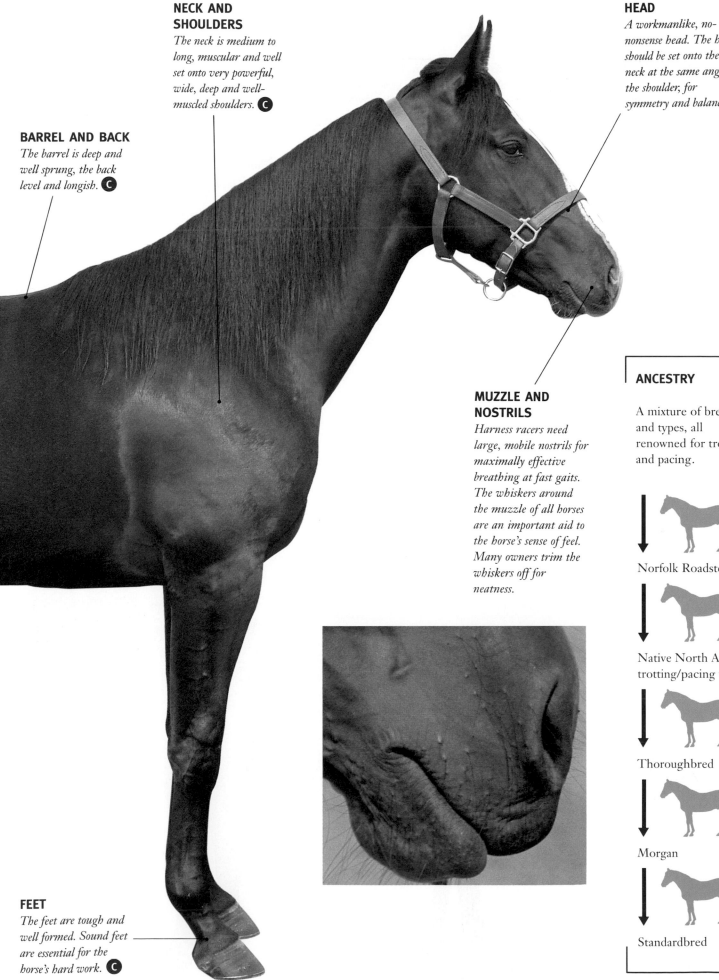

NECK AND SHOULDERS

The neck is medium to long, muscular and well set onto very powerful, wide, deep and well-muscled shoulders. **C**

HEAD

A workmanlike, no-nonsense head. The head should be set onto the neck at the same angle as the shoulder, for symmetry and balance. **C**

BARREL AND BACK

The barrel is deep and well sprung, the back level and longish. **C**

MUZZLE AND NOSTRILS

Harness racers need large, mobile nostrils for maximally effective breathing at fast gaits. The whiskers around the muzzle of all horses are an important aid to the horse's sense of feel. Many owners trim the whiskers off for neatness.

FEET

The feet are tough and well formed. Sound feet are essential for the horse's hard work. **C**

ANCESTRY

A mixture of breeds and types, all renowned for trotting and pacing.

Norfolk Roadster/Hackney

Native North American trotting/pacing varieties

Thoroughbred

Morgan

Standardbred

MISSOURI FOX TROTTER

This breed was developed in the early 19th century in the Missouri and Arkansas regions by settlers who wanted a comfortable, equable-natured, enduring, and speedy horse to get them around all sorts of country. The initial matings consisted of Morgan, early Thoroughbred, Arab, and horses of old Iberian (including Barb) descent. Later infusions of Saddlebred and Tennessee Walking Horse blood gave it considerable elegance and enhanced its fox trot gait.

In the early days, Fox Trotters were raced; when racing was made illegal, the Fox Trotter became more of a utility, all-purpose horse. A stud book was not founded until 1948.

Compared with America's other two gaited horses, the Saddlebred and the Tennessee Walking Horse, the Fox Trotter has a lower, much less extravagant action, and the breed society prohibits the use of any artificial training aids to accentuate the gait; also, the tail is not nicked and set.

Character and care

The Missouri Fox Trotter has a very tractable temperament, great stamina, is sound and tough, versatile, and a willing worker.

The Missouri Fox Trotter today

Today, the breed is used mainly for leisure riding and showing, and also for endurance riding. Unlike its colleague gaited horses, it is usually shown in Western gear.

ANCESTRY

The initial gene base was Morgan, early Thoroughbred, Arab, and old Barb-based Iberian. Later, Saddlebred and Tennessee Walking Horse blood was also used to advantage.

Morgan
Early ▼
Thoroughbred
Arab ▼
Iberian ▼
Saddlebred ▼
Tennessee Walking ▼
Horse
Missouri Fox Trotter

GENERAL CHARACTERISTICS

CONFORMATION A substantial, quite stylish horse. The **neck** is of medium length and well formed, carried fairly low. The **withers** are moderately prominent, the **back** short and level, the **tail** fairly low set. The **legs** are quite fine, the joints are large and well formed, and the **feet** are good and strong.

HEAD Well proportioned and intelligent, rather plain, with a straight **profile**, longish, pricked **ears**, generous, calm **eyes**, and a neat, squarish **muzzle** with open **nostrils**.

COLOR Chestnut in many variations; also brown, bay, black, gray, paint, or pinto (piebald or skewbald), and some red roans. White on head and legs.

HEIGHT 14hh to 16hh.

OTHER FEATURES The fox-trotting **gait** is the breed's distinguishing feature.

This is one of several American breeds with distinctive gaits: its unique gait is the fox trot, in which the front feet walk actively and the hind ones trot. The equable nature of the Missouri Fox Trotter, its hardiness and willingness to work, make it very popular in its homeland, but it is little known elsewhere.

AMERICAN SHETLAND

The first serious importations of Shetland Ponies into America took place in 1885 when Eli Elliot imported 75 of them. The hot, humid climate in the south-eastern states where breeding was concentrated was very different from the bitterly cold sub-arctic conditions of the ponies' homeland, conditions which forged its physical characteristics of small, rotund shape and short legs. It seems, though, that the early imports adapted well, and there are now believed to be around 50,000 American Shetlands in the USA.

The American Shetland Pony Club was founded in 1888.

The American Shetland bears little resemblance to the true Shetland Pony; it has been created to meet local requirements. True Shetlands were crossed with small Hackney Ponies and small Arabian and Thoroughbred blood was also used. The American Shetland retains the thick Shetland mane and tail hair, but has definite horse rather than pony character, and is longer in the body and leg.

Character and care

Tractable enough for children to handle, it is intelligent, and easy to care for.

The American Shetland today

The American Shetland is primarily shown in various harness classes: four-wheeled buggy harness classes, two-wheeled Roadster or driving classes, and harness light sulky racing classes. It is also ridden in general children's show classes, hunter-pony classes, breed classes, and in Western or English tack.

GENERAL CHARACTERISTICS

CONFORMATION A rugged type of Hackney Pony in appearance, it is both workmanlike and showy. The **neck** can sometimes be rather short. The well-set **tail** has luxurious, strong hair. The **legs** tend towards the long side but are correct and strong. The **feet** are often grown unnaturally long to encourage a high, flashy action but, when natural, are strong and well proportioned.

HEAD A definite horse-character to the sometimes plain and long head. The **profile** is straight, the **ears** fairly long and the expression of the **eyes** is horse-like rather than pony-like.

COLOR All solid colors; also roan, cream, and dun.

HEIGHT Up to 11.2hh.

ANCESTRY

Pure Shetland Ponies were crossed with Hackney Ponies and with small Arabs and Thoroughbreds to create this modern breed.

Shetland
Hackney Pony ▼
Arab ▼
Thoroughbred ▼
American Shetland

The American Shetland has been purposely bred to be longer in the body and the leg than the true (Scottish) Shetland with some hot-blood type about it. It has horse rather than pony character, and more scope than the Shetland, but is not as hardy.

MORGAN

Morgan horses are favorite all-round and family horses. They have great personality, but are tractable and willing. All of them, to this day, are very much alike, taking after their founding stallion, Justin Morgan.

The Morgan is probably the most versatile of all American breeds, yet it is not well known outside its home country. The Morgan really does deserve a much higher level of international recognition, for it is a marvelous all-round riding and light harness horse capable of high-level performance.

As with most American breeds, the origins of the Morgan go back to colonial times, but unlike in the creation of most breeds, the Morgan was founded by happy accident. A small bay colt called Figure, foaled in Vermont in 1793, was bought by a schoolteacher called Thomas Justin Morgan. Morgan, impressed by the colt's looks and personality, thought he would try him at stud to see if he was any good as a stallion – with extraordinary results. No matter what kind of mare he was put to, the progeny were invariably the image of Figure, whose fame spread like quicksilver and who was soon renamed Justin Morgan.

Thomas Justin Morgan died not long after buying the horse, and his equine namesake was sold to a truly hard taskmaster, a farmer who worked him mercilessly. Justin Morgan worked on the farm doing chores meant for heavy draft horses: he plowed the fields, worked on the road in harness and under saddle, he serviced mares, and also took part in racing and pulling contests, in which he apparently was never beaten.

Justin Morgan carried on being prepotent as a sire; every single foal was a replica of him, and mares were soon being sent to him from all over the country. He was quite short; only 14hh, but he was of compact build, well muscled with particularly powerful shoulders, elegant legs and feet with some feather around the fetlocks. He had a thick, crested neck and heavy mane, tail, and forelock. He was a bay with black points and a small white star on his forehead.

Justin Morgan was by a stallion called True Briton, which may have been a Welsh Cob. In addition to his Welsh sire, Justin Morgan probably also contained some Oriental blood which was passed on from his dam, about whom nothing is known, except that Justin Morgan was noted for his indomitable spirit, a quality synonymous with Eastern blood which would have been passed on through her.

The Morgan breed became established within the lifetime of its founding father who died in 1821, after some years at an army stud. It is fitting that, until mechanization, the Morgan Horse was the official mount of the U.S. Cavalry. It was also instrumental in founding several other American breeds.

Character and care

Spirit, tractability, and willingness are all hallmarks of the Morgan. They have speed, stamina, and are extremely versatile: it is hard to think of anything a Morgan could not do well. A warmblooded horse, the Morgan is hardy and quite frugal, so is reasonably easy to care for.

The Morgan today

The Morgan is an excellent all-rounder and makes an ideal family horse. It takes part and acquits itself well in any type of equestrian activity and is suitable for professional and amateur riders alike.

Two types of Morgan have now developed, although they do not seem to be able to be bred with certainty. The Park Morgan, shown here, has the neck set high on the shoulders, carries the neck high and has a high, showy action. The Pleasure Morgan is less exaggerated in these features. The difference is mainly seen when the horses are in action.

The head of the Morgan indicates quality with a straight or slightly concave profile, widely flaring nostrils when the horse is in action or excited, and expressive eyes and ears, creating an interested, friendly impression.

MORGAN

Sturdy refinement is a suitable phrase to describe the Morgan's appearance, for it is an elegant, strong horse without any hint of heaviness or coarseness. Two types of Morgan have now developed, although they do not seem to be able to be bred with certainty. The Park Morgan has the neck set high on the shoulders, carries the neck high, and has a high, showy action. The Pleasure Morgan is less exaggerated in these features. The difference is mainly seen when the horses are in action. The symbol **C** *indicates a conformation feature.*

HEIGHT
About 14hh to 15.2hh.

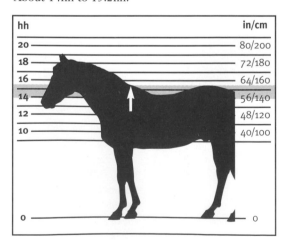

hh		in/cm
20		80/200
18		72/180
16		64/160
14		56/140
12		48/120
10		40/100
0		0

EARS, EYES, AND NOSTRILS
Wide-set, pointed ears, expressive eyes, and flaring nostrils. **C**

WITHERS
The withers are well defined and moderately long and must always be higher than the croup. **C**

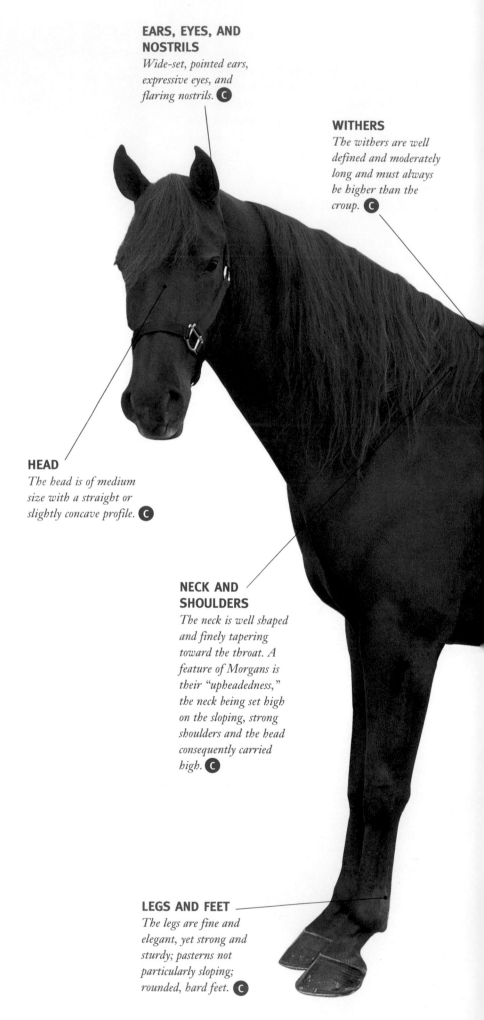

HEAD
The head is of medium size with a straight or slightly concave profile. **C**

NECK AND SHOULDERS
The neck is well shaped and finely tapering toward the throat. A feature of Morgans is their "upheadedness," the neck being set high on the sloping, strong shoulders and the head consequently carried high. **C**

LEGS AND FEET
The legs are fine and elegant, yet strong and sturdy; pasterns not particularly sloping; rounded, hard feet. **C**

ANCESTRY

This is in dispute, but it is likely to be Welsh Cob/ Thoroughbred/native American stock of Iberian/Oriental origin plus imported European breeds.

Welsh Cob/Thoroughbred

Native American of Iberian/Oriental strain

European indigenous breeds Morgan

COAT AND COLOR

The Morgan comes in bay, brown (often attractively dappled, as here), black, and chestnut, with moderate white markings permitted on head and lower legs.

BACK AND QUARTERS

The back is short, level, and strong and the quarters slightly rounded and well muscled with a gaily carried tail. **C**

MANE

The mane is kept long and luxuriant, with a "bridlepath" hogged or roached back several inches from the poll to show off the throat and poll area.

TAIL

Great care is taken of Morgans' tails. They are usually braided in the stable for protection and to encourage wavy fullness, and length, when free. This stretched-down stance, which has to be taught, is common to several American breeds, and now others. It was developed to keep horses still and stable while mounting.

CRIOLLO

The Criollo is extremely hard and tough. This one shows the primitive dun coloring which often occurs in this breed and stems most recently from its Iberian ancestors.

ANCESTRY

Descended from Spanish imports in the 16th century, the breed is based on old Iberian and Oriental strains which have blended together and undergone natural selection, resulting in a distinctive type of tough horse suited to a hostile environement.

Iberian
Barb ▼
Arab ▼
Criollo

When the Spanish explorers Cortés, Pizarro, and their successors brought their Iberian and Oriental horses to the Americas in the 16th century, they had no idea of what the long-term result of their actions would be. From the point of view of the horses, landing on that huge continent meant a completely new way of life for them. It was also the start of the development, by nature and man, of many new breeds and types of horse. Nature and man both create what suits them best out of the available material, and one of the most remarkable breeds in which both man and nature have had a hand is the Criollo of South America.

The breed's ancestors were the Iberian, Barb, and Arab horses which arrived with the *conquistadores*. It is generally believed that the indigenous people of Central America had never seen a horse before the arrival of the *conquistadores* and regarded them initially with terror, but later with a certain veneration.

These horses lived wild on the pampas for around 300 years, where their genes eventually blended together, forming the distinctive Criollo breed with its hardy constitution tailor-made to bear the great extremes of temperature and climate found in South America.

Natural selection meant that the weak and unsound representatives of the breed perished, while the survivors flourished and became even stronger. No doubt it was to the advantage of the horse that it acquired the characteristic coloring of khaki or dun, which was similar to that of its environment – the sandy wastes and burnt-up pastures of the inhospitable pampas.

The Criollo was soon adopted by the South American gaucho for use for ranching purposes, for which this tough little horse was ideally adept.

Character and care

The Criollo is extremely hardy, frugal, and tough, resistant to great discomfort, and a fast and hard worker. Breeding stock now undergo strict selection tests to ensure the continuance of the established breed qualities. One selection test involves marching the horse for 470 miles (750km) while carrying 238lb (108kg) on its back, with no reserves of food or water for the duration of the trek. At the end of it, the horses are then raced for 30 miles (48km).

Most Criollos live in a semi-wild state on the vast ranches of the southern continent, with those being immediately required for work being coraled and broken in. There are now several variations of the breed throughout South America, but they all have the same genetic base.

The Criollo today

The Criollo is used extensively as a cattle horse in South America's beef industry. They are used with great success in endurance riding and as a cross to produce the famous Argentinian polo pony.

GENERAL CHARACTERISTICS

CONFORMATION The horse looks stocky, tough, and primitive, as indeed it is.

HEAD Quite long with a straight or slightly convex **profile**. The **ears** are longish and close-set, and although the **forehead** is broad with alert **eyes**, the face appears long and narrow with a small, tight **muzzle**.

COLOR Mainly primitive dun or mouse-brown, often with a dark cross-stripe over the wither and an eel stripe down the spine. Zebra marks on the legs are not unusual. Brown, bay, black, gray, chestnut, palomino, and roan do occur, as do piebald and skewbald colors. Some white on face and legs is common.

HEIGHT About 14hh to 15hh.

The tough, independent nature of the Criollo is shown clearly in this photograph, although this horse is probably carrying more weight than most working gaucho ponies in South America. Still used on the vast ranches, it is also ideally fitted for endurance riding and is used as a cross for the famous Argentinian polo pony.

AZTECA

Although a new breed, the ancient origins and primitive air of the Azteca can be clearly detected in this photograph. Founded in 1972 for leisure riding and competition work, this breed was specifically intended to be non-Thoroughbred or European warm-blood in character.

ANCESTRY

A judicious blend of Andalusian, Quarter Horse, and Criollo makes up the Azteca.

Andalusian
Quarter Horse ▼
Criollo ▼
Azteca

The Azteca is one of the newest horse breeds in the world. As its name suggests, it comes from Mexico and replaces the Mexican strain of Criollo, which is now believed to be virtually extinct.

Foundation work began in 1972, when Andalusian stallions were crossed with carefully selected South American Criollo and Quarter Horse mares. These breeds were carefully selected as the aim was to create a breed with the best qualities of the Andalusian and of the Quarter Horse. Both breeds are compact in build and are powerfully muscled without being heavy. In temperament they vary, since the Andalusian has a hot nature and the Quarter Horse is more placid. The object of retaining some Criollo blood was to maintain a link with the traditional Mexican horse and to provide the Azteca with hardiness, toughness, soundness, and stamina, all of which abound in the Criollo.

Character and care
The Azteca has the noble attitude and bearing of the Andalusian, with the docility, speed, and agility of the Quarter Horse and the toughness of the Criollo.

GENERAL CHARACTERISTICS

CONFORMATION The Andalusian ancestry of the Azteca is quite obvious. The **neck** is elegantly arched, substantial, and well-muscled. The **legs** are fine and strong with good joints, muscular upper parts, and good riding pasterns and feet. The horse stands naturally square and proud.

HEAD A noble, lean head, **ears** are small and pricked, **eyes** are generous and with a proud spark, **profile** is straight or slightly convex with readily flared **nostrils**.

COLOR All colors are allowed with the exception of particolors.

HEIGHT Mares average 14.3hh, while stallions average 15hh.

The Azteca today
The Azteca was created to provide an impressive, elegant Spanish/Latin-type horse for leisure riding and competition. A European-type warmblood or Thoroughbred type was specifically not wanted.

GALICENO

The Galiceno is probably the least-known breed to be taken across to the Americas by the Spanish *conquistadores*. It is descended from the Spanish pony, the Garrano from Galicia in northwestern Spain, and also from the north Portuguese Minho. It does not have the old Iberian conformation, but is light and narrow in type, probably as a result of the Arab genes in the Garrano.

The original ponies that traveled across the Atlantic landed in Mexico and, although used by man, were allowed to breed indiscriminately among themselves, and so the present type evolved as a result of natural selection rather than artificial selection by man.

It was not until 1959 that Galiceños were brought to North America, where they have turned out to be a very popular in-between type of pony for older children. The breed has adapted to showing and competing with enthusiasm and is also good at jumping. It has great stamina and has a natural fast running walk which means riders can be carried comfortably and speedily over long distances.

Character and care
The Galiceño seems to have inherited many Arab characteristics; it is a tough and hardy quality pony, intelligent, courageous, and a quick learner with a lovely temperament. It is also fast and enduring.

The Galiceño today
In Mexico, the Galiceño is used for ranch work and light harness work. It is ridden by small adults and children. In North America, it excels as a competition pony.

GENERAL CHARACTERISTICS

CONFORMATION A fine, quality type of pony which shows all the best Arab characteristics.

HEAD A quality head, intelligent, with kind, perceptive **eyes**, medium-length **ears**, and open **nostrils**.

COLOR Bay, black, chestnut, dun, and gray. Particolors and albino are not allowed.

HEIGHT 12hh to 13.2hh.

ANCESTRY

Descended from the Garrano and the Minho ponies of Iberia.

Garrano
Minho ▼
Galiceño

Much less famous than its related Iberian breeds, the Galiceño is more Arab in type and is hardy, intelligent, and of light quality with stamina. Its fast, running, four-beat walk carries riders comfortably and fast over long distances. Ideal for ranch work, it has many other talents.

PERUVIAN STEPPING HORSE

The Peruvian Stepping Horse, or Peruvian Ambler/Peruvian Paso, is the blood brother of the Paso Fino, both having exactly the same foundation of Barb and Iberian blood brought to the Americas by the Spanish *conquistadores*, but each breed has subsequently evolved different characteristics to accommodate the climates of their now-native lands. The horse of Peru was developed to carry a rider comfortably for long distances over rough and treacherous mountainous terrain and over narrow, rocky tracks at high altitude.

The Peruvian Stepping Horse has developed an exceptionally large, strong heart and lungs which enable it to perform athletically in an atmosphere with a very low oxygen level. The horse also possesses "mountain sense" or the instinct to pick its way without fear or panic over rocky ground, sliding shale, deep water, and steep inclines.

There are several Paso breeds which all have a natural ability to perform the distinctive, four-beat lateral gaits which mean a rider can be carried at speed for long distances without tiring the horse. There are three major Paso gaits: the *paso corto*, used for practical traveling; the exaggerated, slow, and elegant *paso fino*, used for display and parade purposes; and the extended, fast *paso largo* for speed.

Character and care

Tough and hardy, the Peruvian Stepping Horse is calm, energetic, strong, enduring, and a willing worker.

The Peruvian Stepping Horse today

An excellent riding horse, though it never trots or gallops. Used for parade work and showing, and for travel and ranching in its homeland.

GENERAL CHARACTERISTICS

CONFORMATION Adapted to work in high altitudes: the **legs** are fine and strong, well muscled with very flexible joints, and long, sloping pasterns above hard, open **feet**. The hindlegs are very long.

HEAD The head is of medium size with a Barb appearance. The **ears** are pricked and mobile, the **eyes** bright, the **muzzle** small with flaring **nostrils**.

COLOR Any color but usually bay or chestnut. White on head and legs is permitted.

HEIGHT Between 14hh and 15.1hh.

ANCESTRY

Barb plus old Iberian strains are the foundation of the Peruvian Stepping Horse which has, however, developed its own characteristics due to conditions in the Peruvian mountains.

Barb
Old Iberian ▼
Peruvian Stepping Horse

The Peruvian Stepping Horse has evolved into a slightly different type from its brother breed, the Paso Fino. It works at high altitude and has developed a larger, stronger heart: it also possesses mountain sense and is very independent, calm, and sure-footed.

PASO FINO

A famous breed of Iberian stock, the Paso Fino is best known for its showy, dishing gaits in parades, richly caparisoned and performing the paso corto, *the* paso fino *or* fino fino, *and the* paso largo. *However, it is also a working horse, largely on coffee plantations.*

The Paso Fino is one of the three main types of South American gaited horse which come from the same genetic stock, but which have all developed some minor changes due to having evolved separately in different environments.

The Paso Fino is probably the most famous and comes from Puerto Rico; the others coming from Peru (see Peruvian Stepping Horse) and Colombia. The intended purpose of the Paso Fino was for display and transportation. The Puerto Rican horse has obviously not developed the ability to work in high altitudes (c.f. the Peruvian Stepping Horse), but its gaits are, if anything, even more refined. It performs the *paso corto*, the *paso fino*, and the *paso largo* with breathtaking beauty and skill.

Two other variants of the basic gaits at which the Paso Fino excels are the *sobre paso* and the *andadura*. In the *sobre paso* the horse is relaxed and natural on a loose rein; this gait is not used in the show ring. In the *andadura* the horse performs a fast lateral pacing gait which is not comfortable and used only for shortish distances when speed is of the essence.

Character and care

The Paso Fino has an exceptionally gentle temperament. It is probably the best-looking example of the existing Paso types, having an Arab-type head and an Andalusian body. The horse is intelligent and easy to handle.

The Paso Fino today

The Paso Fino is much in demand for leisure riding, showing, parade and display work, and also for general transportation around the coffee plantations of Puerto Rico.

GENERAL CHARACTERISTICS

CONFORMATION A horse of great quality and style. The **hocks** are particularly excellent and large. The **hindleg** is fairly straight and comes well in under the body to enable the horse to perform his *paso* gaits. The skin is fine and the coat **hair** silky.

HEAD A quality head, with a flat, straight **profile**. The **ears** are quite long and pointed; the **eyes** are expressive and proud; and the **muzzle** has sensitive, open **nostrils**.

COLOR The breed comes in all colors.

HEIGHT Between 14.2hh and 15hh.

POLO PONY

The game of polo is one of the oldest in the world. It originated in Persia shortly before 500 B.C., spreading fairly quickly to other areas and peoples. It is a fast, tough game, and needs a pony with similar qualities.

The British developed a liking for polo during the time of the British Raj in India, from whence it spread to every continent in the world. Today, the best polo pony in the world comes from Argentina.

A polo ground measures 300 yards by 200 yards (274m by 180m), with goal posts at least 10 feet (3m) high, placed 24 feet (7.3m) apart. The game is played with a hard ball made of bamboo root or willow and is hit from the saddle by a mallet measuring 48–54 inches (120–137cm) long with a solid, cylindrical wooden head on the end of the shaft. The object of the game is to hit the ball between the opposing team's goal posts. There are two teams of four players (so eight ponies and riders on the field at once), each game being divided into a maximum of eight chukkas (periods of play) of 7½ minutes.

The ponies, therefore, must be very fast and be able to gallop at top speed for short distances, stop suddenly, and be off again, so suppleness is essential. They inevitably get knocked and hit by sticks, balls, and other ponies, and must also be able to shoulder out of the way an opponent's pony.

It is essential, therefore, for the polo pony to be fit, strong, and determined, with a dominant personality, yet be submissive to its rider. Various breeds have been tried over the centuries, from Asian ponies to Arabs and Thoroughbreds, yet the Argentine Polo Pony is the best. Argentine polo ponies consist mainly of Criollo/Thoroughbred crosses.

A polo pony should be about 15hh to 15.1hh. It needs excellent natural balance; a longish neck with a good ability to flex at the poll and jaw; powerful, sloping shoulders; a strong, short back; a well-ribbed body; very open elbows for free action; and extremely powerful hindquarters.

Polo ponies need to be tough, very agile, and fast over short distances; they must also be intelligent and have lightning responses – a lot to demand in one animal. The best polo ponies are usually regarded as the Argentine ones, although most countries where polo is played breed at least some of their own ponies.

PALOMINO

Surely one of the most beautifully colored horses in the world, the Palomino has always found favor for display purposes – parades, circuses, shows of various kinds. Since it comes in all sizes of horse and pony, a Palomino can usually be found for almost anyone or any job.

Palomino is a color and not yet strictly a breed. Palomino-colored ponies and horses may belong to a registry which records details of their parentage run by their national association, but there is no actual palomino stud book operated by a breed society. The near-exception is found in the United States, where the Palomino Society regards and registers the Palomino as a color-breed with strict requirements as to conformation and type, with a view to creating a strict type in future. In the American registry, one parent must be a registered Palomino, and the other parent must have Arab, Thoroughbred, or Quarter Horse bloodlines.

Unfortunately, there is no way palominos can be made to breed true to color, so their full acceptance as a true breed is unlikely. The color has been well known and admired since ancient times. In the Middle Ages Queen Isabella of Spain encouraged their breeding,

and the horses are still called Ysabellas in Spain. She gave some to Cortés to take to the Americas, who on arrival presented one to Juan de Palomino, hence their name. When California came into American ownership in the mid-19th century, the Palomino was "rediscovered" and soon became known as "The Golden Horse of the West," and its popularity has never waned to this day.

The color of the coat should be that of a newly minted gold coin, or up to three shades darker or lighter, with a white, cream, or silver mane and tail. White is permitted on head and lower legs only.

The Palomino is used worldwide for every job imaginable because the color occurs in most breeds, but not, interestingly, in the Thoroughbred, or in the Arab.

PINTO

The terms "pinto," "paint," or less commonly "calico" are U.S. terms for horses with large patches of white and another color on their bodies. In some other English-speaking countries, they are called piebalds (black and white), skewbalds (any other color or colors plus white) or "colored" or "odd-colored" horses. None of these terms is used to describe horses with mainly spotted markings such as Appaloosas or Knabstrups. Only in the U.S. is the Pinto regarded as a true breed, although various other countries do have registries for colored horses.

In the U.S., Canada, and Australia and, to a lesser extent, New Zealand, colored horses are admired and sought for their uniqueness, no two Pintos being quite the same. They were popular generations ago for trade deliveries because as they were eye-catching, and a good advertisement for business. Romany people have liked them for their bright and showy appearance, and they will probably always be popular on circuses for the same reason.

Pinto-type coloration has been known for thousands of years, and many of the quality breeds now appearing only in solid colors had parti-colored ancestors. The coloring may or may not be primitive, and, despite what has been said about its being eye-catching, it does in fact provide excellent camouflage. The Native American tribes loved pinto types of horses for their showy appearance, but also because their broken outline provided a partial disguise on forays and raids.

The Pinto Horse Association of America has been breeding Pintos for color, good conformation and action since 1956, and the Pinto was recognized as a breed in 1963.

Four types are now recognized in the U.S.: Stock Horses (Quarter Horse type), Hunters (Thoroughbred type), Pleasure type (a good riding horse of Arab/Morgan type), and Saddle type (of Saddlebred type). Height is variable as Pintos can be ponies or horses.

A Pinto of the Tobiano pattern, this well-conformed horse proves that it is quite possible to breed for color and still produce high-quality animals. Pinto coloring was found in previous centuries in several breeds which now appear only in solid colors. In some countries, this horse would simply be called a skewbald.

Another Tobiano-patterned Pinto of a different type from the horse on the previous page, but again of good conformation and quality. As a black and white horse, another name for his coloring is piebald.

There are two recognized Pinto coat patterns: the *Tobiano*, with large, well-defined patches of white and colored coat and normally with a colored head and dark eyes, and the *Overo*, with smaller patches, with the white always appearing to originate from the belly, the back, mane, and tail usually colored and the face white with blue eyes.

AMERICAN WARMBLOOD

This American Warmblood is piebald or pinto, a color pattern which may become familiar in the American Warmblood due to the very wide gene pool on which it is based.

Americans have a reputation around the world for being competitive and when they saw how successful the various continental European warmbloods were in competitive equestrian disciplines, particularly show-jumping and dressage, it was perhaps natural that they would want their own warmblood. They have imported high-class European warmbloods and in the early 1980s started the American Warmblood Society, with a view to creating a superior performance warmblooded horse in the United States.

However, as a warmblood can be technically anything *other* than one hundred percent hot-blood or one hundred percent coldblood, the Americans are free to introduce into their embryonic breed almost anything, from heavy horse to almost completely Thoroughbred or Arab, which gives them an amazing gene pool from which to select. It seems it will be a long time before a recognizable breed-type emerges, but the rest of the world can be sure that whatever animal appears under the banner of American Warmblood in the future, it will certainly be able to excel in competition.

MUSTANG

The Mustang is the feral horse of the North American continent. The word comes from the Spanish *mestengo* or *mesteño*, meaning "stranger" or "outsider."

Horses certainly evolved in the Americas, but they became extinct there, until they were reintroduced by the *conquistadores*. Within a few generations, large herds of small, wiry, and tough Arab- and Barb-based Iberian horses roamed the plains of the species' prehistoric homeland.

Mustangs were caught and used by Native American tribes, which resulted in various tribes developing their own "breeds" such as the Chickasaw Indian Pony, the Appaloosa, and the Cayuse Indian Pony. The Mustang, particularly the wilder type known as the Bronco, has also traditionally been used in rodeos.

The Mustangs and their descendants were subjected to all the hardships of natural selection and so developed incredible toughness at the expense of what we would term quality,

The Kiger Mustang is regarded by its enthusiasts as probably the purest breed of mustang, having more of the features of its Spanish ancestors than any other. They are various types of dun with little or no white, and often show an eel or dorsal stripe plus other typically Spanish/Iberian markings.

despite their aristocratic progenitor base of Andalusians, Arabs, and Barbs. By the turn of the 19th century, the numbers running free were reported to be between one and two million. Merciless culling followed, and there are now only a few thousand running free, with many enclosed on ranches, adopted as domestic riding horses, or being cross-bred with quality breeds to produce a higher-quality riding and ranch horse.

Today, the Mustang is protected by law and regarded as part of America's heritage. Although of no fixed type, those showing original Barb ancestry are favored. The height is generally between 14hh and 15hh.

AMERICAN PERFORMANCE HORSE

The American Performance Horse is a warmblooded horse of high quality. A recognizable breed type and character should emerge sooner than with the American Warmblood because of the narrower progenitor base.

The American Performance Horse is a horse which is technically a warmblood but is not called that, and does not contain the same genes as the embryonic American Warmblood.

This unusual project was started in 1981 with the objective of producing athletic riding horses containing generous proportions of champion Thoroughbred racing blood, and crossing the resulting stock with draft horses, normally Percherons because of their quality, activity, and temperament. The idea was certainly sound, and some excellent and very attractive horses have so far been produced.

In both theory and practice, the American Performance Horse will be able easily to rival the American Warmblood. In any event, because of the stipulation that only high-class Thoroughbreds should be used in breeding, the progeny should be of very high quality, provided similar care is taken in the selection of the heavy-horse component in relation to conformation, action, constitution, and temperament.

ALBINO

White horses have always been regarded by many as spectacular or glamorous, and American Albinos also have the advantage of generally being bred for good conformation and temperament.

White horses, rather like Palomino horses, have always been associated with glamour and show. Albinism in animals is an inherited condition, classified as partial, incomplete, or complete. Affected animals are unable to produce the body's coloring pigment, melanin, which results in pink skin under white hair. Complete albinism results in pink eyes. In other types, the eyes may be dark, blue, or even white, and the coat hair cream. Some albino animals have white or cream hair and cinnamon-colored skin with brown eyes. Albinism is sometimes associated with a weakness in general constitution and proneness to infection, with poor eyesight, deafness, and photosensitization or sunsensitive skin.

In horses, the albino is really a type and not a breed, yet in the U.S. they are regarded as a breed, American Creams, the foundation stallion being Old King, foaled in 1906 and possibly of Morgan/Arab blood. The breed association is favoring stock of Quarter Horse, Morgan, Thoroughbred, or Arab type and various color combinations of white and cream body coat or mane/tail hair, pink or cinnamon-colored skin, and blue or dark eyes.

ROCKY MOUNTAIN PONY

This lovely pony shows the typical coat coloring of the Rocky Mountain Pony which, despite having been developed for only about ten years, shows much more consistent type than many older breeds. It has inherited the amble from its Iberian ancestors.

The Rocky Mountain Pony was founded by Kentuckian Sam Tuttle who felt that his old stallion, Old Tobe, extremely popular with the riders at the stable he ran in the Appalachian Mountains, should be given a chance to pass on his characteristics, and he also wanted to found a breed suitable for riding in the Appalachian foothills – rough, tricky country needing ponies with sensible and calm temperaments, nimble and sure-footed action, with strength, stamina, and comfort for the rider.

The resulting animal has, in ten short years, developed into a remarkably consistent type with all these characteristics (Old Tobe must have been as prepotent as other breed-founders like Justin Morgan). The ponies (usually from 14.2hh to 14.3hh), like Old Tobe, also have coats of a most unusual chocolate brown color, often dappled, with flaxen manes and tails.

As most American native breeds are based on old Iberian stock, Spanish and Barb characteristics frequently come to the fore in one way or the other, and this is the case with the Rocky Mountain Pony, which has inherited the comfortable Iberian lateral gait known as the amble.

The already popular Rocky Mountain Pony is currently numbered only in hundreds, but it seems inevitable that it will, in due course, take its place among the many excellent and distinctive American breeds, and its numbers will subsequently increase.

CANADIAN CUTTING HORSE

People who do not live in North America do not realize that cattle ranching is a major business in Canada and that Canada, although it has no indigenous horse breeds, has long been breeding excellent horses of many types, one of which is a recognized Canadian type – the Canadian Cutting Horse.

This horse, as its name suggests, is used in ranching specifically for cutting cattle out from a herd. It contains much American Quarter Horse blood and is bred along the same lines and for the same qualities, but probably with a wider progenitor base of imported European stock. The resulting Canadian version is larger than most Quarter Horses, but is just as agile, quick off the mark and as fast at the gallop over short distances.

It is a very active, well-balanced, strong, and intelligent horse with instinctive cow-sense. It is longer in the body than the Quarter Horse and has a slightly convex profile. It reaches 16.1 hands in height. It has a very "trainable" nature and good temperament.

Rodeo as a sport and entertainment is increasingly popular in Canada, and the Canadian Cutting Horse is regularly seen taking part in cutting and other contests.

This Canadian Cutting Horse clearly shows the Quarter Horse type sought in the breed but has the typically slightly lighter frame and longer back. This lovely horse is of good conformation and quality.

AUSTRALIA, ASIA, AND AFRICA

ARAB

The horse we now call the Arab or Arabian has probably influenced more other breeds of horse and pony than any other in the world. This breed suffers from a good deal of romanticism, probably because most individuals are very beautiful horses with spirited temperaments, intelligence, and an affectionate attitude toward humans. In practice, it would do the breed a better service if it were respected more for its toughness, individuality, and stamina.

The modern breed is called "Arab" because during the last century and, to a lesser extent, the preceding century, breeding stock was imported to Britain from the Arabian peninsula, but the breed's distant ancestors almost certainly evolved from the small, wiry, Oriental-type ("hot-blooded") wild horses living in Eastern Europe and the Near and Middle East.

Although the breed is claimed to be the oldest and purest, it includes different strains which physically resemble earlier types from which the modern breed developed, and these different physical types can still be seen in the breed today. Whatever its sources, the Arab is a riding horse without equal and is regarded as priceless by those who understand the breed and are willing to treat it as a partner rather than a servant.

Character and care

Arabs are intelligent horses, perceptive, sensitive, and thoughtful, not only in the sense of being considerate and gentle toward people and other animals, but also in thinking out situations for themselves. They do have a reputation for being difficult among those who have tried to force them to do something against their will, but they are extremely courageous and will try their best for someone they trust.

As they originated in hot climates, they are fine-skinned and have all the physical characteristics facilitating easy heat-loss from the body, but tend not to be so sensitive to cold weather as the Thoroughbred. They can

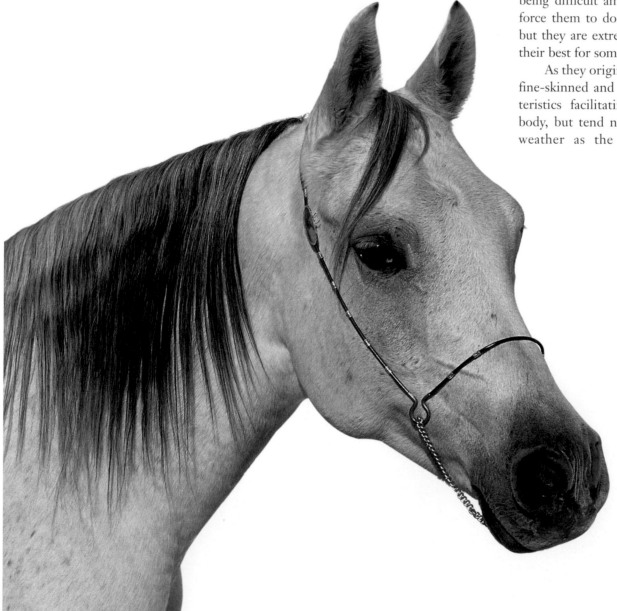

The traditional horse of the desert, the "Drinker Of The Wind," the Arab is the most famous hot-blood in the world but by no means the only horse with similar features. In fact, the breed we now call Arab includes several different strains, families, or types. This head is of the Seglawy or Siglavi type, the type most people imagine as Arab.

usually be handled by novices and children, provided those concerned have a regard for their nature and a sensitivity toward them.

The Arab today

Arabs make excellent all-round riding, and very light harness horses. They are also good family horses because of their affectionate disposition, and their average height which makes them suitable for both adults and older children.

In competition, Arabs should be judged as good riding horses first with their unmistakable type and breed-conformation points second.

In-hand showing classes are extremely popular with many Arab enthusiasts, and they are divided into the normal age and sex groups with overall championships to be won in the different categories.

Increasingly, the Arab is being seen as a saddle horse not only in showing classes, but competitive disciplines involving dressage, jumping, and endurance riding. They are now also raced. In all categories of competition, Arabs compete internationally under the auspices of the World Arabian Horse Organization.

Arabs are sometimes said to be the jacks of all trades and masters of one – endurance riding. Their legendary stamina makes them superb long-distance riding horses in any sphere, working or showing, and Arabs can be found working cattle on a ranch as well as taking most of the prizes in competitive endurance riding.

A common misconception is that Arabs can't jump. Arabs certainly can and will jump, but do not have the scope for high-level eventing or show jumping.

The high-set tail and flattish quarter/croup region indicates natural speed which has resulted in the revival of Arab racing. All in all, they are excellent all-rounders and family horses, and have an inimitable panache in harness.

This chestnut horse has quite a different head, within the type, from the gray horse on the preceding page. It still has those hot-blooded, desert features, though.

The Arab breed is internationally famous for its great stamina and is much in demand as a competition endurance horse today. Arabs can carry heavy weights for their height and love to work with a human partner they respect and trust.

ARAB

Unmistakable body shape and type; should conform to good riding horse first and good Arab second. The Arab breed is internationally famous for its great stamina and is much in demand as a competition endurance horse today. Arabs can carry heavy weights for their height and love to work with a human partner they respect and trust. This is an Arab of the Managhi or Muniqui type, ideally suited for racing. The Darley Arabian, one of the Thoroughbred's ancestors, was believed to be of this type, with the slim body, long legs, and fairly high head carriage. The similarity between this type of Arab and the Turkmene type of Oriental breeds is clear. The symbol Ⓒ *indicates a conformation feature.*

FACE

Concave outline to front of face desirable, often described as "dish faced."

HEAD

Slightly wedge-shaped head, broad forehead, and short overall length. Ⓒ

EARS

The ears are set wide apart and are almost constantly on the move, pricking back and forth toward whatever is interesting the horse.

MUZZLE AND NOSTRILS

The best Arabs are said to have "pint-pot" muzzles, that is, muzzles which would fit into a pint pot. The nostrils are fine, very mobile, and can flare widely for maximum air exchange and exhalation of warm air to help cool the body core. Ⓒ

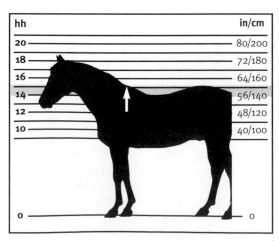

HEIGHT

Mainly between 14hh and 15.1hh.

hh	in/cm
20	80/200
18	72/180
16	64/160
14	56/140
12	48/120
10	40/100
0	0

COAT

Fine, very short in summer, and a little longer and denser in winter.

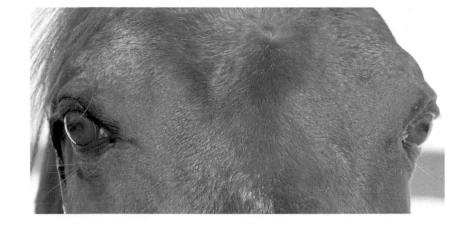

EYES

The Arab's eyes are particularly large, deep, and expressive, and set wide on either side of a broad forehead. They should also be set about halfway down the head or slightly higher.

ANCESTRY

The modern breed we now call the Arab seems to have fewer infusions of other types than most other breeds. Its introduction to Arabia is relatively recent, stemming from the time of Mohammed, for there is no evidence of native Arab stock before that time. Realizing their value as a war weapon, Mohammed imported horses from other Middle Eastern countries in large numbers and encouraged their breeding and improvement.

Asiatic and Eastern European wild stock of hot-blooded type

Arab (modern breed)

TAIL

The tail is set high, sometimes level with or slightly higher than the back, very mobile and gaily carried, sometimes even over the back when excited.

MANE AND TAIL HAIR

The mane and tail hair are naturally long, fine, and silky. The length of the bridlepath or roached/hogged section behind the ears, aimed at showing off the set of head to neck, varies according to the country in which the animal is shown. Sometimes it is done to excess, with almost half the mane removed.

MITBAH

A particularly strong identifying characteristic of the Arab is the mitbah, *the set of the head onto the neck.* **C**

HOOVES

The hooves are normally hard and tough.

COLOR

Solid: chestnut and gray predominate with bay, brown, and black being the other three colors. White markings on legs and head, but not on body.

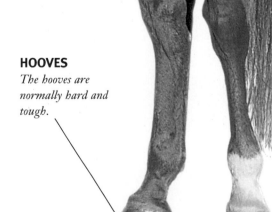

CASPIAN

The Caspian should be regarded as a small horse rather than a pony because it does have horse rather than pony character. Remarkably, despite having been domesticated, it seems to have descended in pure form from an Oriental prehistoric horse, the fossils of which have been found in Iran and match the Caspian's skeletal features. One of the best depictions of this ancient horse can be found on the seal of Darius the Great, ruler of Persia in 500 B.C.

All theories pointed to the horse's extinction in around the 10th century, but in 1965, 40 Caspians were discovered in a remote area of the Elburz Mountains in Iran by Mrs. Louise Firouz, who shipped them to Britain. A breed society was set up to promote and foster the Caspian, and now there are studs in Britain, the U.S., Australia, New Zealand, and Iran.

It is claimed that the Caspian is the oldest pure breed in the world. It is also claimed to be the progenitor of the Arab.

Character and care

The Caspian is a miniature Oriental type, with a free, floating action, alert yet equable and affectionate temperament, and is sensitive without being too highly strung.

ANCESTRY

As a direct descendant of the primitive type, the Caspian is a piece of living prehistory with no known infusions of other blood.

Primitive small Middle Eastern type ▼ Caspian

GENERAL CHARACTERISTICS

CONFORMATION The **neck** is gracefully arched, strong and elegant, the **forelock**, **mane**, and **tail** hair are long, full, and silky. The **legs** are fine and strong, with exceptionally hard **feet** which do not need shoeing.

HEAD Like a miniature Thoroughbred. The **ears** are short and pricked, the **forehead** wide and domed, the **eyes** large, bold, and intelligent. The **profile** is straight, and the low-set **nostrils** readily flared.

COLOR Bay, gray, and chestnut, rarely black or cream.

HEIGHT Between 10hh and 12hh.

The Caspian today

The Caspian makes a superb riding pony for children. Being narrow, responsive, intelligent, gentle, and cooperative, it would be hard to imagine a better beginners' pony. It also makes a good harness pony.

One of the equine success stories of the 20th century, the ancient Caspian, having been believed extinct for about 1,000 years, was rediscovered in Iran in 1965. It is now thriving in studs in Britain, the U.S., Australia, New Zealand, and Iran itself. It makes a superb beginners' pony.

AKHAL-TEKE

The Akhal-Teké from Turkmenistan is the living descendant of the now-extinct old type of Turkmene horse, and is very highly regarded in its home country. It is known to have existed in very much its present type around 3,000 years ago, when it was used as a fast warhorse. Evolved and reared in varying climates from searing heat to killing cold, the breed is one of the hardiest and most enduring in the world.

Historically, the Akhal-Teké is a true desert horse, coming from an arid region with vast expanses of steppe and desert. Although they did (and still do) run in herds under the management of a mounted herdsman, today many are still traditionally tethered and hand-fed barley, eggs, alfalfa, mutton fat, and a heavy fried type of bread when they are needed for work. Heavy covers were used to protect these fine-skinned horses, both from the bitter nights and daytime desert sun. In the past, foals were traditionally weaned at two months, and yearlings were raced hard.

Character and care

Noted for being stubborn, rebellious, somewhat wild, independent, even bad-tempered, and inclined to be vicious.

The Akhal-Teké today

Akhal-Tekés are high-class riding horses: they race, jump, and take part in endurance and dressage competitions. They are a premier sports horse in Turkmenistan, Russia, and other Eastern countries.

GENERAL CHARACTERISTICS

CONFORMATION The Akhal-Teké breaks every rule in the book with its offbeat conformation. The long, narrow **neck** is carried very high, the **withers** are pronounced, the **shoulders** very big, sloping, and narrow. The **body** is shallow, narrow, and rounded; and the fine **legs** are really too long for the body.

HEAD A truly aristocratic head. It is fine, long, and lean, with wide-set and beautifully chiseled **ears**, a wide, flat **forehead** with large, bold **eyes**, a straight **profile**, and widely flaring **nostrils**.

COLOR Bay, gray, chestnut, and black occur, but the most highly prized color is the honey-golden dun with black points. The coat has a peculiar and strong metallic sheen.

HEIGHT 15.2hh, though looks bigger.

The conformation of the Akhal-Teké is being changed, to some extent, by selective breeding for the modern competition horse market. This horse looks much more like a modern Thoroughbred.

PRZEWALSKI'S HORSE

All the Przewalski's Horse herds are considered feral rather than wild.

Przewalski's Horse, or the Mongolian or Asiatic Wild Horse, was discovered, as far as the modern Western world is concerned, in 1881 by the Polish explorer, Colonel N. M. Przewalski. He had been given a skull and the skin of a three-year-old animal by the chief magistrate of Zaisan, who had obtained it from some hunters who had found the remains in the Gobi Desert in western Mongolia. Colonel Przewalski in turn presented the remains to the Zoological Museum of St. Petersburg in Russia, where the naturalist I. S. Poliakoff examined them and pronounced that they belonged to a distinct species of wild horse.

Further investigations and theories went on for years. Today, we know that it has almost certainly been hunted to extinction in the wild, as no sightings of wild Przewalskis have been made since the 1970s. However, from animals caught in the wild earlier, a captive population is being built up, and reintroductions are being made into Russia, China, and France. These animals cannot be regarded as truly wild, but feral. There are also several herds in zoos and parks around the world, and breeding is very carefully controlled through the stud book held at Prague Zoo.

Character and care

Great efforts are made to preserve the Przewalski's Horse in as wild a mental and physical state as possible. They are treated as wild animals in captivity. They are aggressive and afraid of man, yet the stallions are courageous in defending their herds, particularly when foals are present. Naturally, they are extremely hardy and tough.

The Przewalski's Horse today

Przewalski's Horses are not used or tamed by man. Hunting them is illegal, but difficult to enforce; the feral herds are regularly supervised and patrolled to try to guarantee their safety.

Almost hunted to extinction in the wild, reintroduction of this breed to the wild, notably in Russia, Mongolia, and China, with a thriving population in France, is meeting with some success. The Przewalski's Horse is showing its inherent adaptability by acclimatizing apparently effortlessly to whatever region it finds itself in.

GENERAL CHARACTERISTICS

CONFORMATION The horse is very stocky with a ferocious **temperament** when annoyed or disturbed. The **neck** is very short and thick, the **back** can be quite long, and the **legs** are fine with elongated and tough **feet**.

HEAD Coarse and heavy. There is no forelock. The **eyes** are set high up the head and are fairly small. The **profile** is convex or straight. The **muzzle** is small and tight with small, low-set **nostrils**.

COLOR Yellow dun is the most common, but coat color ranges from red dun to creamy dun. The horses have a dark dorsal list or stripe, often with zebra markings on the legs. The lower legs are black. The mane and tail are black. The muzzle and eyes have oatmeal-colored hair around them.

HEIGHT From 12hh to 14hh.

OTHER FEATURES The Przewalski sheds its mane annually and regrows it during the summer, when it stands erect.

TURKMENE

The name Turkmene refers to a family of very similar Oriental horses, all of a type which is not Arab. Turkmene horses were an ancient strain which were largely bred for racing, both for sport and for situations where speed and stamina were needed. They were bred by nomadic tribes around the Gobi Desert more than 3,000 years ago and were much admired by the Chinese during the Han Dynasty period. A strain of them (the Turkoman) is still bred in northern Iran, mainly for racing, as they are accomplished racehorses, and feral herds can still be found on the borders of Iran and Turkmenistan.

Character and care

These horses are the real greyhounds of the horse world. They are true Orientals and are intelligent, independent, courageous, and spirited. Proud, elegant, and aristocratic are other words which describe them.

The Turkmene today

The Turkmene type is used today as a riding horse, and it excels at racing and endurance feats. Turkmenes are used to develop breeds.

ANCESTRY

A member of the old Turkmene family of lean, rangy Oriental horses, the Turkoman descends from the original desert/steppe type of primitive horse. The modern Turkoman is a blend of Oriental breeds.

Indigenous
Oriental types ▼
Turkoman

GENERAL CHARACTERISTICS

CONFORMATION Light-framed, narrow-bodied, long-legged, and fine-skinned, these horses possess phenomenal stamina.

HEAD Long and narrow with a straight **profile**, long, fine **ears**, broad **forehead**, and bright, alert **eyes**. The **muzzle** is fine with low-set, flaring **nostrils**.

COLOR Gray, bay, brown, black, or chestnut, with some white seen on lower legs and head.

HEIGHT Usually about 15.1hh.

BASHKIR

The Bashkir is famous for its long, curly winter coat, a vital necessity in its cold home climate in the Ural Mountains. There the horse is used for transportation, meat, and milk, and for clothing.

ANCESTRY

The pure Bashkir seems to be an indigenous ancient type in itself, with typical cold-climate features, although some other breeds have been crossed into it in recent times to bring in extra size and quality.

Indigenous Russian
primitive type ▼
Bashkir

The Bashkir, or Bashkirsky, is one of the most unusual breeds in the world. It has been bred on the southern slopes of the Ural Mountains in Russia by the Bashkiri people for many centuries. They use it for pulling sleighs and troikas, and for making *kumiss*, an alcoholic liqueur, from the mares' milk.

Its home climate is one of the coldest on Earth. It has the features of a true cold-climate horse – stocky body, biggish head with small nostrils, short legs, and a tail held close to its hindquarters. It also develops a thick layer of insulating fat under its skin in winter. Bashkirs have very small, soft chestnuts on the legs. Their blood is also of a different composition and their heart and respiratory rates are higher than in other breeds.

The most remarkable feature is, however, its long, thick, wavy winter coat: a common variant is tight curls, like Persian lamb, and the most startling of all are tight ringlets up to about 6in (15cm) in length. The summer coat is short and straight.

There are about 1,200 Bashkir "Curlies" (as they are called) in the U.S., where they clean the horse in winter by vacuuming it! The Bashkiri people use the body, mane, and tail hair for spinning textiles and making clothing.

Character and care

Extremely tough, enduring, and hardy, Bashkirs are kind and affectionate, very willing workers.

The Bashkir today

In their home country, they are used for transportation, meat, milk, and clothing. The Mountain type is small and light; the Steppe type is heavier and better in harness. In the U.S., the "Curly" is used for endurance riding and showing.

GENERAL CHARACTERISTICS

CONFORMATION A stocky animal with distinct cold-climate features.

HEAD Big, with a heavy look about it, although the American Bashkir has been purposely changed in this respect to have a smaller and more attractive head. The **ears** are very short and pricked, the **eyes** wide apart with a gentle, intelligent look, a straight **profile**, and small but open **nostrils**.

COLOR Usually bay, chestnut, or palomino, and quite a few have Appaloosa markings.

HEIGHT Around 14hh.

BARB

The Barb is one of the pervading Eastern influences on most of today's horse breeds, particularly old Iberian stock which founded most of the American breeds. The Mustang shown here will contain much Barb blood, although he is not a true Barb color.

ANCESTRY

Possibly from primitive European rather than Asian stock, the Barb is a hot-blooded Oriental type infused with a good deal of Arab blood.

Primitive East European stock
Other Oriental types ▼
Barb

The Barb, or Berber, is one of the old Oriental-type breeds which has, over many centuries, greatly influenced other breeds and helped to found many of the most successful breeds of the world today. Along with the Arab, its place in equestrian history cannot be denied, yet it is little known, has not achieved worldwide popularity like the Arab, and does not even share the status of other lesser-known Oriental types such as the Akhal-Teké and the Turkoman.

The Barb's original homeland is North Africa – Morocco, Algeria, Libya, and Tunisia – the area corresponding to old-time Barbary. Today, it is bred at a large stud at Constantine in Algeria, and at the stud of the King of Morocco. The Tuareg people and some of the nomadic tribes of the remote mountain and desert areas of the region probably still breed a few Barb-type horses.

Character and care

The Barb is renowned for being a tough, tremendously enduring, fast, and responsive horse; and these qualities were required from it when it was bred with other breeds to improve them. It is not as spirited or as beautiful as the Arab and does not have its springy, floating action. Some hippologists believe that the Barb stems from prehistoric European stock rather than from Asian stock, although now it is undoubtedly an Oriental type. Its temperament is not so equable or affectionate as that of the

Arab, to which it is invariably compared.

Exceptionally tough and hardy, it requires little in the way of specialized care.

The Barb today

Today the Barb makes a good riding horse, while formerly it was a superb warhorse. It is also used for riding, racing, and display. The Barb is little known outside its homeland and does not receive the recognition it deserves.

GENERAL CHARACTERISTICS

CONFORMATION A lightly built desert horse. The **neck** is of medium length, strong and arched, and the **legs** are fine but tough. The **hooves**, as with many desert horses, are extremely hard and well formed. The **mane** and **tail** hair is more profuse than in the Arab.

HEAD Long and narrow. The **ears** are of medium length, fine and pointed, the **profile** slightly convex, the **eyes** have a courageous look to them, and the **nostrils** are low-set and open.

COLOR True Barbs are black, bay, and dark bay/brown. Those with Arab blood show other colors.

HEIGHT From 14.2hh to 15.2hh.

AUSTRALIAN STOCK HORSE

This Australian Stock Horse shows much Quarter Horse character but with obvious Thoroughbred influence. The breed has had a fairly checkered history in its short lifetime, but is now established and popular in many spheres, being used for general riding, stock work, rodeos, and as a competition horse.

ANCESTRY

A considerable mixture of old European stock with some Asian and Arab genes. Additional Barb and Thoroughbred infusions make up the present-day Australian Stock Horse.

Iberian
Dutch ▼
Criollo ▼
Basuto and ▼
Indonesian ponies
Mixed European ▼
breeds
Arab ▼
Barb ▼
Quarter Horse ▼
Thoroughbred ▼
Australian Stock
Horse

The Australian Stock Horse, or Waler as it is often called, is a relatively young breed. Horses first arrived in Australia at the end of the 18th century, brought by South African traders from the Cape of Good Hope, and also from Chile. These horses were of mixed European stock plus Arab and Barb blood. Indonesian and Basuto ponies and Criollo horses are also said to have been imported to eastern Australia about that time. These early arrivals are said to have been of poor quality, but with later Thoroughbred and Arab infusions, the resulting New South Wales horse – as it became known – soon became a well-made, sound, and enduring horse. It was used for everything from general riding to light and heavy harness work. It proved to be an excellent stock horse on the outback's massive cattle stations.

After World War II the number of Australian Stock Horses dwindled rapidly as general demand for horses decreased. Until that time, it had been a top-class type of Anglo-Arab. Subsequently, much new blood was indiscriminately introduced, and the breed quickly deteriorated. Now, although the horse is of a mixed type and does not breed true, steps are being made to improve it, mainly with Thoroughbred, Arab, and Quarter Horse blood.

Character and care

The Australian Stock Horse has good temperament, courage, toughness, and stamina.

The Australian Stock Horse today

The Australian Stock Horse is used for stock work, rodeos, and for general riding. It is also often used as a high-quality competition horse.

GENERAL CHARACTERISTICS

CONFORMATION As the type is mixed, the aimed-for type is described here. The **neck** is medium to long, well muscled, and attractively arched. The **legs** should be proportionate to the body, and the upper parts long and well muscled. The joints should be clean, the cannons short and moderately fine with hard, well-defined tendons and hard, well-formed **feet**.

HEAD The head should be a mix of Thoroughbred, Arab, and Quarter Horse. Medium-length pricked **ears** are set well apart, with intelligent **eyes**, straight **profile**, and short **muzzle** with open **nostrils**.

COLOR Bay is common, although all solid colors permitted. White is allowed on head and legs.

HEIGHT 15hh to 16.2hh.

AUSTRALIAN PONY

Australia's children, like children everywhere, wanted their own ponies! Although ponies had been imported with horses during the settlement years, it was not until the late 19th century that any effort was put into developing a set type. A recognizable type emerged by the early 1920s, and a stud book was started shortly afterward.

The Australian Pony is based on small Arab and Welsh ponies. Shetland and Exmoor blood is also present in considerable amounts, but nowadays the pony is so well blended that the only obvious ancestor is the Arab, which shows in the head.

Character and care

The Australian Pony is an excellent riding pony, refined yet not too light. It is renowned for being sound and healthy, robust, responsive, even-natured, and hardy. It shows its "blood" ancestry, but does not require cosseting, and it is easy for children to ride and care for.

One of its most favored features, in addition to its excellent temperament, is its long, free, and flowing action.

The Australian Pony today

The Australian Pony is mainly used as a children's riding pony, but it also makes a good harness pony. It has good jumping ability and has the quality to be shown at the highest level. Its stamina also makes it popular for junior trail and endurance riding.

ANCESTRY

Very mixed, including various European breeds, in particular Shetland, Welsh, and Exmoor.

Mixed European
blood
Hackney ▼
Shetland ▼
Exmoor ▼
Welsh ▼
Timor ▼
Arab ▼
Thoroughbred ▼
Australian Pony

GENERAL CHARACTERISTICS

CONFORMATION A lovely pony. The **neck** is well-shaped, attractively arched with a full **mane**. The fairly fine **legs** are well proportioned, long and strong in their upper parts, and with short cannons, tough tendons, and hard, well-shaped **feet**.

HEAD Its Arab ancestry is fairly obvious in the head. Short, pricked **ears** set well apart, broad **forehead** with wide-set, large and generous **eyes**. **Profile** is straight or slightly concave, with a tapering **muzzle** and flared **nostrils**.

COLOR Gray is very common, but any color is permissible with the exception of particolors. White on head and legs is allowed.

HEIGHT 12hh to 14hh.

The Australian Pony is a mixture of pony blood from Europe and Indonesia, plus the Eastern influence of the Arab and Thoroughbred. It is popular as a children's riding, trail, and endurance pony, and it also goes well under harness.

LESSER-KNOWN BREEDS

BRITAIN AND IRELAND

COACH HORSE COMEBACK
The pure Cleveland Bay is gradually increasing in numbers.

ENGLAND

The **CLEVELAND BAY** was reduced to dangerously low levels in the mid-20th century, but is now being revived. The breed originates from crossing Iberian and Barb horses with a breed of bay pack horse called the Chapman horse, which was found in the northeast of Yorkshire in the Middle Ages. The Cleveland Bay is an excellent agricultural horse and a superb coach horse. It was crossed with the Thoroughbred to produce the elegant Yorkshire Coach Horse, which is now extinct in its original form.

Today crosses of Cleveland Bays and Thoroughbreds are increasing in number and are used in competition for carriage-driving. They are still used in the royal stables in London as carriage horses for state occasions.

Cleveland Bays are usually placid (although some say that they can be stubborn). They are strong and clean-legged, and possess great stamina and substance without being coarse. They are always bay, with no white, and stand between 16hh and 16.2hh.

Probably the best and most influential road horse ever was the **NORFOLK ROADSTER** (also known as the **NORFOLK TROTTER**), which forms the foundation for most trotting breeds. It almost certainly had the same ancestors as the Suffolk Punch. This cob-type animal, which is traceable back to the 15th century, was developed in the flat lands of Norfolk to be a strong, active, smart, short-legged, and tireless fast-trotting horse for use either in harness or for riding. It was mainly used for sustained trotting in light harness and under the saddle, and was often used to carry farmers with their wives riding pillion. For over four hundred years, until the advent of the railroad, the Norfolk Roadster provided an unbeatable mode of long-distance high-speed travel.

By the latter half of the 20th century, numbers were extremely low and the breed almost became extinct until a few enthusiasts gathered together suitable individuals of the Norfolk Roadster type and genes, and began to breed them again.

The **LUNDY** pony resulted from an attempt to breed another British native pony by taking New Forest mares and fillies to the island of Lundy in 1928 and crossing them with Thoroughbred, Welsh, and Connemara stallions. The scheme was not a great success, but a few ponies remain on the island. They have a characteristic dun color and stand around 13.2hh.

EUROPE

FRANCE

The **FRENCH SADDLE PONY** was created during the 20th century by crossing French native pony mares with mainly Arab, Welsh, and Connemara stallions. Other blood has also been used, including New Forest, Selle Français, Merens, Basque, and Landais.

This pony is of good quality and is elegant and spirited yet calm. It stands between 12.1hh and 14.22hh and may be any color. The French Saddle Pony has a light to medium build with good conformation. It makes a good competition pony for jumping and dressage, and is excellent in harness.

The **LIMOUSIN** is a half English Thoroughbred crossed with French native mares from the Limousin region. It also has a good deal of Arab blood. It is now incorporated into the Selle Français and will probably lose its own identity eventually.

The **BASQUE** pony, which is also known as the **POTTOCK** in the Basque language, is a tough, hardy pony from the Basque region, Navarra, and southwestern France, where it lives semi-wild. The Basque people regard the pony as an essential part of their culture. It was formerly used as a mine pony and is now used for riding, trekking, and light farm work.

This willing worker is strong and fertile with a calm, but energetic temperament, and it is an excellent jumper. It is mainly black or brown, but bay, chestnut, and particolors also occur. During the winter months, when it is forced to live on spiny plants, this pony develops a protective moustache. It stands between 12hh and 13hh.

The **COMTOIS** is a coldblooded, heavy horse from the Franche Comté region of eastern France where it has been bred for 1,400 years. It was probably introduced to the region by North German Burgundians who founded the kingdom of Burgundy in

A.D. 411. It was used as a warhorse and for heavy transportation and farm work. This breed has been used to upgrade others such as the Franches-Montagnes. Nowadays it is used for draft work in forestry and vineyards, and is bred for meat.

The Comtois is chunky and muscular with a large, friendly head, a characteristic long, straight back, and strong legs and feet. It has a surprisingly lively, speedy action for a heavy breed and stands between 14.2hh and 15.2hh. The coat is chestnut and bay.

BRITISH/FRENCH COOPERATION
The French Saddle Pony is a liberal mixture of both British and French breeds.

The **LANDAIS** (which incorporates the **BARTHAIS**) is used for riding and light draft work. It comes from the Landes region of southwestern France and is said to descend from the horses depicted in cave paintings in the area. There are now few original purebreds left after the introduction of Arab and heavier blood through the ages. The pony usually has a brown, black, chestnut, or bay coat and stands between 11hh and 13hh.

The heavy **POITEVIN** breed contains much Dutch, Danish, and

Norwegian blood. It is also known as the **MULASSIER** (meaning mule breeder), because it is often crossed with the large Poitu donkey to produce mules. In the middle of the 20th century, the Poitevin was almost extinct, but it was rescued by enthusiasts who are now breeding the horse again.

It is a lethargic and lazy horse, but it is strong, reliable, and easy to handle. It is deep in the body with a rather straight shoulder and stands between 15hh and 17hh. The coat is usually gray, black, bay, or palomino.

The **BOULONNAIS** is a heavy breed from northwestern France that probably descends from Numidian horses brought to France by the

Romans. Some experts believe that it originates from Hun horses left by Attila in the 5th century A.D. Barb and Andalusian blood was introduced and has produced a surprisingly speedy, strong, and elegant heavy horse. It has been used to improve other heavy breeds and to produce foundation blood for competition horses.

The Boulonnais is strong with great endurance and energy. The most usual color is gray, and the horse usually stands at about 16.3hh. It is mainly bred for the meat market.

ACTIVITY AND STRENGTH
Left *This striking coloring is common in the Comtois breed, which is noted for its active movement as well as its compact strength. It is fairly small for a heavy horse.*

THREE OF THE BEST
Above and below
The Trait du Nord is a rare and declining breed of northeastern France, made up of Ardennais, Boulonnais, and Brabant blood.

ROMAN ANCESTORS
Right *The Boulonnais is a heavy breed from northwestern France that probably descends from Numidian horses brought to France by the Romans.*

DUAL ROLE
Right *This is the Poitevin (Mulassier). The breed's second name is due to its success in breeding large, strong mules by mating with the big Poitu donkey. It is also used for farm work and short-haul transportation.*

CHILD'S MOUNT
Right *The bright but calm nature of the French Saddle Pony is shown in this photograph.*

OLD FAMILY
Below right *The striking resemblance of the Ariègios to the British Dales Pony is clear.*

BURGUNDIAN BACKGROUND
Below *The Auxios is another descendant of the original Ardennais as well as of the old Burgundian horse.*

TRUE EUROPEAN
The Franches-Montagnes breed contains blood from several other European countries' horses as well as Arab blood.

The **AUXOIS** stems from the original ancient Ardennais horse and an old Burgundian horse breed. It is larger and more powerful than its ancestors with slightly finer legs.

It is a quiet, even tempered, willing worker with great strength and endurance. Auxois are always a characteristic red roan color and stand between 15.1hh and 16hh.

The **TRAIT DU NORD** heavy horse is the result of crossing the Ardennais, Boulonnais, and the Belgian Brabant. It is hardy and strong, and is particularly well suited to heavy farm and transportation work in steep hilly country. It stands between 15.3hh and 16.1hh, and the coat is bay or roan.

The **ARIEGEIOS** (or **MERENS**) pony is a mountain breed from the eastern Pyrenees and the mountainous Spanish border. It is very similar in appearance to the English Dales pony. This breed is still recognizably related to horses depicted in prehistoric paintings and carvings in its home region, despite the incorporation of blood from Roman heavy horses and some Oriental genes. It was formerly used for transporting lumber and minerals, and is now used as a trekking pony and on farms.

This energetic and willing pony is extremely hardy and can withstand harsh mountain winters. But it cannot withstand heat in summer and must be sheltered. It has a medium-weight, cob-like build with a thick neck, luxurious mane and tail, and cow hocks. The Ariegeios stands between 13hh and 14.2hh.

NETHERLANDS

The old pure type of **GRONINGEN**, of which there are very few still in existence, was used as a heavyweight riding horse, a farm animal, and as a steady, slow carriage horse. It was based on Oldenburg and East Friesian blood and pure Friesian mares, with some influence from imported Suffolk Punch and Norfolk Roadster stallions.

The Groningen stood between 15.2hh and 16hh. It had good conformation, and was docile and economic to keep. Despite its heavy build, it had an elegant action.

Today the Groningen has been almost entirely absorbed into the modern warmblood competition horses of the Netherlands.

SWITZERLAND

The **FRANCHES-MONTAGNES** (also known as the **FREIBERGER**) was developed around the end of the 19th century in the Jura region of Switzerland by crossing native Jura males with Thoroughbreds and Anglo-Norman stallions. Later, Ardennais and Comtois blood was introduced, and Shagya and Arab stallions were used for quality and refinement.

The breed has two strains: one is more suited to medium and light draft work and the other to riding. The horse has an even temperament and is an active, willing performer. It is usually bay or chestnut with some white, though gray and blue roan sometimes occur. The head can be rather heavy on a broad neck. Overall, the Franches-Montagnes is a compact medium-weight horse, standing between 14.3hh and 15.2hh, that is excellent for general use.

The **EINSIEDLER** forms the basis of the excellent Swiss performance horse breeds and types. It is a strong, active horse with good movement and physical strength. It generally has good conformation and an outgoing, willing temperament. It can be bay or chestnut and stands around 16hh.

ITALY

The original **MAREMMANA** was a nondescript, even ugly, horse, which was probably based on the Norfolk Roadster and Neapolitan crossed with local mares. It was, however, an even-tempered and willing worker, and was used as a mount for Italian cattlemen in Tuscany.

Nowadays, the Maremmana has been crossed with excellent Italian Thoroughbred blood and has changed considerably. Although the quality has improved, the hardiness has decreased. Today the Maremmana is popular for general riding. It stands at between 15hh and 15.3hh and occurs in most solid colors.

The **MURGESE**, from Apulia, can be traced back to the era of Spanish rule in Italy. It is a mixture of native Italian, Barb, and Thoroughbred blood. Although it is a good jumper, the Murgese is a mediocre riding horse. It is mainly used for light draft and farm work and for breeding mules.

The breed is tough and frugal with poor conformation and action. It is not of a fixed type and usually stands between 14hh and 15hh, though larger animals frequently occur. Its coat is usually chestnut, but black and gray (sometimes with a black head) also occur.

The **SARDINIAN ANGLO-ARAB**, of the island of Sardinia, stems from the small and wiry local animals crossed with Arabs. Imported Iberian blood was introduced in the 16th century; then in the 20th century, Arab and Thoroughbred blood further improved the breed.

There are small, medium, and large types, ranging from 15.1hh to over 16.1hh. The Sardinian Anglo-Arab is hardy and fast with good endurance and jumping ability. It has an even temperament. Most solid colors occur.

The **SARDINIAN PONY** is highly strung, rebellious, agile, and hardy. Although its roots are untraceable, it is an ancient breed. The few ponies

that remain are sometimes caught and used for light farm work and riding. The ponies are brown, black, bay, or liver chestnut and stand between 12.1hh and 13hh. A similar type of pony exists in very small numbers on the island of Corsica and is known as the Corsican Pony.

There are two types of **SICILIAN** horse – those from the east are of a higher quality and lighter than the inland types, which are slightly more robust. Although this highly strung horse is not particularly hardy, it does have great stamina. It is useful for riding and light draft. Bay, black, chestnut, and gray are the usual

colors, and the average height is between 14.3hh and 15.2hh.

The **SAN FRATELLO** comes from the Nebrodi Mountains in the Sicilian province of Messina. It is bred ferally in the local woods and is a very tough, hardy horse with a lively temperament. Its root stock is unknown, and it has received infusions of Sardinian Anglo-Arab, Anglo-Arab, Salerno, and Nonius blood. Although the head can tend toward being rather large, it is of basically good riding conformation and is used for riding, trekking, and pack work. The coat is bay, brown, or black, and the height ranges from 15hh to 16hh.

The **CALABRESE** from Calabria is a medium-weight riding horse of Arab derivation. In the Middle Ages it was crossed with Andalusian blood, and in the 20th century Thorough-bred blood has been used to increase its height and elegance. All solid colors occur, and the horse usually stands between 16hh and 16.2hh.

The **BARDIGIANO** from Bardi is a medium to heavy pony which seems to derive from indigenous mountain

OUT OF THE DARK AGES

The Bardigiano traces back to the Dark Ages, probably descending from indigenous mountain ponies and Belgian stock.

types plus the barbarian Belgian stock introduced to the area during the Dark Ages. The most common color is black, but bay and brown also occur. The breed has an unmistakable Arab look about the face and eyes despite its chunky build. It is quick and some-times highly strung, but generally docile and willing. It usually stands between 13.1hh and 14.1hh.

The **AVELIGNESE** is the bigger and stockier Italian version of the famous Haflinger. The breed is found in Italy, Austria, Switzerland, and Germany in large numbers. In Italy it is used mainly for pack and draft work.

CHANGE FOR THE BETTER
Below *The original wiry, small horses which formed the foundation for the Sardinian Anglo-Arab were bred up with eastern and Spanish blood; present-day Thoroughbred infusions have greatly improved and changed the type.*

UNKNOWN BACKGROUND
Left and above *The San Fratello's foundation stock is unknown. It is bred ferally on Sicily.*

ITALIAN COW PONY
Left *Originally a plain-looking stock horse, today's Maremmana shows the result of modern infusions of Italian Thoroughbred blood.*

GOOD JUMPER
Right and above right *A ride-and-drive horse, also used for farm work and mule breeding, the Murgese is a surprisingly good jumper and quite a popular riding horse.*

ITALIAN COUSIN
Right and above left *The Italian branch of the famous Haflinger, the Avelignese has the same attractive qualities, but is slightly taller and a little heavier. In Italy, it is used mainly for pack and draft work, not for riding.*

AUSTRIA

The **PINZGAUER** is the Austrian version of the German Noriker. The breed was developed by the Romans about 2,000 years ago, principally in the Austrian provinces of Styria and Carinthia, by mating heavy warhorses with local stock. This produced a hardy, sure-footed, strong horse which was used for war, heavy transportation and agriculture. The breed was further improved in the 16th century by the addition of Neapolitan and Andalusian blood. The coat is usually bay or chestnut. Occasionally roan, black, brown, gray, or spotted coats occur. The Pinzgauer is heavy with a large head and thick sturdy legs, which suit it to heavy work in agriculture and forestry. The mane and tail are luxurious and often wavy. This breed usually stands between 15.2hh and 16.3hh.

POLAND

It is often accepted that the **TARPAN** was one of the two progenitors of all modern breeds of light horses and ponies. The word tarpan is an Eastern European colloquial term meaning wild horse. The animal normally regarded as the true Tarpan became extinct in the wild in 1879 and in captivity in 1887. In the 20th century the Polish government gathered together as many Tarpan-like animals as possible and reintroduced them to the forests of Bialowieza and Popielno.

The modern animal is probably quite like the extinct type, although it is heavier. It occurs in shades of dun with a dark eel stripe down the back and zebra stripes on its legs. It has a full black tail and a bushy, mainly black mane. The head is heavy and can be large. The neck is short and

WILD AND FREE
Extinct in its wild form, this pony is a "reconstituted Tarpan" bred from ponies with Tarpan genes.

thick. The withers are low, and the back is rather long and straight with sloping quarters. The shoulders are short, but sloping, and the chest is deep. The legs are slender and strong. The Tarpan is tough and hardy with an independent and uncooperative temperament. It stands at about 13hh. Quite different is the **SOKOLSKY**, a heavyish, strong horse used for heavy draught and agricultural work in Poland. It was developed during the 20th century, mainly using Ardennais, Breton, Belgian Brabant, Anglo-Norman and possibly Suffolk Punch blood. It is very enduring with a docile, willing temperament. It is usually chestnut, but also brown and bay, standing around 15hh to 16hh.

GERMANY

The **RHINELAND HEAVY DRAFT**, which is also known as the **RHENISH** and the **GERMAN COLDBLOOD**, is extremely rare. This breed was derived from the Ardennais in the last quarter of the 19th century, but also contains much Belgian Brabant blood and lesser amounts of Jutland, Shire, Suffolk, Clydesdale, and Boulonnais blood. It has been used as the foundation of various German and European heavy horse breeds.

The Rhineland Heavy Draft is strong and hardy with a powerful, well-balanced body, short, strong legs, and a characteristic double-sided mane. It has a proud air, and is calm and quiet to handle. The coat can be red roan with black points, chestnut with flaxen mane and tail, or bay. It stands between 16hh and 17hh.

The **BEBERBECK** originated in northwestern Germany where the stud of that name was founded almost two hundred years ago. The breed was produced by crossing local Beberbeck mares with Arab stallions, then resulting mares were crossed with English Thoroughbreds. The next cross was with local Beberbeck stallions to retain type and substance. The result is a heavy Thoroughbred type, which is deep through the girth. It is usually bay or chestnut and stands at 16hh or more. Few Beberbeck horses exist today because the breed has been mostly amalgamated in the German and Eastern European modern warmblood sports horses.

The **NORIKER** (also known as the **SOUTH GERMAN COLDBLOOD**) is the German type of the Austrian Pinzgauer. It contains much Arab, Thoroughbred, Norfolk Trotter, Oldenburg, Norman, Holstein, and Cleveland Bay blood.

One of the rarest native German riding horses is the **HESSIAN AND RHEINLANDER PFALZ**. This heavy-weight hunter-type has now been mostly incorporated into the German warmblood competition horses. The few original types which remain are active, strong, and good-natured. They occur in most colors and stand at about 16hh.

The elegant **WURTTEMBURG** can be traced back to the 16th century when it was developed at the famous Marbach Stud in Western Germany. It was developed by crossing native mares with Suffolk Punch, Caucasian, and Arab stallions, then later by introducing Trakehner, Oldenburg, Nonius, Norman, and Anglo-Norman blood.

This breed was developed as a cobby type of working horse for farmers, but is now much lighter. It is a tough, good-natured horse with a compact body and a good action, popular for riding and draft work. The coat can be bay, brown, black, or chestnut, and it stands at about 16.1hh.

RHINELANDER FROM DRAFT TO RIDING
This Rhinelander is an example of a performance animal bred from the basic stock of the Rhineland Heavy Draft and others to create a warmblooded riding horse.

HUNGARY

The **MURAKOZ**, or **MURAKOSI**, is a Hungarian heavy draft and agricultural horse which was developed during the early 20th century by crossing Brabant, Ardennais, Percheron, and Noriker blood with native animals. It is now bred in two types: one light and one heavy. Both have a well-balanced conformation, which results in great strength. A docile and willing nature is characteristic. The coat is either bay, brown, black, gray, or chestnut, with a lighter mane, tail, and feather. The Murakoz stands at about 16hh.

HEAVY AND LIGHTER TYPES
The Murakoz is bred in two types: a large, heavy type and a lighter, but still draft, type.

pony or for light draft work.

They stand between 11.2hh and 12.3hh and are usually brown or black, with few white markings. The neck is relatively long and thin, the head can be heavy and has a straight profile. The body is rounded, and the legs and feet are tough.

GREECE

The **PENEIA** from the Peloponnese, attractive in appearance and suggestive of Arab blood in its veins, is noted for its stamina and co-operation. It is used as a pack and riding pony and for light farm and draught work. Most colours occur, and it is about 10.1hh to 14hh in height. The stallions are used on donkeys to produce hinnies.

A third Greek pony breed used for similar purposes is the **PINDOS**

SPAIN

The **HISPANO-ARAB** is also known as the **SPANISH ANGLO-ARAB** and the **PENINSULA HORSE**. It is a mixture of Iberian, Thoroughbred, and Arab blood and has strong Arab characteristics. Though it has a slightly higher action than an Arab or Anglo-Arab.

The Hispano-Arab stands between 14.3hh and 16hh, and tends to be bay, gray, or chestnut. Because of its agility and bravery, this spirited and graceful breed is often used to test and herd young fighting bulls. It is also popular as a competition horse for dressage or jumping.

The **BALEARIC** horse from Majorca bears a striking resemblance to the horses illustrated on ancient Greek pottery and coins, and to those illustrated on the Parthenon frieze. It is technically a pony, standing at about 14hh, but has many horse-like characteristics. It has a delicate, but usually Roman-nosed, head with ears that point backward. Its bristly, upright mane adorns a thick, arched neck, and its body is strong, with fine legs. The Balearic moves with a graceful, free action. It is quiet natured and is often used for harness and farm work.

The **GALICIAN AND ASTURIAN PONY**, mainly found living semiferal in the harsh environment of the Asturian Mountains in western Spain, is in danger of becoming extinct. Originating from the Old Celtic pony type, it is suitable for use as a riding

BEST OF BOTH WORLDS
The Hispano-Arab is largely of Iberian and Arab genes.

from Thessaly and Epirus. Attractive in appearance, the Pindos has infusions of Oriental, probably Arab, blood and is a lightweight, tough animal, frugal and hardy with much stamina and a quiet temperament. Mainly gray, it occurs in other solid colors and stands around 12hh to 13hh.

The **SKYROS** pony of the island of that name is probably one of the purest breeds in the world. It resembles the Tarpan, which suggests that it descended fairly directly from that ancient breed. The Skyros has little substance, a ewe neck, and poor front conformation with an upright shoulder and cow hocks. It has a hard life and is mainly used on the island for fetching water and carrying packs, though it is also ridden sometimes. Those animals kept in better conditions improve considerably in strength and appearance. The Skyros may be bay, brown, gray, or dun and usually stands at about 10hh.

BOSNIA-HERZEGOVINA

The **BOSNIAN** pony probably directly descends from the ancient Tarpan with the addition of some Oriental blood. This combination has produced a substantial, hardy pony with a dependable and docile nature. It is used as a riding or pack pony and for farm work and light draft work, and makes an important contribution to the economy of the area. It comes in most solid colors and stands between 12.1hh and 14hh.

BULGARIA

The quality **PLEVEN** horse breed is little known outside Bulgaria. It is basically a European-continental type of Anglo-Arab. It was founded in the 19th century by crossing local half-Thoroughbred and pure Arab mares with Russian Anglo-Arab stallions. Arab, Gidran, and English Thoroughbred blood has also been used. The

Pleven is an excellent all-round riding and sporting horse with particularly good jumping ability.

Although it has good stamina and is quite hardy, this breed requires reasonable care. It is usually chestnut and stands around 15.3hh.

PORTUGAL

Both the Garrano and Sorraia breeds of Portugal played a part in the foundation of other Iberian breeds, and through them have influenced breeds all over the world.

The **GARRANO** pony (also known as the **MINHO**) is an ancient pony breed which originates from the River Minho area along the border with Spain. Animals with its likeness can be seen in local cave paintings and carvings. This substantial pony is used as a pack and riding pony and at one time was used for racing.

ISLAND PONY
The little Skyros of Greece has a tough life, eking out a hardworking existence on poor keep. It probably descends fairly directly from the Tarpan.

The Garrano is strong and hardy with an intelligent, quiet temperament. Its head can be heavy, and the neck is thick on an upright shoulder. It is usually chestnut and stands between 10hh and 12hh.

The indigenous **SORRAIA** pony is a light, Tarpan type of pony with the primitive eel stripe down its back and zebra stripes on its legs. Although this breed generally has an independent character and is not particularly strong, it does have good stamina and is often used for riding and pack work. It is usually dun or gray and stands between 12.2hh and 13hh.

RUSSIA, BALTIC STATES, AND SCANDINAVIA

RUSSIA

The **BEETEWK** was developed as an agricultural heavy horse; few now remain, with most such animals bred in small numbers locally or having been absorbed into individual countries' modern performance warmblood breeds.

The Beetewk breed originated with native heavy breeds in the province of Veronej, specifically around the Beetewk River, which created fertile breeding grounds for horses. In the early 18th century, Tsar Peter the Great imported Dutch stallions to mate with the good local mares and those offspring were crossed with Orlov Trotters. This created an active heavy horse with good trotting ability, able to be used for agriculture and as coach horses.

Their breeding grounds were subsequently turned to arable uses, and their size consequently diminished to a little over 16hh, but they retained great strength along with an enthusiasm for their job, endurance, and good action plus tractability.

A number still existed early in the 20th century, but it is impossible to determine their present-day status.

The **VLADIMIR HEAVY DRAFT** was developed in Russia after the Russian Revolution by crossing existing stock of the Cleveland Bay, Suffolk Punch, Ardennais, Clydesdale, Percheron, and Shire. This produced a strong horse, suitable for heavy draft work, which was registered as a breed in 1946. In order to be registered, each individual is subject to strict selection trials involving heavy draft work and endurance tests.

Although the breed is heavy, it has a majestic air and upstanding posture. It comes in chestnut, bay, brown, or black and stands between 15.2hh and 16hh. It is still used in the former U.S.S.R. for heavy draft work, farming, and transportation.

The **SOVIET HEAVY DRAFT** was developed early in the 20th century to meet demand for a strong, compact animal for haulage and farm work. Native mares were crossed with Belgian and Percheron stallions to establish the type.

The Soviet Heavy Draft has an easy and nimble gait and is hardy and very strong. It has a quiet temper-

UPSTANDING POSTURE
A mixture of English, Scottish, and French breeds, this Russian breed, the Vladimir Heavy Draft, was developed during the 19th century. It has strength without coarseness.

ament, but is energetic and willing. It is usually chestnut or bay and stands at about 15.2hh. This is probably the most common heavy draft type of horse in the former U.S.S.R.

BALTIC STATES

The Toric's ancestor, the **KLEPPER**, was distributed throughout the Baltic States, particularly in Estonia. A small, stocky type about 13hh to 15hh, Kleppers were bred into several different types. All resembled the original wild horse, possessing its characteristics of hardiness, eel stripe, frequent dun coloring, and prepotency in breeding. There are likely to be few, if any, Kleppers of the old type left, their having been absorbed into other breeds as foundation stock.

The **VIATKA** is one breed the Klepper founded. Another member of the original northern pony type, it frequently comes in the primitive dun coloring with eel stripe and dark points, but it is seen in other colors. It is highly resistant to bitter winters, with an exceptionally thick winter coat and apparently a thick layer of fat under the skin.

It has an independent, spirited temperament, is quick-thinking, tough, extremely frugal, and energetic. The Viatka is used for farm work, light draft, general transportation, and riding. They are often seen pulling the famous troikas, harnessed to these sleighs three across, with the outer ones being made to go with their heads turned to the outside. In height, the Viatka is about 13hh to 14hh.

ESTONIA

The **TORIC**, which is also known as the **ESTONIAN KLEPPER** and **DOUBLE KLEPPER**, was developed in Estonia during the 19th century by crossing numerous breeds. These include the Klepper, Arab, Hackney, East Friesian, Ardennais, Hanoverian, Orlov, Thoroughbred, and East Prussian.

The Toric is a sturdy cob type which is an enduring and willing worker with a patient and docile temperament. It comes in both a light and heavy form, the lighter of which is mainly used as a riding horse and can jump well. The heavy form is used for farm work and light and medium draft. The Toric is usually brown, chestnut, bay, or gray, and stands between 15hh and 15.2hh.

LITHUANIA

The **ZEMAITUKA** is an indigenous pony of the area and is thought to have descended from the Asiatic Wild Horse. It is a firmly fixed ancient type and retains the primitive eel stripe on its back. Its harsh environment has made the Zemaituka frugal and hardy, and it seems indifferent to the bitter weather. It also has enormous stamina. Individuals can routinely cover 40 miles (60km) in a day.

The Zemaituka has a compact, muscular conformation. It is usually brown, bay, black, or dun, and it stands at about 13hh. Although it has a spirited temperament, it is co-operative and plays an important part in the local economy as a light draft and farm pony.

SWEDEN

The **NORTH SWEDISH HORSE** is a coldblooded animal with both a light and heavy strain. The lighter strain is also known as the **NORTH SWEDISH TROTTER** or the **NORTH-HESTUR**. Al-though the North Swedish Horse was bred for heavy draft and farm work, the lighter strain has a trotting speed of ⅝ mile (1 km) in 1 min 30 secs – faster than some true trotting breeds.

Both strains are hardy and strong, and have a long life span, and a docile and willing temperament. This breed is well known for its expressive eyes. The North Swedish Horse comes in most solid colors and generally stands between 15hh and 15.2hh.

DENMARK

The **JUTLAND** horse is one of the old, massive types. It dates back to the Viking era (about A.D.800) and is said to have been ridden by knights in armor. When the Danes invaded the British Isles, they took Jutland horses with them to use in agriculture and for heavy transportation, and this breed probably helped to found the Suffolk Punch. Other blood has been used in the Jutland breed over the ages, including the Cleveland Bay, the Yorkshire Coach Horse, and the Ardennais.

The Jutland is willing, strong, and energetic, with a calm and cooperative temperament. It is usually chestnut, although roan, bay, and gray also occur. This massive, docile horse has very strong legs and large feet to carry its heavy frame and stands between 15hh and 16.2hh.

FINLAND

The **FINNISH** (also known as the **FINNISH UNIVERSAL**) is a cold-blooded type of heavy horse. It was developed from native Finnish ponies crossed with other breeds. Originally there was both a light and heavy strain, but only the light type still exists. It is suitable for farm work, light to medium draft, riding, and trotting races.

The Finnish horse is a hard and willing worker with much strength and energy. It has a chunky build with light, strong legs and a smallish, square, heavy head. It has a kind temperament and gentle eyes. Chestnut is the most common color, though bay, gray, brown, and black also occur. The Finnish stands between 16hh and 17hh.

FROM PLOWING TO RACING
The Finnish was formerly bred in a heavy and a lighter type. Today the lighter type can perform as a racing trotter.

THE AMERICAS

The **KIGER MUSTANG** is claimed
to be the purest Barb-descended or
Spanish feral horse in the world today.
They have the conformation of both
the Tarpan and Oriental hotblooded
horses from which the original old
Iberian horses were bred

AMERICAN MINIATURE HORSES
are popular as pets and as
introductory equine for youngsters as
they are no more than 34 inches (86
cm) tall at the withers. The breed now
has a closed stud book managed by
the American Miniature Horse
Association.

UNITED STATES

The **ASSATEAGUE** and **CHINTOTEAGUE**
ponies live on the uninhabited islands
of those names off the coast of
Maryland and Virginia. Although they
are technically ponies, standing at
about 12hh, they have horse-like
characters and heads.

The **CAYUSE INDIAN PONY** and
the **CHICKASAW INDIAN PONY** are two
strains which stem from the earliest
imports to the Americas of Iberian
and Barb horses. The Cayuse Indian
Pony was bred specifically to produce
a hardy, strong animal with great
speed. It has inherited the Iberian's
noble bearing and probably also has
genetic links to the Missouri Fox
Trotter.

A Registry for the **NATIONAL
SHOW HORSE** was started in 1981 by
Gene La Croix mainly to extend the
impact of the Arabian horse through
the N.S.H.R., the breed being a blend
of Arabian and Saddlebred in varying
proportions. Horses can take after
either "parent" breed.

CHECKERED HISTORY
*Containing the blood of several
breeds, the Cayuse itself helped
found several American breeds.*

MADE IN AMERICA
The Cayuse Indian Pony has a very mixed ancestry and history, but the best of them show Iberian ancestry. The Cayuse people developed the breed, and sold and traded them back to settlers.

CANADA

The **SABLE ISLAND PONY** is sometimes referred to as the native pony of Canada. However, Canada has no indigenous horses. The feral Sable Island Ponies derived from a group of French animals which were brought from New England in the 18th century. Since then, the ponies have adapted to the harsh living conditions found off the coast of Nova Scotia – bitter winters, no shelter, and little food. The pony has a heavy head on a short ewe neck. The shoulders are short and the hind-quarters are sloping, often with cow hocks. However, the pony is sturdy with a strong, straight back and tough legs and feet. If it is caught young, it can make a docile and willing riding pony or can be used for light draft work. The usual color is chestnut, and the height is about 14.2hh.

BRAZIL

The **CAMPOLINO** horse is a slightly heavier version of Brazil's Manglarga and as such has a great deal of Arab blood. It is used for light draft work and stands at about 15hh. The coat can be gray, sorrel, roan, or bay.

FRENCH CANADIANS
The Sable Island Pony is descended from French horses brought to Sable Island almost 300 years ago.

AUSTRALASIA, ASIA, AND AFRICA

IRAN

The **PERSIAN ARAB** is one of the oldest Arabian horse strains in the world and is believed to trace back to 2000 B.C. It comes in all solid colors and stands at about 15hh.

Crossing the Persian Arab stallions with Turcoman mares produces an excellent riding horse called the **TCHENARANI**, which is about 300 years old. The **JAF** from Kurdistan and the **DARASHOURI** (also called the **SHIRAZI**) from the Fars region are closely related to the Persian Arab.

The **PLATEAU PERSIAN** is a relatively new breed which has been developed from the Persian Arab, Jaf, and Darashouri. This is a strong, sure-footed riding horse which stands at about 15hh and is gray, bay, or chestnut in color.

The **PAHLAVAN** has been produced at the former Royal Stud in Iran (Persia) since the 1950s by combining Persian Arab and Plateau Persian blood with Thoroughbred blood. It is a bigger horse than the other two breeds (about 15.3hh), which comes in all solid colors and is used for racing and jumping.

TURKMENISTAN

The **IOMUD** is a direct descendant of the old Turkmene breed and has all the qualities of a steppe Oriental horse type. It has developed great resistance to desert conditions, and is a tough horse which can exist on little food and water.

The Iomud is strong, with great stamina. It is enthusiastic but co-operative, and makes a good riding horse, particularly for jumping and cross-country racing. Gray is the most common color, and there are also some blacks, chestnuts, and bays. The Iomud generally stands between 14.2hh and 15hh.

TADZHIKISTAN

The **LOKAI** is a small, desert horse which dates back to the wiry ponies of the Lokai tribe in the 16th century. These ponies were later developed by the Uzbeks, who added Arab, Iomud, and Karabair blood. It is a fine animal which stands on average at 14.3hh. In its homeland it is used for riding and pack work, and elsewhere it is popular for competitive riding.

UZBEKISTAN

The **KARABAIR** is a famous breed of hot-blooded mountain horse which derives its nature from a mixture of indigenous pony stock and Arab

WORK AND PLEASURE
An ancient and typical steppe/desert hotblood, the Lokai is used for both riding and pack work, but makes a good competition horse elsewhere.

blood. There are three types: a heavier one used for harness work, a light type for riding, and an in-between type. The Karabair has itself been used in the development of other breeds, such as the Don.

The Karabair is tough, energetic, nimble, and sure-footed with good stamina. It has a fine conformation and a fiery spirit. It is used for riding and pack work in the mountains and is also suitable for light draft work. The Karabair can be any solid color and stands between 14.2hh and 15hh.

KIRGIZSTAN

The **NOVOKIRGIZ** (also known as the **NEW KIRGIZ**) is a new version of an ancient mountain breed of Mongolian origins used by nomadic tribesmen. During the early 20th century, Don, Anglo-Don, and Thoroughbred blood were introduced, and this mixture has produced a well-muscled, small riding and pack horse.

The Novokirgiz is sensible, sure-footed, and tough, with good stamina and strength. It is an active and willing worker with an easy temperament. It can be bay, brown, chestnut, or gray in color, and stands between 14.1hh and 15.1hh.

In Kirgizstan the Novokirgiz is used for riding, harness work, pack work, and sport (especially long-distance racing). Its milk is used to make kumiss – the traditional alcoholic drink of the region.

MOUNTAIN HOME
A mountain horse shown in its home environment, the Karabair, bred in three types, is extremely nimble, active, and enduring, and is used for riding, pack, and light draft work.

KEEN BUT COOPERATIVE
The long legs shown here are typical of the old eastern Kustanair breed, which is bred in riding and light draft varieties.

KAZAKHSTAN

The **KUSTANAIR** is an old Oriental breed which has been developed by adding other blood. The lighter riding horse type contains Thoroughbred blood, and the light draft type contains some Orlov and Don blood. Both have a well-balanced conformation with long legs. They are strong with good endurance and are easy to keep, with a keen yet manageable temperament. The coat can be any solid color, and generally this breed stands at about 15.1hh.

The **KAZAKII** pony was traditionally used for herding the livestock of nomadic tribes, and its milk was used for making kumiss – the traditional alcoholic drink of the region. It has been developed into two types from its Mongolian origins.

The heavier Dzhabe type, which contains much Don blood, is an exceptionally tough, chunky pony with a short, thick neck. The lighter Adacyev type contains more Karabair, Iomud, and Akhal-Teké blood, and is not so hardy.

The colors found in Kazakhstan are bay, brown, liver chestnut, dun, gray, and light chestnut with a flaxen mane and tail. The average size is between 12.1hh and 13.1hh.

MONGOLIA

The **MONGOLIAN** pony, which was bred by the war-like Mongolian tribes, is probably derived from the ancient Asiatic Wild Horse. It is possibly one of the most influential root sources of breeding stock in the world, and its genes can probably be found in all today's Thoroughbreds, Arabs, and their crosses and derivatives.

In addition to being relatively fast, this compact pony is extremely patient, tough, and hardy, and has good endurance. It is strong with a short, thick neck and a heavy head and sturdy legs. The shoulders are sloping and well muscled, the back is straight and strong, and the quarters are long and sloping. The coat can be black, brown, bay, dun, palomino, chestnut, or gray roan. The pony generally stands between 12hh and 14hh.

The Mongolian is used for riding, herding, farming, pack work, and draft, as well as for the popular Asian sport of polo.

INDONESIA

The **BATAK** pony from the island of Sumatra is a cross between indigenous mares and Arab stallions. The Batak is a lively, light riding pony with a calm temperament and a pleasing appearance. It may be any color and stands between 12hh and 13hh.

The **BALI** pony, from the island of the same name, is probably derived from the Asiatic Wild Horse. It has retained the ancient features of a primitive dun coloring, with an eel stripe down the back and an upright mane.

It is a strong, willing pony with a particularly docile nature. It is mainly used to give pony rides on the tourist beaches and as a pack pony. The Bali pony has low withers, a straight, short back, and sloping quarters and sturdy legs. Its head is rather large, with slanting eyes and small ears. The pony stands between 12hh and 13hh.

The **TIMOR** island pony probably descends from the Asiatic Wild Horse and the Tarpan. It looks similar to the Greek Skyros pony. Although it has poor overall conformation and shows little sign of strength, it is important as a riding pony on the island and is often used for light farm work. The Timor is nimble and enduring with a docile, willing temperament. It may be bay, brown, or black, and stands between 9hh and 10hh.

The **JAVA** pony is similar to the Timor, but it is bigger and stronger with a better conformation, which is probably due to Arab influence. It is used for light draft work (in the two-wheeled taxis that are common on the island of Java), riding, and light agricultural work. The Java may be any color and usually stands at about 12hh.

The **SANDALWOOD** pony of the islands of Sumba and Sumbawa has received considerable amounts of Arab blood in its past. It has good endurance and speed, and is used for bareback racing over distances of around 3 miles (5km), pack work, light draft work, and some farm work. The Sandalwood may be any color and stands about 12hh.

ARAB INFLUENCE
This Java pony has had the benefit of Arab blood, which makes it bigger and stronger than others in this region. It is a widespread "taxi" pony on Java and is also used for riding and other light draft work.

The **SUMBA** pony, from Sumba and Sumbawa, bears a close resemblance to the Mongolian and Chinese ponies. This pony has a heavy head with almond eyes, an upright shoulder, straight back, and sloping croup. The Sumba is most commonly primitive dun with an eel stripe and dark points, and stands at about 12hh. It is this breed that is used for equestrian "dancing" competitions throughout Indonesia in which the horses wear bells on their knees and perform dance steps while carrying young boys.

INDIA

The most common pony in India is the **DEHLI** pony, which is identical to the Indonesian Batak.

The **KATHIAWARI** and **MARWARI** ponies are almost indistinguishable and are taken as one breed. The original native ponies on which the breed is based are said to have descended from animals brought by Alexander the Great (356–323 B.C.). Fifty years ago, the respected equestrian author Reginald Sheriff Summerhays, described the breed as "a wretched little creature, thin, weedy, very narrow . . . but with feet and legs of cast iron, amazing toughness and powers of endurance and the ability to live on next to nothing."

Arab blood has been mixed with this original stock to produce a hardy pony with a light body, sloping shoulders, fine legs, and sickle hocks. The ears point inward and almost meet in the middle. Most colors occur, including cream and particolors. These ponies generally stand at about 14hh.

The **BHUTIA** and **SPITI** ponies from the Himalaya region are almost identical to each other and have common origins with the Tibetan pony. Although they display great endurance in their native highlands, neither is able to tolerate hot, humid conditions.

Both the Spiti and the slightly larger Bhutia are strong, compact, and thick set. Both are gray in color and are noted for their fickle temperaments. The Spiti stands around 12hh, and the Bhutia is usually around 13hh.

The **MANIPURI** is the native polo pony of India. This fast, quick-witted, and eager pony is thought to be a descendant of the Asiatic Wild Horse and the Mongolian pony, and it was probably brought to India by invading Tartars. The Manipuri stands between 11hh and 13hh, and the most common colors are bay, brown, chestnut, and gray.

TIBET

The native pony of Tibet is the **NANFAN** (also known as the **TIBETAN**). It derives originally from the Mongolian pony and the Chinese pony, and is related to the Bhutia and Spiti ponies of the Far East. This strong, robust animal is very versatile and is a willing worker that is easy to handle. The most common color is yellow dun, but most colors occur. The average size is 12.1hh.

The **RIWOCHE** breed was discovered in September 1995 by the French explorer Michel Peissel and is believed to be a missing link in horse evolution. It greatly resembles the ponies depicted in cave paintings in the area. The Riwoche has an angular shape with a heavy head and a bristly mane. The coat is beige with an eel stripe down the back and zebra markings on the legs. The local Bon-po people of the Riwoche valley round up the ponies and use them for work.

CHINA

The **CHINESE** pony (also called the **CHINA** pony) is another breed based on the Mongolian pony and the Asiatic Wild Horse. It is usually a primitive yellow dun with a black eel stripe, dark points, and zebra stripes on the legs, although other solid colors do occur.

This pony is hardy, strong, and sure-footed. It has a deep body and upright shoulders. Its hindquarters are short and sloping, and its legs are sturdy and fine. It has a difficult temperament and is mainly used for light farm work, transportation, pack work and riding. It stands at between 12hh and 13hh.

PRIMITIVE TYPE
Probably closely related to the Mongolian and Chinese ponies, the Sumba shows primitive coloring and markings with a large head. It is noted for "dancing" performances carrying young boys.

JAPAN

The **HOKKAIDO** pony is another offshoot of the Mongolian pony, and has the characteristic dun coloring with an eel stripe and black points. It is tough and frugal, and stands at about 13hh. It is used for general riding, pack work, and transportation.

BURMA

The **SHAN** pony (also called the **BURMESE** pony) was bred by the hill tribes of the Shan states in eastern Burma from descendants of the Mongolian pony. It is a slightly rangy, hardy, sure-footed pony with an

BACK TO THE WILD
The Brumby are feral descendants of introduced stock. Many show primitive coloring, conformation, and spirit.

upright shoulder. It has an unpredictable and uncooperative temperament. It comes in most solid colors and stands at about 13hh. It has been used for polo, but is more suited to pack work and mountain riding.

NIGERIA

The **NIGERIAN** pony is probably descended from Barb horses which were brought to Nigeria by nomadic tribes. Although it is small (standing at about 14.2hh), it is horse-like in character. It is very strong and has good stamina and a quiet, willing temperament. Its main uses are as a pack and riding pony, and for light draft work.

LESOTHO

The **BASUTO** pony is descended originally from the Arab and Barb Cape horses brought to southern Africa by

Dutch settlers. It has deteriorated into a scraggy, badly conformed scrub pony which is very hardy and frugal. It comes in most solid colors and stands at about 14.1hh.

AUSTRALIA

Australia has no natural wild horses. The **BRUMBY** is a feral Australian type of horse which is the result of numerous types of imported horses and ponies being turned free or escaping into the bush. The Brumby has reverted in some aspects. For example, it has primitive coloring, and the average height has reduced over time to about 15hh. Its conformation is poor, with an upright shoulder, big head, and cow hocks. It is naturally independent, intelligent, and cunning.

Although the Brumby was a successful immigrant species, there are now very few left due to culling when attempts were made to control their proliferating numbers during the latter half of this century.

GLOSSARY

Action The way a horse moves. Good, straight action means that the hindlegs follow the forelegs exactly, moving straight from front to back with no sideways deviations; exceptions are Iberian-based breeds which often dish.

Aged Refers to a horse seven years and older.

Airs Movements, usually used in formal dressage. Artificial airs are gaits other than the formal walk, trot and canter, such as piaffe and passage. Airs above the ground are *Haute Ecole* movements performed with two or all feet off the ground such as the capriole, ballotade, etc.

Amble A smooth fast, lateral gait; a less vigorous version of the pace. Both hindleg and foreleg move forward at the same time.

Barrel The body of the horse between the shoulders and hips.

Blood horse A horse of thoroughbred and/or arab blood.

Bloodstock Thoroughbred horses bred for racing.

Blue feet Horn that is dense, blue-black in color.

Bow hocks Hocks which, when viewed from the back, turn outward from each other.

Broodmare A mare used for breeding.

Cannons The lower parts of the horse's legs between the fetlocks and the knees or hocks.

Carriage horse An elegant horse used for carriage-driving; usually with Thoroughbred blood in its ancestry.

Cart horse A large, heavy horse used for pulling carts.

Chestnuts Hard hornlike patches on the inside of the legs, just above the knee and just below the hocks. The shape of each horse's chestnuts is individual, so can be used in identification.

Clean heels/legged Naturally having no excess growth of hair (feather) around the fetlocks.

Coach horse A heavier type of horse than a carriage horse, used for pulling coaches.

Cob A stocky, sturdy type of animal around 15hh. Big-bodied and short-legged, it can carry a substantial weight.

Coldblood A horse, not a pony, of heavy, common or "cart" blood. The basis of warmblood breeds.

Colt A male entire (uncastrated) horse up to four years old.

Confirmation A horse's make-up and shape. The basic requirement of good confirmation is symmetry–the horse should look balanced.

Cow hocks Hocks which, when viewed from the back, turn in toward each other.

Dished face A profile which, when viewed fron the side, appears slightly concaved between eyes and nostrils. Regarded as highly desirable in Arabs. An over-exaggerated dish can hamper breathing at fast gaits due to constricted air passages.

Dishing An action in which the forelegs appear to be thrown outward in an arc. Regarded as a fault in most breeds it is, however, purposely favored in Iberian-type breeds, in which it is regarded as showy. When exaggerated, it can produce an uncomfortable sideways-rocking gait.

Docking The surgical removal of the tail. Now illegal in most countries.

Dorsal stripe Found usually in dun-colored animals, with "primitive" connections, this is a continuous strip of black, brown or dun hair, running from the neck to the tail.

Draft Refers to a horse drawing any type of vehicle, but is mostly associated with heavy breeds.

Elk lip An overhanging and somewhat floppy lip.

Entire A stallion; a horse which has not been castrated.

Ewe neck Where the neck appears to have a slightly concave "sag" to it, rather than an attractive convex arch.

Feather Copious hair around the fetlocks or entire lower legs. The opposite of clean-legged.

Filly A female horse under four years old.

Flexion The yielding of the lower jaw to the pressure of the bit; at the same time the neck is high and arched, and bent at the pole.

Foal A horse or pony under 1 year in age.

Forearm The upper part of the foreleg, above the knee.

Forelock The lock of hair which falls down the horse's forehead or face from between the ears.

Fox trot A gait in which the horse walks with the front feet and trots with the hind, the hind legs stepping into the foreprints and sliding forwards. The horse's head nods and the teeth clack together in time with the hoof beats.

Gait The correct term for the horse's different basic movements in action. Natural gaits are walk, trot, canter, and gallop; artificial ones are the running walk, fox trot, amble, and broken amble, pace, rack, or single-foot. The word "paces" is often incorrectly used.

Gaited horse An American term for a saddle or riding horse which can perform artificial as well as natural gaits. A three-gaited horse must show walk, trot, and canter. A five-gaited horse must also show a slow gait (running walk, fox trot, or amble) and a fast rack.

Gelding A castrated male horse.

Hand The unit of measurement of a horse still used in many countries. A hand measures 4in (10cm). In countries using the metric system, it is unusual to measure horses in hands.

harness horse A horse used for driving in harness rather than under saddle.

Haute Ecole/High School the so-called classical method of riding, practiced in many countries, said to descend from the simple, natural principles evolved, particularly, by the ancient Greeks. Refined and developed in the 17th and, especially, 18th centuries, *Haute Ecole* is today perpetuated most famously by the Spanish Riding School in Vienna, Austria, and the Cadre Noir at Saumur, France.

Heavy horse A horse of big, muscular build, often tall, very strong, and best suited to heavy transportation, forestry, or agricultural work.

Hogged/Roached Refering to the mane, when it has been removed by clipping.

Hot–blood Hot-bloods are horses of desert or steppe ancestry, that evolved in hot, dry climates. Normally taken as being the pure Thoroughbred or Arab breeds.

In–hand An animal being led as opposed to driven or ridden.

Knockkneed A horse in which the knees, viewed from the front, bend in toward each other. This is a confirmation fault.

Loins The kidney area just behind the saddle.

Mare A female equine four years old or older.

On the bit When a horse carries his head near vertically, with his mouth slightly below the rider's hand, he is said to be "on the bit."

Oriental Any breed which comes from the Orient, normally taken as being Asia.

Pacer A harness horse which races at the pace to a lightweight sulky.

Piebald A British and Irish term meaning a horse with large, irregular black and white patches.

Points Normally meaning mane (including forelock), tail, and lower legs. However, it is also used to mean "part", e.g. the points (parts) of the horse.

Race horse A horse bred for racing. Racehorses are mostly Thoroughbreds, although other breeds are used.

Rack The fifth gait of the American saddlebred. It is a four-beat gait, somewhat fast and flashy.

Riding horse A horse used for riding; a saddle horse.

Rig A horse with undescended testicle(s), capable of mating and reproducing. Often sold as geldings, when they can prove dangerous in inexperienced hands.

Roached An American term for *hogged*.

Roadster Now a term used only in showing classes, a roadster was a stylish, cob-type of horse able to trot fast for long periods.

Roan A coat pattern which is evenly sprinkled with white hairs and those of other colors. A blue roan's coat includes black and white hairs, a strawberry roan chestnut and white hairs, a yellow roan dun and white hairs, and a red roan brown with white hairs.

Saddle horse A horse used "undersaddle"; a riding horse.

Scopey/scopy Refers to a horse's action which has "scope" or long, free strides.

Skewbald A British and Irish term indicating a horse which has large, irregular patches of white and any other color, sometimes more then one. A horse that has *only* black and white, however, is called a piebald.

Stallion An "entire", male horse; i.e. not been castrated with both testicles descended.

Stifles The joints at the tops of the horse's second thigh bones or gaskins, the equivalent to the knee joint in humans.

Stud book A book recording the pedigree of individuals of a particular breed.

Type A horse of a particular, recognizable type which is not, however, a formal breed. The word is also used to describe an animal of a specific breed which is a good example of that breed, i.e. "showing good type" for the breed.

Undersaddle *See* Saddle horse

Warmblood In practice, a horse which is a cross between a hot-blood breed or type and a cold-blood breed or type. More specifically, warmbloods are taken to mean warmblooded horses originating from one of the continental European countries.

CARE AND MANAGEMENT

KEEPING A HORSE AT GRASS

Looking after and caring for a horse or pony is perhaps the greatest responsibility any rider faces. Having learned to ride, many riders aim at eventually having a horse of their own. It is worth remembering, though, that looking after a horse unaided—especially if it is stabled—can be a full-time occupation. One answer is to board the horse at a livery stable. Another is to get someone to help out during the day. Most of the other factors involved, such as feeding, watering, exercising, and grooming, are mainly matters of common sense.

Horses can either be stabled, kept at grass or the two systems can be combined. This means that the horse can run free during the day and have the shelter of a stable by night—except in hot weather, when the procedure should be reversed. Whichever system is adopted is a matter of choice, practicality, and the type of horse concerned. Ponies, for example, are usually sturdier and more resilient to extremes of climate than horses, particularly thoroughbreds and

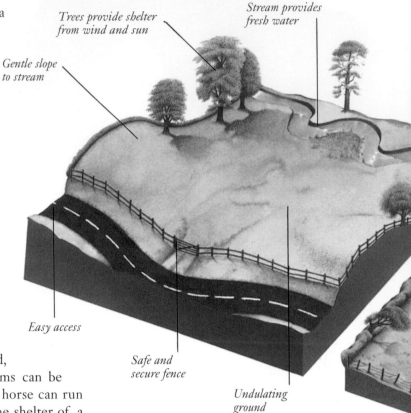

Trees provide shelter from wind and sun

Stream provides fresh water

Gentle slope to stream

Easy access

Safe and secure fence

Undulating ground

Below: Horses may roll to relax after being ridden, or just to deal with an irritating itch. Rolling can also be a symptom of colic, but generally it is simply a sign of pure enjoyment.

partbreds. Some thoroughbreds, for instance, should not be left outdoors over the winter. Nor can a horse being worked hard in, say, competitions be really kept fit enough, except by being cared for in a stable.

A combined system can also be adapted to suit the needs of a rider who is using his or her horse frequently, but cannot spare the time to keep it fully stabled. If the horse is being worked regularly in the spring or summer, say, it is a good idea to bring it into the stable first thing in the morning for the first extra feed that will be required. If the horse is to be ridden more than once a day, the same routine is followed as for a stabled horse until the afternoon, when the animal can be turned out for the night. If only one ride is possible, it can be turned out after the second feed, or, if it cannot be exercised at all, it can be turned out after the first feed.

The right field

Looking after a horse kept at grass is less time-consuming than looking after one kept in a stable. Among the advantages are the natural vitamins and the exercise the horse gets, but equal responsibility is still demanded from the owner. Statistics show that more accidents happen to horses left unattended in a field than those in a stable. They can kick each other, get tangled up in fences or gates, and quickly lose condition either through illness or just plain bad weather. Also, a horse should be visited every day, even if it is not being ridden. Horses are gregarious creatures—ideally, a horse should be kept in company with others—and they require affection. The ideal field is large—between six and eight acres. It should be undulating, well-drained, securely fenced by a high-grown hedge reinforced by post-and-rail fencing, with a clump of trees at one end and a gravel-bedded stream to provide fresh water. But this situation is often hard to achieve. It is usually considered that about 1 to 1½ acres per pony is adequate, provided that the grass is kept in good condition. Because horses are "selective grazers"—that is, they pick and choose where and what they eat—a paddock can become "horse sick." Some places will be almost bare of grass, while others will be overgrown with the rank, coarse grasses the horses have found unpalatable. In addition, the ground will almost certainly be infested with parasites, the eggs of which horses pass in their dung. If action is not taken, the horses are sure to become infected with worms. These fall into two categories, of which nematodes (roundworms) are by far the most important and potentially destructive. Of these, the most dangerous are bloodworms (Strongyles), which, untreated, can lead to severe loss of condition. Even though the horse is well-fed, it looks thin and "poor," with a staring coat; in the worst cases, anemia may develop or indigestion, colic, and enteritis.

As far as an infected horse is concerned, the treatment is regular worming, but it is far better to tackle the problem at its source by making sure that the field is maintained properly. A large field should be subdivided so that one area can be rested while another is being grazed. Ideally, sheep or cattle should be introduced on the resting areas, as they will eat the tall grasses the horses have rejected. They will also help reduce worm infestation, as their digestive juices kill horse worms. Harrowing is also essential as it aerates the soil, encouraging new grass to grow, and also scatters the harmful dung. If this fails, the manure must be collected at least twice a week and transferred to a compost heap.

Mowing after grazing, together with the use of a balanced fertilizer, also helps to keep a field in good condition, but horses should not be returned to their grazing too soon after it has been treated in this way. If in doubt, allow three weeks.

Bots are another problem for field-kept horses. For those affected, veterinary treatment is necessary.

Stagnant water

Coarse rank vegetation—unsuitable for feed

Barbed wire fence

Water trough with main supply

Field shelter

New safe fence

Stagnant pond fenced off

Pasture drained and improved

When selecting a field for a horse, always aim for the ideal (top left), or, if the conditions are bad (center), improve them (above). A good field must be big enough to provide sufficient grazing—about one horse to 1 1/4 acres (0.5 hectare). Grass should be of good quality with no poisonous weeds. A supply of fresh water—preferably running—and some natural shelter are essential. The center field is thoroughly bad, with dangerous fencing, stunted, wind-swept trees, no gate, and a foul pond. What can be done is shown (above). A new gate, sturdy fencing, water trough, field shelter, and improved pasture have transformed it into a suitable field for horses.

KEEPING A HORSE STABLED

There are two main reasons for keeping a horse in a stable. The first is that the horse may be too well-bred to live outside in all weathers, without seriously losing condition. The second is the amount of work the rider requires the horse to do. If a horse is being ridden a great deal, it must be fit enough to cope with its rider's demands without showing signs of distress, such as excessive sweating and blowing. Such a degree of fitness takes time to achieve and can only be maintained in a stable.

The ideal stable is also often easier to provide than the ideal field. It should be roomy, warm, well-ventilated yet draft-free, easy to keep clean, have good drainage and be vermin proof. It should face away from prevailing winds and have a pleasant outlook—preferably onto a stable yard or at least an area where something is often going on. The horse could be spending 22 hours a day in the stable and, unless there is something to hold its attention, it will probably become bored. This can lead, in turn, to the development of vices, such as weaving (rocking from side to side), box walking (a constant, restless wandering around the box), or cribbiting (gripping the manger or stable door with the teeth and drawing in a sharp breath). The first two vices may lead to loss of condition, the third to heaves.

Buying, renting, or building.

Any stable, whether it is bought, leased, converted, or specially built, must conform to certain basic standards which must be followed. An architect can either design a stable to your

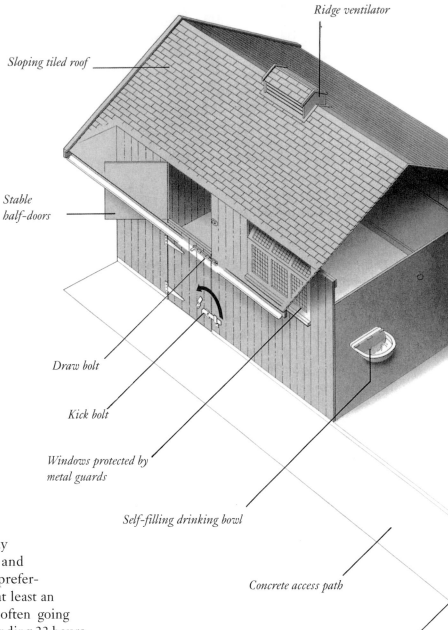

Ridge ventilator

Sloping tiled roof

Stable half-doors

Draw bolt

Kick bolt

Windows protected by metal guards

Self-filling drinking bowl

Concrete access path

Non-slip concrete floor

individual specifications or one can be bought ready-made. This type of stable is usually delivered in sections and erected on a pre-prepared concrete base. But, before committing yourself, always check your plans out with the local authority concerned. They might have to grant planning permission, and will certainly have regulations governing such crucial health factors as drainage.

The choice of site is very important. As far as possible, it should be level and well-drained, with easy access to the electricity and water supplies. The stable itself should be situated with the doorway facing the sun and the general layout should be planned to have all the essential elements—stable, feed room, tack room, and manure heap—conveniently close together.

The stable can either be a plain stall or a loose box; the latter is much more commonly used today, particularly in the UK and USA. The chief advantage of a stall is that it can be relatively small, which makes cleaning easier. But, as it is open at one end, the horse has to be kept tied up. The usual method is known as the rope and ball system, where the halter rope is passed through a ring on the manger and attached to a hardwood ball resting on the horse's bed. This helps to safeguard the horse against possible injury, while still allowing the horse some freedom of movement.

Most horse-owners prefer the loose box, as it allows the horse far more freedom to move around and so more comfort. Size here is all-important; cramming a 16hh hunter into a loose box built for a Shetland pony can only lead to trouble. As a rough guide, 12 ft (3½ m) square is probably the optimum size, rising to 13 ft (4 m) for horses over 16hh. It is worth bearing in mind that a child's first pony, say, will be outgrown in time, so the bigger the box the better.

Boxes should be square rather than oblong, so that the horse can more easily determine the mount of room it has to lie down or to roll. The box must be big enough to minimize the risk of the horse being "cast"—rolling over and being trapped on its back by the legs striking the wall. In its struggles to get up, the horse may injure itself severely. The ceiling height should allow plenty of clearance for the horse's head; 10 ft (3 m) is the absolute minimum.

Brick and stone are both durable and attractive building materials, but solid concrete blocks, or timber may be cheaper. Both walls and roof should be insulated, which will keep the stable warmer when the weather is cold and cooler when it is hot.

The floor must be hard-wearing, nonabsorbent and slip-proof. A well-compacted concrete base is perfectly adequate, provided that it is made with a loam-free aggregate and treated with a proprietary nonslip coating after laying.

Alternatively, roughen the surface with a scraper before the concrete sets. Make sure that the floor slopes slightly—a slope of about one in sixty from front to rear is ideal—so that urine can drain away easily. An alternative is to cut a narrow gully along one inside wall leading to a channel in the wall and so to an outside drain. The channel should be fitted with a trap to stop rats from getting in, and cleared of dirt and debris daily.

The usual type of stable door is made in two halves, the top half being kept open for ventilation. This should be planned to make sure that the horse gets plenty of fresh air but no drafts, as these can lead to it catching colds and chills. The best position for a window is high on the wall opposite the door so that sufficient cross-ventilation can be provided. Make sure it is fitted with shatterproof glass, and covered with an iron grille. Otherwise, vents can be built in the roof to allow stale air to escape. They should be protected by cowls.

Doors must be wide and high enough for a horse to pass through without the risk of injury; 4 ft (1.5 m) is the minimum width, 7½ ft (2.25 m) the minimum height. Make sure that the door opens outward so that access is easy and that strong bolts are fitted to both halves of the door. On the lower door, two bolts are necessary—an ordinary sliding bolt at the top and a kick bolt, operated by the foot, at the bottom. The top half needs only one bolt. Remember that the material used must be strong enough to withstand the kicking of a restless horse. Inside the stable, kicking boards will help with this problem.

Electricity is the only adequate means of lighting the stable. The light itself should be protected by safety glass or an iron grille and all wiring should be housed in galvanized conduits beyond the horse's reach. Switches must be waterproof, properly insulated, and, whenever possible, fitted outside the stable.

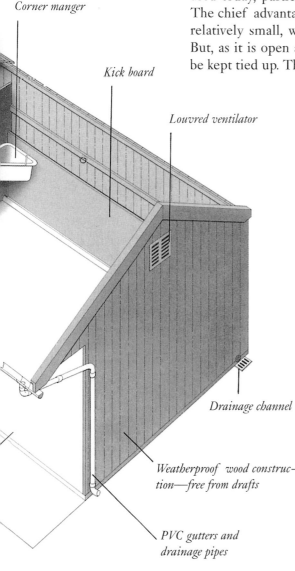

Corner manger

Kick board

Louvred ventilator

Drainage channel

Weatherproof wood construction—free from drafts

PVC gutters and drainage pipes

Above: Inside and outside views of two loose boxes planned with the comfort of the horse and ease of maintenance as the first considerations.

Fixtures and fittings

The basic rule to follow is the fewer fittings, the better, to minimize the risk of possible injury. The only essential is a means of tying the horse up. Normally, this consists of two rings, fixed to bolts that pass right through the stable wall. One ring should be at waist height and the other at head height. All other fittings and fixtures in the stable are a matter of individual preference.

Fixed mangers positioned at breast level and secured either along a wall or in a corner of the loose box are found in many stables. They should be fitted with lift-out bowls to facilitate cleaning and have well-rounded corners. The space beneath should be boxed up to prevent the horse from injuring itself on the manger's rim—this space makes a good storage place for a grooming kit. However, a container on the floor, which is heavy enough not to be spilled and which can be removed as soon as the horse has finished its feed, is adequate.

Fitted hay racks are found in some stables, but they are not really advisable. They force the horse to eat with its head held unnaturally high and hayseeds may fall into its eyes. The best way of feeding hay is to use a hay net. It is also the least wasteful, as hay nets permit accurate weighing. The hay net should always be hung clear of the ground and be fastened with a quick-release knot to one of the tying-up rings.

Water is as essential for the horse in the stable as for a horse in the field. Automatic watering bowls are one way of providing a constant supply—but never position them too close to the hay net and manger, or they may get blocked by surplus food. Buckets are satisfactory, provided that the bucket is heavy enough not to be accidentally upset. Using a bucket means that it is possible to control the amount of water the horse drinks—important after exercise, for instance, when a "heated" horse must not drink too much—and also to check how much it is drinking more easily. This is especially useful in cases where there is suspected illness.

Stable routine

The daily program for looking after a stabled horse takes up a great deal of time (see below). All the stages have to be carried out, though some, such as the number of feeds, will vary from case to case. Skimping will only lead to problems later.

The only way of short-circuiting this routine is to adopt the combined system of care. This has considerable advantages in time and labor, but is not suited to all horses, especially those being worked hard. Otherwise, board or livery is the only alternative. Some riding schools offer what is termed half-livery; this means that the horse gets free board in exchange for use as a hack. The risk is that the horse may be roughly treated by inexperienced riders even, in a supervised lesson. Full livery, however, is extremely expensive. In either case, always check that the stable you choose is officially approved by a recognized riding authority.

The principal areas of a horse-owner's day, however, are not as complex as they seem. They can be broken down into various tasks, all of which are relatively simple to carry out.

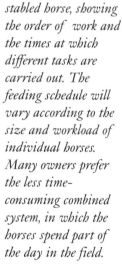

Below: The daily routine for a fully stabled horse, showing the order of work and the times at which different tasks are carried out. The feeding schedule will vary according to the size and workload of individual horses. Many owners prefer the less time-consuming combined system, in which the horses spend part of the day in the field.

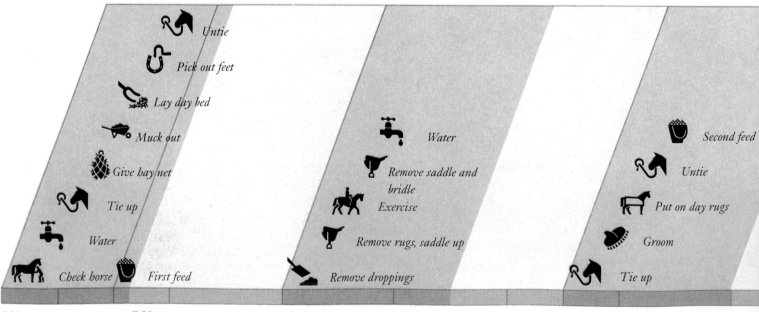

Untie
Pick out feet
Lay day bed
Muck out
Give hay net
Tie up
Water
Check horse   First feed

Water
Remove saddle and bridle
Exercise
Remove rugs, saddle up
Remove droppings

Second feed
Untie
Put on day rugs
Groom
Tie up

6.30 am   7.30 am   9.30 am   11.30 am

1 Mucking out is the first job to be done each morning in the stable. Soiled straw and dung are separated from the cleaner portions of the night bedding by tossing with a fork. The cleaner straw is then heaped at the back of the stall to be used again.

2 The soiled straw and droppings are put into a wheelbarrow for removal to the manure heap. In fine weather much of the night bedding can be carried outside to air in the sun. This will freshen it up, restore its springiness, and make it last longer.

3 When the bulk of soiled straw has been removed and the cleaner straw reserved, the floor should be swept clean of remaining dirt. It should be left bare to dry and air for a while. The clean straw is then spread as a soft floor covering for the day.

4 The soiled straw and dung are tossed onto the manure heap. Take care to throw the muck right onto the top of the heap, as a neatly built heap decomposes more efficiently. Beat the heap down with a shovel after each load to keep it firm and dense.

BEDDING DOWN AND MUCKING OUT

The purpose of bedding is to give the horse something comfortable to lie on, insulate the box, absorb moisture and prevent the horse's legs jarring on the hard stable floor. It must be kept clean—hence the daily task of mucking out. This is usually done first thing in the morning, and, with practice, can be carried out quite quickly.

Straw is the best possible bedding material, though other kinds can be substituted. Wheat straw is excellent, because it is absorbent and lasts well. Barley straw may contain awns, which can irritate the horse's skin. Oat straw should be avoided, because horses tend to eat it and it tends to become saturated.

Of the substitutes, peat makes a soft, well-insulated bed; it is also the least inflammable of all bedding materials. However, it is heavy to work. Damp patches and droppings must be removed at once, and replaced with fresh peat when necessary. The whole bed requires forking and raking every day, as the material can cause foot problems for the horse if it becomes damp and compressed.

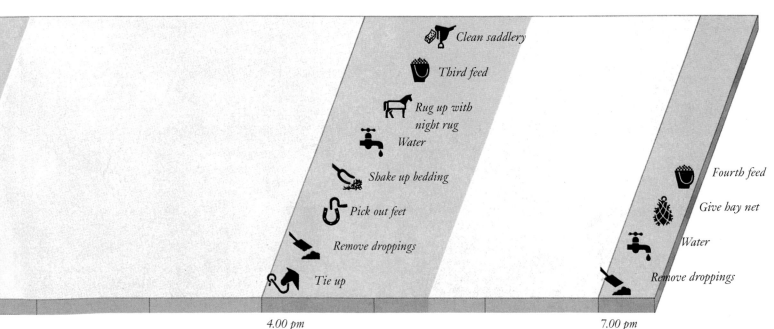

Clean saddlery
Third feed
Rug up with night rug
Water
Shake up bedding
Pick out feet
Remove droppings
Tie up

Fourth feed
Give hay net
Water
Remove droppings

4.00 pm   7.00 pm

Wood shavings and sawdust are usually inexpensive but can be difficult to get rid of. Both need to be checked carefully to see that they do not contain nails, screws, paint, oil, or other foreign matter. Wood shavings can be used alone, but note that they can cause foot problems if they become damp and compressed. Sawdust is best used in combination with other materials.

There are two types of bed—the day bed and the night bed. The first is a thin layer of bedding laid on the floor for use during the day; the second is thicker and more comfortable for use at night. With materials such as peat or wood shavings, laying the bed is very simple. Just empty the contents of the sack on the floor and rake them level, building up the material slightly higher around the walls to minimize drafts.

Below: Paper and straw beds at the Royal Mews, Windsor.

Laying a straw bed requires slightly more skill. As the straw will be compressed in the bale, it has to be shaken so that the stalks separate, and laid so that the finished bed is aerated, springy, and free from lumps. A pitchfork is best for the purpose.

Some owners prefer the deep litter method of bedding, where fresh straw is added to the existing bed every day, removing only droppings and sodden straw beforehand. After a time, the bed becomes as much as 2 ft (60 cm) deep, well-compressed below and soft and resilient on the surface. At the end of a month, the whole bed is removed and restarted. This method should be used only in loose boxes with first-rate drainage. In addition, the feet must be picked out regularly; otherwise there is a major risk of disease.

LAYING A STRAW NIGHT BED

1 Clean straw saved from the day bed is tossed and shaken well with a pitchfork before being spread evenly over the floor as a foundation.

2 New straw is taken from the compressed bale and shaken well to free the stalks and make the bed springy. The floor must be thickly and evenly covered to encourage the horse to lie down.

3 The straw is banked up higher and more thickly around the sides of the box. This reduces drafts, keeps the horse warmer, and gives the animal extra protection from injury during the night.

TYPES OF BEDDING

Above: Wheat straw makes ideal bedding. It is warm, comfortable, easy to handle, and absorbent.

Above: Wood shavings make cheaper bedding and are often laid on a base of sawdust to reduce dampness. Droppings have to be removed frequently.

Above: Paper bedding can be used in cases where horses tend to eat the straw, but paper bedding needs changing more frequently.

FEEDING

1. Tongue
2. Soft palate
3. Gullet
4. Stomach
5. Small intestine
6. Cecum (concealed behind large colon in small diagram)
7. Large colon
8. Small colon
9. Rectum

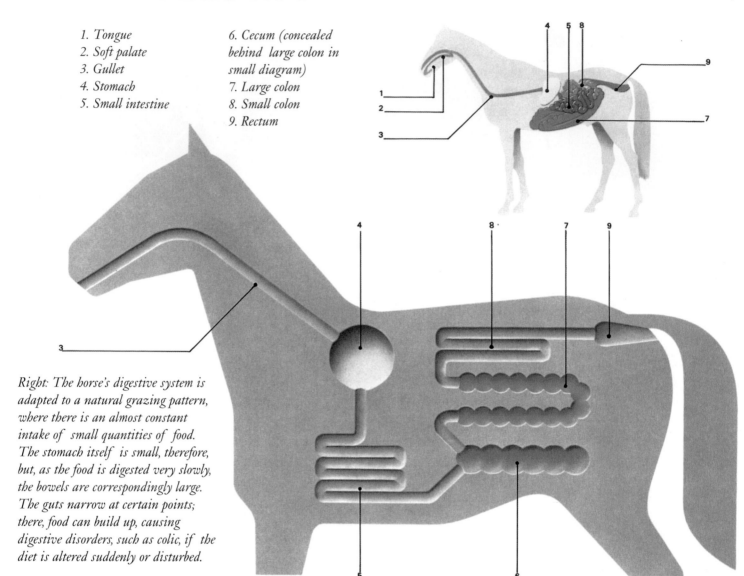

Right: The horse's digestive system is adapted to a natural grazing pattern, where there is an almost constant intake of small quantities of food. The stomach itself is small, therefore, but, as the food is digested very slowly, the bowels are correspondingly large. The guts narrow at certain points; there, food can build up, causing digestive disorders, such as colic, if the diet is altered suddenly or disturbed.

Heredity has given the horse a very small stomach for its size and the food it eats takes up to 48 hours to pass through the digestive system. This system is in itself complex. It depends not only on the right amounts of food at the correct time for smoothness of operation, but also on an adequate supply of water and plenty of exercise. In the wild, horses drink twice a day, usually at dawn and dusk. In between, their day is divided into periods of grazing, rest and exercise. Field-kept horses can duplicate this pattern to some extent, but stabled horses cannot do so.

It is essential to follow a basic set of feeding rules. Otherwise the horse's sensitive digestion might be upset, encouraging the risks of indigestion, impaction, formation of gas in the stomach, or sudden colic attacks.

The basic rules are to feed little and often,

with plenty of bulk food—grass or hay—and according to the work you expect the horse to do. Make no sudden change in the type of food, or in the routine of feeding, once the diet and time has been established. Always water the horses before feeding, so that indigested food is not washed out of the stomach. Never work a horse hard immediately after feeding or if its stomach is full of grass. Let it digest for 1¼ hours or so, otherwise the full stomach will impair breathing. Similarly, never feed a horse immediately after hard work, when it will be "heated."

The staple diet of the horse is grass, or, in the case of a stabled horse, hay. The best type is seed hay, usually a mixture of ryegrass and clover, which is specially grown as part of a crop-rotation program. Meadow fescue, also commonly used, comes from permanent pasture

Left: Basic concentrated foods are an essential part of the diet for horses in hard, regular work. 1. Bran is rich in protein, vitamin B, and salt. Fed as a mash, or slightly damp, with oats, it has a laxative effect. 2. Oats are a balanced, nutritious and easily digested food, high in energy-giving carbohydrate, vitamin B, and muscle-building protein. They are fed whole, bruised or crushed. 3. Sugar beet cubes provide bulk for horses in slow work. They must be soaked before use, or will swell in the stomach and cause colic. There is also a great danger of the horse choking. 4. Corn, fed flaked for easy digestion, is energizing, but low in protein and minerals. It contains vitamin A. 5. Barley, unsuitable for horses in long, fast work, is fed boiled, as a general conditioner; it should be crushed if fed raw. It contains vitamin B.

and so can vary in quality. The best way of judging this is by appearance, smell, and age. Hay should smell sweet, be slightly greenish in color and at least six months old. Blackened, moldy, or wet hay should never be used as fodder.

Of the other types of hay, clover is too rich to be fed to a horse on its own, and the same rule applies to alfalfa, or lucerne, common in the USA and Canada. Alfalfa is extremely rich in protein, so feed small quantities until you can judge how much is needed.

Concentrates for work

Ponies and horses in regular, hard work need additional food to keep them in a fit, hard-muscled condition. In other words, they need energy rather than fatness. This is provided by the feeding of concentrated foodstuffs, usually known as "short" or "hard" feeds. Of these, the best is oats, which can be bruised, crushed, or rolled to aid digestion. Manufactured horse cubes or pellets are a useful alternative.

Oats have no equal as a natural high protein, energy-giving food and are an essential part of the diet for all horses in work. Good

quality oats are plump and short, and pale gold, silver gray, or dark chocolate in color. They should have a hard, dry feel and no sour smell. Do not feed too much, or a horse may speedily become unmanageable. This caution applies particularly to children's ponies, which are often better off without oats at all.

Cubes and pellets are manufactured from various grains and also usually contain some grass meal, sweeteners such as molasses or treacle, extra vitamins and minerals. Their nutritional value is about two-thirds of oats, but they are less heating and so ideal for ponies. Their chief advantage is that they provide a balanced diet on their own, as they do not have to be mixed with other foodstuffs. However, they are expensive.

Other grains can be used in addition or as alternatives to oats, but they are all of lesser quality. Flaked corn is used in many parts of the world as a staple feed. It is high in energy value, but low in protein and mineral content. Like oats, it can be heating for ponies and is usually fed to animals in slow, regular work, such as riding-school hacks. Boiled barley helps to fatten up a horse or pony in poor condition and is a useful addition to the diet of a stale, or overworked, horse. Beans, too, are nutritious, but again, because of their heating effect, they should be fed sparingly, either whole, split or boiled.

OTHER USEFUL FOODS

Right: Proper feeding with the correct balance of vitamins is essential for health. This diagram shows how particular vitamins work throughout the system and what effects they have. Any deficiency of vitamins A, B1, B2, B6, D, and E in the horse's diet will eventually lead to debility and general loss of condition.

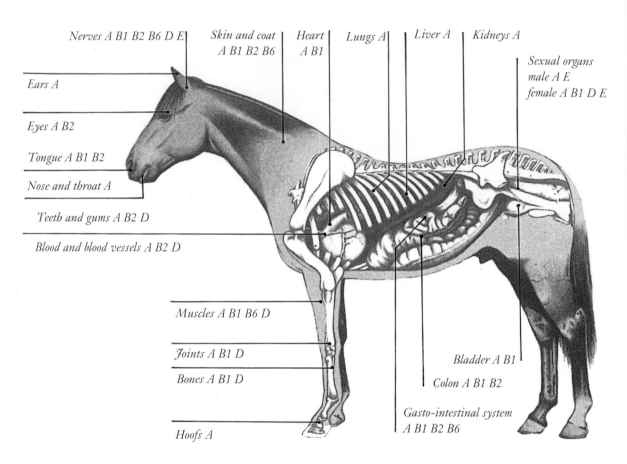

Nerves A B1 B2 B6 D E

Skin and coat A B1 B2 B6

Heart A B1

Lungs A

Liver A

Kidneys A

Sexual organs male A E female A B1 D E

Ears A

Eyes A B2

Tongue A B1 B2

Nose and throat A

Teeth and gums A B2 D

Blood and blood vessels A B2 D

Muscles A B1 B6 D

Joints A B1 D

Bones A B1 D

Bladder A B1

Colon A B1 B2

Gasto-intestinal system A B1 B2 B6

Hoofs A

Bran makes a useful addition to a horse's diet, as it helps to provide roughage. It is either fed dry, mixed up with oats—the combined mixture should be slightly dampened—or in the form of a mash. This is a good "pick-me-up" for a tired or sick horse. The mash is made by mixing ⅔ of a bucket of bran with ⅓ of boiling water and is fed to the horse as soon as it is cool enough to eat. Always remove any remains, as the mash can quickly go rancid. Oatmeal gruel is an alternative. This is made by pouring boiling water onto oats and leaving it to cool. Use enough water to make the gruel thin enough for the horse to drink.

Linseed, prepared as a jelly, mash, or tea, is fed to horses in winter to improve condition and to give gloss to the coat. It must be soaked, then well-cooked to kill the poisonous enzyme present in the raw plant. Dried sugar beet is another good conditioner, because of its high energy content. Most horses like it because of its sweetness. It must be always soaked in water overnight before it is added to a feed. If fed dry, the beet is likely to cause severe colic, as it swells dramatically when wet.

Roots, such as carrots, turnips, and rutabaga, also help condition and are also of particular value to fussy feeders. Always wash the roots first and then slice into finger-shaped pieces. Small, round slices may cause a pony to choke.

Molasses or black treacle can be mixed with food to encourage a finicky feeder. In any case, all feeds ideally should contain about 1 lb (450 g) chaff—chopped hay. Chaff has practically no nutritional content, but it does ensure that the horse chews its food properly, thus helping to minimize the risk of indigestion. It also acts as an abrasive on teeth. Finally, a salt or mineral lick—left in the manger—is essential for all stabled horses. Field-kept animals usually ingest an adequate amount of salt during grazing, but a lick is also a good safeguard.

Left: Foodstuffs should be kept in separate bins and only mixed at feedtime. A scoop is used to measure out each ration. Where several horses are kept a checklist for feeding should be pinned up near the bins. The feed can be dampened slightly with water before being mixed by hand in a bucket and then fed to the horse. Grain keeps fresh and dry in galvanized bins. The lids should be heavy enough to prevent a horse from raising them.

Above: A separate food store is essential. It should be clean, dry, and near to the water supply. Foodstuffs kept in the stable can easily become spoiled or contaminated. The horse is a fastidious feeder, and musty or dusty food, as well as being unappetizing, may be harmful. This simple food store provides a clean, secure, and compact area where foodstuffs can be measured out and mixed. Scales are also useful to check the weight of filled hay nets periodically.

Vitamins and minerals

An adequate supply of vitamins and minerals is vital in addition to the required amounts of carbohydrates, proteins, and fats. Vitamins A, B1, B2, B6, D, and E are all essential; otherwise the horse's resistance to disease will certainly be lessened, and actual disease is likely to result. Normally, good-class hay and grass, bran, and carrots will contain most of the vitamins a horse needs; oats and barley, flaked corn, and sugar beet pulp are also all useful. Vitamin D can only be artificially administered through cod-liver oil, or left to the action of sunlight on the natural oil in the coat.

The absence of a sufficient supply of minerals can be even more serious than a lack of vitamins, especially in the case of a young horse. The essential minerals required are as follows: calcium and phosphorus, for the formation of healthy teeth and bones; sodium, sodium chloride (salt), and potassium, for regulation of the amount of body fluids; iron and copper, vital for the formation of hemoglobin in the blood to prevent anemia; while magnesium, manganese, cobalt, zinc, and iodine are all necessary. Magnesium aids skeletal and muscular development; manganese is needed for both the bone structure and for reproduction; zinc and cobalt stimulate growth; while iodine is particularly important to control the thyroid gland.

However, of all these minerals, the most important is salt. This is why it is vital to provide a horse with a salt lick in either the stable or field.

As with vitamins, the chief source of these minerals is grass or hay, together with the other foods mentioned above. However, if the horse needs extra vitamins and minerals, always take the advice of a veterinarian first—an excess of vitamins or minerals can be as dangerous as an underdose. There are many suitable proprietary products on the market. These usually come in the form of liquid, powders, and pellets, designed to be mixed in with other food.

Signs of lack of vitamins are usually seen on the skin and coat; examination of the teeth, gums, and eyes can also give warning of possible deficiency. But, with sensible and controlled feeding, the problem should not arise.

Quantities to feed

There is no rigid guide as to the exact amounts of food a horse should be fed; much depends on the type and size of horse and the work it is expected to do. However, as far as a stabled horse is concerned, the amount should certainly not be less than the horse would eat if it was grazing freely.

If the horse concerned was 15.2hh, say, it would eat 26½ lb (12 kg) of grass a day. Bigger horses require an extra 2 lb (1 kg) for every extra 1 in of height; smaller ones need 2 lb (1 kg) less.

With this basic total established, it is possible to plan a feeding program, varying the amounts of bulk and concentrated food according to the demands being made upon the horse. Taking as an example a lightweight 15.2hh horse that is being hunted, say, three days a fortnight in addition to other regular work, the emphasis will be on an almost equal balance between concentrated food and hay or grass. The horse should be getting about 14 lb (6.3 kg) of concentrates a day to some 15 lb (6.8 kg) of hay. If, however, the horse is being lightly worked—or not worked at all—the amount of hay will rise and the quantities of concentrated food will diminish.

Remember, too, that most horses feed much better at night, so it is important that the highest proportion of food be given in the final feed of the day. If the horse is being given three feeds a day, for example, the proportions are 10 percent in the morning, 30 percent at midday and 60 percent at night.

The best guide of all is simple observation. If a horse is too fat, it will need its rations reduced; if too thin, it will need building up.

GROOMING

The chief point of grooming is to keep the horse clean, massage the skin, and tone up the muscles. Field-kept horses need less grooming than stabled horses, particularly in winter, but some grooming must nevertheless be carried out.

A good grooming kit is essential. This should consist of a dandy brush, to remove mud and dried sweat marks; a body brush, a soft, short-bristled brush, for the head, body, legs, mane, and tail; a rubber currycomb, used to remove thickly caked mud or matted hair, and a metal one, for cleaning the body brush; a water brush, used damp on the mane, tail, and hooves; a hoof pick; a stable rubber, used to give a final polish to the coat; and some foam-rubber sponges, for cleaning the eyes, nostrils, muzzle, and dock.

Where more than one horse is kept, each animal should have its own grooming kit, kept together in a box or bag and clearly marked. This helps to prevent the risk of infection in cases of illness.

Grooming falls into three stages, each of which is carried out at a different time of the day. The first of these is quartering, normally done first thing in the morning before exercise. Tie up the horse. Then, pick the feet and, next, clean the eyes, muzzle, and dock with a damp sponge. If worn, rugs should be unbuckled and folded back and the head, neck, chest and forelegs cleaned with a body brush. Replace the rugs and repeat the process on the rear part of the body. Remove any stable stains with a water brush. Finish by brushing the mane and tail thoroughly with the body brush.

Strapping is the name given to the thorough grooming that follows exercise, when the horse has cooled down. Once again, tie the horse up and pick its feet. Follow by using the dandy brush to remove all traces of dirt, mud, and sweat, paying particular attention to marks left by the girth and saddle and on the legs. Work from ears to tail, first on the near side and then on the off. Take care to use the brush lightly to avoid irritating the skin.

Right: The grooming kit. Ideally every horse should have its own to reduce the chance of any infection being passed from one to another. Keep the kit in a wire basket or bag so that no item is mislaid. Clean the equipment from time to time with a mild disinfectant.
Top Row: 1. Sponges, one for cleaning eyes, lips, and nostrils, the second for cleaning the dock. 2. Water brush (soft): for laying mane and tail and washing feet. 3. Mane combs are used when mane or tail is braided, trimmed, or pulled. 4. Can of hoof oil and brush, used to improve appearance of hoof and to treat brittle feet. 5. Metal currycomb: for cleaning dirt from body brush (never used on the horse). 6. Body brush (soft): to remove dust and scurf.
Bottom row: 7. Rubber currycomb: removes dirt from body brush and can also be used in place of dandy brush. 8. Hoof pick: for taking dirt and stones from the feet. 9. Dandy brush (hard): to remove dried mud and sweat. 10. Stable rubber: used for final polishing of coat. 11. Sweat scraper: to remove water and sweat from coat.

GROOMING

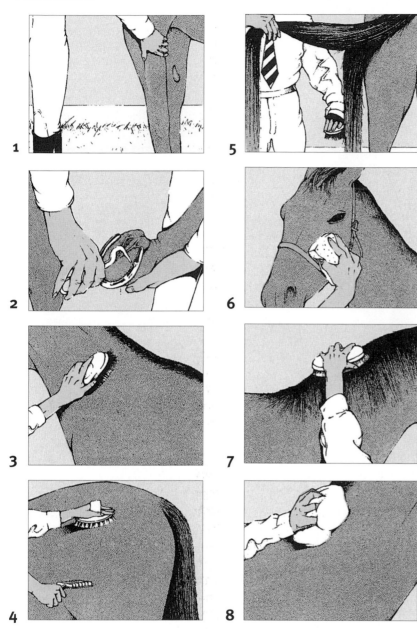

1. To pick up a horse's foot, stand facing its tail. Warn it first by sliding a hand down from its shoulder to its fetlock. 2. Working from the frog to the toe end concentrating on the edges first, use the point of the hoof pick to prize out any foreign objects lodged in the foot. Take care not to push the point into the frog. 3. The dandy brush is used to remove heavy dirt, caked mud, and sweat stains. As it is fairly harsh it should not be used on the more tender areas. 4. A body brush has short, dense bristles designed to penetrate and clean the coat. It should be applied in firm, circular movements. Clear it of dust with a currycomb. 5. The body brush is also used to groom the tail. This should be brushed a few hairs at a time, starting underneath. Remove all mud and tangles. Finally, brush the whole tail into shape from the top. 6. Wring out a soft sponge in warm water and sponge the eyes, taking care around the eyelids. Wring out the sponge and wipe over the muzzle, lips, and nostrils. A separate sponge should be used for the dock area. 7. The water brush is used to "lay" the mane. Dip the tip of the brush in water and shake, then, keeping the brush flat, make firm, downward strokes from the roots. 8 As a final touch, go over the whole coat with the stable rubber to remove any trace of dust. This cloth is used slightly damp and folded into a flat bundle. Work along the lie of the hair.

Next, comes the body brush. This must be used firmly for full effect. Start with the mane, pushing it to the wrong side to remove scurf from the roots. Brush the forelock. Then, start on the body, working from head to tail and grooming the near side first, as before. Work with a circular motion, finishing in the direction of the hairs, and flick the brush outward at the end of each stroke to push dust away from the body. At intervals, clean the brush with the currycomb, which is held in the other hand. The currycomb can be emptied by tapping on the floor occasionally.

Brush the head, remembering that this is one of the most sensitive areas of the horse. So use the brush firmly, but gently, and take particular care when grooming around the eyes, ears, and nostrils. Finally, brush the tail—a few hairs at a time—so that every tangle is removed.

The next stage is wisping, which helps to tone up the muscles and also stimulates the circulation. A wisp is a bundle of soft hay, twisted up to form a rope. Slightly dampen it, and use vigorously on the neck, shoulders, quarters, and thighs, concentrating on the muscular areas. Bang the wisp down hard on these, sliding it off with, not against, the coat. Take care to avoid bony areas and the tender region of the loins.

Sponge the eyes, lips, and muzzle and nostrils. Then, with a second sponge to minimize the risk of possible infection, wash around the dock and under the tail. Lift the tail as high as possible, so the entire region can be adequately cleaned. "Lay" the mane with the water brush. Then brush the outside of the feet, taking care not to get water into the hollow of the heel. When the hooves are thoroughly dry, brush hoof oil over the outside of each hoof as high as the coronet.

Finally, work over the horse with the stable rubber for a final polish. The object is to remove the last traces of dust. Fold the rubber into a flat bundle, dampen it slightly, and then go over the coat, working in the direction of the lay of the hair.

Strapping takes from between half to three-quarters of an hour with practice. It will normally take a novice slightly longer, mainly because of the unaccustomed strain it imposes on the groom's muscles. "Setting fair"—the last grooming of the day—takes far less time. Simply brush the horse lightly with the body brush, wisp and then put on the night rug if one is normally worn.

Checking for injury

The purpose of checking a horse for injury is obvious. You must make sure the horse has not cut, scratched, or bruised himself and check that he appears to be in general good health. Run your hand over his coat to feel for lumps and bumps, paying particular attention to his legs. Bruises will manifest themselves by obviously tender or hot areas, or by swellings. Pick out each foot in turn to make sure no stones have lodged in the hoof, or that the sole of the hoof has not been bruised or pricked by stepping on something sharp.

Any small cuts you may find will generally need very little treatment. Wash them well, preferably using running water from a hose, to clean them and then check the extent of the injury. Dress them with antibiotic powder, which you can get from your veterinarian—you should always keep a supply handy.

If a horse has sustained a more serious wound—from some broken glass someone has tossed into the field, for instance—do not hesitate to call the veterinarian. Proper medical attention in such instances not only speeds recovery, but it often reduces the possibility of the horse being marked by a scar later.

Left: A habit you should get into is checking your horse for injuries. This is especially important if your horse is at grass, as you won't be able to watch him. Whether done while he is still in the field, or in the stable, a thorough check should be made of his entire body, especially the legs and hooves as these are the most prone to cuts, sprains, and infection. Having tethered the horse, move your hands up and down each of the legs, feeling for any swelling, and watching to see if he reacts with pain.

Right: If a minor injury is found, it should first be thoroughly washed with warm water and then sprayed or wiped with antiseptic. Never leave a cut unattended.

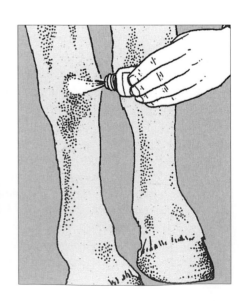

Shampooing a horse

You should always give your horse a thorough grooming or strapping the day before a show. If he has any white socks or stockings, these should be shampooed. The tail, too, will look smarter if it is washed.

Hard, yellow soap available from saddlers should be used when shampooing any part of a horse; never use soft, cosmetic-type soap. To wash the legs, wet them first with tepid water, then rub them with soap to produce a lather. Scrub very gently with plenty of clean water, making sure all vestiges of soap have been removed. Rub the legs as dry as possible with a stable rubber, leave them to dry completely before bandaging them. If you wash your horse's legs frequently, grease the heels periodically to reduce the risk of the skin cracking due to excessive dampness.

CLIPPING

Choosing to clip your horse's coat in winter allows him to work harder and keep him looking smart. The types of clips vary considerably. The trace clip removes just a line of hair from beneath the neck, belly, and tops of legs. The blanket clip is the same as the trace clip but with all hair removed from the neck. The hunter-clipped horse must be kept inside in winter or turned out with a warm New Zealand rug.

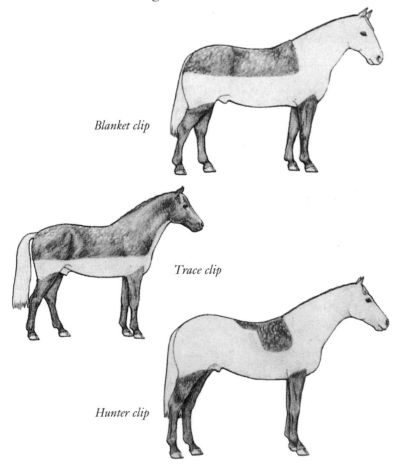

Blanket clip

Trace clip

Hunter clip

To shampoo the tail, first brush it in the usual way to remove any mud and tangles. Then, wet it thoroughly and soap it well. Rub the hairs together with your hands and rinse the tail thoroughly. Run your hands down the length of the tail several times in order to remove as much water as possible. Then, standing by the side of the hindquarters, hold the tail by the bottom of the dock and swing it around in a circle. This helps to dislodge any remaining water in the same way as a dog does when it shakes itself after a bath or swim.

Brush the tail in the normal way, using the body brush and put on a tail bandage (see page 307) which helps to keep the tail clean and makes sure the top hairs dry flat. The bandage should not be left on overnight, as it can constrict the circulation in the dock. Thus, you have washed the tail the day before a show. Remove the tail bandage when you bed down the horse and put on another after brushing the tail in the morning.

If a horse's coat is very stained, it is possible to shampoo him all over, but this should only be done if it is absolutely necessary. Only shampoo a horse's coat if the day is warm, dry, and preferably sunny. Use the same sort of soap described above, with plenty of warm water, and, having soaped and scrubbed the entire coat, rinse it very thoroughly. Remove the surplus water by pulling a sweat scraper across the coat. Then go over the entire body with a dry sponge to "mop" as much remaining water as possible. After this, rub it dry, then walk the horse around until the coat has dried completely. Finally, brush the coat in the normal way with the body brush.

Clipping

Horses are clipped to maintain comfort and, less importantly, for smartness. Removing all or part of the coat by clipping prevents heavy sweating during exercise in winter and therefore lessens the risk of a horse catching a chill. It also enables the horse to dry off more quickly.

There are various types of clip; choice should depend on what the horse is expected to do, and how much it sweats doing it. Remember that a clipped horse will need to wear rugs for warmth during cold weather, whether it is kept in a stable or a field.

SHOES AND SHOEING

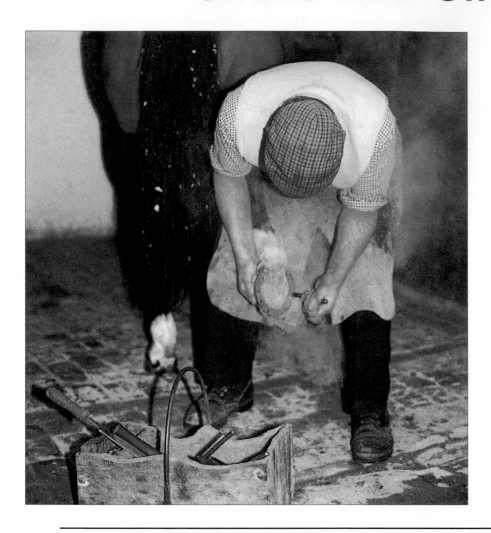

Horse maintenance includes not only the routines of feeding and cleaning, it also includes very important areas such as shoeing and illness for which you should establish a good relationship with a qualified farrier and a veterinarian.

Horses that are being worked to any extent—whether they are being ridden or used to pull a vehicle—must have their feet shod with metal shoes. Riding an unshod horse soon wears away the hard, insensitive horn of the foot and exposes the more sensitive areas. If this happens, these areas become sore and the horse becomes lame within a very short time.

The shoeing of horses is a highly skilled and specialist task, undertaken by a trained craftsman known as a farrier. If the shoes do not fit, or if they pinch the feet in any way, then obviously the horse will not be able to give its best.

To understand how the farrier goes about his task, it is necessary to have some knowledge of the structure of the horse's foot.

Left: The farrier's skill with his tools will mainly determine the fit of the horse's shoe and, consequently, his performance.

TYPES OF SHOES

Right: The care of the horse's feet is probably the most important part of horsemanship, and every rider should know the parts and functions of the horse's hoof.

Cleft of frog

Bar

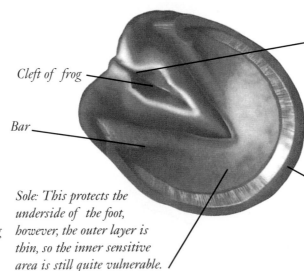

Sole: This protects the underside of the foot, however, the outer layer is thin, so the inner sensitive area is still quite vulnerable.

Frog: The frog is V-shaped and leathery, and provides the foot with a natural shock absorber and non-slip device. The farrier never pares back the frog and it needs daily attention to keep it clean and healthy.

Wall: The wall, like the human fingernail, is insensitive and always growing. Because of the latter, the shoes must be removed regularly and the hoof pared into shape.

Below: Several types of shoes, including a hunter shoe, a grass shoe, a corn shoe, a leather shoe, and a T-shaped shoe for horses with contracted heels or corns.

SHOEING—BEFORE AND AFTER

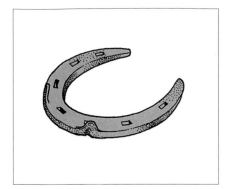

A horseshoe is held in place by nails driven into the tough, horny part of the foot. They are twisted off where they emerge higher up, and hammered down. A horse's shoes should never in any way interfere with the horse's natural actions and movements. Clips help to keep the shoe in place. These are small, triangular points that fit into the wall of the hoof. Usually there is one clip on the foreshoe and two on the hindshoe. Grip is extremely important and there are several methods for improving it, including calks and calking. However, studs are considered the most effective. These are not left in permanently, but screwed in place by the farrier.

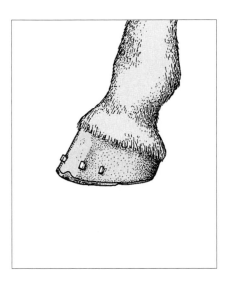

It is absolutely vital that you watch for the signs indicating that your horse needs new shoes. Ideally this should be done on a regular basis, and the shoe and hoof should not be allowed to reach an unhealthy or dangerous state before you get new ones. This horse is badly in need of new shoes. The indications are that the shoe itself has worn thin and rough and the clenches have risen and are standing out from the wall. All of these factors are dangerous and unhealthy for the horse.

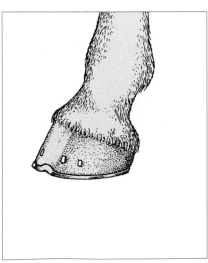

A newly shod foot should show certain points indicating that it has been correctly fitted. The shoe should be fitted to the foot and not vice versa; the foot should be rasped and pared evenly and the frog in contact with the ground; a suitable number of nails should be used—never too many nor too few, and the clenches should be neat and evenly spaced. There should be no space between the shoe and the foot, and the clip should fit well on each shoe.

Hot and cold shoeing

There are two types of shoeing—hot and cold. At one time, the former was virtually the only method practiced, but nowadays it has been largely superseded by cold shoeing. This method enables farriers to go to the horse rather than the horse having to be taken to the smithy, and is thus more convenient. Hot shoeing, however, is said to be superior—the maxim being that the shoe is made to fit the foot, not vice versa, as in cold shoeing.

Whatever method is used, the farrier first removes the old shoe, cuts away the excess growth of horn, and rasps the surface of the foot to make it even. In hot shoeing, he then places the red-hot shoe against the bottom of the foot. It is hard to believe this is not a painful process, but, in fact, no pain is caused. The mark left by the hot metal tells the farrier whether he needs to alter the shape of the shoe, or needs to rasp the surface of the foot further. In cold shoeing, the farrier can only judge by placing the cold shoe against the foot. It is not as easy to alter a cold shoe by hammering as it is to alter a hot shoe, where the metal is more malleable.

In hot shoeing, the blacksmith cools the shoe, once satisfied with the fit. He then hammers it onto the foot using as few nails as possible, but enough to keep it in position; there are usually three on the inside and four on the outside. The points of the nails emerge through the front wall of the hoof and the farrier twists them off with the claw end of the hammer. Finally, he hammers the nail heads against the hoof and rasps them smooth so they lie flush against the wall. The point at which the nails emerge in the front is critical; if too low, they may not keep the shoe in place, tearing down through the outer horn to cause cracking, while, if positioned too high, they can bruise the sensitive inner area of the hoof.

How often a horse needs new shoes will depend to some extent on how hard he is working and on what type of ground. However, most horses should be seen by the farrier once a month, since it may be necessary to cut back the excess growth of horn even if the horse is reshod with old shoes.

Even horses out at grass must be looked at by the farrier once a month. They will not move around sufficiently to keep the horn down to a reasonable length and, if it gets too long, it could cause them to trip. The horn, too, may begin to crack and break.

EXERCISE ROUTINES

All stabled horses must have regular and adequate exercise. Otherwise they can develop swollen legs, azoturia, and colic and will, in any case, be spirited and difficult to manage when ridden. They can also become bored and develop bad habits. The amounts needed vary with the type and weight of horse and the work it is expected to do; a hunter needs more exercise than a hack.

As with feeding, there are a few basic rules to remember. Most importantly, never exercise a horse until 1½ hours after a heavy feed; 1 hour after a small one. In any case, always remove the hay net an hour before exercise. Horses full of hay find breathing difficult when they are being worked hard.

The point of exercise is to get and keep the horse fit enough for the demands being made on it. A horse brought up from grass, say, is likely to be in "grass condition." In such a

SPECIMEN EXERCISE ROUTINE—BASED ON 16HH HUNTER

Exercise	Care and Management	Special Features
Week 1 20 mins walking on the first day, increasing gradually to one hour	Gradually increase concentrated food, begin strapping	During the prework week the horse's feet must be checked and shod. All horses require one rest day each working week
Week 2 Walking for 1¼–1½ hrs over a 6–8 mile (9.5–13 km) circuit	Check conditions of legs and feet, watch for skin galls. Increase corn and vitamin supplements	Quiet lanes and roads with good surfaces are best for road work
Week 3 Always walk the first ½ mile (0.8 km). Then introduce very short periods of trotting, increasing their length gradually	Stable the horse at night and establish a regular routine	Schooling and lungeing in large circles can now be started
Week 4 1½–2 hrs work daily—split into schooling, lungeing, and road work. More frequent periods of trotting	Increase concentrated food	Trotting up gentle slops can commence and increase slowly
Week 5 After first walking and trotting, the horse may have a short, slow canter on soft ground. Then decrease pace gradually	Four feeds a day—increase concentrates and reduce time at grass. Reshoe if necessary	At this stage the coat should shine and the muscles should be hardening
Week 6 A medium canter of reasonable length. Work at a sitting trot can now be started	Increase concentrated food ration. Maintain thorough strapping	Schooling can be intensified by trotting in smaller circles and work at the canter
Week 7 Canters can speed up. A short half-speed gallop may be added at the end of the week (on good ground). Jumping can begin	The horse will sweat and should wear a rug at night	The final phase of building up to full work. It is useful to introduce the horse to traveling and to company at this stage
Week 8 On day 2 the horse can gallop at half speed up a gentle slope. Always walk the final mile	Full rations of concentrate. They horse should gallop on alternate days and do steady work on the others. Renew shoes	When the horse is fully conditioned thorough exercise must be maintained on days when it does not work

Exercise needs always differ according to the size of horse, the type of work it is doing, and what it is being prepared for. Vary the routine accordingly.

Above: It is important to introduce exercises to your horse gradually. Start with a slow walk, as here, then progress to the trot, and canter as and when you feel the horse is ready.

case, fitness can be achieved only through a rigidly controlled program of exercise and feeding. Restrict exercise to walking, preferably on roads, for a week. Then combine walking with slow trotting. Soon, work can start in the school, while the period of road work can also be extended. Increase the amount of grain fed in proportion to the extra work. By the end of six weeks, the horse should be ready to be cantered over distances not exceeding ½ mile (0.8 km). In the ninth week, it can have a gallop for up to ¾ mile (1.2 km), but this should be strictly controlled so that the horse does not gallop flat-out at horse's-speed.

Indications that the program has been successful are an increase in muscle and the disappearance of the profuse, lathery sweat of the out-of-condition horse. Never try to hurry the process; a horse cannot be conditioned through cantering and galloping, but only by slow, steady, regular work. This applies just as

much to stabled horses and ponies.

Always aim to end the exercise with a walk, so that the horse comes back to its stable or field cool and relaxed. Once the tack has been removed, inspect the horse for cuts and bruises, pick out its feet, and brush the saddle and sweat marks. Then rug up or groom. If you have been caught in the rain, trot the horse home so that it is warm on arrival. Untack, and then give the horse a thorough rub down, either with straw or a towel. When this has been completed, cover the back with a layer of straw or use a sweat sheet. It is vital to keep the back warm to avoid the risk of colds and chills.

A thorough drying is essential if the horse is very hot and sweaty, but it will need to be sponged first with lukewarm water. Either restrict sponging to the sweaty areas—usually the neck, chest, and flanks—or sponge the entire body. Then, scrape off the surplus water

Below: Lungeing starts when a trainer feels that the horse is fit enough for a more extensive work program. The horse is led in circles around the trainer at the end of a lunge rein.

with a sweat scraper, taking care to work with, and not against, the run of the coat. Next, rub down and, finally, cover with a sweat sheet. If possible, lead the horse around until it is completely dry.

Horses that have been worked exceptionally hard—in hunting, say, or in competitions—need further care. On returning to the stable, give the horse a drink of warm water. Then follow the procedures outlined above.

Feed the horse with a bran mash and then leave it to rest. Return later to check that the animal is warm enough or has not broken out into a fresh sweat. Check for warmth by feeling the bases of the ears. If they are cold, warm by rubbing them with the hand and then put more blankets on the horse. If the latter, rub down and walk the horse around again until it is completely dry.

LOADING AND TRAVELING

Careful planning when entering for a horse show, say, or going for a day's hunting, is essential if the horse is to arrive fit enough to undertake the tasks demanded of it. The first essential is to plan the journey; a fit horse can be hacked for up to 10 miles (16 km), walking and trotting at an average speed of no more than 6 mph (7.5 kph) (a grass-kept pony's average should not be more than 4 mph [5 kph]). If the distance involved is greater than this, transport will be needed.

Horse boxes or car-towed trailers are the usual method of transport over long distances. Apart from the obvious mechanical checks that should be carried out before each journey, the horse's own requirements, too, need attention. A hay net is one essential; this should be filled with hay and given to the horse during the journey, unless the animal is expected to work hard immediately on arrival. Others include a first-aid kit, rugs (day and sweat), bandages, grooming kit, a head collar, a water bucket, and a filled water container.

The last item is essential if the journey is to be a particularly long one, when the horse will need to be watered perhaps once or even twice en route.

In some cases—when hunting, for example—the horse can travel saddled up, with a rug placed over the saddle, but, in the case of competitions, a rug alone should be worn. Traveling bandages should always be used, as well as a tail bandage to stop the top of the tail from being rubbed. In addition, knee caps and hock boots should be worn as an added protection against injury while the horse is in transit.

Protection of the horse itself must start the night before, with an especially thorough grooming. Both mane and tail should be washed.

A grass-kept horse should be kept in for the night, if possible. The next morning, follow the normal stable routine, with the addition of a drawn-out strapping. Remember that, in the case of a show, the mane should be braided; this can be started the night before to ease the task of getting the mane into shape, but will need to be completed the following day.

Loading the horse

Getting a horse into a box or trailer is an easy enough task, provided that the process is tackled calmly and without undue haste. The simplest way is for one person to lead the horse forward, walking straightforward and resisting the temptation to pull at the head. A couple of helpers should stand behind the horse in case help is required, but out of kicking range.

The main reason for a horse showing reluctance to enter a box is usually its fear of the noise of its hooves on the ramp. This can be overcome by putting down some straw to deaden the sound. Loading another, calmer, horse first, or tempting a horse forward with a feed bucket containing a handful of oats, also act as encouragement.

A really obstinate horse, however, will have to be physically helped into the box. The way to do this is to attach two ropes to the ramp's rails, so that they can cross just above the horse's hocks, with two helpers in position—one at each end of the ropes. As the horse approaches the ramp, they tighten the ropes to propel the animal into the box.

Unloading

To unbox a horse, let down the ramp, untie the halter rope and, depending on the design of the box, push the horse's chest very gently to encourage him to step backward out of the box. In general, it is kinder to tether a horse outside the box (providing it is not in the glaring sunshine) or, better still, under the shade of some trees, than it is to leave him standing in the somewhat cramped conditions of most trailers. Only tether a horse, though, if you are sure he reacts well to such a practice and will not become excited if other horses at the show are ridden past.

Below: Lead your horse up the ramp; a layer of straw on the ramp will prevent him from slipping. Avoid exciting your horse by shouting or waving your hands. Walk in with your horse, looking straightahead and tie him on a short rope. Close the ramp up quickly once inside. Provide your horse with a bowl of feed.

HEALTH

Horses are tough creatures, but, like any animal, they can fall sick or be injured. A healthy pony or horse is alert, bright-eyed, and takes a keen interest in all that goes on around it. Ribs and hipbones should not be prominent, and the quarters should be well-rounded. The animal should stand square on all four legs. The base of the ears should be warm to the touch.

Signs of illness vary, but there are some general symptoms that can give warning of trouble to come. A field-kept pony that stays for a long time in one place, a horse that goes off its food, a willing horse that suddenly becomes "wilful"—all these signs are indications that something is wrong. Other symptoms include: discharge from the eyes or nostrils; stumbling for no apparent reason; restlessness; dullness of eye or general lack of interest; sweating; kicking or biting at the flank; lameness; diarrhea; persistent difficulty in breathing; coughing.

It is essential, therefore, to have a reliable veterinarian, and, if ever in any doubt, to call him without hesitation. Better to pay for a visit than to run the risk of mistaken self-diagnosis leading to a more serious illness, or even death. Nevertheless, all horse-owners should have a practical knowledge of first aid, and a first-aid kit is an essential part of any stable. It should be placed where it can be easily found in an emergency.

Nursing the horse

Like all animals, horses take time to recover from illness. The veterinarian will always instruct the owner in what to do, but, usually, successful nursing is merely a matter of common sense.

AILMENT AND INJURY CHART - SKIN AND COAT

Symptoms	Causes	Treatment
Skin and coat		
Heat bumps (Humor) Various forms of size and shape. Rarely seen all over horse	Probably overheating from too much protein in system	Give bran mash with addition of two tablespoons of Epsom salts
Lice Itching, dull coat, appearance of small gray or black parasites on the coat	Unknown. Appears in spring on grass-fed horses or on animals which have been in poor condition and are now improving	Dust affected areas liberally with delousing powder, obtainable from veterinarian. Keep grooming kit separate
Ringworm Usually circular, bare patches on the skin of varying sizes which may or may not be itchy	Fungus infection that is highly contagious	Apply tincture of iodine to affected parts. Disinfect rugs and sterilize grooming kit. Keep horse isolated
Sweet itch Extreme itchiness of areas around mane and tail, apparent only in late spring, summer, and early fall	Unknown, probably an allergy	Apply calamine lotion to relieve itching. Keep mane and tail clean. Lard and sulphur applied to the area can be soothing. Consult veterinarian
Warbles Maggot of the warble fly	Painful swelling on back	Bathe in warm water which will keep the lump soft and help to "draw" the warble from a small hole on the top of the swelling. The maggot can be gently squeezed out, but do not do this before consulting veterinarian
Digestive system		
Colic Severe abdominal pain, characterized by pawing of the ground, restlessness, sweating, rolling, kicking, biting and looking at the stomach, groaning, cold ears	Poor or irregular feeding, wrong sort of food, exercise or drinking immediately after food, too much food when horse is tired. Worm infestation	Call veterinarian, meanwhile do what you can to relieve the pain. Keep horse warm, apply hot-water bottles to belly. Try to discourage horse from lying down or rolling

AILMENT AND INJURY CHART

Symptoms	Causes	Treatment
Worms Loss of condition, despite careful feeding	There are several types of intestinal parasites collectively known as worms	Regular doses of worming powder or paste, together with regular maintenance of pasture

Feet

Symptoms	Causes	Treatment
Bruised sole Lameness. Horse may ease the weight of the foot when at rest	Bruising by stones or rough-going and hard ground	Rest. If necessary, new shoes. Keep farrier informed
Corns Lameness. Heat in foot. Horse more lame on turn than straight	Ill-fitting shoe causing pinching. Shoe which has moved in. Bruising	Call blacksmith or veterinarian to cut out corn and advise further treatment
Laminitis (Founder) Obvious pain in the feet. Horse is reluctant to move and stands with its front feet pushed forward and its hind legs under it so that its weight is taken on the heels. May shift weight from one foot to another. Possibly a high temperature. Always apparent in front feet first but may affect all four feet	Overfeeding and not enough exercise. Grass-fed horses are especially prone to the disease after eating excessive amounts of new, spring grass. The feet become engorged with blood and the sensitive laminae in the hoof become inflamed and may separate	Call veterinarian at once as prompt treatment can help the condition considerably. In the meantime cool the feet in running water from a hose and try to get the horse to walk, as exercise helps the feet to drain. Remove from grass and give light starvation diet
Nail blind Lameness soon after horse has been shod	Shoe nail driven too close to the sensitive area of the foot	Call blacksmith, who will remove nail and replace it correctly
Navicular disease Intermittent lameness, usually slight, followed by pointing, in which one forefoot is rested in front of the other on the toe. Gradual increase in tendency to stumble. Later, foot will contract at the heels	May be hereditary. Otherwise probably due to jarring of the foot through excessive road work or strain in hunting and jumping. This brings on lesions of the navicular bone	Consult veterinarian
Overreach Cuts and bruises to bulbs of heel	Toe of hind shoe hitting front heel	Bathe wound in salt solution. Call veterinarian if wound is severe. Prevention is better than cure—horse should be fitted with overreach boots
Pedal osteitis Intermittent lameness, later permanent	Severe jarring, brought on by too much road work or by jumping when the ground is very hard. This leads to inflammation of the pedal bone and bony growths on the bone	Rest. Bathing foot in cold water. Special shoeing may help
Quarter crack Crack or split in the wall of the hoof, extending upward into coronet	Mineral deficiency which makes hoof unusually brittle	Consult farrier who may fit special clips to hold edges of crack together, or put on special shoes
Quittor Lameness. Infection breaking out around coronary band	Infection in the hoof working its way upward to form abscess	Consult veterinarian
Seedy toe Revealed when trimming the hoof during shoeing. The outside of the hoof wall appears normal but a cavity is revealed when the horn is pared away	A legacy of laminitis. Tight shoes may also be a cause	Call farrier who will pare away the damaged horn. Then treat liberally with Stockholm tar

Head

Symptoms	Causes	Treatment
Blocked tear duct Tears running down face	Sand, grit, or mucus causing blockage of tear duct	Call veterinarian, who will probably clear blockage by using a catheter to force sterile liquid through the duct

AILMENT AND INJURY CHART

Symptoms	Causes	Treatment
Broken wind Persistent cough, rapid exhaustion, double movement of flank	Breakdown of air vessels in the lung from overworking the horse	Incurable, may be alleviated by keeping horse out, work gently, and dampen food
Catarrh Thick, yellowish discharge from the nostrils	Inflammation of mucous membrane. May be cold infection preceding cough or allergy. Beware of infecting other horses	Clean nostrils with warm boric solution and smear with petroleum jelly. In summer, turn out to grass
Coughs and colds Thin discharge from nostrils; coughing	Infection; sometimes dusty hay or allergy	Isolate animal and keep warm; give doses of cough medicine. Consult veterinarian
Influenza Lethargy, cough, high temperature. Horse refuses food	Virus infection	Isolate. Keep warm. Rest. Call veterinarian. Prevention by inoculation is possible
Strangles Similar to those of influenza, plus swelling of lymph glands under the jaw, which eventually form abscesses	Contact with infected animal or with contaminated grooming kit, feed buckets, etc	Isolate. Call veterinarian. Feed hay and bran mashes and keep horse warm. Rest is essential

Legs

Symptoms	Causes	Treatment
Bog spavin Swelling in the front of the hock and on both sides at the back	Excess fluid in hock joint	None. Bog spavins look unsightly but cause no trouble
Brushing Sudden acute lameness. Injury around the fetlock joints	One leg striking against the other	Rest and hosing the affected part with cold water. Prevent recurrence by fitting brushing boots. Consult blacksmith
Capped elbow Swelling on the point of the elbow, level with chest. If infected, horse may be lame	Persistent irritation or rubbing of the elbow when lying down or because bed is too thin	Cold poultice the swelling and call veterinarian if infected. Special shoeing and provide thicker bed
Cracked heels Sore patches, often suppurating, and deep cracks on the heels at the back of the pastern	An irritant in the soil which affects the heels and legs after they have been covered in mud. White legs are more prone to the condition	Apply ointment, using one with a cod-liver oil or zinc oxide base. Alternatively, dry poultice with dry warm bran, and bandaging
Curb Lameness. Outward bowing of line from point of hock to cannon bone	Sprain to ligament connecting point of hock with cannon bone	Rest. Cold poulticing application of liniment
Ringbone Lameness. Swelling of pastern	Blow, sprain or jarring which causes extra bone to form on the first and second pastern bones, or both	Rest. Seek professional advice and be prepared for pony to be permanently lame
Speedy cutting Sudden fall or lameness. Cuts or bruises just below knee	One leg interfering with another	Rest. Bathe affected part with cold water
Splints Lameness. Heat and swelling in affected leg	Formation of bone between the splint and the cannon bone	Rest. Cold water poultices. Once splint has formed, lameness disappears, leaving a permanent lump
Sprained joints and tendons Heat and swelling. Lameness in some cases	Jarring. Twisting of joint. Inflammation of the tendon	Cold water dousing. For tendons, pressure bandages. Rest
Thoroughpin Swelling just above the hock which can usually be pushed from one side to the other	Strain	Pressure bandage to reduce swelling. Keep soft by massage or by applying goose grease

Giving medicine, for example, can present problems. The simplest way is in the feed, provided that the medicine is suitable and the horse is eating. Soluble medicines can be mixed in with the drinking water. Otherwise the veterinarian will advise.

The golden rules of nursing are gentleness, cleanliness, and the ability to ensure the horse's comfort and rest. When treating a wound, always try to reduce the amount of dust in the stable. Decrease concentrated foods for a horse suddenly thrown out of work by lameness and substitute a mild laxative instead. Gently sponging eyes and nostrils will help refresh a horse running a temperature.

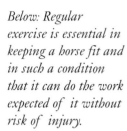

Below: Regular exercise is essential in keeping a horse fit and in such a condition that it can do the work expected of it without risk of injury.

Care when old

Horses and ponies are frequently remarkably long-lived. Some ponies, for instance, are still leading useful lives at thirty, but caring for an elderly horse presents its own set of problems.

Teeth must be regularly filed (rasped), as the molars will probably become long and sharp if left untreated. Select the diet carefully; boiled barley, broad bran, chaff, and good quality hay form the best mixture for an old horse.

Eventually, though, some horses just lose interest in life. If the luster goes out of the eyes or the appetite wanes for no apparent reason, it is then kinder to have the horse put down. A veterinarian will arrange this. A humane killer is used, and death is instantaneous.

TACK AND EQUIPMENT

SADDLES

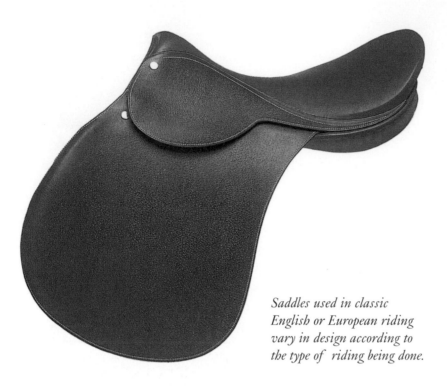

Saddles used in classic English or European riding vary in design according to the type of riding being done.

Below: The most widely used saddle is the all-purpose saddle. The saddle evolved from the style known as the Italian forward seat in which the rider is positioned over the horse's center of gravity, shifting his/her weight with the horse's movements.

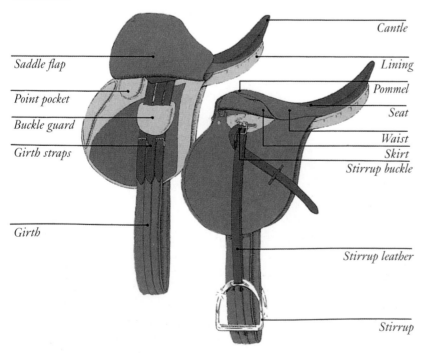

Saddle flap
Point pocket
Buckle guard
Girth straps
Girth

Cantle
Lining
Pommel
Seat
Waist
Skirt
Stirrup buckle
Stirrup leather
Stirrup

The saddle evolved after the bridle. It came into being in order to make riding more comfortable for both rider and horse. Riding bareback is tiring and it is also somewhat insecure for the rider.

All designs of saddle, therefore, have one thing in common—the central gullet directs pressure off the spine and instead distributes the rider's weight evenly on either side of the back over the fleshy, muscular area covering the ribs. They also all assist a rider to control his or her mount by giving a firmer position from which to issue the aids.

The key feature of any saddle is a framework known as the tree, around which all saddles are built. The tree is usually made of lightweight wood. When this has been shaped and glued together, it forms the basis upon which webbing and padding will be bound and attached. Together, they determine the finished shape and, therefore, the purpose of the saddle.

The most widely used saddle in European riding today is the all-purpose saddle. This evolved from the riding style known as the Italian forward seat, which was developed some 60 to 70 years ago. The rider is positioned over the horse's center of gravity, shifting his or her position as the center shifts. An obvious example is leaning forward when a horse is jumping. Before this style was developed, a rider sat well back in the saddle, his legs pushed forward; if he had to jump, he would lean further back.

The design of saddles then in use encouraged such a position, so, to further their new ideas, the Italians developed a saddle that encouraged their new style. As this method of riding became widely adopted and practiced, most nations began to produce their own version of this saddle and now there is an enormous range of them.

Sidesaddles

Sidesaddle riders are faced with a much smaller range of saddles—if, indeed, they can find one at all. Nearly all sidesaddles are secondhand, since, until the revival of the last decade or so, the art of aside riding—and thus the art of making sidesaddles—had almost died out. Most sidesaddles were made to fit a specific rider and this is an important point to bear in mind when buying a secondhand one.

PUTTING ON AN ALL-PURPOSE SADDLE

PUTTING ON A SIDESADDLE

1 Place the saddle in position, so the pommel is just behind the withers, with irons up and girth across.

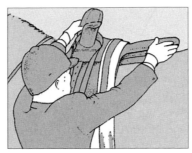

1 Standing by the horse's near-side shoulder, lift up the saddle and place it on the horse slightly forward of the withers.

5 The girth, surcingle, and balance strap are now hanging down on the horse's near side and must be brought over to the off side.

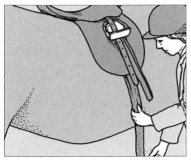

2 Check that the coat is smooth under the saddle flap. Then move around to the off side of the horse and let down the girth.

2 As the girths, surcingle, and balance strap are all attached to the near side of the saddle, undo these and take them down.

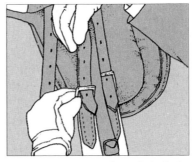

6 Bring the surcingle and girth through and buckle them. Make sure that the hook on the saddle flap is secured on the off side.

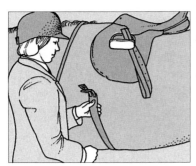

3 Return to the near side and pass the girth under the horse's belly. Check carefully to make sure that it does not get twisted.

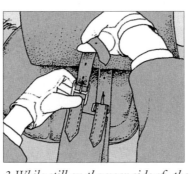

3 While still on the near side of the horse, check to make sure that the girth is buckled sufficiently high up on the saddle.

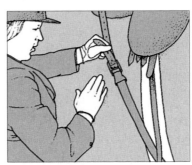

7 Pull the balance strap under the horse's belly, slotting it through the keeper on the girth. This will help to keep the strap in place.

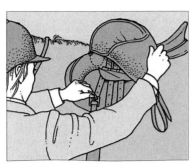

4 Buckle the girth to hold the saddle securely in position. Adjust stirrup leathers and tighten the girth again. Then mount.

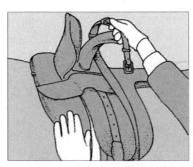

4 Unhook the surcingle from the pommel. If your horse is jumpy, ask an assistant to hold the saddle. It is not yet secured on the horse.

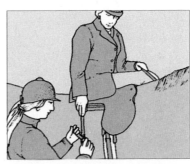

8 Mount and ask an assistant to adjust the girth, balance strap, and surcingle, in that order, on the off side of the horse.

WESTERN SADDLES

There are almost as many designs of Western saddles as there are European ones. The basic design features—the high horn, deep, wide seat and high cantle—were born out of practicality and are present to some extent in all Western saddles. However, over the generations, they have been subjected to endless variations and modifications.

The first stock saddle was said to have originated in Mexico, from whence it traveled to Texas, where it was copied. It continued to spread across the country, as ranchmen and cattle began to invade what had previously been buffalo territory. Alterations were made in different places to the rigging (the system of straps and girths that keeps the saddle in place), the horn and the swells (the padded area directly in front of the rider's knees, which varies in degree according to taste and the rider's job). In addition, tremendous variations occurred in the actual esthetic appearance of the saddles, according to the extent

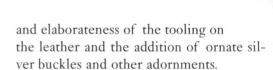

and elaborateness of the tooling on the leather and the addition of ornate silver buckles and other adornments.

The cowboy's working stock saddle on the home range differs from that used for Western pleasure riding, or more classic Western riding. Similarly, it differs from the saddle used by another ranchman, whose job involves him spending long hours of each day riding over the range. The cowboy working cows—roping them and jumping out of the saddle hundreds of times a day—uses a saddle with a very strong, reinforced horn that can withstand the strain of a twisting, bucking cow. The saddle also has almost flat swells, so that these do not get in his way as he leaps quickly from his horse's back. The ranchman riding the range prefers a saddle with very pronounced swells and a deep seat, which makes the long hours in the saddle a great deal more comfortable.

Left: The Western saddle was designed for practicality. While some are very elaborate, most, like this one, are simple, sturdy, and functional. The horn is designed to withstand the stress of roping cattle and most saddles will have a deep seat and pronounced swells that allow the rider to sit relatively comfortably for long hours out on the range.

Unlike European saddles, the Western, or stock, saddle has no padding. This is because the extreme heat of the climate, which would often cause the horse to sweat profusely, would soon affect the padding by shifting it about and making it hard and lumpy. For this reason, Western saddles are always worn with pads and blankets underneath (these were often used as bedding for the rider when he had to sleep out on the range). Once again, though, the saddle must still fit the horse correctly; an ill-fitting Western saddle can no more be made to fit a horse by putting extra blankets underneath than a European saddle can be.

Left: Western saddles are much heavier than English or European saddles. They were designed to carry a person long distances, so they were often padded for additional comfort. When putting on a Western saddle, begin by making sure that the hair around and under the saddle is lying flat and smooth. Standing on the near side, fold a blanket in half or thirds and put it high up on the withers, making sure it is evenly placed across the back. Place the saddle pad towards the front and position the saddle, pulling the blanket and pad up into the gullet so that they are not drawn too tightly across the horse's back.

PUTTING ON A WESTERN SADDLE

1 Go to the other side and take the cinch and other straps down from the side of the saddle.

3 Then buckle or tie the cinch. The rear cinch does not have to be secured as tightly as the main cinch.

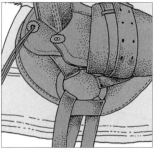

2 Return to the near side and pull these through under the horse's belly.

4 Finally, pick up each of the forelegs in turn and pull them forward to make sure the cinch is not pinching the skin behind the elbow.

WESTERN SADDLE VARIATIONS

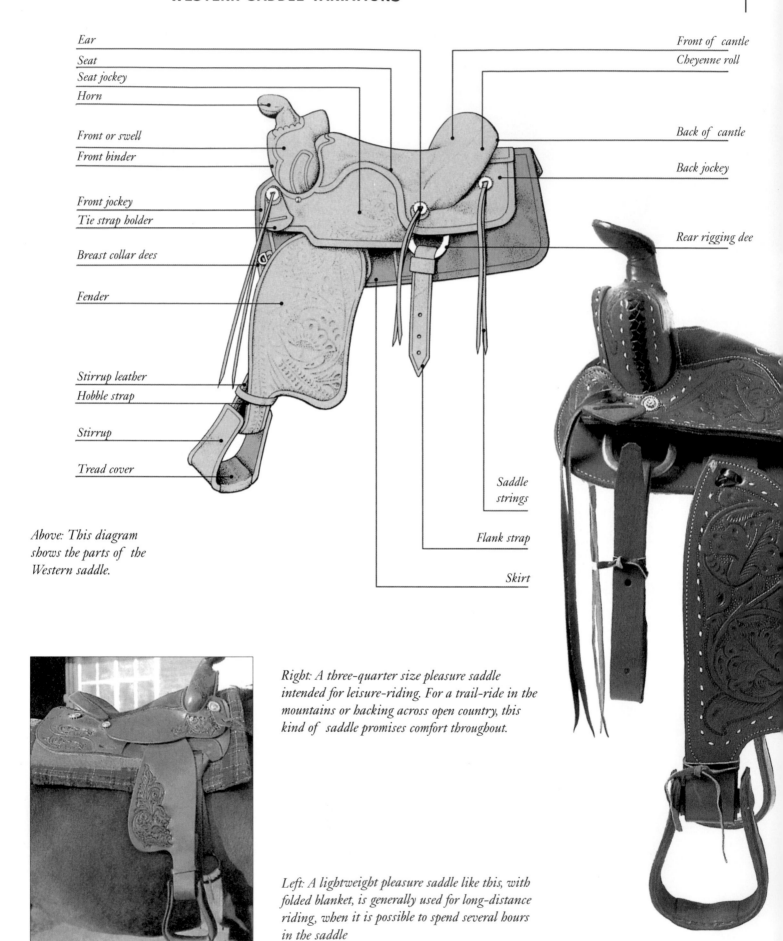

Ear

Seat

Seat jockey

Horn

Front or swell

Front binder

Front jockey

Tie strap holder

Breast collar dees

Fender

Stirrup leather

Hobble strap

Stirrup

Tread cover

Front of cantle

Cheyenne roll

Back of cantle

Back jockey

Rear rigging dee

Saddle strings

Flank strap

Skirt

Above: This diagram shows the parts of the Western saddle.

Right: A three-quarter size pleasure saddle intended for leisure-riding. For a trail-ride in the mountains or hacking across open country, this kind of saddle promises comfort throughout.

Left: A lightweight pleasure saddle like this, with folded blanket, is generally used for long-distance riding, when it is possible to spend several hours in the saddle

Above: A lightweight saddle with hand-tooled leatherwork and a padded seat. This is a typical example of the kind of saddle that would be used for barrel-racing). Note the wooden stirrups sheathed in steel.

BITS

The snaffle is the simplest type of bit. Its mouthpiece may be jointed or unjointed, smooth or twisted, straight or curved, according to its individual design and purpose. At each end, it has a circular or D-shaped ring to which the reins are attached. Depending on how the rider uses his or her hands, the bit can be used to exert pressure on the outside of the bars of the mouth, the tongue, and the corners of the mouth.

The mouthpiece of a curb bit can also be jointed or unjointed; alternatively, it may have a raised section in the center known as a "port." It may be "fixed," in that it is rigidly secured at either end to the cheekpieces, or movable, which means the cheekpieces can move a little, independently of the mouthpiece. The slight flexibility this affords tends to lessen the severity of the bit. It also encourages the horse to play with it in his mouth, which helps to create saliva. This, in turn, helps to protect the sensitive tissues of the horse's mouth.

The curb bit has long cheekpieces extending down either side of the mouthpiece, with the rings to take the reins placed at the bottom. In addition, a curb chain or strap, resting in the "curb groove" under the horse's chin, is fastened to either side of the bit. The lever action produced by the reins exerts pressure on the horse's poll through the headpiece and also on the curb groove through the curb chain or strap. The mouthpiece of the bit exerts pressure on the tongue, the bars and—in the case of very high ports—the roof of the mouth.

Above left: the bit contributes to the overall control of the horse and is used in conjunction with a number of other aids. The pressure exerted by the rider on the horse's mouth sends instructions, and the horse's reaction should be one of relaxation and not one of fear or pain. There are numerous types of bits ranging from the simple to the complex; however, it is still the skill of the rider that will determine the horse's movements and cooperation.

Left: 1 German snaffle; 2 straight bar snaffle; 3 rubber snaffle; 4 eggbutt snaffle; 5 Fulmer snaffle; 6 gag-bit; 7 loose-ring snaffle; 8 Kimblewick; 9 flexible rubber mouth Pelham; 10 Weymouth bridoon and curb bits; 11 Pelham bit; 12 Scamperdale

TYPES OF BIT

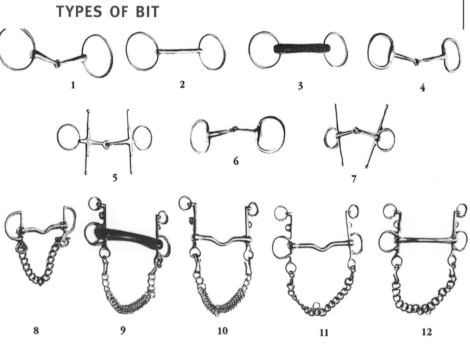

1 2 3 4

5 6 7

8 9 10 11 12

HOW THE BRIDLE AND BIT WORKS

To understand how and why the bridle enables the rider to control and direct his horse, it will help to look at the parts of the animal's head that are affected. The bit and bridle can be used to exert pressure on eight parts of the head.

Poll: Pressure is applied here by the head-piece when used with a curb or gag bit.

Roof: Affected only by bits with very high ports.

Bit

Tongue: All bits apply pressure here and the design of the bit determines the extent of the pressure.

Bars: Sensitive, fleshy area on either side of the mouth between front and back teeth mainly affected by curb bits.

Lower jaw: Very little flesh-covering the bone. Only affected by the bosal bitless bridle.

Nose: The front is extremely sensitive and affected by some types of noseband. Bitless bridles concentrate pressure on this point.

Corners: A very sensitive area only thinly covered by skin. Affected by snaffle bits.

Curb groove: Extremely sensitive area easily affected by the curb chain or strap.

Below: This is a loose ring cheek snaffle, known as the "Fulmer" snaffle in the UK.

The position adopted by a young horse in the early stages of training. The mouthpiece acts in an upward direction against the corners of the lips.

An intermediate position. The action of the bit is divided between the lip corners and the bars of the lower jaw.

The position obtained at a later stage in training. The mouthpiece of the bit now bears across the bars of the lower jaw.

NOSEBANDS

In almost every instance the nosebands fulfills some practical function connected with increased control of the horse. The only exception is the plain cavesson noseband which, unless it is used as an anchorage for the standing martingale, serves no more than an esthetic purpose. In its normal position the cavesson is fitted so that two fingers can be inserted between it and the jawbone. If fitted tightly and a little lower than usual it can partially close the mouth, but not to the same extent as the drop noseband.

The drop noseband

The drop noseband is without doubt the most important type of noseband in the context of modern riding, whether it is being used in the schooling of a horse or in competition. The nosepiece is fitted some 3 in (7.5 cm) above the nostrils, just below the termination of the facial bones. The back strap is then secured under the bit, so as to lie in the curb groove. Positioned in this way and adjusted fairly tightly, the noseband stops the mouth from being opened and, as a result, also prevents the horse from evading the action of the bit in that manner. For the same reason, its use ensures that the bit remains central in the mouth, since the horse cannot slide the bit over to one side or the other.

The pressure of the noseband therefore assists and strengthens the action of the bit. Pressure on the rein is transmitted to the nose as the horse's lower jaw gives to the bit action. In turn such pressure causes the horse to drop his head, allowing the bit to bear across the bars of the lower jaw, in which position it will have the greatest effect. However, it is also the

Above: Drop noseband, fastening below the bit—a very common modern bitting arrangement

case that the pressure exerted on the nose—if sufficiently strong—can cause a momentary check to the breathing, which will contribute to the dropping of the head.

Variations on the basic drop noseband also exist. One widely-used type is called a "Flash" noseband, after a jumper who wore it, and another is the Grackle, Figure 8, or "cross-over" noseband. The former is designed for use with a standing martingale, the two crossing straps sewn to the center of the cavesson, which fastens under the bit, being the means by which the mouth is kept closed. It is not, however, as effective in lowering the head as the straightforward drop, since the point at which pressure is put on the nose is higher than in the true drop noseband. Far less nose pressure can be applied as well.

The Grackle was named after a horse of that name who wore one when he won the British Grand National in 1931. In fact, the Crackle has lost the chief features of its design in recent years and has become merged into the general concept of a cross-over noseband. In its general form, the top strap, fastening above the bit, was carefully shaped, so that it and the lower strap, fastening under the bit, were kept exactly in place; this being assisted by the connecting strap at the rear. Nose pressure was localized at the point of intersection of the straps, but could be adjusted at the headpiece so the point was raised.

The cross-over nosebands are possibly not as precise as the conventional drops, but they are probably more suited to some horses. This is because of their reduced degree of restriction, particularly in relation to the respiration, which make them suitable for the hard-pulling cross-country horse and for the steeplechaser.

The Kineton, or Puckle, noseband goes to the opposite extreme. It has no pretensions to be other than a strong stopping agent for use on very hard-pulling horses. It makes no attempt to close the mouth, the metal loops, fixed behind the bit, transmitting the very considerable pressure that can be obtained directly to the nose by means of the nosepiece which is adjusted both low and fairly tight. The nosepiece is frequently reinforced with a core of light metal.

A noseband popular in racing and other equestrian circles is the sheepskin-covered

DIFFERENT TYPES OF NOSEBAND

Australian racing cheeker

Grackle, or Figure 8, noseband

Sheepskin noseband derived from the harness racing shadow noseband

Kineton, or Puckle, noseband

Plain cavesson noseband

Flash noseband

A raised, show-type noseband with a snaffle bridle

noseband, which originally was used with harness trotters as an "anti-shadow" or "anti-shy" noseband. In the context of the trotting horse the "shadow roll," as this noseband is termed, has a definite purpose. In conjunction with the characteristic extended nose position of the trotter moving at speed, it prevented the horse from seeing shadows on the track or variations in the surface color, which might cause him to check or break his gait. It has far less to commend it in the context of the riding horse, and very little in the context of racing, either. No firm opinion, for example, is held as to whether the use of the sheepskin-covered noseband is supposed to encourage a horse to put his head up or down.

The Australian Cheeker

A final, useful piece of equipment is the noseband referred to as an Australian Cheeker, which, for no very good reason, is confined largely to the racing scene. Usually made of rubber, the Cheeker fits over the bit rings on either side and then joins into a central strap that runs right up the face and fastens to an attachment on the headpiece of the bridle, right between the horse's ears.

Correctly fitted, the noseband lifts the bit in the mouth, which makes it more difficult for a horse to get his "tongue over the bit," thus evading its action and causing even more serious trouble by "swallowing" the tongue. This, however, is not its only effect. For some reason that is still not satisfactorily understood, anything running up the center of a horse's face exerts some form of psychological restraint and is a very effective ploy to use in the case of hard pullers. In more elaborate forms, the system can be seen incorporated into the Rockwell bridle and the Norton Perfection, or Citation; these are bridles of American origin used in racing.

BRIDLES

The various parts of the bridle are virtually common to all types, although they may not look the same or employ the same method of fastening.

The head of the bridle, passing over the horse's poll, has, attached to it, the cheeks to which the bit is secured. The throatlatch (pronounced throatlash) is usually incorporated in the head, though, in some instances, it is a completely separate strap attached to the head by a loop fixed between the horse's ears, as in some American patterns.

Certain types of bridle, however, omit the throatlatch completely. There are, for instance, no throatlatches on the bridles used in the Spanish Riding School in Vienna. The reason for this is that a throatlatch, if it is too tight, can discourage a horse from flexing at the poll, because of the discomfort it would cause. The Spanish School Lipizzaners are, in any case, naturally thick through the jowl and, since they are unlikely to get into situations in which the bridle may be pulled off, there is no need for a throatlatch. Its other purpose is to prevent the bridle coming off in the event of a fall, for instance. A number of Western bridles also dispense with the throatlatch, preferring to keep the bridle in place by a slit passed over either both ears or a single ear.

The browband, or "front" as it is sometimes known, is fastened by loops to the headpiece and serves to keep the latter from sliding backward. There is then, in most bridles, but not in all, a noseband and then finally a pair of reins.

Above: The double bridle, comprising curb bit and bridoon (i.e., a light snaffle bit) generally goes under the name Weymouth.

Right: Parts of a double bridle. The extra pair of reins is also a requirement of the Pelham and Gag bridles.

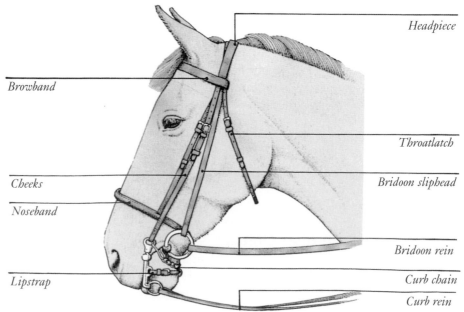

Headpiece

Browband

Throatlatch

Cheeks

Bridoon sliphead

Noseband

Bridoon rein

Lipstrap

Curb chain

Curb rein

Double bridles and Pelhams

The above describes the composition of a snaffle bridle, but, in the case of double bridles and Pelhams, additions are needed.

On a double bridle, for instance, there has to be a sliphead, from which the bridoon is suspended. A sliphead is a strap and one cheekpiece passed through the loops of the browband under the headpiece. The cheek of the sliphead is placed on the off side so that its buckle matches that of the noseband on the near side.

In both the double and Pelham bridles, a pair of extra reins is necessary, the curb rein always being the narrower of the two. There is also the addition of a lipstrap, which is attached to the dees halfway down the cheeks of the bit and through the "fly" (flying) link in the center of the curb chain. Its purpose is to keep the curb chain in place.

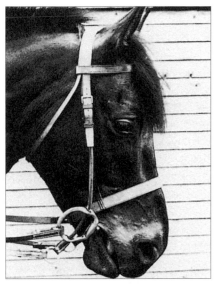

Above: Gag Bridle

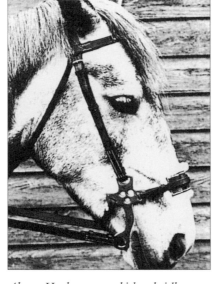

Above: Hackamore or bitless bridle

Above: Pelham, which can be converted to a single rein with a leather rounding joining the bridoon and curb rings.

Above: Hunting snaffle

Above: Fine leather, lightweight show bridle with raised and swelled noseband.

Above: Weymouth bridle in hunting, general-purpose weight. Bridles can be attached to bits by sewing, hook studs or, very occasionally, buckles.

MARTINGALES

All martingales share the common objective of assisting the action of the bit by restraining in one way or another the positioning of the horse's head and neck. In some cases they may go further by accentuating a particular action, or even by altering the character of the bit.

These auxiliaries can be regarded conveniently in two sections. There are those that seek in the simplest ways to prevent the head from being raised out of the control of the hand, and those that are intended as serious, long-term schooling aids, designed to affect the whole outline of the young horse or to attempt the correction of that of the older animal. In effect, the martingale is an aid to improved balance—although it would not be considered so by the purist.

Simple martingales

The simplest form of martingale is the standing or "fast" martingale. Essentially this is an adjustable strap attached at one end to the girth between the forelegs and at the other to the rear of a plain, stout cavesson noseband. To keep the strap in place it is fitted with a neckstrap, which can also be used by the rider in case of emergency to stay in the saddle.

The martingale prevents the horse, very effectively, from throwing up his head and, depending on how it is adjusted, places the bit below the hand and acting squarely upon the bars of the lower jaw. Adjusted to a sensible length there is no reason why it should restrict the horse when jumping, since the head and neck are then stretched forwards and downwards—not upwards.

The martingale, in a very much strengthened form, is a virtual essential in the equipment of the polo pony, but sometimes appears as the more colorful pugaree martingale. This piece of equipment comes from India. It is, in fact, a length of colored turban cloth.

Occasionally, in some areas of Western riding, the standing martingale acts directly on the mouth, rather than the nose, being divided at the top end of the strap and the bifurcations being fitted with snap hooks to fasten to the bit. A similar device was once in vogue in Europe.

Running martingales

The running martingale is slightly more complex. Again, this has the central strap divided, the ends of the two branches being fitted with rings through which the reins are passed. When the horse attempts to throw up his head, the action is countered by pressure on the bars of the lower jaw through the bit. The tighter the martingale is adjusted, the greater is the restriction on the position of the head. In theory, it is recommended that the martingale is fitted so that the rings are in line with the withers, but in practical terms the adjustment is usually somewhat tighter. In show jumping, for instance, the rein frequently forms a distinct angle between the mouth and the hand. In both instances the martingales, whether standing or running, alter the action of the snaffle bit, since it must be presumed that without the restraint imposed by them, the horse's head would be held higher, so that the bit would act more upon the corners of the lips than otherwise. Using the martingales, the bit is placed over the bars of the lower jaw, the action being more direct in the case of the running martingale.

Racehorses very often wear a running martingale in which the branches are joined by a triangular-shaped piece of leather. This is called a "bib" martingale and is fitted as a precaution against an excited horse getting caught up or even getting his nose between the two branches. Racing trainers also use a small piece of equipment, which, despite being called the Irish martingale, is an intruder within the martingale family, since it has none of the group's familiar objects or characteristics. It consists of a short strip of leather joining two rings together, through which the reins are passed, and its use has no influence on the head position at all. Its purpose is to assist the correct direction of the rein pull and to prevent the reins being brought right over the horse's head in the event of a heavy fall.

It is usual to fit "stops" on the rein with which a running martingale is used. These are shaped pieces of rubber or leather that are slid on to the rein and fit tightly. Ideally they are positioned about 8–10 in (20–25 cm) from the bit. They prevent the rings of the martingale from running too far forward and becoming caught on the bridle in some way, or even

Above: Standing or "fast" martingale controlling position of head by pressure on the nose.

Above: Running martingale, imposing control by pressure on the mouth. The "stops" prevent the rings sliding forward and becoming caught on the bridle or over a tooth:

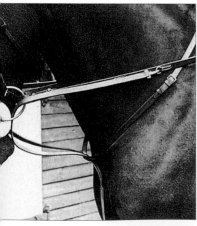

Above: The Market Harborough or German rein, which is a much improved version of the old draw rein.

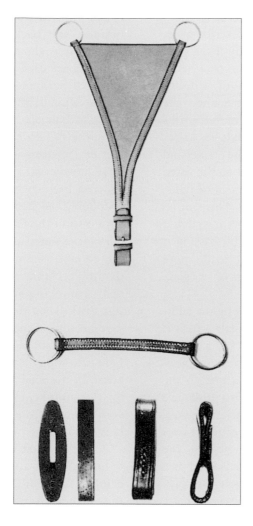

Bib martingale and (above) Irish martingale, and rein stops made from rubber and leather

becoming caught over one of the horse's teeth.

In theory again, the running martingale should not be used with a double bridle, since the latter, on a schooled horse, provides, without outside assistance, all that is necessary to obtain the required head position and degree of control. In practice, however, the martingale is on occasion used with the bridle. In this instance, it should logically be placed upon the curb rein to assist the lowering of the head, which is the purpose of the latter. As often as not, it is to be seen on the bridoon rein, when it becomes a contradiction in terms; sometimes with both reins passed through the rings. This last may constitute an effective braking system, but makes a nonsense of the reasons why the double bridle is used by riders.

The German rein

Another pattern of martingale much used in showjumping goes under the name of Market Harborough or German rein in Britain, though, in Germany, it is often called an English rein. The rein derives from the more straightforward draw rein that fastens to the girth on either side, then passes through the bit rings back to the rider's hand. Though it is termed a rein, it is much more like a martingale in its action.

The martingale has two strips of leather attached to a ring on the chest and passing through the bit ring to a fastening on the rein. The adjustment is made either with a buckle or by clipping the leather strip to one of three or four small metal Ds set on the rein. The action is quite simple. So long as the horse carries his head acceptably, the rein operates in the normal fashion. A downward pressure on the mouth only occurs when the horse throws up the head, causing the leather strips to tighten and to pull down on the bit rings.

For the moment, outside of polo, the standing martingale is out of favor, although it is used as a training aid for jumping. The running martingale, however, is widely used in all competitive events, with the natural exception of dressage.

The pulley martingale

The older generations of horsemen and women seem to have given much more thought to bitting than is usual in these days of universal horsemanship based on the snaffle and drop noseband. One older type of running martingale such riders used was the pulley type, in which the rings were attached to a cord that passed through a pulley at the top of the body strap. Its advantage was that, in making sharp turns and so on, the horse was allowed to bend his head in the direction of the movement, without the kind of restriction on the opposite side of his mouth that is inevitable to some degree with the conventional pattern.

THE WESTERN HACKAMORE

Above: A variation of the bitless bridle, misnamed hackamore, now in general use. It achieves its object by putting pressure on the nose. The sheepskin padding on the nose and rear strip is to prevent chafing. It is also necessary to vary the fitting frequently to avoid callousing the nose.

In Europe, "hackamore" is often used mistakenly to describe a bit-less-type bridle, usually fitted with metal cheekpieces. The true hackamore largely consists of a heavy, braided rawhide noseband, the shape of a réal tennis racket, with a large knot at the end that lies under the horse's chin. The noseband itself is called a bosal and is fitted to the horse by means of a light-weight latigo headstall. This may be slit at an appropriate point so that it can be kept in place by passing it over an ear, or may be made more secure by the addition of a brow-band, or cavesada.

The hackamore is completed by the addition of a rope made from mane hair, which is called the mecate and usually by a fiador, made from the same material or sometimes from cotton. The mecate is attached to the heel knot by a system of "wraps" to produce a delicately balanced and sophisticated control device, the heavy rope reins and the heel knot combining to act as a counterweight to the substantial nosepiece. The fiador is used as a throatlatch and adjusted short enough to prevent the heel knot from bumping annoyingly against the lower jaw as the horse moves.

From hackamore to bit

Initially, the hackamore is used with both hands, but, as the horse's schooling progresses, the reins are used in one hand only. The fully schooled hackamore horse can carry out all the movements required of him in a state of constant balance and at high speed. He can make the sudden stops, the pivots (the equivalent of the dressage pirouette, though not the same movement), the turns and the rein-backs, all on a looping rein and without his mouth ever being touched. The final stage is the graduation from the hackamore to the bit, usually, but not always, a fairly long-cheeked high-ported curb (the port is the inverted U in the mouthpiece that allows room for the tongue and permits the bearing surface of the bit to rest directly on the bars). This transition is a gradual one, made with the help of a much lighter hackamore fitted with a pair of very light rein ropes. It is often known as a two-rein bosal. In the final stages, control passes to the bit, the latter being supported by a bosal of the very lightest proportions acting independently without reins.

The finished Western horse is ridden in a light curb bit bridle without a bosal or noseband of any sort, and a floating, or looping, rein, which exerts no more than a minimal contact on the mouth. Sometimes the reins are weighted by the addition of small decorative pieces of metal, but the ideal is for the horse to ride on the weight of a plain ¼ in (6 mm) rawhide rein.

Right: The parts of the hackamore including the fiador, the throatlatch which prevents the heel knot from bumping annoyingly against the lower jaw.

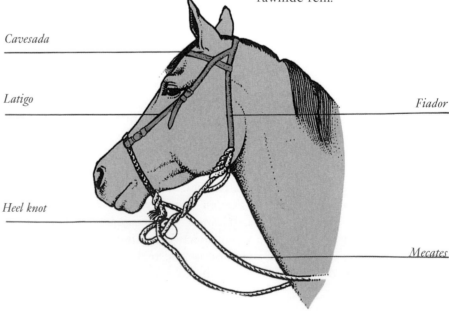

Cavesada

Latigo

Heel knot

Fiador

Mecates

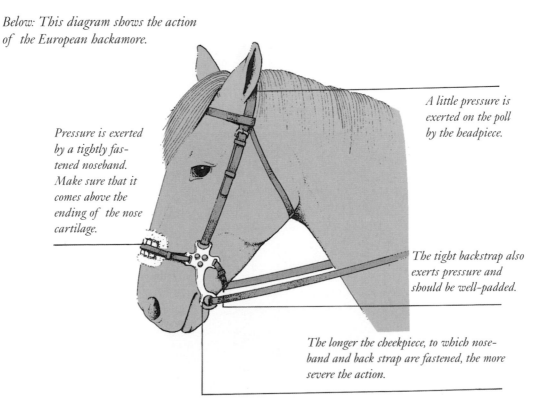

The European hackamore

The European equivalent of the hackamore is the variety of bitless-type bridles, deriving from the hackamore system. Of these, the best known is Blair's pattern. This bridle consists of the usual type of headpiece, a noseband, a curb, or back strap, and a pair of long metal cheeks to which the last two items are attached. Control is effected by exerting pressure on the nose and on the back strap embracing the lower jaw, the potential severity of the action being dependent upon the length of the cheek. Since nosepiece and back strap must be adjusted tightly to be effective, both must be soft and well-padded. The nosepiece should rest, as in the case of the bosal, above the ending of the nose cartilage, so as not to restrict the breathing, and its position needs to be altered continually.

Contrary to the general view, the bitless bridle is not suitable for novice use, since a novice could do far more damage with it than with a metal bit. Nor will it produce sudden and miraculous results. It is the precision tool of the expert horseman with a pair of delicate hands. Ideally, it, too, should operate from a floating rein, changes of direction being made by carrying the required rein outward and combining that action with a shift of body weight in the same direction.

Less severe and often effective on a horse whose mouth, for whatever reason, precludes the use of a bit are the shorter cheeked bitless bridles, but they have little in common with the hackamore system.

An interesting bitless bridle is that perfected by William Stone, a lorimer in Walsall, Britain, who worked for many years with the firm of Matthew Harvey Ltd. It is called the W S Bitless Pelham and it, or something very similar, is still available today. The bridle employs two reins—hence the term "Pelham"—the top rein acting on the nose and the lower one on the curb groove by means of a curb chain. The metal cheeks of the bridle, which are comparatively short, move independently and thus allow a certain finesse in the action, which is not found in other patterns in current use.

The advantages of the hackamore system are obvious enough in the schooling of polo ponies, for instance, but perhaps less so in regard to the modern, competitive, horse world. This is considered to be unfortunate by many, because there is much to commend this older and infinitely skilful school of riding to the present-day rider.

*Below: This diagram shows the action
of the European hackamore.*

*Pressure is exerted
by a tightly fas-
tened noseband.
Make sure that it
comes above the
ending of the nose
cartilage.*

*A little pressure is
exerted on the poll
by the headpiece.*

*The tight backstrap also
exerts pressure and
should be well-padded.*

*The longer the cheekpiece, to which nose-
band and back strap are fastened, the more
severe the action.*

RUGS

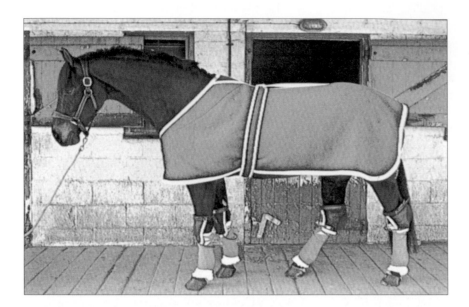

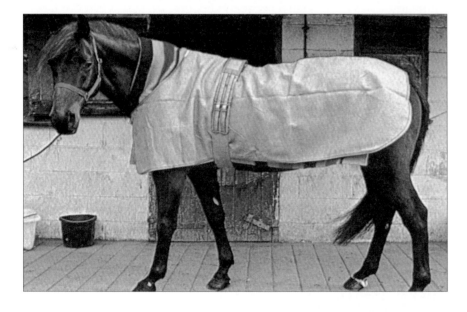

If a horse is worked during the winter, he will normally need clipping to avoid excessive sweating. The corollary of this is that his natural coat must be replaced by an artificial one, if he is not to catch cold. Winter stable rugs exist for this purpose and come in a number of varieties. The traditional pattern, made of jute or finely woven canvas and fully lined with a gray wool-mixture blanket, is probably the most successful. The rug is kept in place by a leather buckle fastening at the chest and either by a jute surcingle attached to the rug, a plain leather roller, or an anti-cast roller. The last is an adaptation of the ordinary leather roller, as it is fitted with a metal arch that goes over the horse's spine. It prevents the horse rolling over in his box and perhaps getting cast—that is, unable to get up unaided.

For added warmth, a "pure new wool" blanket can be placed underneath the rug. These blankets are traditionally fawn in color, with black, red, and blue stripes at either end. They weigh approximately 8 lb (3.6 kg). Lighter-weight blankets, made of "all wool" as opposed to "pure new wool" in similar colors, are also on the market, plus gray or brown wool-and-fiber mixture varieties.

An anti-sweat sheet, similar to a string vest, can also be used under the night rug for extra warmth. The sheet, made of cotton mesh, creates air pockets next to the body to insulate the horse against extremes of heat or cold. Its normal use is with a sweaty horse. For best results, it should be put on the hot animal next to the skin, with a day rug or summer sheet on top of it, to prevent the horse from getting chilled.

Top: A horse ready for traveling, wearing a headstall, wool day rug, roller, tail guard, kneecaps, hock caps and protective bandages.

Above: A jute night rug worn over a striped underblanket and secured by a body roller.

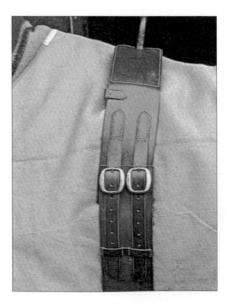

Left: Leather stable roller fitted with anti-cast hoop.

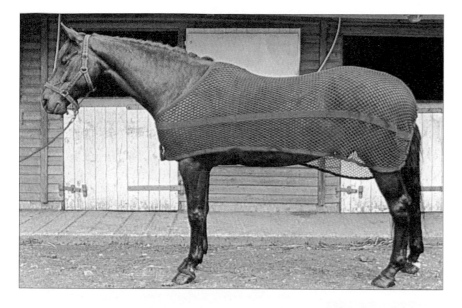

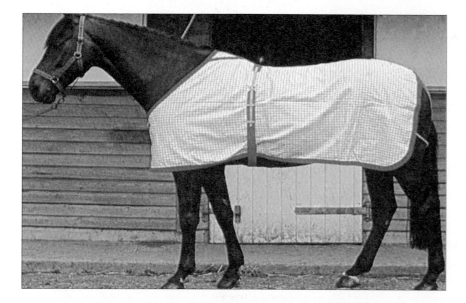

Other rug varieties

A range of nylon quilted rugs, similar to the anoraks worn by people, are available. Most are made of nylon with polyester filling, with either a brushed nylon or cotton lining. They are extremely light and warm at the same time. These rugs are again kept in place by a surcingle or roller, with a nylon and metal fastening at the chest.

An alternative method of fastening is particularly popular in the USA. Here, the rug is fastened at the front with a chrome box clasp, with a cross-surcingle, designed on stress engineering principles, to keep the rug in place. The two webbing straps sewn on the rug equalize the tension by starting from the points of each shoulder, crossing under the horse in the normal roller position to the top of the hindquarters.

A rug, made of a very light fabric called Thermatextron, has a similar cross-surcingle fastening. Laboratory tests have demonstrated that this fabric has a higher degree of thermal insulation than any other. Thermatextron also absorbs less moisture.

Both these factors mean that the heat generated by the horse's body is conserved. For the maximum benefit, the rug should be worn next to the skin. It can be put over a wet or sweating horse, the damp evaporating through the fabric.

A further type of rug with cross-surcingle fastenings is known as a "banner blanket." It is made of triple-thickness woven acrylic fabric and keeps horses warm and the dampness out, even in the cold US winters for which it was designed.

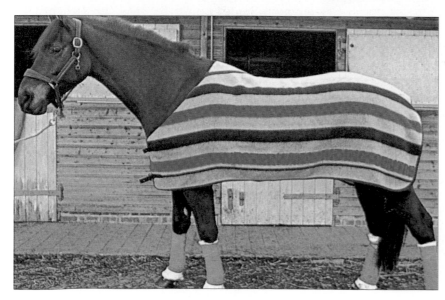

Top left: Mesh anti-sweat rug.

Center: Linen/cotton summer sheet with fillet string and light surcingle.

Bottom: Striped blanketing, originally used by the Hudson Bay Company for trading with the North American Indians, is traditional to the horse clothing industry.

BANDAGES

Horses wear bandages for a number of reasons. Principally, bandages are used to protect the horse's tail and legs when traveling; to prevent injury to the limbs, should the horse knock himself in the field or when being ridden; as a support for the tendons during exercise; to keep the horse warm in the stable; and to hold dressings in place when veterinary treatment is required.

The type of tail bandage commonly used is made of a strip of elastic gauze, about 8 ft (2.5 m) long and 3 in (7.5 cm) wide. This is bound around the tail to keep the hair flat and in place. Such a bandage should always be worn during traveling to prevent the horse from breaking his tail hairs, if he rubs his tail

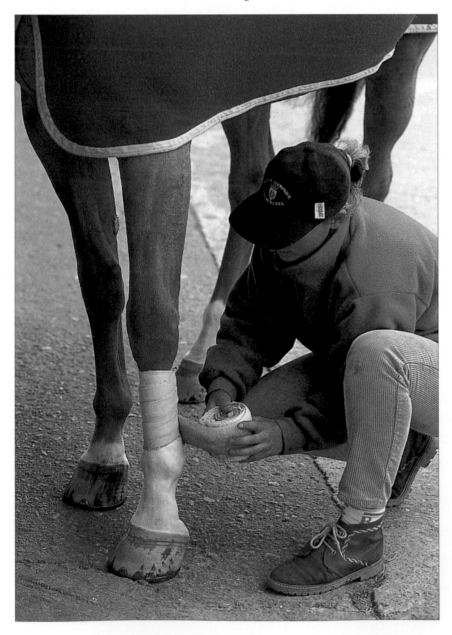

on the back of a trailer or against the side of a box. The tail hair should be dampened before the bandage is applied; the bandage itself, however, should not be wetted, as it might otherwise shrink when in place, causing both discomfort to the horse and damage to the tail. It should be wound around the tail, from the top down to the end of the dock, and then up again for a few inches, before being secured.

The same 3 in- (7.5 cm-) wide gauze bandages are also used as exercise bandages to support the tendons. Here, they are worn over a layer of Gamgee tissue, thick cotton batting, pads of cotton, felt, or other similar materials. Such bandages are applied at the top of the cannon bone under the knee and extend down to above the fetlock joint. The tapes of the bandage are fastened securely on the outside of the cannon bone with a knot. Bandages fastened on the inside of the leg are more likely to come undone while the horse is working, since the knot can be caught by a blow from the opposite leg.

The purpose of the bandages is to help to absorb concussion and to make sure that the pressure ridges, which could damage the tendons, are evened out. When used on horses taking part in strenuous activity, such as competing cross-country, show jumping, or hunting, it is advisable either to sew the bandages in place after tying the tapes, or bind them round with surgical tape. This ensures that the bandage will not come undone, while, if the surgical tape is used, this will also supply a waterproof covering.

Support must be given to each pair of legs, if it is to be effective—that is, both forelegs have to be bandaged, or both hindlegs. The horse can be bandaged all around if this is considered necessary.

Left: This show jumper is bandaged in front for protection and support; the bandages are firmly secured by a wrapping of surgical tape. The tape covering also protects the bandages from the consequences of being immersed in water, which can cause the bandage to shrink and become uncomfortably tight. It is for this reason, as well as for that of security, that surgical tape is so frequently used in the sport of eventing.

FITTING A STOCKINETTE TAIL BANDAGE

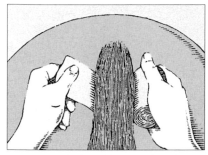

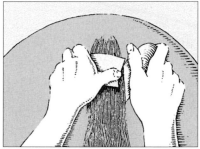

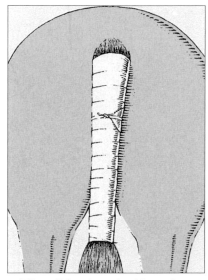

1 Dampen hair with water brush. Unroll short length of dry bandage and place this beneath the tail, close to dock.

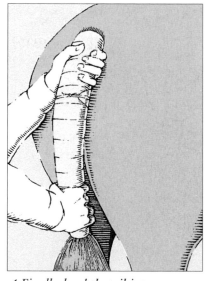

2 Holding the end of the bandage against the tail, make one turn to secure the bandage. Then continue the bandaging evenly downward.

3 The tail bandage should stop just short of the last tailbone and the remaining length should be bandaged upward and secured with tapes.

4 Finally, bend the tail into a comfortable position. Tail bandages should not be left overnight. Slide them off, downward, with both hands.

Gauze bandages can also be used to keep dressings in place, or as a cold water bandage for sprains and swellings. A type of proprietary elastic sock can also be used for this purpose. Another recent innovation is the "self-stick" variety of gauze bandage. Its use eliminates the need to use tapes.

Woollen stable bandages, approximately 5 in (12.5 cm) wide and 18 ft (2.5 m) long, are particularly useful for keeping a stabled horse warm in winter and protecting the legs of horses in a box or trailer. In the second case, it is particularly important to make sure that the bandage and its padding come down completely over the coronet, thus giving protection to the heel. Gamgee or similar padding is again used, though, in the case of some bandages, this is unnecessary. This type is made of thick, padded wool, with stockinette at each end.

The bandages are applied between knee or hock and continue down over the fetlock joint, this giving more warmth and protection than exercise bandages. They are fastened with strips of Velcro (as in the case of the padded bandages described above), or tapes. Velcro strips are quick and easy to apply, but their use can present a problem. The noise of the Velcro being unfastened can startle a young or nervous horse and therefore care should be taken. If tapes are used, they should be fastened on the outside of the cannon bone.

Below: Four stages in fitting a stable bandage. Pad beneath all bandages with cotton or an equivalent. Wool stable bandages are rolled evenly down from below the knee or hock to the coronet, then upward to the start and tied on the side of leg.

Below: Placing of gauze exercise bandage to support back tendons and protect the leg. These bandages are applied firmly and often stitched in place for greater security.

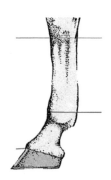

CLEANING TACK

Left: The necessary equipment. This consists of (1) Chamois leather; (2) Dandy brush; (3) Saddle soap; (4) Round sponge for soaping; (5)Flat sponge; (6) Bucket of tepid water; (7) Two cloths, one for polishing; (8)Metal polish; (9) Two stable rubbers.

Ideally, saddlery should be cleaned each time it is used; it should at least be given a quick cleaning, with a thorough one once a week. If the leather is allowed to dry out, it will become brittle.

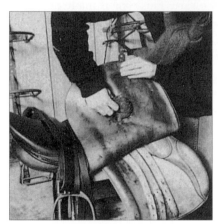

1 The lining of the saddle is washed with a damp sponge. Only leather-lined saddles should be washed like this.

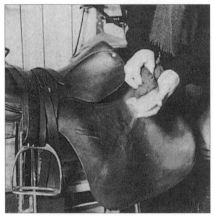

2 Applying saddle soap to the seat. Care must be taken not to overwet the leather, or water may seep into the stuffing.

3 Cleaning under the flap. This area attracts dirt and sweat, so it needs a thorough cleaning with a damp sponge.

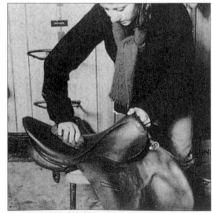

4 Rubbing the seat and flaps with a damp sponge, then they are dried with a chamois leather to remove surplus soap.

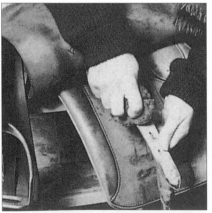

5 Washing the girth straps. These should be checked thoroughly for wear, since they are vital to the rider's safety.

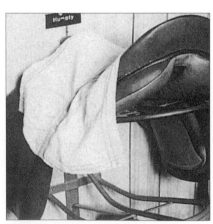

6 After polishing the saddle, it is replaced on its bracket or saddle horse and covered with a stable rubber.

CLEANING BRIDLES AND BITS

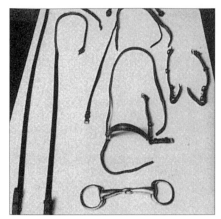

1 *A dismantled bridle, consisting of reins, snaffle bit, noseband, headpiece, browband, and cheekpieces.*

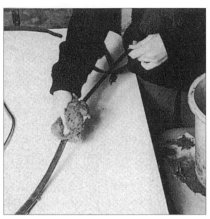

2 *Rubbing the reins with a damp cloth. All leather parts should be cleaned similarly and then dried.*

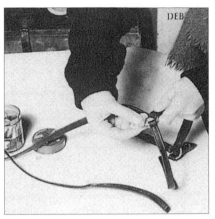

3 *If the bridle is fitted with metal rings or studs, these should be cleaned with metal polish.*

4 *Washing the bit thoroughly to remove all traces of stains and saliva.*

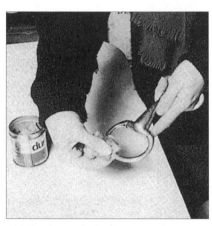

5 *The rings of the bit—not the mouthpiece—should be polished with metal polish.*

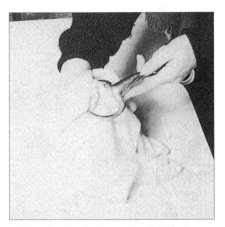

6 *The final polishing. The bridle is then reassembled and hung up ready for use.*

7 *Cleaning the girth. The method varies—webbing is brushed and scrubbed, nylon and string scrubbed.*

8 *Cleaning the stirrup leather. This is done in the same way as the saddle, checks being made for wear.*

9 *Cleaning the stirrup irons. After the dirt has been removed, the irons should be cleaned with metal polish.*

LEARNING
TO RIDE

FIRST LESSONS

In the early stages of your riding career, try to establish and maintain a regular pattern of lessons. If you can only manage to ride once a week, book a course of six half-hour lessons. This is usually sufficient to give you the initial feel of riding, and after these you can move on to one-hour lessons.

The more frequently you have lessons, the more quickly your riding will progress: it is far better to have a half-hour lesson each week than a one-hour lesson once a fortnight. Moreover, you will find it far too tiring to try to ride for a full hour at a time at first. If you have been working properly for the first few weeks, your muscles will be aching and your legs will feel as if they are ready to drop off after considerably less than a half-hour. Much of the technique of riding depends on developing the correct muscles and, until you have done so, you cannot hope to begin to realize your potential as a rider.

Mounting the horse

Once in the school, your nervousness or apprehension may well heighten with the thought of actually getting on the horse. There is no need whatsoever to worry about this, provided that you think logically about what you are doing.

The first step is to take up the reins. Even though the assistant will be holding the horse's head, you should get into the habit of holding the reins sufficiently tightly yourself to discourage the horse from moving forward. Take them up in your left hand—together with a lump of mane if you feel the need for security—and stand by the horse's shoulder facing towards his tail. Take hold of the stirrup iron with your right hand, turn it toward you and put your left foot into it. Hop forward and turn to face the saddle. Then, with your right hand across the seat of the saddle, spring up off your right foot, trying to avoid hitting the horse's back as you do so, and sit down lightly in the saddle. Put your right foot in the stirrup iron.

The stirrup leathers should lie flat against your legs; if they are twisted, one edge will dig into your legs and this will soon be very painful. You must adjust the stirrup leathers too, so they are the right length. It is impossible to give exact instructions as to how to judge the correct length, as this will alter as you settle deeper into the saddle and become more confident. As a guide—always providing that this length does, in fact, feel comfortable—hang your legs straight down and adjust the leathers so the bottom of the iron is level with your anklebone. The leathers must be of equal length; if your legs are lopsided, you will have no hope of sitting straight and being equally balanced in the saddle.

LEG POSITIONS

Above: Your lower leg should be in contact with the horse's side at all times. To apply the leg, close lower leg and ankle against horse's side.

Above: The inside lower leg is applied to create impulsion and to instruct the horse to bend around that leg when making turns.

Above: The outside lower leg is applied behind the girth, to make sure that the hindquarters follow the line of the front end.

Above: The stirrup iron is under the ball of the foot, and the heel is lower than the toe. This makes it easier to apply the legs correctly.

COMMON FAULTS

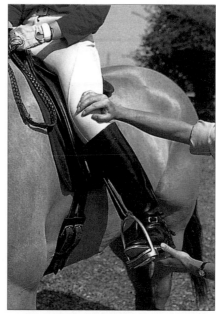

Left: Do not ride your lower leg sticking out from the horse. If you try to apply the leg aids from this position, your horse will have a bad fright.

Above: If the rider's hands are uneven, the bit will not lie correctly in the horse's mouth, and the tension on its mouth will be wrongly distributed.

Left: The horse is reacting to a stiff arm and unyielding hand by tilting its head, grinding its bit, putting its ears back and refusing to walk on actively. The rider's stiffness is causing the problem. This can be solved by working on developing a secure, independent seat.

Position in the saddle

There are two things to be said straightaway about adopting the correct position in the saddle. The first is that it is of paramount importance, for it is only by sitting correctly at all times that you can become an effective and good rider, and the second is that you should not expect it to feel comfortable until you have got used to it.

If you are sitting up sufficiently straight with your head held high, it will feel as if you are sitting as straight as a ramrod, with your head and shoulders forced back. If you could see yourself, you would see that this was not actually so; in any event, the importance of keeping your head up cannot be sufficiently stressed. Your head is the heaviest single part of your body and its position determines much of the positioning of the rest of it. If you look down, your weight automatically shifts forward. A horse already carries two-thirds of his weight on his forehand, so the last thing he wants is your extra weight on this area.

Your body weight should be on your seat bones, evenly distributed on either side of the saddle, so that you and the horse can balance freely. Your seat is maintained at all times by balance, not by grip. If you grip with your thighs and knees, you are automatically impeding the horse's freedom of movement and pushing your seat upward in the saddle. Try to relax your knees and hips, which will demand some conscious thought and effort.

Your legs should hang straight underneath you, making a straight line from the shoulder and hip to the heel. This should not be done by bending more acutely at the knee, so the lower part of your leg is forced back, but by bringing that part of the leg directly underneath you. Finally the weight of your legs should fall into the heels. In doing this, the temptation is often to stick your toes out, which results in gripping the horse's sides with the back of your leg. Instead of thinking of pressing your heel down, think of bringing your toe up, pointing directly forward.

313

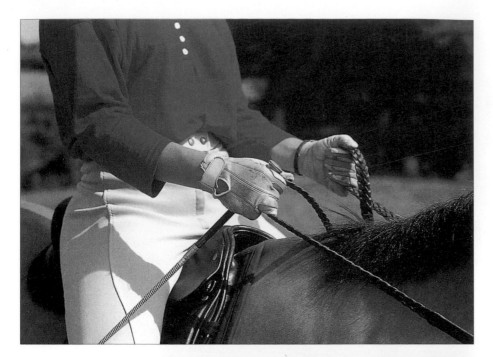

Left: The horse's mouth is very sensitive, and your hands must be sympathetic if it is not to become hardened or damaged. You hold the reins by wrapping the fingers around the rein, almost closing the hands to make a fist. This gives you a firm grip on the reins without having to use your arms. The arms remain soft and relaxed. The horse's movement is contained by putting pressure on the bit through the reins. The severity of the aid will depend, to some extent, on the sensitivity of the horse. You must match what the horse offers you.

The first movements

Even before you learn to hold the reins, your instructor will probably ask the assistant to lead the horse forward, so that you can get the feel of the walk. With your hands on the pommel, close the insides of your legs against the horse's side, and by doing this you will encourage the horse to move forward.

A horse walks by picking up and putting down each foot separately, so that four distinct hoofbeats can be heard. This results in a pace that has a gently swinging or swaying movement and, as your aim at all times is to move with the horse, you should let your body sway gently in time with the movement. This is not a conscious movement. If you think about it, you are likely to sway too much, so concentrate instead of maintaining the correct position in the saddle. Keep sitting on your seat bones, with your back straight and your head held up so you look between the horse's ears, and your legs hanging easily beneath you.

Even though you are now in the saddle, you will either be led by an assistant or lunged by your instructor. This means he or she will stand at a given spot—the center of a circle—and control the horse from the end of a long rein attached to his bit, guiding him around and around. In either case, you do not yet have to worry about controlling the horse; you can concentrate completely on sitting correctly. Until this becomes second nature, this will take all concentration.

Above: The rider is using her inside leg to create good forward movement and at the same time is maintaining a steady contact with the horse's mouth. It knows it is not going to be jabbed in the mouth by the bit, so it is going forward confidently into the rider's controlling hand.

Above: The rider drops the reins so that the horse can stretch out as it walks. This is a good way to reward a horse and allow it to relax when it has been working strongly in walk and trot.

Holding the reins

Although you do not need to concern yourself with controlling the horse yet, you must know how to hold the reins. Pick up a rein in either hand, so that they run through your little and third fingers, across the palms of your hands and emerge between your thumb and first finger. Your thumbs—pointing straightforward—are on the tops of the reins holding them down onto your first finger.

Hold your hands in front of you about 4 in (10 cm) above the withers with elbows bent and supple. There should be a straight line from the bit, through the reins, hands, and arms up to your elbow. You will find this necessitates holding your hands quite forward and apart about the width of the bit. Think of holding a book in front of you, your thumbs on top of the pages.

Always remember that the reins are for guiding the horse and not to be clutched for security, to maintain your position, or to correct your balance. Think of the reins as delicate threads: if you pull on them too hard, they will break.

As soon as the horse moves forward—remember you make him do so at this stage by closing the inside of your leg against his sides—you must make sure you follow the movement of his head with your hands. If you keep your hands rigid, you will naturally impede his head movement, thus making it difficult for him to balance properly. To do this, he needs to be able to move his head freely. You will find that, at a walk, his head moves quite considerably, so let your hands move as well. Again, do not try to move them consciously; just let them follow the movement, so it is the horse's head that moves your hands rather than the other way around.

When you want the horse to slow down or stop, you must pass on your intention to him. Clearly you have to discourage or restrict his forward movement; you do this by pushing him forward with your legs and then squeezing the reins gently so that he meets resistance. In other words, your legs push him up to meet your hands. Do not tug on the reins, leaning backward as you do so; instead, brace your back muscles, so you are no longer following the horse's movement, and close your hands on the reins, so that they, too, are no longer following the movement. This should be done gently, as though you were squeezing a sponge.

COMMON FAULTS

1 The rider has let her reins go, losing all contact with the horse's mouth. She is slouching in the saddle and is not pushing the horse on with her leg. As a result the horse is ambling along with his head dropped, rather than walking out with even steps.

2 The rider's arms are straight and stiff, her hands are too low, and they are not giving with the horse's movement. The horse is fighting against this restriction by raising its head and tipping it to one side.

3 The rider has crept up on the horse's neck so that her weight is a long way out of place, and she is holding the horse on a very short rein. This makes the horse anxious and it starts to jog.

Left: The rider uses her legs to create impulsion and the horse steps out well. Its hind leg comes well underneath its body, showing that its hindquarters are engaged and working actively.

This makes it a much bouncier gait, so prepare to be bounced around in the saddle.

As you progress, you will learn to ride at this pace, both by sitting down in the saddle to the movement and rising up and down with it. For this first time, however, take hold of the pommel firmly with both hands, ask the horse to move into a trot by closing the inside of your legs against his sides and then try to maintain your balance as he moves forward. When you want him to return to a walk, try to sit very tall in the saddle—this helps you to maintain your balance as the horse slows down—and ask him to walk by closing your legs against his side and bracing your back muscles.

The rising trot

By now, you should be confident enough in the saddle to learn how to rise at the trot. From your previous experience, you will know that the trot is a very bumpy pace, so, to avoid any unnecessary damage to the horse's mouth, take hold of the neck strap before moving.

At first, it helps to practice the technique of the rising trot while the assistant holds the horse still. Gently stand up and sit down again in the saddle, using your knees as hinges to push you up rather than relying on the stirrup irons to support your weight. Thinking of this

From walk to trot

If you feel reasonably confident and comfortable at a walk in your first lesson, your instructor may suggest that you try a few strides at the trot. This is a very different pace from the walk. It is a two-time pace—that is, the horse moves its opposite diagonal legs together and springs from one pair of diagonals to the other.

COMMON FAULTS

1 The rider is behind the horse's movement. Her body is no longer upright, her arms have become stiff and she is balancing by hanging onto the reins. In response the horse has raised its head and neck and indicates that it is not comfortable with the rider's position.

2 The rider has let her reins go long and is sitting too far forward. The energy she is creating by using her legs, is wasted as she has lost contact with the horse's mouth and therefore cannot contain the horse's movement. As a result, the horse's weight is falling onto its forehand.

DISMOUNTING

action as a forward and backward movement from your hips helps resist the temptation of rising too high. As you rise forward and backward count "one, two," keeping the counting and the rising as regular as possible.

This may seem easy, but transferring it to the actual action is more difficult, although it soon comes with practice. Therefore, if you find you are rising in time with the movement for a few strides and bumping for double the number, you can be pleased, for it shows you are making progress. In these early stages, only trot for short distances at a time—down one side of the school, for example.

The trot is a very tiring pace for you until you get used to it: if you get overtired, you will find it even more difficult.

Dismounting

The last stage of any lesson is dismounting. To do this, take both feet out of the stirrup irons and collect the reins in your left hand. Put your right hand on the pommel, or the side of the horse's neck, and swing your right leg up behind you and over the back of the saddle. As gently as you can, slide yourself down to the ground, letting your knees bend to take the jar as you land. Be warned—after even a half-hour on a horse, it takes a second or two to regain your usual muscles, and you will probably find your first few steps are somewhat staggering ones. It is not unknown for people to find themselves sitting down on the ground.

Thank your horse for the ride by patting him. Then, with the reins looped around your arm so that he cannot walk off on his own, run the stirrup irons up the side of the leather closest to the saddle so they rest against the top sides of the saddle. This will prevent them from banging against the horse's sides as he walks. Take the reins over the horse's head and, holding them together with the leading rein, lead him away.

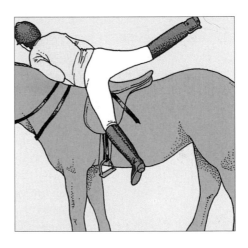

1 Leaning forward slightly, take both of your feet out of the irons.

2 Leaning forward with the left shoulder, swing right leg up and behind.

3 Still holding onto the saddle, bend your knees as you land, to prevent jarring.

POSITIONAL EXERCISES

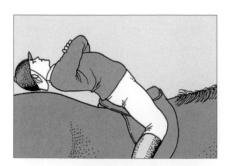

1 Cross arms and bend forward from the waist keeping your lower body still. Slowly straighten up and lean backward the same way, making sure your legs do not shoot forward. This will help supple your waist.

2 Put one hand on the pommel and circle the other arm from the shoulder. Think of trying to pull your hips out of their sockets as you lift your arm upward. Keep your legs absolutely still and in the correct position. Repeat with the other arm.

3 With both arms outstretched at shoulder level, turn from the waist, first to the right and then the left, so that your hands point to the horse's ears and tail.

The sitting trot

Once you can maintain the rising trot, you can begin to learn the sitting trot. For this, as the name suggests, you sit in the saddle all the time; this is far more difficult than it sounds, particularly if your horse has a very springy action. Try sitting for a few strides and then going back to a rising trot, gradually increasing the amount of time spent sitting as you begin to feel more comfortable. Relax your body, sitting deep into the saddle, but sit even more upright than for the rising trot. The tendency is to become careless in an attempt to relax into the movement, but you will find, in fact, that this throws you out of the saddle even more vigorously.

The sitting trot is a tiring pace for horse and rider, particularly when you are learning it. Therefore do it only for short bursts at a time. Rise to the trot down the long sides of the school and sit along the shorter ones. Remember with all trotting exercises—both sitting and rising—to work evenly on both reins.

Positional exercises

It was briefly mentioned earlier that the position in the saddle should be maintained by balance at all times.

This is very important; if you grip with your thighs and knees, you will automatically make the horse tense his back and shoulder muscles. This, in turn, restricts the freedom of his movements. It also pushes you upward in the saddle so you come off your seat bones. To help you achieve an even balance across the horse's back, let your arms hang down by your sides. Then, without rounding your shoulders, imagine you are carrying two heavy shopping bags—one in either hand—which, by definition, require you to be evenly balanced.

To maintain a balanced position, all parts of your body must be perfectly relaxed and supple. Even though your back is straight and your shoulders are pulled squarely back, they should both still be relaxed and so should your hips and pelvis. Your knee, hip, and elbow joints should all be supple. It is essential to coordinate body movements—that is, moving one part of the body in harmony with another—but you must also be able to move one part of your body independently of the other parts. To begin with, you will probably find this extremely hard to do; as you use your legs, your hands will automatically jerk upward or make you lean backward, but, as you think about it and practice it, you will find it becomes easier.

Every lesson or schooling session should include some exercises, for they are invaluable in developing the position in the saddle. They will help you to coordinate your body movements as well as use each part independently; they will help you to become supple and reduce stiffness; and they will help to develop the correct riding muscles.

Some of the exercises pictured here are designed to help you learn to move one part of your body independently. Provided that the assistant is still leading you, you can do them at a walk as well as at a halt.

EASY EXERCISES WITHOUT STIRRUPS

1 Swing your legs backward and forward from the knee.

2 Keeping legs still, circle each arm from the shoulder.

COMMON FAULTS

1 Hanging onto the reins to maintain balance.

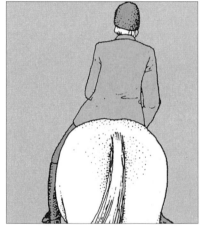

2 Moving out of position while doing exercises.

COMMON FAULTS

1 The rider has shifted forward. The horse has its weight on its forehand. The rider is in the wrong position to communicate with the horse.

2 The rider is leaning back and pulling on the reins to bring the horse down a pace. The horse becomes resistant to the rider's action.

Rising without stirrups

From an early stage, you should get accustomed to riding without stirrups. This will help you with your balance; it also teaches you not to rely on your stirrup irons to help you maintain your position.

With the horse halted, take both feet out of the stirrups and cross the leathers over in front of the saddle, the irons resting on either side of the horse's neck. The usual order from your instructor for this will be to quit and cross your stirrups. Ask the horse to walk on in the normal way and let your legs hang down in a relaxed fashion for a few paces. Put your legs in the correct position, then raise your toes, letting the weight fall down to the heel again. Keep your hands on the pommel initially, but when you feel secure, take up the reins as you would normally. You must be even more careful now not to rely on your reins to balance you.

A good exercise to do while riding without stirrups is to swig your legs from the knee backward and forward, either together or alternately. Alternatively, try swinging one leg forward and the other back at the same time, making sure you keep your hands still and do not bounce in the saddle. This exercise helps to supple your knees.

Always remember that, as the majority of exercises are designed to develop muscles, always to repeat those that involve just one side with the other one. By the same token, it is very important to ride evenly at the same pace on both reins, otherwise both you and the horse will develop a preference for riding one way. Largely because they are ridden by so many people, most riding-school horses do have a preference for one side and you will soon feel this: they will always be a little stiff and more reluctant to cooperate on the other rein.

COMING TO A HALT

With a young horse, aim to bring the horse up with front legs square, and hind legs nearly square.

Above: The rider's position is good for this trotting exercise. Her weight is slightly forward, her hands are in contact with the horse's mouth, she is sitting down in the saddle, and squeezing the horse forward with her lower legs.

Above: Here the rider is cantering over poles and she has folded forward, closing the angles. Her lower legs are on the girth and are maintaining a good contact with the horse. Her body is forward and, as she is not leaning on her hands, they are in active contact with the horse's mouth. She is driving the horse on with her lower legs.

The art of control

Now that you are gaining strength, confidence, and a sense of balance, think more about controlling your mount. The time has come when the position you have worked so hard at has also to be effective in making the horse obey and work for you. Combining a correct position with effectiveness is often one of the hardest aspects of learning to ride.

The signals that have been devised to help a rider transmit his wishes to his mount are known as the aids. Natural aids are those given with parts of the rider's body. The chief ones are the hands and the legs; in addition, shifting the body weight slightly or bracing muscles are included. The voice also counts as a natural aid, though this should be used sparingly and never in anger. Artificial aids are the additional items of equipment a rider can use to help to encourage or control the horse. These consist of a cane or whip, spurs and ancillary items of tack, such as a martingale, which are used for specific reasons to do with control.

The most important point to remember about aids is that they should always be given firmly and decisively, but never roughly. A half-hearted aid is useless, and the horse will not understand what he is meant to do. Aids should be given together, that is, a leg aid should be supported by a hand aid.

If you want your horse to move forward more quickly, you would tell him by squeezing his sides with the inside of your leg. At the same time, you must relax or yield with your hands in order to give him the freedom to move forward. Similarly, if you want him to slow down, you push him forward with your legs so that he gathers himself together, then stop the forward movements by resisting with your hands and bracing your back muscles.

At this time, you should learn to carry a whip during lessons. Choose either a cane or a riding crop. Hold it in your hand along the rein so that the top emerges from the crook of your thumb and forefinger. The remainder of the whip rests across your lower thigh.

When riding in a school, a whip should generally be held in the inside hand. This is because a horse will automatically move away from it when it is used and he should move always toward the outside of the school, not in toward the center. If you are carrying a whip, therefore, you must remember to change it to the other hand when you change the rein. Do this as you cross the center of the school.

COMMON FAULTS: WALK TO TROT

1 The rider's legs are away from the horse's sides, completely out of contact with the horse, so the instruction to change pace surprises it. The rider has let the reins go loose as well. The horse reacts by hollowing its outline and shortening its steps.

2 The rider has anticipated the transition by tipping forwards and dropping contact with the reins. As a result there is no controlling hand for the horse to go forwards into. It jumps into the next pace rather than stepping forwards into it.

3 The rider has failed to achieve a good, active pace before the transition, and is also leaning forwards. As a result, the transition is sluggish.

4 The rider has let the reins go loose, losing contact with the horse's mouth, and she is not creating impulsion in the horse's hindquarters. The horse's weight is on its forehand, and the transition is poor.

1

2

3

4

From trot to canter

Once you have truly mastered the sitting and rising trot, the next pace upward is the canter. This is executed by the horse in quite a different way from a walk or trot and has a very different feel from the paces so far discussed. It is a pace in three-time in which one hind leg strikes off, to be followed by the diagonal of the opposite hind leg and foreleg, and then by the opposite foreleg. There follows a moment of suspension when all four legs leave the ground before the pattern is repeated.

To go from trot to canter, sit deep in the saddle, close your hands slightly on the reins to stop the horse from going into a faster trot, and press both legs against his sides. Lean forward slightly from the waist to counter the horse's

movement, but this should be barely perceptible.

As the horse breaks into a canter, try to sit deep in the saddle. Make no conscious effort to move; let the rhythm of the pace move you. Avoid using your hands to balance as, at the canter, more than any other pace, you need to let your hands move with the horse to give his head the freedom it needs.

To return to the trot, slow the horse down by pushing forward with your legs, then resisting with your hands and bracing your back muscles. Then try to pick up the rising rhythm as soon as he begins to trot.

Only attempt the canter for a few strides at the beginning. Concentrate on relaxing into the saddle, then performing smooth transitions from a trot to a canter and a canter back to a trot.

COMMON FAULTS: TROT TO CANTER

1 The rider is holding the horse on too tight a rein, and her hands are not allowing the movement of the horse's head. The horse is fighting against this restriction by raising its head and neck and resisting the movement.

2 The rider is standing up in the saddle and leaning forward. From this position she cannot push the horse forward into a canter.

1

2

TURNS AND CIRCLES

Left: The rider closes the inside leg against the horse to ask it to move forward away from the leg while using the outside leg behind the girth to prevent the horse's hindquarters swinging out. At the same time she uses the inside hand to ask the horse to turn and controls the degree of bend with the outside hand. She looks in the direction in which she wants the horse to travel. She is applying the aids in a well coordinated way to produce a good turn; the horse's head is just inclined in the direction of the movement and the hind legs are following in the path of the front legs.

point between the three-quarter points and the center of the school—between H and E, K and E, or M and B and F and B according to which way you are going. Then go on to X (the center of the school) and next to a point between the other three-quarter marker and the center of the school. Finally, go back to C or A.

Riding a perfect circle is not easy, so concentrate and make sure your horse is properly bent around your inside leg all the time. Bear in mind that his body should be bending around the art of the circle—at no point are you attempting to turn him. Watch that he does not "fall in" to the center of the circle so the circle becomes imperfect. It is helpful to ride on soft ground, as you can check hoofprints to measure the accuracy of the circle.

When you have ridden a few circles, change the rein and ride in the opposite direction, so neither you nor the horse favor one side. Also, try riding smaller circles, always remembering that your aim is to form the horse's body into a perfect arc throughout the exercise.

The serpentine tests your control and ability to ride accurately to the full. This involves riding down the school from C to A, making four perfect loops, the extreme point of which is about 10 ft (3 m) from the side of the school. The whole movement should be smooth and fluid, not jerky or uneven. Try the exercise at a walk first, and then progress to a trot, checking your tracks in the school to see how accurate you have been each time.

If you are riding with others in the school, there are several exercises and movements you can perform together, which will help to improve your skill, control, and accu-

A recognized riding school measures 40 x 20 ft (12 x 6 m) and is usually marked with a standard series of letters. So far you have concentrated in riding around the outside and changing the rein across the center of the school or from the three-quarter markers, but there are other ways in which you can use the school.

The first school figure to practice riding—at a walk, then a trot and finally a canter—is a 20 ft (6 m) circle. The command from your instructor to ride a 20 ft (6 m) circle and then to return to the outside track will be: "At C (or A) go forward into a 20 ft (6 m) circle. As you return to C (or A), go large." Leave the track at the center of the short side of the school (C or A) and ride in a perfect arc to a

Left: The aim, when turning through a bend, is to keep the horse looking in the direction in which it is moving. Its neck should have no more bend in it than the body.

racy. Such maneuvers include, for example, being told by your instructor to position yourself at a letter and then changing places with another rider standing at a different letter. If there are several of you in the school at one time, this maneuver can be quite a test of your riding. The code in passing other riders head-on is to pass right-hand to right-hand.

In addition, practice riding holding both reins in one hand, so that this will not present a problem to you, if it should ever be necessary on a ride. If you are holding the reins in your left hand, for example, hold the left rein normally, then bring the right one across the top, so that it enters your hand between the thumb and forefinger, crosses the palm, and emerges beneath your little finger. When riding like this, you must control the horse more actively with your legs, bending it around your inside leg if you want to turn corners. Do not attempt to guide it too accurately with your hand—this is bound to confuse.

To help you think less actively about the hand holding the reins, put your reins into one hand in order to allow you to do something else with your other hand—such as blowing your nose, doing up a button on your coat, or adjusting the length of a stirrup leather.

RIDING CIRCLES AND TURNS

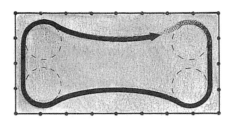

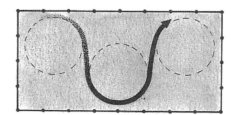

1. When riding a circle, imagine a diamond shape on the ground. Ride around the diamond, rounding off each point. This should give you a correct circle. Turns consist of a section of a circle, and are ridden in the same way.

2. Shallow loops made on the long side of the area will teach the horse to change the direction of the bend and make it more supple. You can introduce a small circle at the end of the loop.

3. Once you are progressing well on circles and loops, you can also introduce serpentines into the routine, across the width of the area.

COMMON FAULTS

1 The rider is trying to make the horse bend into the corner by holding it out with her outside hand, instead of using her legs to control the movement. As a result, the horse is looking in the wrong direction.

2 The horse is bending its neck too much to the inside of the circle. If the correct degree of bending is being maintained, the rider should be able to see the corner of the horse's eye, but this horse has far more of its head turned in.

3 The rider is looking too far around the circle, so her head and upper body are turned too much to the inside of the circle. The rider should be looking through her horse's ears, with shoulders and hips parallel to those of the horse.

LEARNING TO JUMP

Above: The shortened leathers have the effect of moving your seat toward the back of the saddle so that the lower leg and knee can sit firmly around the horse. Your seat comes slightly out of the saddle and your body folds forward from the hips. Keep your back straight and look ahead. Your elbows remain bent and your hands must follow the movement of the horse's head.

Right: You must keep your weight over the horse's center of gravity by folding forward over a jump. The shoulder, elbow, hip, and ankle remain in a straight line.

Although the aim is always to produce one continuous flowing movement, the horse's jumping action can be broken down into five elements—approach, takeoff, suspension, landing, and recovery. During the approach, the horse, having seen and summed up the obstacle in front of him, will balance and prepare himself for the jump by stretching his neck and lowering his head. He may begin to lengthen his stride, but he should continue at the same even pace, without altering his speed.

At the point of takeoff, the horse brings his head up as he lifts his forehand off the ground. The power for the leap forward comes from the horse's hocks, which are tucked well beneath him to act like a spring. During the moment of suspension, the horse's body forms an arc over the jump with the head and neck stretched forward. As the descent begins, the horse extends his forelegs, his head and neck down towards the ground and tucks his hindlegs under him, so that they will clear the jump. As the forelegs touch the ground—usually one just in front of the other—the horse balances himself by bringing his head up and shortening his neck. The hind feet touch down immediately behind the forefeet, one forefoot often moving into the next stride before the hind feet land.

At all times the rider must remain in complete harmony with the horse, taking particular care not to interfere with the free movement of the animal's head. The jumping position described in the following section has been designed to fulfill this aim.

If jumping is to be included in a lesson, it should come toward the end. This will give the horse time to loosen and limber up and make sure that the rider is sitting deep in the saddle and is loosened up enough to be riding at his or her best.

The jumping position

The first thing to learn and practice, until it becomes second nature, is the jumping position. Assuming that you will have dropped your stirrup leathers a hole or two for general school work by now, you will need to take them back up again for jumping. The stirrup leather should still remain vertical to the ground, which means that your knee and ankle will be bent a little more deeply. This allows them to do their work as "hinges" and "shock absorbers."

CLOSING DOWN THE ANGLES

The stirrup leathers are shortened for jumping, closing down the angles at hip, knee, and ankle. Think of your body as being a "W" turned on its side: shoulder to seat, seat to knee, knee to heel to toe. In the correct jumping position, you flatten the W as much as possible.

In the jumping position, the rider's upper body bends forward in a folding movement from the waist. The back remains straight and supple—there should be no slouching or rounding of the shoulders—while the head is still held high, looking straight between the horse's ears and never down at the jump. The seat should remain in light contact with the saddle throughout the approach, although it may lift up during takeoff. The body weight is taken on the knee, thigh, and heel, but resist any temptation to straighten the knee and to stand up in the stirrup irons. There should still be a straight line from your elbows, which are bent and remain close to your sides, through your arms and hands, along the reins to the bit. Your shoulders, elbows, and fingers have to be even more supple in order to follow the movement of the horse's neck. In fact, your hands should stay in the usual position throughout a jump and it is better to move them forward rather than run any risk of jabbing the horse in the mouth.

In the early stages of jumping, make sure a neck strap is buckled around the horse's neck and hold onto this. It will make you feel more secure as well as guarding against you jerking the horse's mouth. Practice moving into the jumping position in the saddle, first at a halt and than at a walk and trot. When you can bend forward and sit up straight without losing your balance at a trot, try doing the same exercise at a canter. Your aim is to achieve a smooth rhythm.

COMMON FAULTS

1 The rider's seat has come too far out of the saddle, causing her legs to straighten and push forward and her back to round. Her weight is too far back, and she will get behind the horse's movement over the fence.

2 The rider has folded too far forward, causing her to hollow her back. It is impossible for her to keep her leg in the correct position. The lower leg has moved too far. She cannot communicate well with the horse from this position.

3 By standing in her stirrups the rider has opened up the angles at hip, knee, and ankle, and raised her hands too high, so that her position in the saddle is made very insecure.

Above: The rider's position is good for this trotting exercise. Her weight is slightly forward, her hands are in contact with the horse's mouth, she is sitting down in the saddle, and squeezing the horse forward with her lower legs.

Pole work

This is a very good exercise for developing rhythm when teaching a horse to jump, or when improving the performance of an older horse. It is also excellent for practicing the correct jumping position.

It is important that you have the distances between the poles correct. A horse will take two strides at the trot to one at the canter. If you have the poles double-spaced, that is, correct for the canter, they will be correct for the trot as well, and you will not need to keep dismounting to move the poles each time you change pace.

The distance between the poles will depend on your horse's size and stride. The table gives a guide to distances.

When the horse is happy and at ease going over one pole, move up to three poles or more. Do not work over just two poles, as it might encourage the horse to jump both poles together.

Begin by walking over the poles, and then go over them at a rising trot. Cantering to poles should not be attempted unless the horse has mastered them at the trot. In canter, the horse should just bounce along without taking any steps between the poles.

COMMON FAULTS: TROTTING

1 The rider's leg is too far forward and has straightened, and her back has rounded. This often happens when the horse rushes the poles.

2 The rider approaches the poles with her legs too far back along the horse's side and is using the reins to balance. She cannot give the horse precise instructions from this position, and the horse is showing its concern at the lack of communication from the rider by raising its head and hollowing its

3 The rider is resting her weight on her hands and is not making use of the horse's impulsion, which she is trying to create with her legs. The horse is not taking a full stride as it approaches the poles.

DISTANCES FOR POLE WORK

size of horse	length of stride trot	length of stride canter
14½ hh	4 ft 1.2 m	8 ft 2.4 m
16hh	4½ ft 1.4 m	9 ft 2.75 m

Above: Here the rider is cantering over poles, and she has folded forward, closing the angles. Her lower legs are on the girth and are maintaining a good contact with the horse. Her body is forward and, as she is not leaning on her hands, they are in active contact with the horse's mouth. She is driving the horse on with her lower legs.

COMMON FAULTS: CANTERING

1 Although the rider's leg is in the correct position, her body is collapsing forward and to one side. She is leaning on her hands and looking down. As a result, the horse's movement is restricted.

2 The rider is sitting too upright, which puts her weight too far behind the horse's movement. The horse's balance and judgment are adversely affected, and it does not stride cleanly over the poles. Instead, its forefeet are either side of the pole.

The first jump

The next step is to hop over a small jump, which should be no more than about 10 in (25 cm) high: you can use proper jump supports or improvise by using stout poles on wooden boxes or barrels. Most riding establishments, however, will probably use a type of pole known as a cavalletti. If you do not use a cavelletti, make sure the poles are thick and solid with no rough parts or sharp nails protruding. Horses show far more respect and jump better and more boldly over solid objects than flimsy, unimposing ones.

Even though the horse is quite capable of stepping over the cavalletti at a trot, he will probably prefer to hop over it, so make sure you are prepared. The first "jump" you take is bound to throw you off balance; remember to hold onto the neck strap, so that you do not jerk the horse's mouth by mistake. When you are reasonably confident and able to maintain your balance and rhythm at the trot, approach the cavalletti at a canter. Keep the pace calm and let the horse bounce over the jump, offering no interference so he can take it in his stride.

After this, try placing another cavalletti or low jump, perhaps slightly higher, several strides further on, so you have time to return to the normal position before resuming the jumping position for the next one. If you have approached the first one calmly and quietly, there should be no need to check the horse between jumps. It is better not to interfere with the reins between jumps as both of you will probably lose your balance.

Having achieved good rhythm and balance over a couple of small jumps positioned some distance from each other, bring them closer together, so that they are separated only by a couple of strides. Again, allow your horse to judge the takeoff points and distance between the jumps: you should concentrate yourself on keeping your balance and not interfering with his movement in any way.

TAKING THE POLES AND JUMP

1 The horse is approaching on a good stride and is looking intently at the fence. The rider is keeping a good conversation going with the horse via her lower legs.

2 The rider is closing down the angles at her hip, knee and ankle as she prepares for the moment of takeoff. The horse is reacting to her positive instructions by coming into the jump

3 The rider has folded her body down well and is looking straight ahead. The horse has its weight over its hocks and is beginning to lift its forelegs.

4 The horse take the fence in its stride.

COMMON FAULTS

1 The rider is standing in her stirrups, straightening her body. She is keeping her balance by bracing her hands against the horse's neck. Her whole position is weak and insecure. If the horse chose to swerve out or stop, she would find it very difficult to counteract such misbehavior.

2 Lack of communication: The rider stands in her stirrups and keeps her body upright, reducing her chance of communicating properly with the horse. Her hands are too high, and the horse is on too long a rein. The rider's lack of positive signals is causing the horse to lose impulsion. Its back feet are trailing behind and it does not look committed to jump. The horse tackles the jump, but its ears are back, its outline is hollow, and it is taking off unevenly from its hocks.

Above: The rider is balanced well over the horse. She has folded her body right down. Her lower leg and ankle are wrapped around the horse and are staying in position in the region of the girth. Her hands have moved forward to allow the horse to stretch out its head and neck over the fence.

Individual fences

As you gain confidence through working on grids of poles with a small fence, you can move on to tackle larger, individual fences.

When practicing over larger fences you should retain the last pole on the ground in front of the fence to act as a placing pole. It will bring the horse to the fence in the correct spot for takeoff.

In order to approach a fence correctly you need to concentrate on establishing a good, rhythmic canter with plenty of impulsion, and should wait for the fence to come to you. As with the previous exercise, it is important that you maintain the same rhythmic stride throughout both the approach and the jump itself. You should not need to check the horse at all as you approach the fence.

Present the horse to the fence with your legs wrapped around the horse. Try to have your lower calf and ankle in contact with the horse's sides, applying a steady pressure to tell the horse that you want it to continue. If the horse is confident that you will allow its movement with your hands, it will jump without you needing to force or yank it into the air. Keep your body relaxed and stay in balance with the horse over the jump.

If the horse does not give a good jump, it could be for a variety of reasons. The placing pole could be at the wrong distance from the jump, bringing the horse in incorrectly, so check that you have it in the right place. It could be that the horse has had a bad experience in the past. Or it could be that the horse lacks confidence in its rider. As with other riding problems, always ask yourself if you are doing everything correctly.

Above: The rider has stood up in her stirrups before reaching the fence and is unable to use her legs correctly. At the same, time she has dropped the contact through the reins. A horse may well take advantage of this lack of contact to refuse the fence.

Types of jump

From this point, the only way to improve and develop your jumping is to practice it over as many different types of obstacles in the greatest number of different conditions as possible.

Jumps fall into two basic categories. These are uprights, such as walls, gates, hurdles, narrow hedges, and poles placed in a vertical line on top of one another, and spreads, such as parallel or triple bars and overs. In addition, ditches and banks should also be included in your practice jumping sessions. In the early stages, concentrate on jumping low jumps well, rather than raising the poles higher and higher and jumping badly.

Practice jumps—you can easily construct these yourself with a little imagination—should not be more than about 3 ft (90 cm) high and many should be smaller. It is far better to increase the width of a fence, so that the horse has to stretch himself over it, than to keep testing his high-jump ability by raising the height—better for him and better for you to get the feel of the jumping movement.

A ground line placed in front of a jump, particularly an upright, will help you and your horse to judge the takeoff point more easily. The takeoff point should be approximately the same distance away from the jump as the height of it. This will vary according to the height of the fence and the speed of the approach; a horse approaching a small jump quite fast, for example, will take off far further in front of it than the height of that obstacle.

If the establishment where you are learning to ride has a jumping lane, or if you are jumping in the confines of a school, a useful exercise is to negotiate a line of low poles with your arms crossed and the reins knotted around the horse's neck. This will show you how much you are relying on the reins to balance you. Pick up the reins quickly at the end of the line; then try riding it again doing something like buttoning your coat or knotting a piece of string. This helps to encourage you to ride by "feel" and instinct.

An even more testing exercise is to quit and cross your stirrups as well as riding with no reins, so that now you can only rely on the balance of your position to keep you sitting correctly. This is a useful and practical exercise, since there are few riders who never lose their stirrup irons at some time in the middle of a jumping course. It is comforting to know that you will not be unhorsed immediately.

COMMON FAULTS

1 It is easy to get left behind over a jump. The horse may surprise you by taking off early, or it may make a bigger jump than you expect it to. The rider copes by slipping the reins, that is,

letting them run through her fingers, so that the horse is not restricted at all as it puts in a large jump. This will ensure that she does not catch the horse in the mouth.

2 By looking down and to one side of the horse, the rider is losing her balance, and has allowed her leg to move back so that her leg aid will be less effective. As she is looking down, she will be unable to give instructions on landing.

Jumping doubles

When you have negotiated poles and different types of individual fences, you can move on to doubles. These consist of two fences positioned close together, usually with one non-jumping stride in the middle. As you have to negotiate two fences within a short space of time it is even more important that you maintain the correct position, so that you can communicate effectively and positively with the horse throughout the whole jump.

As you approach a double, aim your horse at the center of the fences and look to the second part. This will stop you looking down or to one side as you go over the first part.

You have to judge the correct amount of impulsion carefully coming into a double. If you ride in with too much impulsion your horse will jump too far in over the first part, and find it difficult to jump over the second part. On the other hand, if you let your horse crawl over the first element you will be leaving it with too much to do to get out of the combination neatly. In either case, the horse may respond by running out at the second element.

If the combination consists of a spread in and an upright out, it will be more difficult to jump because the spread will encourage the horse to jump big, and it may not be able to collect itself and shorten its stride enough to jump the upright.

When you are building practice fences, bear in mind that if the first element consists of cross-poles, it will help you to come in correctly and set you up well for the second element.

JUMPING A DOUBLE

1 The rider's lower leg is on the girth, and her body is folded forward. Her hands are maintaining a good contact with the horse's mouth.

2 The rider is ready to push the horse on using her lower legs. You must not rest on your hands, or you will not be ready to correct any steering problems ready for the second part.

3 The rider's legs are on the girth, applying pressure, to give the horse precise instructions on how to approach the second element. There is no hesitation on the horse's part as it prepares for the spread.

4 The cross-poles at the second element help to guide the horse to the center of the fence, and it jumps well lifting its shoulders and tucking its forelegs up neatly. The rider is still looking ahead.

5 *The rider has folded forward, her lower leg has stayed in position, and she is looking ahead. Her hands are relaxed but in contact, allowing the horse the freedom to use its head and neck as it jumps.*

COMMON FAULTS

In pushing onto the second part of the double, the rider is leaning too far forward, and her seat is coming out of the saddle. In this position she will find it difficult to give precise instructions to the horse as they come into the second element.

Above: A horse can sense the way you are feeling, and a bad jump may result from your own lack of confidence. Be patient, and attempt to make the jump again.

Coping with a refusal

Generally, horses jump badly or refuse to jump for one of two reasons—either they have been badly schooled or they are being badly ridden. At this point, it is more likely that the latter reason will apply. Always try to analyze what it is that you are doing wrong and work at putting it right. Have you interfered with his stride on the approach, jabbed him in the mouth on takeoff, or shifted back into an upright position too quickly on landing, for instance? Any of these errors might make him reluctant to jump for you. If he refuses or runs out, is it because you were uncertain yourself and did not ride him at the jump as if you really meant him to go over it?

If a horse refuses a jump, ride him in a small circle and come straight into the jump again. Horses that constantly run out at fences can often be discouraged from doing so by building high or elaborate "wings" on either side of the fence.

Always finish with a good jump from both you and the horse—however small it may be. This is the one you and your mount will remember for the next session.

RIDING OUT

Having achieved mastery over the sitting trot, the rising trot, and the canter, together with confidence in your ability to control your horse and use the aids properly, there is no reason why you should not take a break from the formality of the school for a ride or two. Bear in mind, though, that this is going to be completely different from the conditions you have so far encountered. Riding on roads, or even across tracks and fields, is very different from riding around a school under the constant, watchful eye of an instructor—even though a qualified person will accompany you.

Most situations you will meet with can be dealt with by your riding experience coupled with common sense, but this is something that people often seem to lose when on horseback.

It is vitally important to be constantly alert. This does not mean that you cannot relax, but you must be ready for the unexpected. Somebody may suddenly emerge from a concealed driveway or something may flutter in the hedge, taking you by surprise and making your mount jump or shy. Control him gently, talking to him to reassure him, and then turn

Below: Allow time for exercising across open country in your routine. It helps to keep a horse fresh and prevents it from becoming bored.

him, to see whatever has startled him.

Do not underestimate the size of your horse when going through gates, or when skirting parked vehicles. The latter should be given a wide berth, but not so wide that you end up riding in the middle of the street. In the same vein, it is wise to ride around man-hole covers, which can be both slippery and potential hazards for the horse to trip over, but do not take this to extremes by going to the other side of the street. Remember you have to steer and control the horse at all times; he will do what you tell him to do and, if you do not steer him around a stationary truck, for example, he may well either walk into the back of it or just come to a halt behind it. Try not to get into the habit of expecting him to get you both out of difficulties; you are the one in control.

Coping with falls

Something you are bound to experience sooner or later in your riding career is a fall. It may have already happened during one of your riding lessons, or it may be that the ignominy will occur when you are out for a

ride. Ignominy is what it is—nine times out of ten when you fall off a horse, the only thing to be hurt is your pride.

Falls occur in all sorts of ways. They may be a gentle slide to the ground when you have lost your balance in the saddle and have reached the point of no return. They may be caused by not ducking low enough or in time to avoid an overhanging branch, or they may be a seemingly dramatic toss and tumble as the horse trips, halts unexpectedly, or throws you off his back as part of a display of high spirits.

Whatever the cause or type of fall, try to get up as quickly as possible if you are not hurt, to show your instructor or companions that you are all right. Then, no matter what your personal feelings and wishes are at this moment, get back up into the saddle immediately. This is important for your confidence as well as from the point of view of establishing who is master. If a horse senses you are reluctant to remount, this will bring out the worst in him, and he is likely to behave badly. It may help you to analyze the reasons for the fall; was it that you lost your balance, for instance, or was it the result of some other cause that could equally well be worked at and therefore avoided in the future?

Experts differ on whether or not you should make a conscious effort to hold onto the reins when you fall. Often, you have no choice, as they are wrenched from your hand; equally, you sometimes have no time to think. Within the confines of the school, it is generally better to drop them; the horse is not able to escape, as he might do in the open, and letting go of the reins lessens the risk of the horse trampling you.

If a companion falls off when you are out for a ride, the whole ride should stop and wait for him to pick himself up, regain composure, and remount. Help to catch the horse, if necessary, and hold it still for the fallen rider. If a loose horse decides to turn the escapade into a game and refuses to be caught, never chase after him. This will only heighten his excitement and make him even more determined to evade capture. Instead, try to corner him; when he realizes all escape routes are blocked, he will soon give in.

Even though a hack is obviously less formal than school work, do not let your riding deteriorate as a result. Concentrate on maintaining the correct position at all times and on making the horse go well for you. Practice smooth transitions from a walk to a trot, a trot to a canter, and back to a trot and walk again. Make sure the horse does only what you want him to do at the times you ask him to do it. If he displays whims of his own—perhaps to canter at a spot where he usually does—you must correct him. You are still the boss.

OPENING AND CLOSING A GATE

1 Position your horse parallel to the gate with its head facing the latch, take the reins and whip in one hand and, with the hand nearest the gate, undo the latch.

2 Use your leg nearest the gate to ask the horse to move away from it (the horse will be turning on its forehand).

3 Open the gate far enough for you to pass through, remembering that some horses become upset and try to rush. If you do not give yourself enough room you could get badly knocked against the gatepost, or perhaps be unseated.

4 Once through, position the horse parallel to the gate again so that you can pull the gate shut, and fasten the latch. Always watch where your horse's head is—a horse can quite easily catch its bridle on a gate latch.

Above: Hill work is beneficial for improving the horse's strength and endurance whatever area of competition you are involved in. Uphill work is of particular value.

Above: When riding uphill at a canter it is important to keep your weight well forward, to allow the horse maximum freedom of movement.

Across country

Just as there are rules to observe when riding on streets and roads, there are rules to follow when riding across the countryside. There are also elementary codes of good manners to observe towards any pedestrians you meet.

In the country, always close gates behind you, whether the field they border contains livestock or not. Always pass single file through a gate, making sure you leave sufficient room for your knees—a rap on a gatepost can be extremely painful. It helps if one person on the ride holds the gate open for the others, but remember to return this courtesy by waiting on the other side until the gate has been closed and everyone is ready to proceed.

In many country areas, you are the "guest" of a farmer, in that you are riding over his land. Behave as you would if you were a guest in someone's house, by observing basic good manners. Do not canter or gallop across a sown field; indeed, you should not ride at speed across any field, particularly if the ground is very wet. You could cut it up and damage it considerably. If by any chance you do some damage, knock down a fence, or let some animals out, find out whose land it is and tell them what has happened. It is inexcusable to leave someone else to discover the damage, whatever it is; by the time they do so, it might have worsened.

Show consideration for the others on the ride. The pace should always be adjusted to the least experienced and most nervous rider. Never ask or expect your fellow riders to do things they neither want to, nor are ready to do. It would be like asking you to jump a gate or hedge at this stage. Later, when you have learned to jump, never jump every obstacle in sight; if you do, you will become the farmer's enemy, rather than friend. If, you want to jump, jump only those obstacles that you know you are allowed to and which, should you crash through them or knock them down, will cause no serious damage—for example, knocking down the boundary fence of a field containing livestock could be disastrous.

When riding through wooded areas, lean well forward—not back—when passing beneath low, overhanging branches. This may sound obvious, but you would be surprised how many people forget to do it. Similarly, if you encounter a swinging branch, do not release it so that it flies into the horse or rider behind. If you meet pedestrians on a narrow track, slow down and go past them at a walk.

Right Horses always enjoy the opportunity to relax that riding out provides, whatever the conditions.

If your horse goes lame for any reason, get off immediately and see if you can determine the cause. The most likely reason is a stone lodged in his hoof. If this is so, remove the stone and he will probably be quite sound again. If you cannot find out the reason, run the stirrup irons up the leathers, take the reins over his head and lead him home. All the points mentioned are no more than common sense and good manners. Do not lose sight of either of these just because you are sitting on the back of a horse.

Right: If you find that your horse becomes rather strong, you will be able to control it better if you bridge the reins by bracing them against the withers. If the horse pulls, it will be pulling against itself, and cannot pull the reins out of your hands.

Bottom right: If your horse is going too fast, and your position in the saddle is stable, you can slow it down by anchoring one hand in the horse's mane and giving a series of tugs with the other rein. If you pull continuously against a horse, it will only pull harder against you.

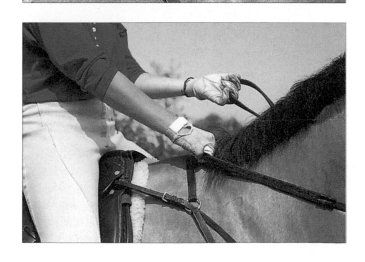

WESTERN RIDING

Contrary to the popular image of Western riding conveyed by the cowboys of the movie screen (galloping furiously across the prairie with legs straight in the stirrups and arms flapping), classical Western riding differs only fractionally from English or European classical riding. The two styles certainly come from the same historical roots, because before the Spaniards landed in Mexico in the 16th century—the first Europeans to reach the continent—the people who lived there had never even seen a horse. Thus, the riding style practiced by the Spaniards—the style followed throughout Europe at the time—must have been the example that the inhabitants of the country learned or copied.

The differences that developed in riding styles came about through practical reasons. The early settlers of the Americas were faced with vast tracts of land, which were largely uninhabited, uncultivated, and unfenced, even by natural boundaries. These conditions were entirely new to them, as nothing similar existed in their European homelands and so they were forced to adopt new riding habits. Now, they had to spend hours, if not days, in the saddle, working with their horses to establish farms and ranches. As a result, the saddle was adapted to ensure maximum comfort and greater control. From the native Indians who soon mastered the art of riding on horses that escaped from the early settlements, they learned how to use the lariat to rope stampeding cattle. They soon practiced the technique from horseback, and it is now an essential part of Western riding.

Classical Western riding today is still closely linked to the riding of the cowboys. The point to bear in mind, however, is that, to the cowboy, the horse is merely a tool, part of the essential "machinery" of his work. As long as the animal allows the cowboy to do his work with the maximum speed, ease, and efficiency, he is generally not concerned as to whether or not he achieves a classically correct performance.

Schools and differences

There are two recognized schools of Western riding today—the South Western, or Californian, school and the Texan school. In general, the Californian style is more classical, calling for somewhat more refined movements

While Western riding may differ only slightly from English or European riding, it was developed much more for reasons of necessity than for esthetic considerations. Above: Western saddles are also unique in having a high horn, a deep, wide seat, and a high cantle.

and precision in performance from the horse. Contact with the horse's mouth, although still very light, is more dcfinite than it is in the Texan school. For this reason, the reins are more often very slightly weighted close to the bit—the weighting consisting of no more than a length of braiding of the reins—to make this part fractionally heavier. The Texan school generally demands a little less collection from the horse through the paces, so, to the observer, the horse has a longer "outline"—that is, it is less gathered together.

The most obvious difference between Western and European riding is that, once horse and rider have been trained correctly, the Western rider holds the reins in one hand only, since, quite often, the other hand is needed to hold a lariat. This means that, in order to be able to control the horse, the horse has to be trained to understand the aids and principles associated with neck-reining. In the initial stages, however, it is better for a beginner to hold a rein in each hand. This gives the rider a far greater opportunity to establish a correct and stable position in the saddle. Holding the reins in just one hand tends to pull you out of the saddle and generally plays havoc with what is probably a none-too-secure and well-established position.

The commonly held belief that the Western rider rides with a perfectly straight leg is totally incorrect. To do so would give him no flexibility in his knee or control over his lower leg. Both of these are, of course, extremely essential in any style of riding.

Left: The rider also looks different from the European or English rider because of his riding outfit, which would include a wide-brimmed hat for protection from the sun, a brightly colored shirt, blue jeans, leather or suede chaps, and boots with high heels and pointed toes. Again, Western dress is often criticized by European or English riders as being informal and sloppy. However, when one considers the environment and conditions under which most of these riders must perform, the particular Western habit is well-suited to the type of riding.

Clothing and tack

Western riding kit differs markedly from the European equivalent; like the style of riding itself, the kit is the subject of much misconceived criticism. Critics of Western riding claim the clothes are untidy and sloppy—a description that they also apply to the riding style. This is not necessarily so, however; apart from the traditional gear described here, specially designed riding suits are now being worn by more and more Western riders, particularly in the show ring. These are well-cut and tailored suits, designed in the traditional style of Western riding clothes, but with particular attention paid to matching and coordinating colors. Unlike traditional European gear, however, they are often very brightly colored, which has also led to criticism from some traditionalists in the riding fraternity.

The tack worn by horses in Western riding is also different from that used in European classical circles. Once more, it has evolved from equipment developed to suit the conditions of the Western prairies and to give the cowboy every possible assistance and comfort in his work. The bridle is generally "skeleton" in design—that is, it consists of the minimum number of straps and other gadgets. This is partly because leather and metal do not mix well in burning hot conditions, tending to react badly with each other. Bridles traditionally associated with Western riding are either bitless or possess a spade or ordinary Western curb bit: many Western riders, however, prefer to use one of the Western snaffle bits, which is a type of joined mouth curb bit. The English jointed Pelham is similar, but without a rein for a snaffle bit.

Both horse and rider need to be extremely well-trained if a spade bit is used. This bit has a high port, which moves fractionally in the mouth as thc reins are moved. The horse feels this movement on the tongue, and also very slightly on the roof of the mouth. Such bits usually have a curb strap made of leather, rather than the chain one usually used in European riding. This, again, keeps the mixture of leather and metal to a minimum.

There are many different designs of Western saddle, the designs varying to suit the work the cowboy has to do. The type most frequently used for recreational Western riding is known as the Western Pleasure Saddle. This is lighter than most stock working saddles, but still possesses the traditional high horn.

Mounting

Getting to know the horse on which you are going to learn to ride Western-style is just as important as in any other riding style. Before attempting to mount, therefore, find out the horse's name and pat and make a fuss over him, before leading him to where your lesson is to be. When you are ready to mount, check that the rigging is sufficiently tight to prevent the saddle from slipping.

Mounting Western-style is not very different from mounting European-style. Standing on the horse's near side, hold the reins in your left hand sufficiently tightly to stop the horse from moving forward. Get into the habit of doing this from the start, even though someone will be holding the horse's head during your early lessons. Face obliquely to the horse's hindquarters—that is, not directly toward the tail, as in English equitation, but in such a way that a sideways glance over your left shoulder means you can keep an eye on the horse's head. Turn the stirrup toward you and put your left foot in it. Move your right hand over to the off side of the saddle and rest it against the swell; then spring up off the ground and throw your right leg over the horse's back and saddle. Remember that the extra height of the Western saddle means you will have to lift your leg slightly higher than normal. Settle into the middle of the saddle and put your right foot in the stirrup.

The advantage of putting your right hand against the off-side well means first of all that you eliminate any danger of pulling the saddle toward you, as you would if you took hold of the cantle. It also means that you can leave it in this position until you are sitting in the saddle. If you placed the hand further back, you would have to move it forward as you brought your leg across the saddle, which means that, momentarily, you would be balancing in space.

Such precautions as holding the reins sufficiently tight to discourage any forward movement from the horse, and placing your right hand in a way that you do not have to move it while you mount, stem from the early days of Western riding. The worst thing that could happen to a Western rider on the range was to lose his horse. If, for example, it shot forward while he was mounting, so that he lost his balance and let go of the reins, he was often as good as dead. With the horse would go, not only his transport, but also his canteen of water and his emergency food rations.

MOUNTING

1 Facing obliquely to the horse's hindquarters, put your left foot in the stirrup iron. Hold reins tightly.

2 Hop around to face the horse's side and put your right hand across the seat of the saddle.

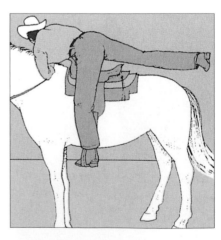

3 Jump up off the ground and swing your right leg over the horse's back, settling gently into the saddle.

As mentioned earlier, it is often thought that Western riders ride with a perfectly straight leg. In fact, the stirrup leathers should be about the same length as that used for dressage; that is, slightly longer than for normal, European-style, recreational riding, but not so long that, if you stood up in the stirrups, your seat would not lift off the saddle. An exercise that will help you initially to find the right length is to put your feet in the stirrups and let the leathers down until your legs are hanging straight down on either side of the saddle. Remember, however, not to point your toes downward, too. Then, take the leathers up one hole—in most Western saddles, these are positioned about 2 in (5 cm) apart. If they are set closer together, take them up two holes. It is impossible to adjust the leathers on a Western saddle when mounted.

Above: The rider's position in Western riding is similar to that of European. The rider sits evenly in the center of the saddle with the body weight distributed on either side and body weight and thrust directed downward into and out of the heels.

The Western seat

As in European equitation, the Western rider sits in the middle and center of the saddle, so that his or her weight is evenly distributed across the horse's back and directly over his center of balance. In just the same way, the rider's head is held high and the weight of the body falls down onto the seat bones. The residue falls down onto the knee and out of the heels; in other words, the rider's weight is all directed downward. The feet should not be braced hard against the stirrups, as this lifts the seat upward out of the saddle.

Dismounting

To dismount Western-style, put the reins in your left hand and place them just in front of the saddle. Put your right hand on the saddle horn and take your right foot out of the stirrup. Lean forward and swing your right leg up behind you over the back of the saddle and across the horse's back. Looking toward the front of the horse, step quickly and gently down to the ground. As soon as your right foot touches the ground, take your left foot smoothly out of the stirrup.

DISMOUNTING

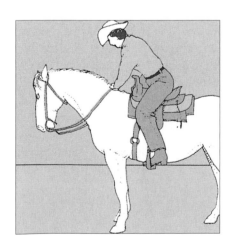

1 Take your right foot out of the stirrup iron, keeping a tight hold of the reins, resting your hand on the horse's neck.

2 With your right hand resting against the right-hand side of the saddle, lean forward and swing your right leg up behind you.

3 Step down to the ground by the horse's side, then take your left foot out of the stirrup iron.

Above: The walk in Western equitation is asked for in exactly the same way as in European riding. Ask the horse to move forward from a halt by gently tapping his sides with the inside of your legs and heels, at the same time yielding very slightly with your hands to allow the forward movement. He should move forward freely and smoothly, maintaining an even pace.

Below: The jog is the Western equivalent of a trot. Although the movement is the same as in European styles of riding, the pace tends to be rather more bumpy. The rider should sit deep into the saddle, keeping the waist and loins very supple, in order to allow him to relax with the movement.

The walk and the jog

As in all types of riding, the most important aspect of Western riding is to get the feel of the horse—to know the feel of sitting correctly in the saddle and to learn to recognize the feel of the horse's legs beneath you. Not only is that difficult to explain but very difficult to teach. The only way to understand even the meaning of this feel is to practice riding continually and extensively. Practice continually the walk, even before you move onto the jog, aiming to achieve smooth turns and perfect circles. Give the aids to turn in exactly the same way as you would normally, feeling gently with the rein in the direction you want the horse to move, with your inside leg pressed against his side close to the cinch and the outside leg applying pressure just behind this. Remember that the pressure you put on the reins should be no more than the slightest squeeze. Your aim is to achieve a smooth, flowing turn, with no jerkiness or violent head reaction from the horse. If you pull on the reins, rather than feel, your mount will inevitably react jerkily and violently.

The Western rider asks his or her horse to move forward into a walk from a halt in exactly the same way as a rider practicing any other style of equitation—that is, by closing or nudging the legs against the horse's side and opening the fingers to allow the horse to move forward. As the horse goes into a walk, the rider must follow the movement by allowing his body to move in time with the rhythm of the pace.

In Western riding the trot is called a jog. The correct jog calls for engagement of the hocks, so the horse is coming from behind with energy and rhythm. Ask for it in the usual way, making sure first that your horse is walking out well and is attentive and obedient to your aids. Stay seated in the saddle, as for the sitting trot, relaxing your body so that you are able to follow the horse's movement. Do not brace your body against the saddle—if you do, you will inevitably bounce out of it—but, equally, do not relax enough to become sloppy. Sit up straight and let your loins and waist absorb the movement.

As with the walk, do lots of practice work at the jog, trying to maintain a completely even and steady pace for three or four circuits of the school at a time, and then through smaller 65 ft (20 m) circles and figure-eights. This is considerably more difficult to achieve

Left: Again, at a lope, the rider should follow the movement of the horse, by sitting deep in the saddle and relaxing the waist and loins.

strange, but, if you think consciously of what you want your horse to do, you are far more likely to transmit your wishes to him clearly. The philosophy is just the same as looking ahead in the direction in which you want to travel, particularly when asking for a turn. Look where you want to go, think about the pace you want from your horse, and the battle is halfway won.

The canter or lope

In Western riding, the canter is called a lope. It is exactly the same pace, although when it is executed correctly, with the horse moving very smoothly, it tends to look a little easier and more relaxed than the European version. Though there is a considerable amount of power coming from the hindquarters, it is a very light pace, so the contact with the reins should be similarly coinsiderate. Such lightness, however, can tempt the horse to fall back into a jog, so the rider must ensure against this by urging him gently forward with the legs all the time.

The aids for the lope are the same aids as in the European canter. If you are moving counterclockwise around the school, you would ask for a lope with the near fore leading; if you are riding round the school on the right rein, or clockwise, your aids should be directed toward making the horse's off-fore lead.

Ride at the lope in the same way as you would at a canter, sitting deep in the saddle with your loins and waist really supple, so that they can absorb the movement. Once more, you should be sitting bolt upright, your head held high, and looking in the direction you want to go. It is also another pace in which the smoothness and evenness of rhythm can sometimes encourage the unwary rider to become sloppy. When you want to return to a jog, "think jog" and give the aids for a downward transition.

than it sounds on paper, but it is extremely good practice. You should bear in mind constantly that the Western jog is a collected movement in which the horse's hindquarters are active and tucked well beneath him, giving an alert and active pace.

Traditionally the Western rider always rides at the jog, and not rising like the European rider. However, particularly if you intend to go Western trail riding (pony trekking, Western-style) when you may spend many hours a day in the saddle, it is a good idea to be able to rise to the trot, too. On long rides, this is essential for at least some of the time; sitting in the saddle for very long periods is exceptionally tiring for both horse and rider. You will also find that practicing the rising trot will help you in recognizing feel, as you think more consciously about the legs moving in diagonal pairs beneath you.

Slowing down and stopping

Just as the aids for moving forward, or going from a walk to a jog, are the same in Western riding as they are in other classical styles of equitation, so, too, are the aids of slowing down and stopping. To go from a jog to a walk, close the inside of your lower leg against the horse's side and squeeze on the reins to discourage the forward movement. You should think of "walking"—this advice may sound

COMPETITIVE RIDING

DRESSAGE

Above: Blenheim Palace, UK, provides a wonderful backdrop for a dressage competition.

Below right: The smaller-sized arena is used for tests up to Medium level, the larger arena for international events. It is useful to practice in a large arena when you are working on advanced movements. The arena is marked with letters that indicate where the movements being performed should begin and end.

The term "dressage" covers all training done on the flat, and dressage movements and exercises are used for training all horses regardless of which area of the sport they compete in. Its aim is to produce a horse that is strong, supple, well-developed, and obedient to its rider.

You have to teach the horse to move in the different paces, progressing gradually from one to the next. In doing this, you must always take into account the horse's stage of development and training. In the demonstration sequences in this section, most of the movements are shown first by a novice horse that is still learning some of the paces and then by an advanced horse, to illustrate what can be expected at different stages of a horse's development. The advanced horse also demonstrates the self-carriage that all dressage horses must develop. It is essential to build up gradually, as the horse needs to develop the muscles necessary to perform each action. A horse can be ruined if he is asked to do too much too early.

The rider also has to undergo an intensive training program. You have to work on your position in the saddle. You have to learn to use the leg, seat, and hand aids independently of each other but correctly balanced for the movement you are executing, so that you control the whole horse all of the time. And you need to learn to work with a relaxed but positive mind, as any tenseness or indecision on your part will instantly communicate themselves to the horse. A young horse should be worked for about a half-hour a day, and you should include hill work and grid work in the training routine to get the horse fit and keep its mind fresh. Always remember that your horse is not a machine. Do not drill him, and do not just sit on top and try to dominate him. The horse must want to work with you if you are to get the best out of him.

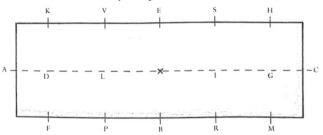

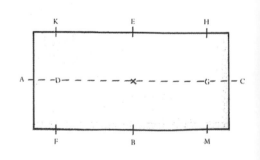

Left: If your horse is very lively, you are well-advised to turn it out for a half-hour, or to lunge it before beginning a schooling session.

Below: The aim of dressage training is for the horse and rider to learn to work together.

The walk

In walk, the horse must have good forward movement, be straight, and responsive to your aids. He must be moving forward symmetrically, with the power coming from behind. You must be as still and relaxed as possible and allow, with your hands, to let the horse take a full stride.

There are four types of walk: free, collected, medium, and extended. The free walk is a walk on a long, loose rein. The horse takes long, easy strides and can relax and stretch out his neck.

In collected walk you are looking for increased flexing in the hocks and activity in the joints to give short, elevated steps. The outline should be shortened, and the hind feet should fall just in, or slightly behind, the prints of the front feet. The collected walk is created by using the half-halt repeatedly while maintaining the pace.

The medium walk comes between free and extended. The horse begins to lengthen and extend his stride and the hind legs slightly over-track the forelegs. He also begins to lengthen his body, although the outline remains compact and rounded overall. The horse's steps should be free and active, and you should maintain a light contact with the horse's mouth.

In extended walk the horse must just release the outline and become longer and lower. He must cover as much ground as possible with each stride while maintaining regular steps. You ask for the extended walk by increasing the pressure from your seat and closing your legs against the horse. At the same time you allow the horse to stretch his neck forward and take the rein.

Above: The rider has given the horse the freedom to lower and stretch out its head and neck.

Above: By using her legs and seat, the rider asks the horse to lengthen its stride a little. She has a light contact with her hands. The horse's outline remains rounded.

Above: In this collected walk the rider is using her legs to create more activity in the hindquarters, at the same time using a series of half-halts to ask the horse to shorten and heighten its stride.

Above: The rider is closing her lower legs to ask the horse to stretch out and lengthen its stride, and allows it to take the rein as it does so. In extending its body, this novice horse has flattened out too much.

Right: In this medium walk, this advanced horse has a shorter stride than the younger one. It needs to drop its neck a fraction and lengthen out.

Right: This advanced horse's hind leg is coming through well from behind and is overtracking the print left by the front foot. Again, it needs to drop a little lower in the neck and lengthen out. Then its hind leg would come through further, lengthening its strides into a good extended walk.

Above: For this working trot the horse is attentive, it has a good outline, and a nice length of stride.

Above: Moving towards collection the horse has good flexion in the back, and is coming up in front. It is beginning to make its stride shorter and more active, and its outline rounder.

The trot: working and collected

In trot you should aim for free, active, regular steps, and a general impression of elasticity and suppleness, with the hind legs engaged. The trot is a difficult pace to do correctly, and young horses, in particular, tend to hurry, causing themselves and their riders to lose their balance.

There are four types of trot: working, collected, medium, and extended. You must be able to follow the movement of extended and collected trot very closely. If your seat is not deep enough, the rhythm of the pace will probably be lost.

The working trot is used for horses that are not ready to learn collection. It demonstrates whether the horse is properly balanced, has good hock action, and is on the bit.

As with all collected paces, collected trot requires plenty of impulsion coming from the hindquarters. You then contain the energy with the half-halt as it comes through from behind, to create springy, elevated paces. The horse's hind legs should be very active, with increased flexion in the hocks, so that they come well under the horse.

The horse's ability in collected trot will depend to a certain extent on his conformation and natural action, as well as his stage of development. Some horses have a very round, natural trot action, and can achieve the required flexion up and hold more easily than others. A horse that has a straight, flat action will have difficulty achieving the same degree of flexion and roundness.

Above: The rider has her feet lightly balanced in the stirrups, and her lower legs are wrapped around the horse's body. She is relaxed and independent of her hands, and rises with the horse's movement.

Above: Here, however, the rider's body is stiff, and she is leaning slightly backward. Her hands are raised, and the reins are too long, so she has lost the contact.

Right: The rider is asking for impulsion and using the half-halt to create a very elevated, collected trot. The horse is flexing well and moving with a rounded action.

COMMON FAULTS

1 The stride is shorter but the horse has too much weight on its forehand. The rider is slightly forward, and looks as if she is trying to carry it. She needs to sit upright and half-halt to sit the horse down and release and lighten the front.

2 The horse is arguing with the bit. The rider is asking it to start to collect, and is possibly using too much hand, as opposed to using her back and seat properly to ask for the pace. She needs to sit up straight and push the horse forward.

1

2

The trot: medium and extended

Medium trot comes between working and extended in length of stride. There should be plenty of impulsion from the hindquarters, and the horse should be taking energetic strides. His neck should be slightly extended. The horse must be overtracking, and the stride must be of equal length in front and behind. Uneven strides show that the horse is not working actively behind.

In extended trot, the horse lengthens his outline to the maximum, to produce long strides. Prepare for the extended trot with the half-halt. Then give strong aids, pushing with the seat and closing the legs firmly against the horse, and release the movement through the reins. Go with the stride as you ask for it. If you do not go with the movement, you will get behind it and end up pulling on the reins.

Above: The rider is asking for a lengthened stride into a medium trot with her seat and legs, and is keeping a light contact with her hands. The horse is working actively, and the strides in front and behind are of equal length.

Above: The rider is fractionally behind the horse's movement. However, as she went with the movement, she is not interfering with the horse's stride.

COMMON FAULTS

Above: The horse has its head up, is resisting the bit and going onto the forehand. It is "running" and the rider is having to balance it with her hands. In asking for the pace, she should have used her legs more to engage the horse's hindquarters and push it forward, and then allowed the movement with her hands.

Above: The length of the stride is good in this extended trot. The novice horse is still learning this pace, and is going into it too much, with its weight on the forehand. The rider is leaning fractionally forward in an attempt to help it. However, she is allowing the movement to come through. The pace is very active, but a little unbalanced.

Left: The rider has asked for the pace by preparing this advanced horse with a half-halt, pushing the horse on strongly, and then releasing the forward movement with her hands, keeping a light contact with the horse's mouth. The horse is responding with a smooth, active, extended stride. You can see how much it has lengthened compared with the medium trot.

Above: The horse is starting collection. Its neck is raised, its hindquarters are rounded and lowered, and it is starting to sit. The rider is slightly against the horse, twisting and pulling back on the inside rein.

The canter

In canter you are aiming for a general impression of regular steps, lightness, roundness, and acceptance of the bit. The horse should be light in the forehand so that its shoulders are free and mobile, and he should demonstrate good hock action. The horse's back should be round and swinging, and you should be relaxed in the saddle, absorbing the movement. In addition, you must keep the horse going straight, that is with the inner hind foot in line with the inner front foot.

The four canter paces are: working, collected, medium, and extended.

The working canter is used for horses who are not ready to learn collection. It demonstrates a free, balanced pace.

Collected canter should have a clear 3-time beat. The horse should be on the bit, moving forward with its neck raised and arched. He should bring his hindquarters well underneath him, shifting his weight back and lightening his forehand to produce short, springy strides.

In medium canter, again the 3-time movement should be well-marked. The horse should lengthen a little, and his hind leg should come well under his body, producing an active stride.

In extended canter, the hind leg should come well under the horse's body in order to lengthen the stride as much as possible and produce a longer outline. However, apply the pushing aids gently, so that the horse does not go forward in a series of jerks. Extended canter is a difficult pace to maintain because the horse has a natural inclination to rush its strides rather than lengthen them.

Left: The rider is in a good position, and the horse is achieving a good stride in this extended canter. It is on the forehand a little because its hindquarters are not quite engaged enough. Although it is lengthening well, it should not drop its head, but must remain in self-carriage as the advanced horse has done.

It can be difficult to keep a horse straight in canter. If you find this a problem, you should first think about your own position. If you are not sitting square in the saddle you will make the horse go crooked. Next, think about the aids you are giving. If you are not balancing them correctly, the horse will not go straight. For example, if your outside leg is too far back, it can make the horse's quarters swing in. If your inside hand is too strong, creating too much bend in the horse's neck, you will lose control of the shoulders and the outside shoulder will fall to the outside.

Above: The horse's outline is shortened and rounded in this collected canter. In the middle of a stride it is like a coiled spring ready to unwind.

Above: The stride of this medium canter is a little shorter than the extended canter direct. The rider has simply gone forward with the movement of the horse. She is using her legs to push the horse on and has a good position in the saddle.

Above: The horse is making a good long stride in this extended canter, but it is a little flat behind the saddle. It needs to engage the hindquarters more by bringing the inside leg a little further under its body.

COMMON FAULTS

1 The horse is not using its hindquarters actively enough, with the result that they are not properly rounded. This can be seen behind the saddle, where it is flatter than in the picture above.

2 The horse is on the forehand, resisting the rider. She needs to use her legs to increase the activity in the horse's hindquarters.

1

2

HOW THE HORSE TURNS

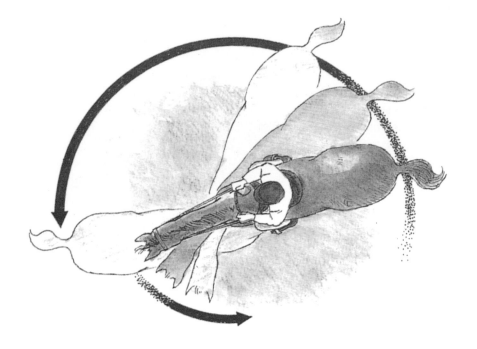

Turn on the forehand

The turn on the forehand is used in the early part of a horse's training. It increases the horse's suppleness, and teaches him to be obedient to the rider's aids. The movement is also valuable in teaching the rider to control the whole horse.

You ask the horse to fix his shoulders and, using your leg on the girth, you push the horse's hindquarters around. The horse's hind legs step across each other so that he pivots on his forehand.

The turn on the forehand is done from a standstill. Move in a little way from the side of the arena so that the horse has enough space in which to turn.

The horse pivots on its forehand through 180 degrees. It is done from the standstill and has little impulsion or forward movement.

TURN ON THE FOREHAND: ADVANCED HORSE

1 Starting from halt, the rider applies her left leg on the girth to ask the horse to move sideways. At the same time she restrains the horse with her hands to keep the forehand in the same place.

2 The horse's hind legs step across each other as it pivots on the forehand. The rider continues to apply the leg aid in rhythm with the movement, while her hands control the horse's shoulders.

3 The horse has turned through 180 degrees while remaining on the same spot.

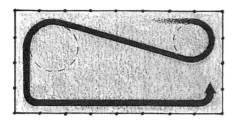

Above: Ride a small circle and come back to the track in counter canter, then bring the horse back to the walk, or change back to true canter using a simple change. When the horse can do this on both reins, continue the counter canter through the corner of the arena.

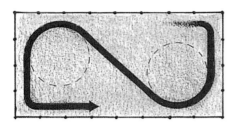

Left: When the horse can hold counter canter through the end of the school, ride a figure-eight, maintaining counter canter through the whole movement.

Counter canter

In counter canter the horse leads with his outside foreleg, and his body is flexed slightly toward the outside of the arena. It should be just as fluid and controlled as the true canter.

The aids for counter canter are the opposite to those used for true canter. The outside leg is used on the girth and asks for strikeoff, while the inside leg is used behind the girth to create impulsion and maintain the movement. The outside rein directs the horse and maintains the bend to the outside, while the inside rein helps to balance the horse and controls his speed and direction.

To begin with, practice counter canter on a shallow loop on the long side of the arena, maintaining the bend toward the direction of the leading leg. You can then move onto the two exercises illustrated here.

COUNTER CANTER: ADVANCED HORSE

1 The rider has asked for strikeoff in counter canter by using her outside leg on the girth.

2 The rider uses her inside leg slightly behind the girth to maintain the pace, and her outside leg stays on the girth.

3 Her inside hand controls the horse's direction while her outside hand helps to maintain the bend.

4 The counter-canter stride: the outside foreleg leaves the ground as the inside hind leg comes well under the horse.

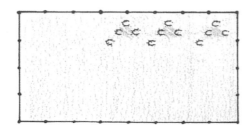

Left: To achieve the correct angle to the track and to make sure that the horse moves on two tracks, the horse's outside hind leg should fall in the print left by the inside foreleg.

Shoulder-in

In shoulder-in the horse moves forward and sideways down the track. His forehand is a little inside the track, with his shoulders turned in, while his hindquarters remain on the track. The horse's body is bent around the rider's inside leg, away from the horse's direction of travel, and his shoulders should form an angle of about 30 degrees to the track. You should aim to have the inside hind leg falling in the track left by the outside foreleg, and the horse should be flexed slightly away from the direction he is going. This will give you the correct angle to the track.

Shoulder-in is a good exercise for making the horse more supple. It is particularly good for loosening up a horse's shoulders for jumping. It also teaches the horse to listen to the rider's legs.

The best way to practice shoulder-in is to start it coming off a small circle at one end of the arena. Come around the circle imagining you are going to do another circle. As the horse's shoulders come off the track to start the second circle, resist a little with the inside rein or do a half-halt. Contain the bend with the outside hand so that the horse does not come too far around. Keeping this degree of flexion, push the horse forward down the track with your inside leg on the girth, controlling the hindquarters with your outside leg behind the girth.

Shoulder-in is a small movement. Many people tend to think they do not have enough angle to the track, so they overdo it. Experience will teach you the angle correctly.

CORRECT SHOULDER-IN: NOVICE HORSE

1 The rider is using her inside leg to push the horse down the track. Her outside leg is a little behind the girth to keep the horse's hindquarters straight. Her inside hand asks for flexion in the horse's body while her outside hand controls the amount and the horse's direction.

2 The inside hind leg is falling in the print left by the outside forelegs. This young horse is showing the movement well, and has a good angle to the track, but it needs to develop a little more flexion in the body.

COMMON FAULTS

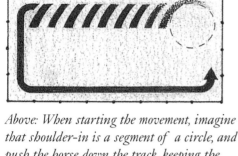

Above: When starting the movement, imagine that shoulder-in is a segment of a circle, and push the horse down the track, keeping the same degree of flexion.

1 The rider is not using her legs and hands to ask the horse to flex.

2 With too much angle to the track, the horse makes too many tracks with its feet. Adjust the angle by controlling the shoulders through the reins.

Above: In order to perform the more advanced paces well, horses must spend time doing elementary exercises such as shoulder-in when they are young so that they learn to be obedient to the rider's leg.

The half-pass

In this movement the horse moves forward and sideways down the arena on two tracks. The horse's body should remain parallel to the sides of the arena overall, although it must be flexed toward the way it is going, unlike shoulder-in, when it is flexed away from the direction in which it is going. The straighter hindquarters must neither trail behind nor get ahead of the shoulders. This exercise shows whether the horse is loose in the hips.

To practice half-pass, come around the track and ask the horse to bend in the way you are going by using the inside hand, and controlling the direction of the horse with the outside hand. Your outside leg goes behind the girth to push the horse away, while your inside leg is just on the girth to make sure that the hindquarters do not lead the movement. Look in the direction in which the horse is going.

You must aim for a good, active crossover with the forelegs, with the hind legs stepping out as well, and you must maintain impulsion and rhythm as the horse carries out the movement.

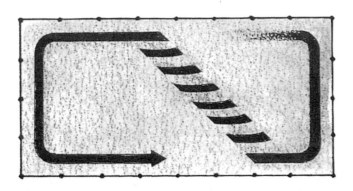

Above: As you start to come down the long side of the arena, move away from the track toward the center in half-pass.

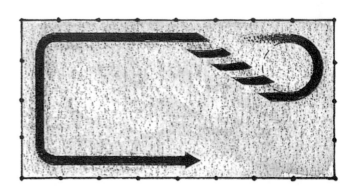

Above: Turn to come down the center of the arena and then move in half-pass either left or right back to the track. The horse should be straight as you come onto the track again.

HALF-PASS: NOVICE HORSE

1 The rider is using her outside (left) leg behind the girth to push the horse forward and sideways, while her inside leg controls the hindquarters.

2 The horse is performing this adequately for its stage of training, but is not yet loose enough in the shoulders to perform it well.

3 This horse needs to develop more crossover with the forelegs, and more "expression" in the movement as a whole.

COMMON FAULTS

Above: The horse is using a good through action to make this half-pass, stepping over well with its forelegs. The outside bind is also moving well.

Above: The horse's hindquarters are moving across the arena fractionally ahead of the shoulders because the rider is not controlling them enough with her inside (right) leg.

Above: As a horse becomes stronger and more supple, through schooling, it develops self-carriage, or the ability to perform paces and movements with "expression," as demonstrated by this horse.

Leg-yielding

In this movement the horse again travels forward and sideways down the arena. He should have flexion away from the direction in which he is going. As in half-pass, aim to keep the horse parallel overall to the side of the arena. The hindquarters should neither lead nor trail behind the shoulders.

Your outside leg should stay near the girth so that it controls the horse's shoulders. If it goes too far back, it will throw the hindquarters over too much. Feel the outside rein to ask for slight flexion away from the direction the horse is going in. Your other hand controls the degree of flexion.

LEG-YIELDING CORRECTLY

1 The rider is using her outside (left) leg to push the horse sideways, while the inside (right) leg stays near the girth in order to prevent the horse's right shoulder from falling out.

2 At the same time the outside (left) rein is asking the horse for flexion away from the direction in which it is moving. The inside (right) rein is against the horse's neck, helping to support the shoulder and controlling the amount of flexion.

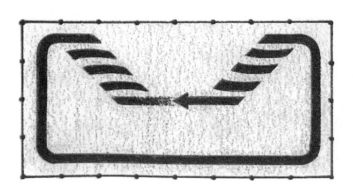

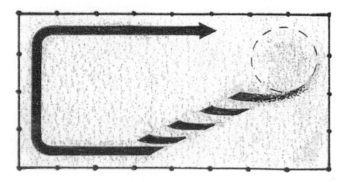

Above: To ride loops when leg-yielding, ride a shallow loop down the side of the arena leg-yielding towards the center. Go straight ahead for a few strides, then leg-yield in the other direction back to the track.

Above: To ride circles when leg-yielding, ride a small circle, and begin leg-yielding across the arena to the far track as you come off the top of it.

Walk pirouette

In walk pirouette the horse pivots on his hindquarters. You push the horse as if to move on but bring him around with the reins at the same time. It is done from the walk, and the horse should move smoothly forward into walk without hesitation as he finishes the movement. The hind legs mark time, while the forelegs step across one another. The horse must bend around your inside leg, maintaining flexion in the direction in which he is going, and must pick up his hind feet as he turns.

Prepare the horse with a half-halt and begin the movement as the inside hind stops moving forward. Push the horse on using the outside leg behind the girth, and the inside leg on the girth. At the same time use the rein to ask the horse to step around, while the outside rein controls the degree and speed of the turn.

This exercise should not be done until the horse is working in collected paces and has good impulsion.

A GOOD WALK PIROUETTE

1 The rider is using her seat and legs to push the horse on. She is showing it the way round with the inside rein, while the outside rein comes to the horse's neck to help bring it round.

2 The rider keeps applying the aids in rhythm with the horse's steps. The horse shows good flexion and is looking in the direction it is going.

3 The horse's weight is back on its hindquarters, and its forelegs are crossing over well.

4 The rider is using her leg behind the girth in case the horse's hindquarters are about to swing out.

The halt and rein-back

When a horse becomes more obedient and responsive to the aids for both upward and downward transitions, the halt becomes easier to master.

Although a young horse soon learns to halt and stand still when asked, it is not until he is really accepting the aids that he can perform a true halt from walk or trot. In a correct halt, the weight of the horse should be distributed evenly on all four legs while he remains steadily on the bit and ready for movement forward or backward.

In the rein-back, the horse steps backward with his legs moving in diagonal pairs. He should lift his feet well off the ground and not drag them backward. His weight should be taken on his hind legs without any sinking in the back or lowering of the forehand. He should not resist the hand and should move backward in a straight line. You must be careful not to ask a horse to rein back before he is sufficiently strong in his back and capable of a true halt. Once he has accomplished this, ask him to rein back slightly, lightening your seat and closing the lower leg as if to move forward but, at the same time, restraining the forward movement with your hand. As soon as the horse steps back, reward him with praise and a lighter hand. No more than one or two steps should be asked for in the early stages.

Only when the horse is obedient to the aids should he be asked to step back. If he resists the rein aids, push him up with the lower leg and seat until he realizes that it is simultaneously a restraining but allowing hand. The horse must stay on the bit throughout.

Any tendency to run back out of control must be quickly, but quietly, corrected with forward-driving aids and, if necessary, a touch of the whip. Running back is caused by a desire to drop the bit, so the movement should be ridden with slightly more leg aids and a light rein contact throughout. If the horse raises his head and hollows his back when asked for rein-back, then this should be corrected first. In this position, the horse cannot move backward comfortably with your weight on his back, so do not ask for rein-back until the horse has returned to the correct stance.

Care and patience is required in teaching the horse the rein-back. With some fine or thoroughbred horses, you have to take a noticeable proportion of his weight off the horse's back and transfer some of it to his knee and thigh, although without leaning forward. In really difficult cases, it may be advisable to teach the horse the rein-back without your weight. This can be done using long reins, and, once the movement is established, the rider can be reintroduced. This lesson must be learned over a period of time; in no circumstances should it be hurried.

If the horse does not move back in a straight line, this should be corrected with a little more pressure of the leg or rein aid on the side the hindquarters are moving out.

The Rein-back

1. Rider lightens the seat.
2. The lower legs are placed behind the girth.
3. Hands are gently restraining, but yielding with the steps.
4. The horse moves backward in two-time, taking diagonal steps.

THE AIDS FOR HALT AND REIN-BACK

- *To halt, lighten the seat, close lower legs, and push horse forward into a restraining but allowing hand.*
- *As horse steps back, keep rein aid light and slightly yielding with each step.*
- *After a few steps, halt, then close legs to ask for forward steps.*
- *Care must be taken not to hurry the horse forward after rein-back, because this can lead to anticipation and tension in the movement. Ask for a few seconds' halt every now and then after a rein-back.*

HALT AND REIN-BACK

1 Here the horse is in a true halt, squarely placed, with its weight distributed over all four legs. It is on the bit and listening for the rider's next command.

2 Now it takes its first steps backward for the rein-back. Note how its legs are moving in diagonal pairs, and the steps are well-raised.

3 Backward movement continues, now on the other diagonal, although the footfall is now not quite in two-time. The foreleg has come to the ground just before the hind leg.

4 Here the horse is better balanced, taking a little more weight on the hind legs, so that the hind foot is now just about touching the ground at the same time as the foreleg.

5 The horse is about to complete the fourth step of the rein-back, after which it will be quietly ridden forward, perhaps after a pause.

Travers

Travers and renvers are movements in which the horse's body is bent in the direction of motion. In travers, the hindquarters are brought in from the track with the horse bent around your inside leg. In renvers, the shoulders are brought in from the track and the horse is bent around your outside leg. Viewed from the front, the angle is greater than that of shoulder-in, so four feet are seen, not three. Travers and renvers are more demanding than shoulder-in and often used with other gymnastic exercises such as shoulder-in and half-pass.

The aids for travers down the long side of the arena are as follows. Before the corner, half-halt, then ride into the corner with the inside seat and leg. As you come out, allow the inside leg to become more passive while the outside leg, placed well behind the girth, asks the horse to move sideways. The inside hand should keep the flexion, with the outside hand regulating the bend and maintaining the balance of the horse. The inside leg should be placed at the girth to give the horse stability, and used more strongly only if the horse's hindquarters come in too much.

Like shoulder-in, travers should sometimes be ridden on the center line, and in fact it is a useful movement when ridden in conjunction with shoulder-in. A good exercise is to ride the horse in shoulder-in, followed by an 8½- or 11-yd (8- or 10-m) circle, a travers, and then a half-circle and half-pass. These movements flow well together and help to establish a positive bend throughout the horse's body, giving him the opportunity to achieve a real balance and rhythm.

COMMON FAULTS

1 *The horse has its hindquarters in from the track.*

2 *The horse is not bent correctly—its body is straight and only its neck is slightly bent.*

3 *The rider should place the inside leg on the girth for the horse to bend around.*

4 *The rider should sit straight and use much less outside leg—the inside leg has been forgotten.*

Travers

1 *Rider looks ahead in the direction of the movement.*
2 *Rider's seat is used firmly but lightly to ride horse forward into the movement.*
3 *Inside (right) leg is placed on the girth asking for the inside bend, and also riding horse forward into the movement.*
4 *Right rein asks for inside (right) flexion.*
5 *Outside (left) leg is placed behind the girth to move the hindquarters into the movement.*
6 *Left rein controls the balance and regulates the bend.*
7 *Horse's outside (left) hind leg moves forward and under the horse to cross in front of the right hind leg.*

RIDING TRAVERS IN TROT

1 You can see clearly in these pictures that the travers is a four-track movement. Here the outside hind and inside forelegs are on the ground, with the horse well-bent throughout its body.

2 Because the horse's weight is on the inside hind leg and outside foreleg, the bend through the body appears much greater. This is an illusion brought about by the placement of weight.

3 Here you can see clearly how the outside hind leg is brought forward and under the horse to step in front of the inside hind leg.

EXERCISES FOR TRAVERS

Travers is often performed down the center line, but these movements are useful for training.

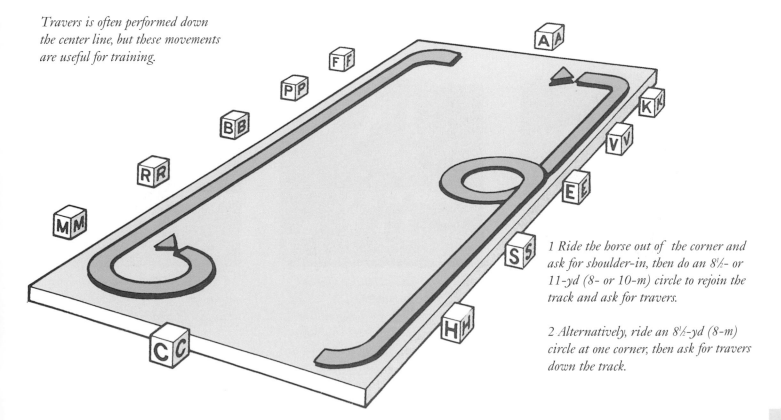

1 Ride the horse out of the corner and ask for shoulder-in, then do an 8½- or 11-yd (8- or 10-m) circle to rejoin the track and ask for travers.

2 Alternatively, ride an 8½-yd (8-m) circle at one corner, then ask for travers down the track.

Renvers

1 Rider looks in the direction of the movement.
2 Left leg is on the girth for the horse to bend around.
3 Left hand asks for left flexion.
4 Right leg is placed behind the girth.
5 Right hand controls the shoulders and the bend, and balances the movement.

Renvers

Renvers is, perhaps, a more difficult movement to achieve than travers, because you have to position the shoulders and then ask for the bend when riding it on the track. It is, in fact, easier to ride renvers down the center line, especially if coming out of a 11-yd (10-m) circle, as you hold the hindquarters on the center line, while keeping the shoulders and bend beyond it.

The aids for renvers are as follows. Half-halt at the three-quarter point of the circle, slightly weighting the inside seat bone. Place the inside leg passively on the girth, using the outside leg behind the girth to drive the horse forward and round the inside leg. The hands should regulate the bend in the direction of the movement. Keep the horse forward and on the line with the inside leg.

To ride renvers on the track, start as if riding shoulder-in, then change the bend to the direction of motion by weighting the other seat bone and changing the flexion and bend.

RIDING RENVERS IN TROT

1 The horse has just come round the corner of the arena and the rider is asking for left flexion for the renvers. The horse is pictured almost in the moment of suspension in trot.

2 The horse has established the bend and angle of the renvers. The outside (left) hind leg is being placed just in front of the inside (right) hind leg, and the inside (right) foreleg is crossing in front of the outside (left) foreleg.

3 The inside (right) hind leg and outside (left) foreleg are being brought forward and under the horse.

EXERCISES FOR SHOULDER-IN AND RENVERS

Renvers is a useful exercise to perform when a horse is reluctant to finish the half-pass. Ride the half-pass nearly to the track, keeping the bend and the hindquarters pushed over on to the track and take renvers on for several steps. The sequence half-pass, renvers, a reverse half-circle and half-pass again is a useful exercise to establish and reinforce the correct bend throughout all these movements.

1 Begin with shoulder-in (then half-pass) across the arena, leading into renvers to rejoin the track.

2 Or half-pass and renvers: come out of the corner in half-pass, at the track go into renvers, ending with a reverse half-circle. You could go into half-pass again after this, if you wish.

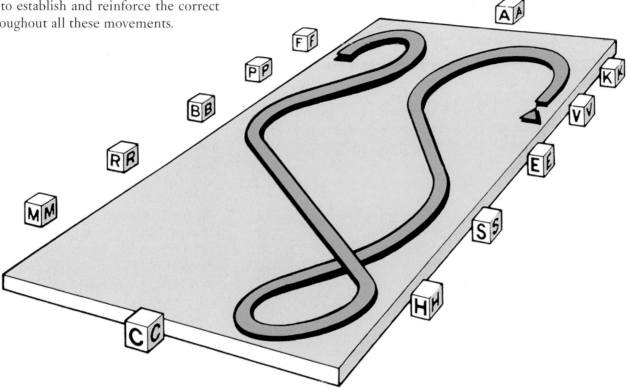

1 Before making the change, the rider has asked for a half-halt to make the horse pay attention. You can tell by its ears that it is listening for the next instruction.

The flying change
The flying change is a natural pace when the horse jumps from one canter leading leg to the other during the moment of suspension in the canter. Horses with very good, active canters find the flying change very easy to execute. Horses lacking jump in the canter will find it more difficult because the moment of suspension is lacking. You are aiming to achieve lightness and expression in the flying change, and for this you need a canter that is collected, active, straight, and springy.

To execute this movement well, you must be able to feel the exact moment to ask for the change. Make sure your legs are correctly positioned closely round the horse, and, because the change takes place at the moment

2 *The horse has just performed the flying change. The rider has lightened her seat slightly to allow the horse to jump into the air to make the change.*

3 *The horse has landed on the left leg, and is now in the second stride of the canter. The rider allows it to go forward, while maintaining the left canter position.*

of suspension, you must give the horse sufficient warning.

A preparatory half-halt is important to get the horse to listen to the correct aids for a flying change. Move the original outside leg forward just before asking for a change with the new outside leg, which moves back with stronger contact behind the girth. The seat rides the horse on while allowing him to jump, the new inside seat being pushed slightly forward. The legs can then ride the horse forward and straight or give a half-halt if required. The flexion is minimal and is used only to keep the forehand straight. There should be no flexion to the new inside leg, contrary to popular belief. The reins are used only to keep the balance and to give support.

It is important to keep the change straight from the start: swinging the quarters is a bad fault and will affect the horse's later training. A high croup is another fault that must be corrected early in the horse's education: this can turn into a major problem and is an evasion of the aids. With a horse who changes with a high croup, begin by several half-halts, then change with plenty of freedom, riding forward during the actual jump. You may have to give a half-halt soon after the change because, while correcting the balance of the change itself, he may have lost balance generally. The flying-change aid must be given quietly, but firmly—any throwing of your weight upsets the horse's balance and makes it more difficult for him.

EXERCISES FOR FLYING CHANGE

1 *Circle from the track in right canter, then ask for a flying change at point marked X, and circle to the left. Ask for another change at the lower point marked X, and half-circle again.*

2 *In left canter, leave the track and ride a 21-yd (20-m) half-circle: ask for a flying change at point marked X in the diagram. Circle to the right to rejoin track.*

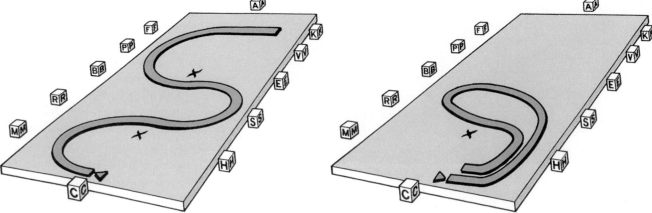

It is easy for a horse to become upset with careless riding of the flying change. You must be sure to keep balance and straightness while releasing the new inside leg sufficiently early, so as not to confuse the horse. If the horse increases his speed into the change, it is likely that the change will be late behind. In this case, more collection is needed. Working on a circle with transitions from counter canter to true canter with simple changes can help eradicate this fault.

Teaching the flying change

When teaching a horse the flying change, using a manège can be an advantage. Changing the rein on the short diagonal and asking for the change before arriving at B or E is a good place to start. Alternatively, ride a canter half-pass to the track and, when fully straightened up, the horse will be ready and well-balanced for a flying change. Make sure you ask for the movement well after the half-pass or anticipating could creep in. When the horse fully understands the aids and is happy and settled performing the flying changes while changing the rein and other variations, then practice off the track, changing to counter canter and then back to true canter. At this stage, the counter-change of hand can be practiced in canter but you must always make sure the horse is straight before asking for the change.

Take time to build up collection throughout the whole training of the horse before teaching the canter pirouette. Transitions in canter are an important part of establishing the required collection. Ride in working canter with many transitions to collected canter. Next, give a few half-halts in collected canter, always checking the horse's straightness by riding in a position right or left. Then ride forward to working canter again. Some steps riding in shoulder-fore in canter help to activate the inside hind leg of the horse; then, from this, the large canter half-pirouette can be asked for. Your chief concern must be the correctness of the steps and the balance of the horse—not the size of the pirouette. Any tendency to throw the shoulders around must be corrected with the outside rein and inside leg, and the pirouette made larger. Once a large half-pirouette can be performed with the horse in balance, you can practice a circle with the horse bent in the direction of the pirouette. Ride travers on the circle, then make a correct circle and ask for a few steps of smaller pirouette, and so on until the horse can accept the collection and balance.

Correct pirouettes are obtained through careful training and not from forced riding. Horses that are short coupled and with a naturally good canter pace find the pirouette easier than a large, long-backed horse. Any tendency for the horse to raise the forehand and come above the bit in little jumps on the hind legs should be corrected by riding the horse strongly with the legs into the hand and making him come into canter with more energy from the hind legs. Some flexing of the neck before riding the pirouette can help to loosen the horse.

Work should not become too repetitious. Changing the pirouette sometimes to a half-pirouette, a three-quarter pirouette, or even two pirouettes help to make the horse listen to the aids.

When the horse is in true collection and balance, the rider can begin to aim for the correct size of pirouette—although even with a highly trained horse the perfect pirouette is achieved only occasionally. Usually, the horse is capable of performing the movement if he is correctly muscled and fit, but it is the rider who needs so much practice in collecting and balancing the horse and in using the aids correctly. Every horse is different, and one may need more inside or outside leg and seat than another. It is this "feel" and sense of timing a good rider develops that is so important when riding advanced dressage.

EXERCISES FOR HALF-PASS AND FLYING CHANGE

Cantering right-handed, turn down the center line, then half-pass out to the track. Canter straight for a few strides, then ask for a flying change at point marked X. This is a very good exercise, because the horse will be well-collected with its hind legs really under it in the half-pass, and with good right flexion.

INTERPRETING YOUR DRESSAGE MARKS

In competitions, whatever your level you will be marked on a scale of 0–10. The judges award marks based on the expected performance for the class you have entered.

0	Not Performed.
1	Very bad.
2	Bad.
3	Fairly Bad.
4	Insufficient
5	Sufficient
6	Satisfactory
7	Fairly Good.
8	Good.
9	Very Good.
10	Excellent

Dressage tests require the horse to be active and free while still displaying all the qualities of power and speed that are its inherent characteristics. It must be light in hand so that the rider can control it with a light contact on the reins and almost invisible aids. It must be supple and obedient, and adjust its paces without resentment. It must remain straight from its head to its tail when moving on a straight line, bending slightly in the direction it is traveling on a curved line. All paces must maintain a regular rhythm with the correct footfall.

In addition, all changes of pace and other movements must take place at the specified markers, your circles must be circles, serpentines must be evenly spaced, and circles and loops must be the specified size.

Competitions are judged by one to three judges, and by five at international level. Each judge has a writer to note down the points scored and comments for each movement. Each movement is marked out of 10 points. In addition, extra points are given for different aspects of your overall performance: for example, general impression and calmness; accuracy of the paces and impulsion; and the position and seat of the rider, and correct application of the aids.

You should aim to arrive early at a competition to give yourself and your horse plenty of time to relax and unwind after the journey. This is not the time for a final practice. Do a few, simple movements to warm up and get the horse listening to you.

After the test, study the judges' remarks on your score sheet carefully and work extra hard at the movements you have been marked down on before the next time.

Above: Horse and rider have a final brush-up and warm-up before going in for their test.

EVENTING

The cross-country position

A cross-country course is ridden at speed. As the horse gallops around, it stretches out and its center of gravity moves forward. The key to riding a course well is to adopt a forward seat in order to stay balanced with the horse.

You should fold forward from the hip, with your seat out of the saddle, and keep your lower leg securely in position all the time. As you come into a fence, sit lightly in the sad- dle in order to drive the horse on over it.

It is vital that your legs remain in the cor- rect position, firmly on the girth, all the time, if you are to remain secure in the saddle. If they slide out of position, or flap against the horse's side, you will not be able to maintain a secure position.

Work all the time to balance yourself with the horse, not getting either ahead of, or behind, its movement.

Above: The rider's weight is forward, and she is well-balanced over the horse. Her lower leg is vertical, and is steady against the horse's side. She is pushing her weight down into her heel. She is keeping a straight line from her elbow through her hands to the horse's mouth, keeping firm contact and good communication.

Above: A good, secure position in the saddle will enable you to tackle any type of obstacle with confidence. Here, the rider is leaning back to keep his weight over the horse's center of gravity as they tackle the big drop, but he is still keeping his leg firmly in position on the girth.

COMMON FAULTS

The rider's leg is too far back, and she is leaning forward to compensate. This brings her ahead of the horse's movements, shifting her weight too far forward and making it difficult for her to apply her lower leg properly. She has lowered her hands, so the line of contact from her elbow to the horse's mouth has been broken.

Gridwork

Gridwork is as valuable in training the event horse as it is in the other areas of competition. It builds the horse's confidence by teaching him to think for himself, and to shorten and lengthen his stride coming to a fence. It is particularly good for practicing combinations, as it teaches the horse to maintain his concentration over a series of fences.

Grids can be used to practice different types of fences and to solve specific problems, as you can vary the jumps and the distances between them. You can bring two fences close together to create a bounce fence. Or you can space the fences apart, with poles on the ground between them, to make an overeager horse concentrate.

Start with one pole and a single fence and build up gradually from there, but do not confront your horse with a mass of poles. It saves a lot of time if you can have a helper to hand, to move fences and put back fallen poles for you.

It is very important that you get the distances in the grid right for your horse. All horses are different, so you need to work out the length of your horse's stride in relation to your own paces, in order to assess distances accurately.

A STRAIGHT FORWARD GRID

1 The grid starts with cross-poles, which guide the horse into the center of the grid and encourage it to round over the fence.

2 The pole on the ground brings the horse to the second fence correctly. It is looking confident and alert as it takes off.

3 The canter poles between the fences teach an overenthusiastic horse to bring its head down and concentrate. They also discourage it from rushing at the next fence.

4 The horse jumps well over the last element. The rider is balanced, with her weight forward, lower legs on the girth, and hands maintaining good contact with the horse's mouth.

SETTING UP A PRACTICE GRID

← One non-jumping stride → ← Two non-jumping strides →

Above: Practice on this type of grid helps you and the horse to judge the length of stride. The distance between the elements depends on whether you are in trot or canter.

APPROXIMATE DISTANCES FOR SETTING UP A GRID

Approach	In trot	In canter
Bounce	9–11 ft 2.75–3.3 m	11–14 ft 3.3–4.25 m
One non-jumping stride	18–24 ft 5.5–7.3 m	24–26 ft 7.3–7.9 m
Two non-jumping strides	30–32 ft 9–9.75 m	34–36 ft 10.4–11 m

Right: You need to know the length of your horse's stride in relation to your own. You can then set up a grid to suit your own horse.

COMMON FAULTS: RUSHING THE FENCE

1 *As the horse rushes at the last fence in the grid, it takes its rider by surprise. She is almost sitting back in the saddle, having been left behind the horse's movement.*

2 *Because the horse rushed at the fence, it has flattened out over it, raising its head and hollowing its back, and risks knocking it down. The rider is still behind the movement.*

TAKING A BOUNCE FENCE

1 *The rider is sitting down and using her seat, legs, and hands to bring the horse in on a short, bouncy, controlled, well-balanced stride. Its hocks are well underneath it and it has plenty of impulsion.*

2 *The horse lifts itself up well over the fence, although the rider's position is a little forward of the movement.*

3 *As the horse lands over the first part, it brings its hocks well underneath it in preparation to spring off over the second part. The rider sits up slightly, applies her lower leg and allows the horse's movement with her hands.*

Bounce fences

On a cross-country course you are quite likely to meet a "bounce" fence. This is a form of combination fence where there is no nonjumping stride between the elements. The horse lands over the first part and immediately takes off for the second.

You can practice riding a bounce either on its own or as part of your grid. As your horse grows in confidence and experience, you could even try a double bounce.

This type of fence places great demands on a horse's athleticism and coordination. As his forelegs touch the ground over the first element, he must bring his hindquarters as far underneath it as possible to take off for the second part.

To tackle a bounce fence successfully, the horse needs to be supple and agile. You need to bring him in on a short, controlled stride, well-balanced and with plenty of impulsion. If the horse comes in long and flat, he will probably land too far over the first element and have trouble with the second. You should sit up slightly between the elements so that you do not push the horse onto its forehand as he lifts himself up over the second element.

With this type of fence in particular, it is very important that your position follows through with the jump of the horse so that you do not get ahead of or behind it. You must keep your weight pushing down into your heels and let your hands go forward with the horse's movement, keeping in communication with the horse all the way.

DOWNHILL BOUNCE

1 Horse and rider take off over the first part of a downhill bounce fence. A straight approach and neat, athletic jumping are essential for this type of fence.

2 The rider has her weight back as they land over the first part. The partnership looks confident and well-balanced.

3 The horse has brought its hocks under and taken off close to the second part. They look set to clear it comfortably.

COMMON FAULTS: POOR CONTACT WITH THE REINS

1 Rather than going forward with the horse's movement, the rider has dropped her hands, so that they pull down on the horse's mouth and prevent it from stretching its head and neck forward sufficiently.

2 As a result, the horse has flattened out over the fence, raising its head and hollowing its outline. Its hindquarters are trailing over the fence and might knock it down.

JUMPING A CORNER FENCE

1 Horse and rider approach toward the center of the fence. The rider is sitting well down in the saddle and pushing firmly with her legs. She is sticking to her line of approach, and the horse is quite clear about what is being asked of it.

2 At the point of takeoff the horse's weight is well balanced over its hocks. The rider keeps her weight pushing down into her heels as she starts to fold forward.

Left: Approach a corner fence straight ahead but near the corner.

Corner fences

Corner fences can be awkward obstacles when you first meet them in competition. Approached correctly, however, they shouldn't cause too many problems.

Try setting up a practice jump, using a couple of poles and three jump stands. Start with the jump quite low and the angle between the poles quite narrow. As your schooling progresses, and you and your horse become more confident, you can open out the angle and increase the height of the jump as necessary.

This type of fence can easily confuse your horse if you are not clear in your approach to it. Cut across the corner and you run the risk of the horse running out (remember that in a competition there won't be a jump stand—possibly just a flag). Approach the jump riding across, but away from, the corner and you still present the horse with problems. He will have to tackle the widest part of the spread, and the front pole will be angling outward toward him, making takeoff difficult.

The best way to tackle this type of fence is straight on but toward the corner, so that the spread is not too great. It is particularly important that you keep the horse going straight and forward for this type of fence, which has a wide spread and can be quite demanding. If the jump becomes an effort, the horse will start to lose confidence.

COMMON FAULTS

1 The approach to the fence is on the side away from the corner, and the horse is backing off. The rider needs to push the horse forward more in order to encourage it to lengthen its stride into the fence.

2 Indecisive approach: The horse is heading toward the corner instead of meeting the fence straight ahead and is approaching in a hesitant manner. The rider is not using her whip enough, nor is she sitting down in the saddle. She needs to use her outside leg much more to keep the horse straight. She also needs to maintain firmer contact with the outside rein.

3 Lack of confidence in the approach is communicated, with the result that the horse runs out.

3 As they go over the jump, the rider's position is good. Her hands are forward but haven't dropped, and she has folded forward from the hip, making it easier for the horse to stretch out over the spread and tuck up its front legs.

4 Horse and rider land well-balanced and ready to ride onto the next fence.

Table fences

These big, solid fences are always found on a cross-country round. Although they appear solid and imposing, they are easier to jump than they look. If you approach them with plenty of impulsion and plenty of control they should ride well.

A table fence should be treated in the same way as a spread. That is, you should come in on a lengthening stride and get close in for takeoff. However, although they have a very solid top line, they usually do not have to come in too close. You need to judge the take-off point very carefully.

With any type of fence you need to bear in mind that you should always adjust the way you ride to the temperament and ability of the horse you are riding. If you do this, you will be able to help the horse to jump to the best of his ability. If you have an impetuous, overeager horse, sit up a little to control him as you approach a fence, and let the fence come to you. If you are on a more sluggish horse, sit down in the saddle and drive the horse on hard with the legs, in rhythm with the horse's strides, in order to create the necessary speed and impulsion. Fold right down over the fence so that the horse can really stretch out over it.

Above: Lucinda Green on Shannagh at Badminton, UK. Table fences of all sorts require strong, accurate riding, but are quite straightforward.

SLUGGISH HORSE

1 *This horse lacks natural impulsion, and has to be encouraged over the fence. The rider drives the horse on hard with her legs as they approach takeoff.*

2 *As they go over the fence she folds down as much as possible to allow the horse to stretch to its maximum, to make up for any lack of impulsion on takeoff.*

IMPETUOUS HORSE

1 *This horse needs a little encouragement to jump. The rider is asking the horse to take the jump steadily, by remaining slightly upright in the saddle in order to hold the horse's natural exuberance in check.*

2 *The horse springs out well over the fence. The rider's leg position remains secure, and he is folding forward from the hip.*

TAKING A DROP FENCE

1 This is a cautious horse, and it is coming in steadily. The rider is sitting down in the saddle and is squeezing with her legs to create an active pace, while keeping good contact, through her hands, with the horse's mouth.

Drop fences

A drop fence, that is, a fence where the ground is lower on the landing side than on the takeoff side, can strike terror in the heart of even experienced cross-country riders.

The secret is to come in very steadily—preferably at the trot—making sure that the horse is balanced and that his weight is well back on his hindquarters. The horse must not be in danger of falling onto his forehand. Bring the horse in as close as possible to the fence, with his hocks well underneath. Keep fairly upright to help the horse lift himself up, and aim for a neat jump over the top. If you take the jump slowly you reduce the risk of the horse jarring himself on landing.

If the horse stands off at a drop fence, he will land a long way out from the fence, where the ground will fall away more steeply. The horse may jar himself as he lands, and an inexperienced rider whose balance and position are not quite secure will be thrown forward.

You can easily be thrown out of position over this type of jump if you do not go with the horse's movement all the way. Keep your leg position secure and do not interfere as the horse stretches over the fence. Allow with your hands, letting the reins slip through your fingers so that the horse can stretch his head and neck as far downward as he needs to, to balance himself on landing.

LACK OF CONTROL

1 The horse is approaching at a trot, but it is "running" at the fence because the rider is not controlling the pace. The rider is too far back in the saddle and is pulling back on the reins. He needs to use his legs to make the horse bring its hocks underneath it and to contain the horse's movement with his hands.

2 The rider is pulling on the reins in an attempt to contain the horse's movement. The horse is trying to stretch out against the pull of the rider's hand, and is having difficulty lifting its forehand up over the fence.

2 By pushing on with her legs the rider has made the horse bring its hocks well underneath it, close into the fence, for takeoff. The rider has her weight well-balanced above the horse as it rounds over the fence.

3 Because the horse took off close to the fence it lands reasonably close in and is not jarred by the landing. The rider is allowing the horse to stretch its head and neck right out in order to balance itself, but at the same time she is maintaining good contact with the horse's mouth.

3 The rider has fallen behind the horse's movement, with his weight right back in the saddle. However, he is allowing with the reins as much as he can from this position.

4 Horse and rider have remained in balance, but they have landed a long way out from the fence, where the ground is falling away.

Downhill fences

Downhill fences require a similar style of riding to drop fences. However, the approach may be downhill for a while before you reach the jump, and it can be difficult to maintain a good, balanced approach. You should come in on a controlled stride and always take a downhill fence straight.

It is very important to follow the natural movement of the horse, keeping a more upright position in the saddle so that your weight does not move forward ahead of the point of balance for the horse. Allow with the hands so that the horse can stretch his head and neck down without restriction to keep his balance on landing. You must remain balanced and independent of your hands throughout the jump.

Make sure that you get in close to this type of fence. If the horse stands off, he cannot see where he will land and may be reluctant to jump.

Below: The rider has his weight back when jumping downhill and is giving the horse its head so that it can balance itself on landing.

1 Horse and rider have made a balanced approach. The rider is driving with his legs as they come into the fence, and the horse has brought its hocks well underneath it. They arrive close in for takeoff.

Right: The rider has his weight well back as the horse lands on this steeply sloping obstacle.

2 The rider has stayed slightly upright as they go over the fence and his leg remains in a secure position, keeping him balanced, and allowing him to follow the natural movement of the horse. His hands have a good contact with the horse's mouth.

3 On landing, the rider lets the reins slip through his fingers, so that the horse has complete freedom to balance itself. His legs have remained in position, and he is completely balanced and secure in the saddle.

Uphill fences

Uphill fences require a lot of impulsion in the horse, to give him the necessary thrust to bring his hocks underneath and spring up and over the fence.

You and your horse must be well-balanced coming up the hill on the approach, and you must be coming in with a very bouncy stride. You create this by squeezing hard with the legs and controlling the horse's forward movement with your hands.

The key to jumping this type of fence is to keep with the horse all the way up the hill, and to keep your weight forward over the horse as he jumps the fence, so that you do not interfere with his natural action.

You can easily get left behind on takeoff, which will throw your weight back over the horse's hindquarters and make it difficult for the horse to spring up off his hocks.

TAKING AN UPHILL FENCE

1 Although the rider has got a little behind the horse's movement as it took off, he is aware of the problem and has extended his arms right forward, in order not to restrict the horse.

2 The rider is still too far back in the saddle but his legs are securely on the horse, and he is well-balanced over it. He is not restricting the horse, which is stretching out well over the fence.

3 The rider has remained secure in the saddle. This has enabled him to recover to a good position quickly on landing.

COMMON FAULTS

The horse is having to twist itself up over the fence because it has come in on an unbalanced stride.

Steps: downhill

Many riders are worried by steps when they first come across them. However, they are really a series of downhill or uphill fences in quick succession, and should be approached in the same way.

Approach downhill steps on a controlled, well-balanced stride. Take them steadily and do not try to do a big jump. Between each step come upright, and put the leg on firmly to tell the horse that you want him to keep going. Keep your hands flexible, following the horse's movement as it stretches over each part.

TAKING DOWNHILL STEPS

1 The rider's contact is good, but he is not pushing the horse on quite strongly enough with the legs, so the horse falters at the top of the first step.

2 The horse's hesitation was momentary. The rider is secure and well-balanced in the saddle, staying with the action of the horse. He has come more upright in the saddle and is using the leg firmly to encourage the horse to keep going down the second step.

3 As the horse takes off, the rider has come forward of the movement.

4 The rider has recovered his position in the saddle and lands in balance and with the movement. If you are ahead of the movement, there is always the danger that you will be pitched forward on landing.

Steps: uphill

Steps uphill are jumped in the same way as other uphill fences. You need to have tremendous impulsion and to drive the horse on with a strong leg, so that you do not lose momentum halfway up. Keep your lower leg firmly on the girth and your weight well forward. Once you begin to get behind the movement, you will fall further behind with each jump up.

TAKING UPHILL STEPS

1 As they approach the bottom step, the rider is sitting down in the saddle and is pushing hard with the seat and legs, to create plenty of impulsion.

2 As they land over the first step, the rider has got behind the movement, with his weight a long way back in the saddle. This is restricting the horse's forward movement.

3 The horse takes off strongly up the second step, but the rider's weight is hanging back and his lower leg is starting to creep forward.

4 As they land over the second step, the rider's weight has fallen even further back in the saddle than over the first. However, he is stretching forward with his hands in order not to restrict the horse's movement as much as possible.

SHOW JUMPING

Above: Aim for this shape over a fence. The hocks are deep to the fence, the shoulders are raised high, the neck is arched, the head dropped, and the front legs are folded up well.

SETTING UP A GRID

2.75m
(9ft)

5.5-7.3m
(6-8yds)

A straightforward grid consisting of a placing-pole and two sets of cross-poles. The placing-pole should be positioned about 9 ft (2.75 m) in front of the first fence, and the cross-poles should be 6–8 yd (5.5–7.3 m) apart to allow for one stride between them. After practicing over the cross-poles, you can change the second fence to an upright or a spread, because the horse will always arrive at it in the perfect position to jump it.

Gridwork

A grid is a series of practice fences set up at related distances, giving the horse a set number of strides between each fence. Gridwork teaches the horse to set himself up right for a fence and to think for himself, as well as increasing his athletic ability. It strengthens the horse and makes him more supple so that he makes the correct shape over the jump. In particular, it helps the horse to loosen his shoulders and raise them up over the fence, at the same time arching his neck, dropping his head, and folding his forelegs up tight, rounding himself over the fence as he jumps.

You can set up a simple grid consisting of a pole on the ground, the placing-pole, followed by two sets of cross-poles. You should work at the trot until you have developed a good, collected, balanced canter. By trotting over the placing-pole, you ensure that the horse arrives in the correct place to take off for the fence. By arriving consistently in the right place, the horse learns how to set himself up to jump a fence correctly, whereas if you come in at an uncontrolled canter the horse will be too far off one time, and too close in the next. You also do not want to allow the horse to develop the habit of always coming into fences fast and sailing through them on a long, flat stride.

You can shorten or lengthen the distance between the fences to teach the horse to adjust his stride. If the horse gets into the habit of meeting fences correctly, he will start to think for himself rather than depending entirely on your instructions. If he lands a little long he will shorten his stride for the second part and vice versa.

Although gridwork is done mainly for the benefit of the horse, you should practice always maintaining the correct position.

TACKLING A GRID

1 Coming in on a balanced, controlled trot, the horse breaks into a canter over the pole.

2 The rider is in complete control on landing.

3 He increases leg pressure to encourage the horse to lengthen to the second part.

4 The horse lifts its shoulders and rounds well over the second fence.

COMMON FAULTS

The horse has taken off too early. This is making it difficult for it to lift its shoulders and to snap up its forelegs neatly.

TAKE-OFF POSITION

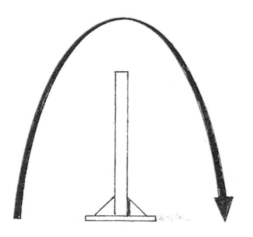

In training, get the horse deep into the fence so that it learns to make a very rounded shape.

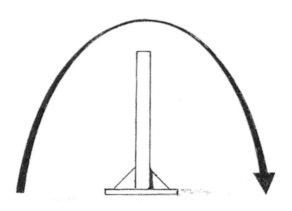

In competition, give it a little more room so that it can take the jump in its natural stride.

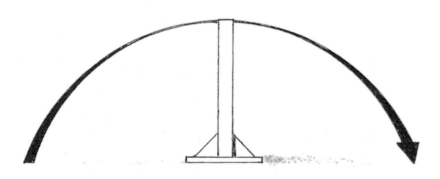

If you takeoff too early, the horse will flatten out over the fence and risk having it down.

Uprights

These jumps can take the form of planks, a gate, a single pole between two jump stands, a series of poles one above the other, or a wall. What they all have in common is that they are built vertically to the ground and have no spread.

They are the easiest fences to have down because they encourage the horse to flatten out rather than to make a good shape, whereas a spread is built in a way that complements the horse's bascule, encouraging him to round over the fence.

To jump an upright successfully, your approach must be balanced and collected, with plenty of impulsion. If anything, you want to come in on a lengthening stride to teach the horse to get in deep and come back onto his hocks, really using his hindquarters to make a very round shape in the air. Allow the horse's movement with your hands and squeeze the horse up into the air with your legs. If the horse stands off, he will have to stretch to get over the fence, thereby losing the correct, rounded shape. Jump like this regularly, and the horse will get into the habit of jumping flat.

When practicing over verticals, always get in close so that the horse learns to round over them properly. When riding in competition, give the horse a little more room so that he can take the jump in his natural stride but still make a good shape. This will be easier for him, and may also save valuable seconds in a jumpoff. However, don't stand off so far that the horse jumps long and flat.

Verticals are particularly tricky when they come at the end of a course. Horse and rider are eager to finish, and may have been pushing on hard over previous fences, so there is a great temptation to rush them. Be particularly careful to control your approach in this situation so that you jump clear.

JUMPING AN UPRIGHT

1 By applying pressure with the legs, the rider has the horse coming in on a lengthening, but collected, stride, and getting deep into the fence. Its hindquarters are positioned well underneath it to get the necessary upward and forward thrust.

Left: Lisa Jacquin on For the Moment in Paris.

STANDING OFF

1 The horse is taking off too early. It is having to reach for the fence, and its front legs are dangling.

2 The horse has lifted its shoulders well, arched its neck and dropped its head on takeoff, and folded up its front legs. The rider has folded forward over the jump. His hands have given, but still maintain contact.

3 As the horse prepares to land it maintains its rounded shape. Notice that the rider's leg stays in the same position, applying pressure behind the girth, throughout the jump.

2 The horse is at its maximum height, but it is not over the top of the upright.

3 The horse is coming down too early. It is dropping its shoulders, raising its head, and hollowing its back in trying to clear the fence.

THE CORRECT SHAPE

Spreads

Spread fences have width as well as height. They include parallel bars, triple bars, overs, and a wall with rails behind. Fences that slope up away from you are easier to jump than true parallels. For any spread, the horse has to jump wide and high, yet the wider a horse jumps, the less easily he can achieve height.

In order to gain optimum height as well as width over a spread, the horse must get deep into the fence on takeoff and bring his hocks well underneath him. If he stands off, he will clip the top.

You should approach the fence on a deep, lengthening stride. Accurate jumping is essential over this type of fence. You need to be able to see the stride, because the horse must have room to lengthen into the fence. He must not be shortening his stride at the last minute in order to get close to the rail. This ability to see the stride highlights a good ride. It cannot be taught, although it can be developed by practice over poles.

If the horse is supple from flatwork and jumping exercises over grids, he will be able to get his hindquarters right in underneath, bringing his hocks close to the front rail. From this position he springs out over the fence in a good, round shape.

You can get away with standing too far off a parallel only if the fence is not very wide or high—or if your horse is a brilliant jumper. Do not try to train over large fences. Set up a simple, small parallel spread and practice jumping it perfectly.

The width of the horse's jump is measured from the point where its hocks take off to the point where its front feet land. It should make an arc over the fence, the highest point of which must be over the highest part of the fence.

Left: The horse has come up strongly off its hocks. It is lifting its shoulders up over the fence and is rounding well. A horse needs to be very supple in the shoulders in order to jump spreads well.

JUMPING A SPREAD

1 The rider has judged the approach accurately. The horse's hocks are well underneath it and close into the front rail. The rider applies the leg continuously to maintain balance and impulsion.

2 The horse is centrally positioned as it reaches optimum height at the top of the parallel.

3 The horse lands in balance the same distance beyond the fence as it took off in front of it.

COMMON FAULTS: TAKING OFF TOO EARLY

1 The rider has asked the horse to take off too soon, and its forelegs are not folding up neatly.

2 The horse is beginning its descent while it is still over the top of the fence, and is flattening out.

Above: Neat, controlled jumping, with horse and rider concentrating on the fence at hand. If the elements of a combination are approached in the same way, they should not cause you concern.

Combination fences: doubles

Combinations are difficult to jump because, when faced with a line of fences, riders tend to panic, which in turn makes the horse panic. As a result they rush at the fence, making it more difficult to come to it correctly. As they go over the first element, they are worrying about the second. The horse raises his head to look at it before landing over the first, causing him to flatten out over the first part and risking bringing it down.

It is up to you to steady your horse and keep his concentration fixed on the element you are jumping until you have landed over it.

Always jump combinations one fence at a time. Do not gallop into them, but ride very firmly. Apply pressure with the leg in order to create impulsion, but do not confuse impulsion with speed. You need to apply more pressure and create a stronger rhythm if the first part is a spread than if it is an upright. Practice jumping the first part really well, to keep the horse concentrating and give him confidence.

Your landing should be controlled and balanced. You should not be leaning on your

COMMON FAULTS: LACK OF CONCENTRATION

1 The horse has just realized that there is another fence ahead and has raised its head to look at it. As a result it is flattening out as it comes down.

JUMPING A DOUBLE

1. Horse and rider have come in on a controlled stride, and the horse is arching well over the first element, an upright.

2 The rider is applying pressure with the leg, and the horse is lengthening its stride in order to get in close to the second element, a spread.

hands, and they should not move on the reins. Recover your position in the saddle immediately. You will then be able to ask for any adjustments to stride or pace in preparation for the next element.

When practicing, concentrate on achieving a rounded, balanced approach, and teach the horse to take the jumps steadily so that he learns to relax. Do not let him rush on just because there is another fence ahead.

2 The horse lands short over the first element, and has a lot of ground to gain if it is to get close enough into the parallel.

3 The rider is completely forward and is really having to push the horse on to reach the second element. They risk standing too far off from it and landing in the middle.

Combination fences—trebles

Exactly the same approach applies to trebles as to doubles. Jump the first element as if it were a single fence. When you land over it, put pressure on with the leg if you need to lengthen to the next element, and contain with the hands if you need to shorten. Whether the second part is a spread or an upright, meet it like an individual fence. Once over it, do whatever is needed in order to meet the third element correctly.

Accurate and balanced riding are more important than ever with a treble fence. You should remember that the faster your approach, the more likely it is that you will have problems, because the horse will not be able to set himself up right for the different types of fence in the combination.

As with all practice jumping, keep the fences small and build up the horse's confidence gradually.

COMMON FAULTS: RUNNING OUT

1 The horse is surprised on seeing a third element to jump, and the idea of running out has just occurred to it. It is moving to the right and twisting its body, while the rider is pulling it to the left to try to keep it straight on to the fence.

2 To correct this, the rider sits down in the saddle, and rides with a strong outside leg, so that the horse is in no doubt that it is going to jump the fence.

JUMPING A TREBLE

1 The horse takes off well over the first element, a vertical. The rider's lower leg is squeezing the horse into the air, his hands give with the movement, but they are still in contact with the horse's mouth.

2 Horse and rider are balanced and controlled on landing. The rider sits down in the saddle and applies pressure with the legs to encourage the horse to lengthen into the second element, a spread.

3 The spread has been cleared, and the rider is applying pressure with his legs and containing the movement with his hands in order to meet the third element, another vertical, on a shorter stride.

4 The horse has brought its hindquarters underneath it and rounds well over the vertical.

JUMPING A WATER TRAY

Spooky fences

Fences with water or ditches under them, fluttering flags, brightly painted poles or planks, or odd colors can all spook a horse, making him hesitant about jumping them. Very narrow fences, and ones that have little filling-in material, may also worry a horse.

When taking this type of fence, don't make the mistake of galloping at it in the belief that the faster you go, the more likely you are to clear it. If you are approaching at speed, the horse is far more likely to take fright and back off at the last moment, when it sees what he is being asked to jump.

The correct approach is to come in at a slow pace so that the horse can see where you are pointing him and take a good look at what's coming. At the same time, squeeze hard with the legs to create plenty of impulsion and give him confidence.

It is better to come in at a trot and "pop" over the fence, than to come galloping in.

As long as the horse is not frightened by these kinds of fences, he will learn to trust you and respond to your instructions. Construct small versions of some of these fences at home to accustom your horse to taking unusual-looking jumps. For example, you can put a white board on the ground underneath a simple upright to simulate a water tray.

Top: On the approach the rider is pushing the horse on in a firm but controlled manner, squeezing with the legs to reassure the horse.

Middle: The horse is a little concerned, but is picking itself up well.

Bottom: The horse has been given confidence by the rider's positive approach, and it makes the optimum shape with its shoulders over the fence.

COMMON FAULTS: BACKING OFF

1 The horse's approach is unsure and hesitant. The rider is having to increase the pressure quietly with his legs to persuade the horse to take the fence.

2 The horse's position as it takes off is crouched and tense, with its hindquarters close to the floor.

Above: You should prepare your horse for water jumps before meeting them in the ring. When training your horse to jump water. Start with a small, inviting jump and increase the width gradually. Do not gallop at this type of fence, but approach it with plenty of impulsion to encourage the horse to stretch out over it.

John Whitaker (center) checks the fences for stability

PLANNING A ROUND

1 Start on the left rein.
2 This vertical needs a collected approach.
3 Be on the left rein here.
4 The upright first element requires a collected approach.
5 Lengthen the stride for the second element.
6 Pace off the distance between the fences to calculate the number of strides.
7 Lead on the left leg here.
8 Collect for this combination.
9 Apply leg to lengthen the stride.
10 This was also the first fence.
11 Pace off the distance. There may be room to shorten the stride.
12 Keep on the right rein.
13 Be careful to approach the fence straight ahead after this awkward turn.

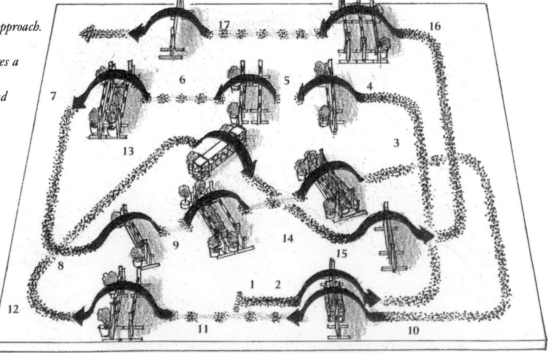

14 Make a proper square turn so that the horse has time to see the next fence.
15 The horse may be tired and could flatten out over this vertical. Collect and jump carefully.

16 Approach on a lengthening stride to take off as close as possible.
17 Collect for a steady approach to the last fence.

*Above: The
Olympic Stadium,
Seoul, 1992.*

Riding a course

It is one thing to jump any amount of single fences, but show-jumping is about completing a course. To do this successfully you need to combine a controlled, rhythmic pace with the ability to execute tight turns and changes of speed and direction smoothly and calmly, but at the same time getting the optimum ability out of your horse over the different types of fence. You should aim for a smooth, controlled round, in which all these elements merge into one fluid, balanced performance.

When practicing at home, aim to be able to canter around ten fences in a controlled way, maintaining the same rhythm throughout the round. A horse only has a certain number of jumps in him, so do not ride him over a course too much at home, and do not practice over large fences—keep them for the ring. Alter the type and sequence of the fences from one session to the next to keep both you and horse alert.

When setting up a practice course, incorporate several turns and changes of direction to keep the horse balanced and to keep yourself thinking. Experienced horses will automatically put themselves on the correct leg after jumping a fence.

Others, with help from their rider, will perform a flying change. However, don't be afraid to bring your horse back to a trot if you need to, in order to change direction. Then ask for canter again with the correct leg leading.

Think about what you ask the horse to do in the ring. For example, do you ask him to approach fences short, at an angel, or on the turn? Then create these problems over little fences at home, so that the horse can learn to cope with them without frightening himself.

RIDING A COURSE (CONTINUED)

1 The course begins with an upright. The horse is on the right rein and is being brought in on a bouncy, collected canter, with the aim of maintaining that rhythm throughout the round.

2 After clearing the first fence, horse and rider begin to make a right-handed turn to the next. Ride the turns smoothly to maintain rhythm and to keep the horse balanced.

6 The horse is now leading with the left leg. The rider has asked it to change, in anticipation of a left turn after the next fence, the water tray.

5 The horse jumps out well over the spread. The rider is well-balanced and looking straight in front.

3 Horse and rider make a fairly wide turn to come into the parallel bars. There is no need to cut corners unless you are in a jumpoff, as long as you keep within the allotted time. The horse is leading with its inside (right) foreleg.

4 The turn has enabled them to meet the parallel with a good central approach, well-balanced, and getting in close to the front rail.

RIDING A COURSE

7 The rider pushes the horse on with a straight, positive approach and rhythmical, balanced stride that encourage the horse to jump.

8 It clears the water tray without any problems.

9 After the water tray, they turn on the left rein to approach the double. The horse is nicely balanced, maintaining its rhythm, with the left leg leading.

10 They come in toward the double with a good, straight approach and at a steady, collected pace.

LEADING OFF ON THE CORRECT LEG

You can teach a young horse to lead off from a jump on the correct leg for the way you want to turn. Jump a small fence in a figure-eight, coming in at a slight angle. As you come over the fence, you swing your body weight in the direction you want to go. The horse will soon learn to tell from this which way you are going to turn, and will lead off on the correct leg on landing.

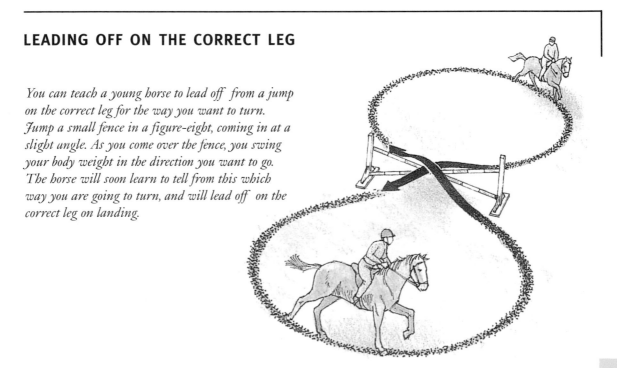

RIDING A COURSE

11 *The horse stands back a bit at the first element, an upright. The rider applies pressure with the lower leg to encourage it over the fence.*

MAKING A FLYING CHANGE

This movement will be a great help in the ring. Use your outside leg strongly behind the girth to ask the horse to strike off with that outside hind. By doing this it will be leading with the inside foreleg. At the same time, shift your weight to the inside of the saddle in the direction of the bend. With regular practice the horse comes to recognize these aids and will respond by changing its leading leg.

12 *It lands well out over the upright, going forward, and has not been distracted by the second element.*

13 *The horse has adjusted to meet the parallel correctly, and springs out over it in a good shape.*

INDEX

Page numbers in *italics* refer to illustrations and/or their captions

A
accidents, at grass 259
action *see* gait
age 27
agriculture 15, 28, 44, 96, 105, 234
  see also forestry; heavy horses
Ahlerich (Westphalian dressage horse) 139
aids 320, *320*
ailments 282–4
airs 255
Akhal-Teké 13, *13*, 225, *225*
Albino 215, *215*
Altér Real 150, 154–5, *154*, *155*, 205
amble 216, 255
Ambler, Peruvian 208, *208*
American breeds 180–209, 248–9
American Creams 215
American Miniature Horses 248
American Performance Horse 215, *215*
American Saddle Seat 185
American Shetland 38, 197, *197*
American types 209–17
American Warmblood 213, *213*, 215
ancestors of the horse 10–13
andadura gait 209
Andalusian 96, 114, 150–3, *150*, *151*, *152–3*, 205, 206
  gait 19
Andrade, Dr Ruy d' 154
anemia 259, 271
anger, showing 25
Anglo-Arab 68–71, *68*, *69*, *70–1*, 144
Anglo-Arab, French 68, 95, *95*
Anglo-Arab, Hungarian *see* Gidran
Anglo-Arab, Polish 126, *126*
Anglo-Arab, Sardinian 239
Anglo-Arab, Spanish 68, 244, *244*
Anglo-Norman 88, 89, 92, 147

Appaloosa 186–9, *186*, *187*, *188–9*, 191
Arab 29, 95, 220–3, *220*, *221*, *222–3*
  and other breeds 54, 58, 96, 133, 139, 144, 231
  and Thoroughbred 50, 68–9
Arab, Managhi-type *13*
Arab, Persian 161, 250
Arab, Shagya 146, *146*
Arab, Strelets 68, 164
Ardennais 102, *102*, 105, 120
Argentine breeds 204, 210
Argentine polo pony 210
Ariegios *237*, 238
Arrogante (Spanish mare) 149
Asiatic Wild Horse *see* Przewalski's Horse
Aslan (Arab stallion) 95
Ass, Somali Wild *11*
Assateague 248
asses 11, 15
Australian breeds 230–1, 254
Australian Cheeker (noseband) 297, *297*
Australian Pony 231, *231*
Australian Stock Horse 230, *230*
Austrian breeds 118–19, 242
Auxios 102, *237*, 238
Avelignese 118, 239, *241*
Azerbaijani breeds 168
azoturia 278
Azteca 206, *206*

B
Babieca (El Cid's horse) 151
Babolna Stud, Hungary 115, 133, 146, 149
balance 18, 313, 318, *319*, 324, *331*
Balearic 244
Bali 255
bandages 306–7, *306*, *307*
  for traveling 281, *304*
Barb 13, 114, 202, 208, 229, *229*, 234
Bardigiano 239, *239*
barley 20, 269, *269*
barrel 255
barrel-racing, saddle for *293*
Bars I (trotting stallion) 160
Barthais 235

Bashkir (or Bashkirsky) 228, *228*
Basque 235
Basuto 254
Batak 255
beans 269
beasts of burden 14
Beberbeck 243
bedding 265–6, *266*, *267*
Beerbaum, Ludger *141*
Beetewk 246
behavior 24–5
Belgian breeds 120–3
Belgian Heavy Draft Horse *see* Brabant
Berber *see* Barb
Bhutia 253
Bialowieza reserve, Poland 124
birth dates, offical 27
bits 294
  cleaning *309*
  effects of *295*
  "on the bit" 255
  types 294, *294*
  Western 339
Black Allan (Standardbred stallion) 190
Black Carthorse, Old English 44
Black Hand I (Walker stallion) 191
blacksmiths 21
Blake's Farmer (Suffolk Punch ancestor) 55
Blaze (Norfolk Roadster stallion) 193
Blenheim Palace, UK *346*
blood horse 255
bloodstock 255
bloodworms 259
blue feet 255
bog spavin 284
bones 271
Boomhower, Leslie 191
Bosnian 245
bots 259
Boulonnais 102, 138, 235
bow hocks 255
box walking 262
Brabant (or Brabançon) 102, 105, 120–3, *120*, *121*, *122–3*
bran *269*, 270
Brazilian breeds 205, 249
breaking in 25, *25*
breeding of horses 16–17
Breton 100, *100*, 138
breweries 33, 44, 105
bridles 298–9

bitless *299*, 302, *302*, 303, *303*
  cleaning *309*
  effects of *295*
  parts *298*
  types 298–9, *298*, *299*
  Western 339
British breeds 32, 32–71, 44, 55, 234
British Show Hack, Cob and Riding Horse Association 81
British Sports Horse 82, *82*
British types 78–85
British Warmblood 79, *79*
British Warmblood Society 79, 82
broken wind 284
Bronco 214
broodmare 255
Brumby 254, *254*
brushing (injury) 284
Budyonny, Marshall 162, 164
Budyonny (or Budenny, Budyonovsky) 162, 164
Bulgarian breeds 157, 245
bullring horses 94, 149, 151, 156
Burmese 254
Byerley Turk (stallion) 50

C
Cadre Noir, Saumur, France 255
Calabrese 239
calcium 271
Camargue 94, *94*
Campolino 249
Canadian breeds 217, 249
Canadian Cutting Horse 217, *217*
cannons 255
canter 18, *320*
  in dressage 354–5, *354*, *355*
  counter canter 357, *357*
  flying change 369–71, *369*, *370*
  over poles 326, *327*
capped elbow 284
Caprilli, Federico 112
Cardi Cob *see* Welsh Cob
Carpathian Pony 127, *127*
carriage-driving 29
  see also coach horses; harness horses
  breeds used for 104, 115, 132, 144, 147, 148, 169, 175, 234

Carthorse, Old English Black 44
carthorses 33, 119
  see also heavy horses
Carthusian 149, 150
Carthusian monks 149, 151
Caspian 13, 224, *224*
Castilian 150
catarrh 284
cattle 259
cattle horses 181, 203, 207, 217
  see also stock work
cavalry horses 102, 112, 144, 146, 149, 162
Cayuse Indian Pony 248, *248, 249*
Celle Stud 135
Celtic Pony 12
  descendants 36, 43, 54, 56, 72, 76, 171, 173, 177
chaff 270
Chapman horse 234
Charentais 89
Charles II of Austria, Archduke 114
Charles VI, Emperor 115
chestnuts 255
Chicksaw Indian Pony 248
children's mounts:
  British breeds used for 37, 39, 43, 57, 58, 80
  other breeds used for 171, 177, 191, 197, 224, 231
Chinese (or China) pony 253
Chintoteague 248, *248*
Church Stretton Hill Pony Improvement Society 57
circles, riding 322–3, *323*
circus work 164, 176, 212
Classic Touch (Holstein show jumper) *141*
clean heels/legged 255
Cleveland Bay *19*, 132, 134, 141, 234, *234*
clipping 275, *275*
clothing, Western 339, *339*
Clydesdale 32–5, *32, 33, 34–5*
Coach Horse, Yorkshire 132, 141, 234
coach horses *15*, 140, 145, 234, 255
  see also carriage-driving
coal industry 32, 39

coat:
  see also color
  ailments 282
  Bashkir 228
cob 78, *78*, *235*, 255
Cob, Norman 89, 101, *101*
Cob, Welsh *see* Welsh Cob
cobalt 271
coldblood *13*, 255
Coldblood, German 119, 243
colds 284
colic 20, 259, 268, 270, 278, 282
color:
  Albino 215, *215*
  Appaloosa 186
  Knabstrup 176
  Palomino 211, *211*
  Pinto 212–13, *212, 213*
Colosses de la Mehaigne 121
colt 255
communication, horse 25
competition horses 16, 19
  European breeds used for 69, 79, 95, 106, 110, 125, 126, 129, 139
  other breeds used for 162, 166, 169, 174, 206, 207, 221, 230
competitive riding 345–409
  see also dressage; endurance riding; eventing; show jumping
"dancing" 255
Comtois 235, *236*
concentrates 269–70, *269*
Confidential Cob 78, *78*, *235*
conformation *18*, *19*, 255
Connemara 76–7, *76, 77*
conquistadores 151, 202, 207, 214
controlling horse 320, *320, 337*
  at jumps 380, *381, 382*
copper 271
corn (grain) 20, 269, *269*
corns 283
Corsican Pony 239
coughs 284
counter canter 357, *357*
covert hacks 85
cow hocks 255
cracked heels 284
Creams, American 215
crib-biting 262

Criollo 202–3, *202, 203*, 205, 206
Crisp, Mr Thomas 55
cross-country riding 336
  see also eventing
  seat 373, *373*
curb bit 294, *294*
curb (lameness) 284
"Curly" Bashkir 228
Cutting Horse, Canadian 217, *217*
Czech breeds 145

D
Dales Pony 36, *36*, 43
"dancing" competitions 255
Danish breeds 174–6, 247
Danish Warmblood 174, *174*
Danubian 157
Darashouri 250
Darbowski-Tarnowski 126
Darley Arab (stallion) 50
Dartmoor Pony 37, *37*
Dda, King Hywel 56
Delhi 253
desert horses 13, 26, 250
digestive system 268, *268*
  ailments 282–3
Diluvian (Forest) Horse 12, 120
  descendants 94, 102, 167
dished face 255
dishing action 19, 255
dislike, showing 25
dismounting 317, *317*
  Western style 341, *341*
docking 101, 255
Dole Trotter 172, *172*
Dole-Gudbrandsdal 172
domestication of the horse 14–15
Don 161, *161*
donkeys 15
dorsal stripe 255
Double Klepper 247
draft breeds 255
  see also heavy horses
Draft Breton 100, *100*
Draft, Dutch 105, *105*
Draft, Irish *see* Irish Draft
Draft, Latvian 167
dray horses 33, 45, 105
dressage 16, 29, 346–72
  arenas for *346*
  breeds used for 79, 106, 134, 139, 164
  canter 354–5, *354, 355*
  counter canter 357, *357*

flying change 369–70, *369, 370*
  half-halt *369*, 370
  half-pass 360, *360–1*
  halt 364, *365*
  interpreting competition marks 372, *372*
  leg-yielding 362, *362*
  pirouettes 371
  rein-back 364, *364, 365*
  renvers 366, *369*
  shoulder-in 358, *358–9, 369*
  training routine 346, *347*
  travers 366, *366, 367*
  trot 350, *350, 351*, 352, *352–3*
  turns on forehand 346, *346*
  walk 348, *348–9*
Dutch breeds 103–9, 238
Dutch Draft 105, *105*
Dutch Warmblood *see* Warmblood, Dutch

E
East Bulgarian 157
East Friesian 133, *133*
East Prussian *see* Trakehner
eel stripe 49, 170, 173, 247
Einsiedler 110, 238
El Bedavi XXII (Arab stallion) 118
elbow, capped 284
elk lip 255
Elliott, Eli 197
endurance riding 29
  breeds used for 161, 162, 164, 177, 203, 221, 227
English Black Carthorse, Old 44
enteritis 259
entire 255
Eohippus 10
Equus 11
  asinus 15
  caballus 12
    gmelini Antonius *see* Tarpan
    przewalskii przewalskii Poliakov *see* Przewalski's Horse
    sylvaticus see Diluvian Horse
  hemionus onager 14
Estonian breeds 246, 247
Estonian Klepper 247
European breeds 72, 96, 100, 101, 102, 105, 111, 119, 120, 138, 167, 235, 238, 242, 243, 246, 247
feeding 45

eventing 29, 79, 373–88
 bounce fences 376, *376*, *377*
 corner fences 378, *378–9*
 downhill fences 384, *384–5*
 downhill steps 387, *387*
 drop fences 382, *382*
 gridwork 374–5, *374*, *375*
  distances 375
 rushing fences 375
 table fences 380, *380*
 uphill fences 386, *386*
 uphill steps 388, *388*
evolution of the horse 10–13, *10*
ewe neck 255
exercise 20–1, *21*
 daily routines for horse 278–80
exercises:
 for flying change *370–1*
 for half-pass *371*
 for jumping 331
 positional 318, *318*
 for renvers *369*
 for shoulder-in *369*
 for travers *367*
 without stirrups 319, *319*
Exmoor Pony 12–13, 37, 42, *42*
Extremeño 150

F
Falabella 204, *204*
falls, coping with 334–5
farm work *see* agriculture
farrier 276, *276*
fear:
 flight reaction *24*
 showing 25
feather 255
feed and feeding 20, 21, 268–71
 concentrates 269
 foals 27
 heavy horses 45
 quantities 271
 Shetland Pony 39
 storing food *270*, 271
 supplementary 260
feet:
 ailments and injuries 283
 structure 276, *276*
Fell Pony 36, 43, *43*
fences:
 individual 330
 rushing 375
 taking bounce fences 376, *376*, *377*
 taking combination fences:
  doubles 396–7, *396–7*

trebles 398, *398–9*
 taking corner fences 378, *378–9*
 taking downhill fences 384, *384–5*
 taking downhill steps 387, *387*
 taking drop fences 382, *382*
 taking spooky fences 400, *400*, *401*
 taking spread fences 394, *394–5*
 taking table fences 380, *380*
 taking uphill fences 386, *386*
 taking uphill steps 388, *388*
fencing round field 261, *261*
feral horses *24*, 214, 226, 239, 254
field *see* grass, keeping horse at
Figure (colt later called Justin Morgan) 198
filly 255
Finnish 247, *247*
Fire (Westphalian show jumper) 139
Firouz, Mrs Louise 224
fitness 21
Fjord *12*, 13, 173, *173*
Flaebehingsten (Knabstrup stallion) 176
Flaebehoppen (Iberian mare) 176
Flanders horse 120–1, 134
flat racing 28–9
 see also racing
flehmen 25
flexion 255
flying change 369–71, *369*, *370*
 exercises for *370–1*
Flyinge, Swedish Royal Stud 169
foals 27, 255
food *see* feed and feeding
forearm 255
forelock 255
Forest Horse *see* Diluvian Horse
forestry 97, 119
 see also agriculture
founder *see* laminitis
fox trot 196, 255
Fox Trotter, Missouri 196, *196*
Franches-Montagnes 235, 238

Frederick Wilhelm I, King 128, 129
Frederiksborg 175, *185*
Frederiksborg Stud, Denmark 174, 175
Freiberger 235, 238
French Anglo-Arab 68, 95, *95*
French breeds 88–102, 235–8
French Saddle Horse *see* Selle Français
French Saddle Pony 235, *236*, 237
French Trotter 88, 92–3, *92*, *93*
Friesian 43, 103, *103*, 132
Furioso 126, 148, *148*
Furioso (Thoroughbred stallion) 148

G
gait 18, *18–19*, 19, 216, 255
 see also trotters and trotting
 Dartmoor Pony 37
 Hackney 48
 Icelandic 177
 Mangalarga 205
 Missouri Fox Trotter 196
 Paso 208
 Saddlebred 184
 Tennessee Walking Horse 190
gaited horse 255
Galiceño 207, *207*
Galician and Asturian Pony 244
gallop 18
Galloway, Scottish 43
Garrano 207, 245
Garron 49
gas in stomach 268
gates 261
 opening and closing *335*
Gayot, E. 95
Gazal (Arab stallion) 133
Gelderlander 104, *104*, 106
gelding 26, 255
General Stud Book 16, 53
genes 10
Gentlemen's Gentleman 78
George II of England, King 135
German breeds 132–44, 243
German Coldblood 243
Gibson, M. *128*
Gidran 68, 126, 149
Gidran II (stallion) 149
Gidran Senior (Arab stallion) 149

Godolphin Arab (or Barb) 50, 181
Gotland 170, *170*
Gower Union Pony Association 57
Grand Breton 100, *100*
grass 20, 27, 259, 271
 eating before work 268
 types 260, *260*
grass, keeping horse at 258–61
 choosing field *258–9*, 259
 feeding 260
 fencing and gates 261, *261*
 shelter 260, *260*
 water supply 260, *261*
Great Horse 102, 134
Greek breeds 244–5
Green, Lucinda *380*
gridwork:
 for eventing 374–5, *374*, *375*
 for show jumping 389, *389*, 390
Gris de Nivelles 121
Groningen 106, 238
grooming 272–5, *273*
grooming kit 272, *272*
Gros de la Dendre 121
Grunox Tecrent (Hanoverian dressage horse) *135*

H
Hack 57, 85
hackamore:
 European 303, *303*
 Western 302, *302*
hackamore (bitless bridle) *299*, 302, *302*, 303, *303*
Hackney 48, *48*, 92, 100
Hackney Horse 48, *48*
Hackney Pony 48, *48*, 197
Haflinger 118, *118*, 239
half-ass 14
half-halt *369*, 370
half-livery 264
half-pass 360, *360–1*
 exercises for *371*
halt, in dressage 364, *365*
hand (measurement) 17, *17*, 255
Hanover, House of 134
Hanoverian 106, 133, 134–7, *134*, *135*, *136–7*, 139, 144
haquenée (riding horse) 48, 85
Harddraver *see* Friesian
Harness Horse, Latvian 167
harness horses 14, *14*, 18, 197, 221, 224

see also carriage-driving; pacing; trotting
Haute Ecole (High School) 255
    breeds used for *103*, 112, 114, *114*, 155, 156, 175
hay 20, 21, 268–9, 271
haylage 20
head, ailments 283–4
health 282–4
heat bumps 282
heaves 262
Heavy Draft Horse, Belgian *see* Brabant
Heavy Draft, Italian 111, *111*
Heavy Draft, Rhineland 243
Heavy Draft, Schleswig 138, *138*
Heavy Draft, Soviet 246
Heavy Draft, Vladimir 246, *246*
heavy horses 12, 13, 15, 19, 28, 33, 255
heels, cracked 284
herd instinct 24
Hessian and Rheinlander Pfalz 243
Highland Pony 13, 49, *49*
Hispano-Arab 68, 244, *244*
Hobbye, Irish 76
hock boots 281, *304*
hogged 255
Hokkaido 254
Holstein 135, 140–3, *140, 141, 142–3*
horse types 12, 13
    Horse Type 39 *13*
    Horse Type 49 *13*
horse-drawn vehicles 15, *15*, 32, 44
    see also carriage-driving; harness horses; heavy horses
hot-bloods *13*, 220, 255
Huçul 127, *127*
humor 282
Hungarian breeds 146–9, 243
Hunter 57, 68, 73, 83, *83*
    see also Working Hunter
hunter type, pony of 84
Hunters (Pinto) 212
hurdling 29
Huzul 127, *127*
Hyracotherium *10*
Hywel Dda, King 56

I
Iberian horses 13, 112, 150, 181, 208, 234

see also Portuguese breeds; Spanish breeds
Icelandic *12, 13*, 177, *177*
illnesses 282–4
impaction 268
impetuous horse, controlling 380, *381*
in-hand 255
Indian breeds 253
Indian Pony, Cayuse 248, *248, 249*
Indian Pony, Chickasaw 248
indigestion 259, 268, 270
Indonesian breeds 255
influenza 284
injuries:
    chart of 282–4
    checking for 274, *274*
    treating 274, *274*
interest, horses showing 25
iodine 271
Iomud 250
Iranian breeds 224, 250
Irish breeds 72–7
Irish Draft 72–5, *72, 73, 74–5*, 78, 79
Irish Hobbye 76
Irish Horse Board 73
Irish hunter 73
Irish types 78
iron 271
Italian breeds 111–13, 239
Italian Heavy Draft 111, *111*
Italian Saddle Horse 112

J
Jaf 250
Janus (Thoroughbred stallion) 181
Japanese breeds 254
Java 255, *255*
joints, sprained 284
Julius Caesar 56
jumping 10, 16, 164
    see also show jumping
    bounce fences 376, *376, 377*
    combination fences:
        doubles 332, *332–3, 396–7, 396–7*
        trebles 398, *398–9*
    common faults 329, 331, *373, 375, 377, 379, 386, 395, 396–7, 398–9*
    control 380, *381, 382*
    corner fences 378, *378–9*
    doubles 332, *332–3*, 396–7, *396–7*
    downhill fences 384, *384–5*
    downhill steps 387, *387*
    drop fences 382, *382*

first jump 328
individual fences 330
lack of concentration *396–7*
leading off on correct leg *407*
lessons in 324–33
    pole work 326, *326–7, 328*
    distances 327
    position 324–5, *324, 325, 328*
    refusals 333
    spooky fences 400, *400, 401*
    spread fences 394, *394–5*
    table fences 380, *380*
    trebles 398, *398–9*
    types of jumps 331
    uphill fences 386, *386*
    uphill steps 388, *388*
    water jumps 400, *400, 401*
Justin Morgan (Morgan stallion) 198–9
Jutland 138, 174, 247

K
Kabardin 165, *165*
Karabair 250, *251*
Karabakh *20*, 168, *168*
Karacabey 144
Kathiawari 253
Kazakii 251
Kentucky Saddler 184
Kiger Mustang *214*, 248
Kirgizstan breeds 251
Kladruber 145, *145*
Klepper 246
Klepper, Estonian (or Double) 247
Knabstrup 176, *176*
knee caps 281, *304*
knights 102, 134
Knights of the Teutonic Order 129
knockkneed 255
Konik 124, *124*, 127
Konrad of Masovia, Prince 129
Kranich (stallion) 132
kumiss (alcoholic drink) 228, 251
Kustanair 251, *251*

L
La Croix, Gene 248
Ladies Hack 85
Ladies' Hunters 83
lameness 337
laminitis 39, 260, 283
Landais 235
Large Hack 85

Latvian 167, *167*
Latvian Draft 167
Latvian Harness Horse 167
Latvian Riding Horse 167
leg-yielding 362, *362*
legs:
    ailments and injuries 284
    bandaging 281, 306–7, *307*
    swollen 278, 307
Lesotho breeds 254
lice 282
licks 270, 271
life cycle of the horse 26–7
light harness *see* carriage-driving; harness horses
Limousin 89, 235
linseed 270
Lipizza (Lipica) Stud 114, 115
Lipizzaner 114, *115, 116–17*, 298
Lithuanian breeds 247
livery 264
Lokai 250, *250*
Louis IV of Germany, King 118
Lundy 234
lunge rein 25, *25*
lungeing *280*, 314, *347*
Lunn, Major Villars 176
Lusitano 150, 156, *156*

M
Macken, Eddie *89*
magnesium 271
Malopolski 126, *126*
management, good 20–1
Managhi-type Arab *13*
manège riding 114, 135
manes 173, 227
    braiding 281
Mangalarga 205, *205*
manganese 271
Manipuri 253
manure 259
Marbach Stud, Germany 243
marcha (or *marchador*) gait 205
Maremmana 239, *241*
Marengo (Napoleon's horse) 95
mares 26, *26, 27*, 255
    broodmare 255
Marsh Horse 140
Marske (Oriental stallion) 54
martingales 300–1, *300, 301*
Marwari 253
mash 270
Masirem 125, 126
Massoud (Arab stallion) 95

maturity 27
measurements:
    conformation *18*
    hands 17, *17*, 255
meat *100*, 111, 228, 235
Mecklenburg 134, 144
medicine, preventive 21
Merens *237*, 238
Messenger (Thoroughbred
    stallion) 193
Métis Trotter 160, 163, *163*
Mexican breeds 206
Mezöhegyes Stud, Hungary
    147, 148
Midnight Madness (Dutch
    Warmblood show jumper)
    106
military uses *see* cavalry
horses; warfare
minerals 270, 271
Minho 207, 245
Miniature Horses, American
    248
Miss Fan (Selle Français
    show jumper) *89*
Missouri Fox Trotter 196,
    196
molasses 269, 270
Mongolian 253, 255
    see also Przewalski's Horse
Morgan 198–201, *198*, *199*,
    200–1
Morgan, Thomas Justin 198
mountain horses 165, 173,
    208
Mountain Pony, Welsh *see*
Welsh Mountain Pony
mounting 312
    Western style 340, *340*
mouthing 25
movement *see* exercise; gait
mucking out 265–6, *265*
Mulassier 235, *237*
Murakoz (or Murakosi) 243,
    244
Murgese 239, *241*
Mustang 214
Mustang, Kiger *214*, 248
mutation of genes 10

N
nail blind 283
Nanfan 253
Nang-Chen 12
Napoleon Bonaparte 95,
    102, 151, *161*
National Pony Society 57
National Show Horse 248
navicular disease 283
Neapolitan 112, 132, 135
nematodes 259

New Forest Pony 54, *54*, 234
New Kirgiz 251
New South Wales horse 230
Nez Percé tribe 186, *186*
Niatross (Standardbred
    trotter stallion) 192
nicking (of muscles under
    the dock) 185
Nigerian 254
Nonius 144, 147, *147*, 148,
    157
Nonius Senior (Norfolk
    Roadster stallion) 147
Norfolk Roadster 48, 92,
    100, 148, 193, 234
Noriker 119, *119*, 243
Norman 88, 92
    see also Anglo-Norman
Norman Cob 89, 101, *101*
North American breeds
    180–201, 248–9
North Star (Norfolk
    Roadster stallion) 148
North Swedish Horse
    (or Trotter) 247
North-Hestur 247
Northern Pony *see* Celtic
Pony
Northlands 171, *171*
Norwegian breeds 171–3
nosebands 296–7, *296*, *297*
Novokirgiz 251

O
oatmeal gruel 270
oats 20, 269, *269*
Oberlander 119, *119*
old age 27
Old English Black Carthorse
    44
Old King (Morgan/Arab
    stallion) 215
Old Shales (stallion) 193
Old Tobe (Rocky Mountain
    Pony stallion) 216
Oldenburg 103, 132, *132*, 133
Oldenburg, Count Anton
    von 132
Olympic Games *15*
onagar 14

Oppenheim LXII (stallion)
    138
Oriental horses 50, 95, 96,
    118, 146, 165, 220, 227,
    255
    see also Arab; Barb
Orion (stallion) 147
Orlov, Count Alexei
    Grigorievich 160

Orlov (or Orloff) Trotter 92,
    160, *160*, 163
Overo Pinto coat pattern 213
overreach 283
overtracking 19
oxen 15, 44

P
pacers 255
paces *see* gait
pacing races 192, 193
pack horses 36
Pahlavan 250
Palomino 16, 211, *211*
Panje ponies 129
pannier ponies 36, 43
parade work 209
Parahippus 10
park hacks 85
Park Morgan 199
Partbred, care 258
paso corto gait 208, 209
Paso Fino 19, 208, 209, *209*
paso fino gait 208, 209
paso largo gait 208, 209
Paso, Peruvian 208, *208*
pedal osteitis 283
Peissel, Michel 12, 253
Pelhams 299, *299*, 303, *303*
Peneia 244
Peninsular Horse 68, 244,
    244
Pennine ponies 36
Perche, Comte de 96
Percheron 96–9, *96*, *97*, *98–9*,
    102
Performance Horse,
    American 215, *215*
Perow (Trakehner dressage
    horse) *128*
Persian Arab 161, 250
Persian, Plateau 250
Peruvian Stepping Horse
    208, *208*
pet breeds 204, 248
phosphorus 271
Piber, Austria 115
piebalds 212, 255
Pindos 244–5
Pinto 212–13, *212*, *213*
Pinzgauer 119, 242
pirouettes 371
Plantation Walking Horse
    190, *190*
Plateau Persian 250
Plateau Pony *see* Celtic Pony
plates 21
Pleasure Horses 81, *81*
Pleasure Morgan *199*
pleasure riding 28
    see also riding

Pleasure type (Pinto) 212
Pleven 245
Pliohippus 10–11
point-to-point 29
points 255
Poitevin 235, *237*
Poitiers, Battle of (732 AD)
    134
police horses *28*
Polish Anglo Arab 126, *126*
Polish breeds 124–8, 242
Polkan (stallion) 160
polo 181, 210, 255
polo pony 51, 57, 210, *210*,
    253, 300
Polo and Riding Pony
    Society 57
ponies 258
Pony of the Americas 191,
    191
pony of hunter type 84
pony types 12–13
    Pony Type 1 12–13, *12*
    Pony Type 2 *12*, 13
Pony, Welsh *see* Welsh Pony
Portuguese breeds 154–6,
    245
Postier-Breton 100, *100*, 111
potassium 271
Pottock 235
Powys Cob 59
Powys Rouncy 59
Poznan 125, *126*
pregnancy 27
prepotent animals 16
prey animals 14, 27
primitive type horses 12–13
Proto-Arab 13, *13*
Przewalski, Colonel N. M.
    226
Przewalski's Horse 12, 13,
    173, 226–7, *226*, *227*, 247,
    253
psychology 24–5
Puerto Rican breeds 209

Q
quarter crack 283
Quarter Horse 29, 180–3,
    180, *181*, *182–3*, 206, 217
quarter pathers 181
quartering 272
quittor 283

R
race horses 255
racing 28–9, 50, 51, 162, 168,
    227
    see also trotting
    in America 180, 181
    martingales for 300

nosebands for 297, *297*
shoes 21
rack gait 184, *185*, 255
ranch work *see* cattle horses
refusal, coping with 333
rein-back 364, *364*, *365*
reins:
  holding 315, *315*
  Market Harborough
    (German) *300*, 301
renvers 366
  exercises for *369*
Rhenish 121, 243
Rhineland Heavy Draft 243
riding:
  across country 336
  coming to halt *319*
  common faults *313*, *315*,
    316, *319*, *321*, *323*
  competitive 345–409
  control 320, *320*, *337*
  coping with falls 334–5
  dismounting 317, *317*
  exercises without stirrups
    319, *319*
  first movements 314, *314*
  hill work *336*
  holding reins 315, *315*
  jumping 324–33
  leg positions *312*
  lessons in 312–41
  mounting horse 312
    Western style 317, *317*
  position in saddle 313, *313*
  riding out 334–7
  rising trot 316–17
  sitting trot 318
  trot to canter 321
    common faults *321*
  trotting 316–17, 318, *320*
  turns and circles 322–3,
    322, *323*
  walk to trot 316
    common faults *321*
  Western 338–41
  without stirrups 319
riding cob *see* cob
Riding Horse, British 81, *81*
Riding Horse, Latvian 167
Riding Horse, Ukrainian
  166, *166*
riding horses 14, *18*, 19, 48,
  255
  American breeds 187, 206,
    208, 209, 221, 225, 229
  British breeds 48, 69, 81,
    85
  European breeds 106, 126,
    139, 157
  other breeds 165, 174, 175,
    176

Riding Pony, British 80, *80*
rigs 26, 255
Rimfakse (Northlands stal
  lion) 171
ringbone 284
ringworm 282
Riwoche 12, 253
roached 255, *255*
Roadster 255
Roadster, Norfolk *see*
  Norfolk Roadster
roan 255
Rocky Mountain Pony 216,
  216
rodeos 214, 217, 230
rolling 258, *258*
Roman (Westphalian show
  jumper) 139
Romans 56, 59, 102, 103, 119
roots 270
Rotrou, Comte de 96
Rouncy 59
roundworms 259
Roussin 100
Royal Frederiksborg Stud,
  Denmark 174, 175
royal horses 103, 112
rugs 304–5, *304*, *305*
running walk 185
Russian breeds 160–5, 228,
  246
Russian Trotter 160, 163,
  163

S
Sable Island Pony 249, *249*
saddle horse 255
Saddle Horse, French *see*
  Selle Français
Saddle Horse, Italian 112
Saddle Pony, French 235,
  236, 237
Saddle type (Pinto) 212
Saddlebred 184–5, *184*, *185*
saddles 288–93
  all-purpose 288, *288*
    putting on *289*
  cleaning *308*
  design 288
  parts *288*
  pleasure 292–3, 339
  sidesaddles 288
    putting on *289*
  stock 290
  Western 290–3, *290–1*, *338*,
    339
    parts *291*
    putting on *291*
    variations *292–3*
Sadecki 126
Salerno 112–13, *112*, *113*

salt lick 270, 271
Sampson (stallion) 193
San Fratello 239, *240*
Sandalwood 255
Sardinian Anglo-Arab 239
Sardinian Pony 239
Schleswig Heavy Draft 138,
  138
Schweiken ponies 129
scopey/scopy action 255
Scottish Galloway 43
seedy toe 283
Seglawy Arab strain 146,
  149, *220*
Selle Français 88–91, *88*, *89*,
  90–1, 106, 235
Seoul, Olympic Stadium *403*
setting fair 273
Shagya Arab 68, 146, *146*
Shagya (stallion) 146
shampooing 275
Shan 254
Shannagh (eventing horse)
  380
shape *see* conformation
sheep 259
shelter 260, *260*
Shetland, American 38, 197,
  197
Shetland Pony 38–41, *38*, *39*,
  40–1, 191, 197
Shirazi 250
Shire 33, 44–7, *44*, *45*, *46–7*
shoes and shoeing 21, *21*,
  276–7, *276–7*
  hot and cold shoeing 277
  types of shoe *276*
shoulder angles *18*
shoulder-in 358, *358–9*
  exercises for *369*
Show Horse, National
  (USA) 248
show jumping 16, 29,
  389–409
  breeds used for 79, 89, 106,
    134, 139, 141

  combination fences,
    trebles 398, *398–9*
  gridwork 389, *389*, 390
  leading off on correct leg
    407
  planning round *402*
  practice courses 404
  riding course 403, *404–9*
  spooky fences 400, *400*,
    401
  spread fences 394, *394–5*
  water jumps 400, *400*, *401*
Show Pony, British 80, *80*

showing and show classes
  221
  Britain 80, 81, 83, *83*, 84,
    85, 187
  USA 185, 190, 228
Sicilian 239
sidesaddles 288
  putting on *289*
Siglavi Arab strain 146, 149,
  220
sitting trot 318
skewbalds 212, *212*, 255
skin, ailments 282
Skogruss 170, *170*
Skyros 245, *245*
slow gait 185, 193
sluggish horse, encouraging
  380, *381*
Small Hack 85
Smetanka (Arab stallion) 160
snaffle 294, *294*
"snaking" motion of stal-
  lions 25
sobre paso gait 209
sodium 271
Sokolsky 242
Somali Wild Ass 11
Sommier 100
Sorraia 150, 245
South American breeds
  202–10
South German Coldblood
  119, 243
Soviet Heavy Draft 246
Spanish Anglo-Arab 244, *244*
Spanish breeds 96, 114, 149,
  244
Spanish Riding School,
  Vienna 114–15, *114*, 255, 298
Spanish Trot *151*
speedy cutting 284
Spiti 253
splints 284
sport 28–9
  see also competition horses;
    racing

sprained joints and tendons
  284
stable:
  design 262–3, *262–3*
  fixtures and fittings 264
  requirements 262
  site 262–3
stable, keeping horse in 258,
  262–7
  routine 264, *264–5*
stadium jumping *see* show
  jumping
stallions 25, 26, *26*, 255
Standardbred 29, 92, 160,

163, 192–5, *192, 193, 194–5*
steeple-chasing 29, 72
steppe horse 13, 161
    see also desert horse
Stepping Horse, Peruvian
    208, *208*
stepping pace 185
stifles 255
stirrups, cleaning *309*
Stock Horse, Australian 230,
    230
Stock Horses (Pinto) 212
stock work 205, 207, 230
    see also cattle horses
    Western saddles 290
strangles 284
strapping 272–3
Strelets Arab 68, 164
strength 21
    Shetland Pony 38
Strongyles 259
stud books 17, 255
submission signs 25
Suffolk Punch 55, *55*, 138
sugar beet *269*, 270
sulkies 192, 193
Sumba 255, *253*
Swedish breeds 169–70, 247
Swedish Pony Association
    170
Swedish Trotter, North 247
Swedish Warmblood 169,
    169
sweet itch 282
Swiss breeds 110, 238
Swiss Warmblood 110, *110*

T
tack and equipment 287–307
    cleaning *308–9*
Tadzhikistan breeds 250
tail:
    bandaging 281, 306, *307*
    docking 101
tail-braces 185
Tarpan 12, 13
    descendants 124, 127, 129,
        165, 170, 245
    modern 242, *242*
Tchenarani 250
tear ducts, blocked 283
teeth 27, *27*, 271
Tencteri tribe 134
tendons, sprained 284
Tennessee Walking Horse
    190, *190*
Tersky (or Tersk, Terskij,
    Terek) 164, *164*
Tesio, Federico 112
Theodorescu, Monika *135*

Thoroughbred 16, 50–3, *50,
    51, 52–3*
    American type 50
    and Arabs 68–9, 95
    birth dates 27
    and British breeds 39, 54,
        234
    care 258
    and European breeds 89,
        106, 112, 134, 135, 138,
        141, 157, 176
    and Irish Draft 72, 73, 79
    racing 28–9
    shape 19
thoroughpin 284
threats, horses' reactions to
    25, *25*
three-day eventing *see*
    eventing
thyroid gland 271
Tibetan 12, 253
Timor 255
Tobiano Pinto coat pattern
    212, 213, *213*
tølt gait 177
Toric 247
tracking up 19
training of horses 24, 25, *25*,
    27
Trait Du Nord 102, *236*, 238
Trakehner 128–31, *128, 129,
    130–1*
transportation 15, 28, 32, 44,
    97, 165, 228
    loading and traveling 281,
        281
    protective wear for *304*
travers 366, *366*
    exercises *367*
    in trot *367*
treacle 269, 270
trekking 36, 43, 173, 177
trickle feeding 20
trot 18, 19, 48, 316–17, *320*
    in dressage 350, *350, 351,
        352, 352–3*
    over poles *326*
    riding travers in *367*
    sitting 318
    trot to canter 321
        common faults *321*
    walk to trot, common
        faults *321*
Trotter, Dole 172
Trotter, French 88, 92–3, *92,
    93*
Trotter, Missouri Fox 196,
    196
Trotter, Norfolk *see* Norfolk
    Roadster
Trotter, North Swedish 247

Trotter, Orlov 92, 160, *160,
    163*
Trotter, Russian 160, 163,
    163
Trotter, Yorkshire 48
trotters and trotting 13, 92,
    97, 170, 192–3, 247
    breeding trotters *16*, 48
Trotting of the Cobs 59
troughs 260, *261*
True Briton (Welsh Cob
    stallion) 198
Turkish breeds 144
Turkmene breeds 13, 225,
    227, 250
Turkoman 227
turns on forehand 346, *346*
Tuttle, Sam 216
types of horses 17, 255
    see also horse types

U
Ukrainian Riding Horse 166,
    166
undersaddle 255
USA *see* North American
    breeds
Uzbekistan breeds 250

V
Vendées 89
Vestland *see* Fjord
veterinary care 21
Viatka 246
Vikings 173
vitamins 271
    effects *270*
Vladimir Heavy Draft 246

W
Waler 230, *230*
walk 18, 19, *314*
    in dressage 348, *348–9*
Walker 190, *190*
warbles 282
warfare 14, *15*, 28
    breeds used in 102, 134,
        140, 144, 151, 229
    Rouncies 59
Warmblood, American 213,
    213, 215
Warmblood, British 79, *79*
Warmblood, Danish 174, *174*
Warmblood, Dutch 104,
    106–9, *106, 107, 108–9*
Warmblood, Swedish 169,
    169
Warmblood, Swiss 110, *110*
warmbloods 13, 79, 128, 132,
    134, 255

water:
    in field 260, *261*
    in stable 264
water jumps 400, *400, 401*
weaving 262
Welsh breeds 56–67
Welsh Cob 56, 58, 59, *59,
    60–1*, 78
Welsh Mountain Pony 56–7,
    56, 58, 66–7
Welsh Pony 56, 57–8, *57,
    64–5*
Welsh Pony and Cob
    Society 56, 57
Welsh Pony of Cob Type
    56, 58, *58, 62–3*
Western riding 338–41
    clothing 339, *339*
    dismounting 341, *341*
    mounting 340, *340*
    saddles 290–3, *290–1,
        292–3, 338, 339*
        putting on *291*
    schools and differences
        338
    seat *340–1*, 341
    tack 339
Westphalian 139, *139*
whips 320
Whitaker, John *402*
Whitaker, Michael *106*
white horses 215, *215*
Wielkopolski 125, *125*
Wild Ass, Somali 11
Wild Horse, Asiatic *see*
    Przewalski's Horse
wild horses 20, 226
working horses 28, *28, 29*
    see also carriage-driving;
        competition horses;
        heavy horses
Working Hunter 82, *82*
Working Hunter Pony 84, *84*
World Arabian Horse
    Organization 221
worms 259, 283
Wurttemburg 243

Y
Yankey (trotter) 193
Yorkshire Coach Horse 132,
    141, 234
Yorkshire Trotters 48
Ysabellas 211

Z
Zapatero 150
zebras 11, *14*, 15
Zemaituka 167, 247
Zetland *see* Shetland Pony
zinc 271